Educational Linguistics/TESOL/ICC
Graduate School of Education
University of Pennsylvania
3700 Walnut Street/C1
Philadelphia, PA 19104

Library of Congress Cataloging in Publication Data

BAKER, CARL LEE, 1939-
   Introduction to generative-transformational syntax.

   Includes bibliographies and index.
1. Grammar, Comparative and general—Syntax.
2. Generative grammar.   3. English language—Syntax.
4. English language—Grammar, Generative.   I. Title.
P291.B29 1978   415   77-22537
ISBN 0-13-484410-6

To Mary Farr Jordan

Printed in the United States of America

10   9   8   7   6   5   4   3

Prentice-Hall International, Inc., *London*
Prentice-Hall of Australia Pty. Limited, *Sydney*
Prentice-Hall of Canada, Ltd., *Toronto*
Prentice-Hall of India Private Limited, *New Delhi*
Prentice-Hall of Japan, Inc., *Tokyo*
Prentice-Hall of Southeast Asia Pte. Ltd., *Singapore*
Whitehall Books Limited, *Wellington, New Zealand*

INTRODUCTION TO GENERATIVE-TRANSFORMATIONAL SYNTAX

C. L. BAKER

The University of Texas at Austin

PRENTICE-HALL, INC., Englewood Cliffs, New Jersey 07632

Contents

Part III

SOME ALTERNATIVES FOR THE ANALYSIS OF ENGLISH 257

11. THE BASIC STRUCTURE OF SIMPLE SENTENCES   259

12. HELPING VERBS   280

13. PRENOMINAL MODIFIERS   308

Preface

This book is designed to introduce the reader to generative syntax and English transformational grammar. Although it presupposes some familiarity with the terminology of traditional school grammars, it does not require any previous preparation in modern linguistics.

The book has two basic objectives. The first is to give a clear outline of some of the specific ideas that have played an important role in writing and discussion on generative syntax. The second is to provide a coherent picture of the overall logical structure of syntactic investigation. Special emphasis has been given to a careful definition of the fundamental goals of syntax and also to a clear characterization of the connection between the study of individual languages and the complementary investigation of "universal grammar," the system of abstract properties common to all human languages.

Chapter 1 gives a brief introduction to the basic problems of syntactic study, and offers an initial discussion of the kinds of data that the grammar of an individual language should account for and the kinds of data that a universal grammar might be expected to explain. In Part II (Chapters 2 through 10), two projects are carried out simultaneously. One is the development of a set of syntactic rules for English; the other is the construction of a general abstract framework for grammatical description—in effect, a tentative theory of universal grammar. With some qualifications, the general framework is roughly the theory of transformational grammar sketched in Noam Chomsky's 1965 book *Aspects of the Theory of Syntax.*

Each of the four chapters in Part III (Chapters 11 through 14) is devoted to a detailed discussion of a single basic issue in English syntax. The general purpose of this group of chapters is to give some examples of relatively complex arguments for and against particular transformational accounts of English syntax. In Part IV (Chapters 15 through 18), the focus shifts to universal grammar. Chapter 15 deals with the relationship between the syntactic rules of a language and the rules that determine certain aspects of semantic interpretation. Chapter 16 deals with interactions between syntactic rules and phonological rules. Chapter 17 offers arguments in favor of a syntactic framework that is much more restrictive than the transformational framework developed in the first half of the book. The line of reasoning introduced in this chapter is applied in Chapter 18 to an important controversy, that concerning the proper treatment of nominal constructions.

Exercises have been provided at the end of most of the chapter subsections. Some of these exercises are designed to test the reader's understanding of new material. Others introduce new material, and provide an opportunity for critical evaluation and original analysis.

This book should not be taken as a summary of established results in generative syntax. As in other scientific fields in which significant questions are being vigorously studied, there is always a healthy variety of views in evidence. Each year sees the publication of many interesting new proposals, some of which have a profound impact on subsequent work. At the same time, many ideas occupy a prominent place for a few years, but then cease to attract adherents in any appreciable numbers. These considerations have a clear practical implication: instead of trying simply to memorize the various rules and hypotheses discussed here, the reader should place primary emphasis on understanding them, on assessing their relative strengths and weaknesses, and on following the arguments given in support of them or against them. This approach will foster analytical and critical skills whose usefulness will continue long after many of the specific rules and hypotheses have been revised or replaced. These skills will in fact provide the reader with the best possible basis for finding his own way among the variety of conflicting views that he is certain to encounter in any subsequent reading that he does in this field.

Many people have helped me in the preparation of this book. Among those who commented on individual chapters are Sidney Cochrane, Bob Harms, Lauri Karttunen, Asa Kasher, W. P. Lehmann, Hsin-hsiung Lin, and Tom Roeper. In addition, I owe a special debt to Tom Wasow and Arnold Zwicky; each of them read the preliminary version of the manuscript in its entirety and offered many valuable criticisms and suggestions. Finally, I have benefited enormously from questions and objections raised by the many students in introductory syntax courses at the University of Texas who have used various portions of the book in preliminary form.

C. L. BAKER

Part I

INTRODUCTION

1

The Study of Syntax

1.1 THE GRAMMAR OF A LANGUAGE

The fundamental aim of a linguist seeking to describe a certain language is to give an account of what it is that a person knows when it can be said of him that he knows that language. If English is the language under study, the linguist will be attempting to say exactly what a person knows when he knows English, that is, what knowledge he possesses that distinguishes him from the people in the world who do not know English. Syntactic description has as its fundamental aim the spelling out of one facet of this knowledge, namely, what the speaker of the language in question knows about combining words together into sentences. A complete description of a language would include not only a description of its syntax, but also descriptions of its *phonetics* (the sounds of the language), its *phonology* (the way in which these sounds combine), its *morphology* (the formation of words), and its *semantics* (the meaning of words and sentences).

At first glance, it may seem that there is little here to study, especially in the case of a language such as English, which has been discussed with such seeming thoroughness in an enormous number of textbooks. Many speakers of English can quote a handful of rules from these textbooks. For instance, a speaker might state that the verb *lay* is used if there is a following direct object, whereas *lie* must be used otherwise:

(1) a.   John will lay the book on the table.   CORRECT
     b.   The book is laying on the table.   INCORRECT
     c.   The book is lying on the table.   CORRECT
     d.   John will lie the book on the table.   INCORRECT

After he has stated a few additional rules, including perhaps a rule for choosing between *who* and *whom*, and one for choosing the correct pronoun from pairs such as *I–me* and *they–them*, the typical English speaker may believe that he has exhausted what there is to say about English grammar.

Suppose now that he is presented with two pairs of sentences:

(2) a.   I am knowing the answer now.
     b.   I know the answer now.
     c.   I am writing the answer now.
     d.   I write the answer now.

The speaker will immediately report that only the second and third of these sentences "sound right," whereas the first and fourth do not. Other speakers of English presented with the same sentences will almost uniformly agree with the first speaker. What is curious about this second group of sentences is that there is no common textbook rule that would account for the speaker's preferences.

Similar responses will be elicited if a third group of sentences is presented to the speaker:

(3) a.   Where he has gone?
     b.   Where has he gone?
     c.   I don't remember where he has gone.
     d.   I don't remember where has he gone.

Again, only the second and third of these sentences will "sound right" to a fluent speaker of English, whereas the first and fourth will not. As in the previous case, other speakers of English will almost certainly agree with him in his judgments, even though none of them may be able to quote a textbook rule that would dictate these judgments.

We will henceforth refer to the types of judgments illustrated above as *judgments of grammaticality*; furthermore, we will apply the term *grammatical* to sentences that a speaker of English finds "good" or "normal" or "okay," and the term *ungrammatical* to sentences that he feels to be "bad" or "abnormal" or "not good English." Interesting examples of such judgments could be multiplied indefinitely, and they suggest what may seem to be a surprising view: below the small handful of principles that English speakers can quote by memory from their grammar school textbooks, they have unconscious knowledge of a vast system of rules which do not correspond to any rules that they learned in school. It is this system of rules that is responsible for the ability to make firm judgments about whether a given sequence of words qualifies as a normal, well-formed English sentence.

How might we go about discovering these rules? The first possibility that might suggest itself is simply to ask speakers of English what the relevant rules are in the cases of the sort we have just presented. As can be readily ascertained by anyone who cares to put such a question to a group of English speakers, there will be a bewildering variety of vague and mutually conflicting answers. Some of the respondents may simply restate original judgments, saying, for example, that some of the sentences "sound better than the others," or that some of the sentences "are just not good English." Both of these remarks are undeniably true, but they would provide no illumination at all for a student in a beginning English class who had spoken or written one of the incorrect sentences. He would have been given no help in avoiding similar mistakes in the future. Other respondents may assert that the incorrect sentences are judged incorrect because "they don't mean anything." Such a charge would be not only unilluminating, but incorrect as well; fluent speakers of English, if they were to hear any of the incorrect sentences presented above, would have no difficulty at all in understanding what the person uttering them was trying to communicate.

If a speaker's unconscious system of rules cannot be discovered by direct questioning, what alternative approach is available? The approach that has been most widely adopted throughout the history of linguistic studies is to try to infer something about the unconscious rules of a language by studying the conscious judgments in which the rules are manifested. What a linguist attempts to do is to formulate explicitly a set of rules which mirror the effects of the native speaker's unconscious system of rules. Such a set of rules is frequently referred to as a *grammar*. We often say that a certain grammar *generates* a certain sentence, by which we mean that the rules of the grammar allow the formation of that sentence.

The most basic condition that a grammar must satisfy, if we are to claim that it mirrors the unconscious system of rules of the native speaker, is that the rules of the grammar generate all of the sentences that the native speaker would judge grammatical, without generating any sentences that he would judge ungrammatical. We thus look on grammars as yielding predictions about judgments that speakers will make. If the speaker's actual judgments of grammaticality are consistent with the predictions deduced from the grammar, then the grammar is to that extent successful. On the other hand, if the predictions are not consistent with the judgments of the speaker, then the grammar is to that extent unsuccessful, and some attempt must be made to modify the set of rules in such a way as to bring the predictions that it makes into line with the speaker's judgments.

As a simple illustration of a syntactic rule that enjoys some successes and suffers some embarrassments, let us consider the following informal rule for number agreement of subject and verb in English:

(4)   An English verb in the present tense agrees in number with the noun most immediately preceding it, taking an -*s* ending if the noun is singular and no ending if the noun is plural.

This statement would of course require some previous listing of verbs and nouns, and some indication of how to tell whether a certain noun was singular or plural. Let us imagine for the purpose of discussion that these preliminary matters have already been taken care of. We can then inquire whether or not this rule gives good results.

Suppose that we start with the simple sentences given in (5), indicating the critical noun and verb by means of italics:

(5) a.   The *man sells* bread.
     b.   The *sailors leave* soon.
     c.   The *men sells* bread.
     d.   The *sailor leave* soon.

As can be readily verified, the rule in (4) gives just the right results for these four sentences. The first two conform to the rule in (4), whereas the last do not. Hence we are led to predict, and correctly so, that a native speaker of English would judge only the first two grammatical. This correspondence between predicted and actual judgment can perhaps be seen more clearly in the following table:

(6)

Sentence	*Predicted Judgment*	*Actual Judgment*
The man sells bread	grammatical	grammatical
The sailors leave soon.	grammatical	grammatical
The men sells bread.	ungrammatical	ungrammatical
The sailor leave soon.	ungrammatical	ungrammatical

In the case of these four sentences, rule (4) gives good results: in every instance the predicted judgment and the actual judgment coincide.

Let us look at some slightly more complicated sentences. Again, we mark the key noun and verb in each sentence with italics:

(7) a.   The child and the *man sells* bread.
     b.   The child and the *man sell* bread.
     c.   The parents of the *man leaves* soon.
     d.   The parents of the *man leave* soon.

In (a) and (c), the choice of verb form is that dictated by rule (4), so that we would expect them to be judged grammatical. On the other hand, (b) and (d) are predicted to be ungrammatical. Unfortunately, these predicted judgments are precisely the reverse of the actual judgments, a state of affairs summarized in the following table:

(8)

Sentence	*Predicted Judgment*	*Actual Judgment*
The child and the man sells bread.	grammatical	ungrammatical
The child and the man sell bread.	ungrammatical	grammatical
The parents of the man leaves soon.	grammatical	ungrammatical
The parents of the man leave soon.	ungrammatical	grammatical

If we are to have a chance of avoiding these incorrect predictions, we must try to formulate an alternative rule to replace the rule stated in (4). As a matter of fact, most traditional studies in English grammar contain rules of agreement that are more sophisticated than rule (4). For instance, these traditional rules specify the "head noun" or "simple subject" as determining the number of the verb. In the sequence *the parents of the man*, the word *parents* would be classed as the head noun, and thus it would be used to determine the appropriate verb form. Similarly, a special statement might be given to specify that subjects that consist of two parts conjoined by *and* automatically require the plural verb form. A description that included these more traditional rules would give much better predictions for (7) than did rule (4).

What we do when we attempt to formulate a description of some language is very nearly parallel to what we would do if we wanted to formulate laws or hypotheses about the physical universe. In order to make this parallel clear, let us imagine briefly that we are trying to develop an account of the relation between the distance a body falls when it is dropped, and the time that it takes to fall that distance. We might try to express this relation by means of a mathematical equation relating time and distance, from which we could arrive at a set of predictions, each one taking the form: "If the body falls for ——— seconds, then it will fall a distance of ——— centimeters." Suppose that an initial test has been made, in which an object that fell for one second was found to have traveled 49 centimeters. A natural first guess as to the relation between time and distance might then be that the distance in centimeters is just the time in seconds multiplied by 49. In equation form, this is just

(9) $d = 49t$

From this equation, we can derive the following predictions, among others:

(10)   a.   If a body falls for 2 seconds, it will fall 98 centimeters.
          b.   If a body falls for 5 seconds, it will fall 245 centimeters.

The table in (11) exhibits the relation between predicted distance and actual distance for the times tested:

(11) Time	Predicted Distance	Actual Distance
1 second	49 centimeters	49 centimeters
2 seconds	98 centimeters	190 centimeters
5 seconds	245 centimeters	1187 centimeters

From the huge disparity between the predictions of our equation and our actual measurements, we are forced to conclude that something must be wrong with our equation. After a certain amount of reflection, we might hit upon the idea of specifying that the distance is related to the *square* of the time (that is, to the time multiplied by itself):

(12) $d = 49t^2$ (i.e., $d = 49 \times t \times t$)

From this equation, we derive a new set of predictions:

(13) a.   If a body falls for 1 second, it will fall 49 centimeters.

b.   If a body falls for 2 seconds, it will fall 196 centimeters.

c.   If a body falls for 5 seconds, it will fall 1225 centimeters.

Again, we can compare the predicted distances and the actual distances in a table:

(14)	*Time*	*Predicted Distance*	*Actual Distance*
	1 second	49 centimeters	49 centimeters
	2 seconds	196 centimeters	190 centimeters
	5 seconds	1225 centimeters	1187 centimeters

This second set of predictions, while not coinciding exactly with the experimental results, is close enough to indicate that the second equation is quite promising. We might hope eventually to account for the minor discrepancies in terms of some additional factor (for instance, the force of friction exerted by the air through which the object passed). In any case, our new equation gives much more accurate predictions than the old one gave.

Let us summarize here what the linguistic investigation and the physical investigation have in common. In the first place, in each investigation there is some particular body of data to be accounted for. In the linguistic investigation, the data consist of the judgments that speakers of a language make regarding the grammaticality of various sentences that are presented to them. In the case of the physical investigation, the data consist of observations in which both time and distance are measured. In the second place, in both instances we try to set up general rules or laws from which can be deduced predictions that coincide with actual data. The linguistic hypothesis may be a rule like (4); the physical hypothesis may be an equation like (9) or (12). Finally, in both instances we are forced to abandon or revise our hypothesis when we find a significant discrepancy between predictions and available data.

The most basic condition that a grammar must satisfy, then, is that it generate all of the grammatical sentences of a language and no ungrammatical sentences. We will use the term *descriptively adequate* to refer to grammars that satisfy this condition.[1]

There is a further requirement that we will try to satisfy: the set of rules in a grammar must be *revealing*, rather than *unnecessarily complex*. The rules should be as general as possible, so that they do not make the language appear to be more complicated than it actually is. This second requirement might seem so natural that it requires no justification. However, as we will see in the final section of this chapter, there are compelling reasons for setting this requirement.

The difference between a revealing grammar and an unrevealing one can be made clear with a simple illustration. We will compare two different miniature grammars for some simple data from English involving the sentence environments in which certain nouns appear. (In this discussion, as in the remainder of the book, we mark ungrammatical sentences with asterisks.) The first grammar is like most traditional grammars in that it makes crucial reference to the notions *singular* and *plural*:

(15)   Description I

    a.   In general, English nouns form their plurals by adding *-s* or *-es* to the singular form. For example, the plural of *dog* is *dogs*. Exception: the plural of *man* is *men*, instead of **mans*.

    b.   Singular nouns permit the numeral *one*, but no higher numerals (*two, three,...*). Plural nouns do not permit the numeral *one* but do permit the higher numerals.

We saw one dog.	We saw one man.
*We saw three dog.	*We saw three man.
*We saw one dogs.	*We saw one men.
We saw three dogs.	We saw three men.

    c.   Third-person present-tense verbs agree with their subjects in number. If the subject noun is singular, then the verb must have an *-s* or *-es* suffix. If the subject noun is plural, then it must have no suffix.

The dog eats meat.	The man eats chili.
*The dog eat meat.	*The man eat chili.
*The dogs eats meat.	*The men eats chili.
The dogs eat meat.	The men eat chili.

    d.   There is a distinction among demonstratives, depending on the number of the following noun. A singular noun can only have *this* or *that*; a plural noun can only have *these* or *those*:

This dog grew large.	This man grew large.
*These dog grew large.	*These man grew large.
*This dogs grew large.	*This men grew large.
These dogs grew large.	These men grew large.

(A similar set of examples can be constructed for *that* and *those*.)

The second description, by contrast, accounts for the same data with rules that refer only to the *form* of nouns, without any reference to more abstract, less tangible notions such as *singular* and *plural*:

(16)   Description II

    a.   In general, English nouns that do not end in *-s* or *-es* are matched by nouns that do end in one or the other of these suffixes. For example, corresponding to the noun *dog* we find another noun, *dogs*. Exception: neither the noun *man* nor the noun *men* have corresponding forms **mans* or **mens*.

b.   Nouns without an -*s* or -*es* suffix may be preceded by the numeral *one*, but exclude higher numerals (*two*, *three*,...). Nouns with an -*s* or -*es* suffix exclude *one*, but permit higher numerals. Exception: the noun *men* excludes *one*, but permits higher numerals.

We saw one dog.	We saw one man.
*We saw three dog.	*We saw three man.
*We saw one dogs.	*We saw one men.
We saw three dogs.	We saw three men.

c.   If a subject noun does not have the ending -*s* or -*es*, then a present-tense verb must have an -*s* or -*es* suffix. If a subject noun does have an -*s* or -*es* suffix, then the verb must not have an -*s* ending. Exception: if the subject noun is *men*, then a present-tense verb must not have an -*s* or -*es* ending.

The dog eats meat.	The man eats chili.
*The dog eat meat.	*The man eat chili.
*The dogs eats meat.	*The men eats chili.
The dogs eat meat.	The men eat chili.

d.   A noun without an -*s* or -*es* ending can be preceded by *this* and *that*, but not by *these* and *those*. Just the reverse is true for nouns having an -*s* or -*es* ending. Exception: *Men* can be preceded by *these* and *those*, but not by *this* and *that*.

This dog grew large.	This man grew large.
*These dog grew large.	*These man grew large.
*This dogs grew large.	*This men grew large.
These dogs grew large.	These men grew large.

The predictions made by the second grammar are no different from those made by the first, at least with regard to the common set of illustrative examples given with both grammars. What does it mean, then, to say that the first is "more revealing" than the second? In the first, the number of descriptive statements is kept to the absolute minimum necessary to yield correct predictions about the illustrative data. In particular, there is only a single exceptional statement, that concerning the peculiar plural form for the noun *man*. In the second description, on the other hand, a total of four exceptional statements is required. Worse yet, each of the statements, as if purely by coincidence, happens to make reference to the word *men*. The second description, then, has the defect of making English appear to be more irregular and complicated than it actually is.

1.2   COMPETENCE AND PERFORMANCE

At this point, many readers may be tempted to ask why we should take a fluent speaker's judgments about sentences as the data of our investigation, rather than studying his actual utterances. Might we not arrive at a more accurate idea of what he "knows" about his language by observing the actual utterances that he produces, instead of merely asking him to make judgments?

In most instances, it is useful to prefer the judgment to the actual utterance. The chief reason is that many kinds of additional complexity are introduced when we examine actual utterances. For instance, in actual recorded speech, we find all of the following types of utterances at one time or another:

a.   sentences that are interrupted short of their termination;
b.   sentences that are halted by the speaker and begun a second time;
c.   sentences in which the order of two words is altered through some slip of the tongue;
d.   sentences in which some actual unconscious grammatical rule is violated.

It would be well-nigh impossible to start with such utterances as a basis for describing the language in question. Imagine, for instance, the difficulties that a linguist who knew no English would have in describing English if he had to assign an equal status to the following utterances:

(17)   a.   I don't think that Mark brought the book.

b.   Mark didn't bring — I don't think that Mark brought the book.

c.   I don't think that Mark...(interrupted by other speaker)

He would have a much easier time of it if he simply checked the judgment of a native speaker of English, who would tell him that only (a) was a good sentence in its own right. After the linguist had written a description of the sentences judged good, he would then be in a strong position to describe the utterances in (b) and (c) by stating the respects in which they failed to satisfy this norm. In fact, this is just the type of description that we gave when we listed types of deviant utterances above.

These considerations appear to suggest what at first may seem a paradoxical conclusion: the study of actual utterances should ideally be preceded by a study of grammaticality judgments. The study of these judgments, in this view, will lead to a generative grammar, the function of which is to specify the grammatical sentences of the language. This generative grammar then defines a *norm*, or standard, toward which people unconsciously aim, with greater or lesser success, in their actual speech. We can then describe the irregularities of actually occurring utterances in terms of their deviation from this norm.

In the literature in psychology and linguistics, a distinction is often made between a speaker's *competence* and his *performance*. Performance is concerned with the production and comprehension of utterances by the speaker of a language, and the psychological processes which are involved in these two activities. Competence, on the other hand, is concerned with what the speaker knows unconsciously, his knowledge of the principles by which the sentences of his language are constructed. This abstract knowledge of sentence construction can to a large extent be studied independently of the other psychological mechanisms involved in the actual production and comprehension of sentences.[2] By contrast, any successful study of these performance processes will require a prior understanding of the competence which provides a basis for them.

This has, in any case, been the position assumed in recent years by many generative grammarians. The reader should be warned that it is not an entirely uncontroversial position. While the issues are quite complex, a general word can be offered here about the justification for such a distinction between competence and performance. The distinction is justified to the extent that an approach to the study of language and language use that makes this distinction is more fruitful than any approaches that do not. The distinction can thus be effectively attacked only by devising an approach that is successful to at least the same degree as the one that we have sketched, but that does not make such a distinction.

1.3   NONSTANDARD COMPETENCE

In the preceding section, it was argued that judgments of grammaticality provide better data for the study of a person's knowledge of his language than do actual utterances of the speaker. There is one situation, however, in which the actual utterances may provide the more accurate indication. Suppose that you ask a speaker of English to make judgments of grammaticality concerning the following three pairs of sentences:

(18)   a.   It was I.
       b.   It was me.
(19)   a.   John is taller than I.
       b.   John is taller than me.
(20)   a.   Whom did you see at the party?
       b.   Who did you see at the party?

Most English speakers will immediately report that the (a) sentences are grammatical, whereas the (b) sentences are not. Yet in their unguarded moments, the vast majority of them will utter the (b) sentences rather than the corresponding (a) sentences. These discrepancies between judgments and utterances are much more systematic and predictable than were the discrepancies exhibited in (17). Moreover, the present discrepancies are easily described in terms of grammatical concepts such as "nominative case," "objective case," "understood object," and so forth, whereas such concepts would not have been at all useful for describing the difference between (17a) and (17b–c). In the present situation, then, it appears that instead of a contrast between competence and performance, we have evidence of a conflict between two varieties of "knowledge of English." The first variety, which is responsible for the judgments in favor of the (a) sentences, is knowledge consciously acquired in school or from books. The second variety, which is responsible for the appearance of the (b) sentences in ordinary conversation, is unconscious knowledge of the type we discussed in section 1.1. In instances where we find a conflict of this sort, we obtain a clearer idea of a person's unconscious knowledge of his language by discounting his judgments and concentrating instead on what he actually says. The unconscious knowledge that manifests itself in these utterances that even the speaker himself may not approve of could be described as "nonstandard competence." Contrary to what might appear to be the case, it is just as readily describable by linguistic rules as is the conscious knowledge reflected in the judgments.

A similar situation may occur when sentence pairs containing reflexive pronouns are presented for an English speaker's judgment:

(21) a.   He hurt himself.
      b.   He hurt hisself.

(22) a.   They hurt themselves.
      b.   They hurt theirselves.

We may find many people who, when asked for judgments of grammaticality, state a preference for the (a) sentences above, but who in their normal speech tend to use *hisself* and *theirselves*. Unlike the difference in the previous set of examples, the difference here is not merely a conflict between schoolbook knowledge and unconscious knowledge. Rather, it is a difference that can be attributed to the existence of two slightly different kinds of English, that is, to the existence of two different *dialects*. We can account for the behavior of the person reacting in this way if we assume that the unconscious rules of his *native dialect* of English give the (b) sentences, whereas his conscious preference for the (a) sentences arises from his familiarity with the rules of another dialect, one that he has learned later in his life and does not control so thoroughly. The forms represented in the (a) sentences in fact have a sociologically privileged position, being those found in the most socially prestigious English dialect, often referred to as the *standard dialect*.

Although it would take us too far afield to discuss the historical emergence of standard dialects and their relation to other dialects, we should report here on one important conclusion that has arisen from the long tradition of scholarly work in the study of grammar. This is that, contrary to an opinion nearly universal in England and the United States, the standard language does not in the least owe its privileged position to any sort of logical superiority over the nonstandard dialects of English. In fact, if logicality is equated with regularity, then it will frequently be found that a certain nonstandard dialect may be more "logical" than the standard.

A very striking example in which a nonstandard dialect shows greater regularity than the standard dialect is afforded by the reflexive pronouns illustrated earlier. The full lists of words are the following:

(23) | Standard | Singular | Plural |
|---|---|---|
| First person | myself | ourselves |
| Second person | yourself | yourselves |
| Third person | himself | themselves |
| | herself | |
| | itself | |

(24)   *Nonstandard*   *Singular*   *Plural*
       First person   myself   ourselves
       Second person   yourself   yourselves
       Third person   hisself   theirselves
                         herself
                         itsself

A reasonable rule for the standard dialect is the following:

(25)   The reflexive pronoun is formed in the first and second person by prefixing the possessive form of the pronoun to *self* or *selves*, and in the third person by prefixing the objective form of the pronoun to *self* or *selves*.

For the nonstandard forms, by contrast, it is not necessary to distinguish third-person reflexives from first- and second-person reflexives; one rule will give all of the forms correctly:

(26)   The reflexive pronoun is formed by prefixing the possessive form of the pronoun to *self* or *selves*.

The set of nonstandard forms thus show a greater degree of regularity than the standard forms.

1.4   UNIVERSAL GRAMMAR

The aim of a grammar of a language, as we have presented it in section 1.1, is to describe the competence of a fluent native speaker of the language, that is, what he knows that distinguishes him from nonspeakers of his language. In attempting to frame a grammar, then, a linguist seeks to find rules for the language in question which will generate exactly the sentences that the fluent speaker of the language judges grammatical.

Universal grammar, in effect, goes one step farther back. It is concerned with a much more fundamental kind of unconscious knowledge, the knowledge that a human being has of language in general, knowledge that he possesses not by virtue of any linguistic experience, but rather by virtue of his genetic endowment as a human being. The term *innate* is often used in referring to knowledge or capacities that exist in an animal or human independently of experience.

Again, just as when we defined the subject matter of a linguistic description of English, it might appear at first glance that there is really nothing here to study. This objection could be formulated as a question: What reason have we to assume that humans actually have any innate language capacity? The answer that we will present here is quite a surprising one: unless we are willing to assume that such an innate language capacity exists and make some specific hypotheses about it, we face severe difficulties in explaining how a person's childhood linguistic experience with his native language suffices to determine his competence in that language.

If this assertion is to be believable, we must first give critical attention to some "common sense" accounts of language learning that do not require us to assume any general language capacity. Perhaps the simplest such account is the following:

(27)   A child becomes competent in his language by *imitating the adults and older children with whom he comes in contact.*

There is, of course, an obvious element of truth in this account; the utterances that a child hears around him play an absolutely essential role in determining the competence that he will eventually show. A child reared in an English-speaking environment will become a speaker of English, a child reared among speakers of Japanese will become a speaker of Japanese, and similarly for any other language that we could mention. It would obviously be folly to attempt to account for a child's language learning without making reference to the linguistic environment in which he is reared.

Once this obvious element of truth is acknowledged, however, a further consideration will show that the above statement, if taken literally, comes nowhere near to being sufficient. The basic reason is quite simple: given this account, we would be led to expect that no fluent speaker of a language could produce or understand a sentence, or even make a judgment about it, *unless he had encountered it before.* Under these circumstances, a person judged to be fluent in English would be little better than a parrot or mynah bird, in that every one of his utterances would simply be an imitation. The most basic test of a person's competence in a language, however, is the ability to deal with sentences that are completely new in his experience. Even though most speakers of English have never heard or seen either of the sentences below, few of them would have any difficulty at all in determining that the first sentence is grammatical and the second is not:

(28)   a.   Production of oranges in Alaska is more systematic this year than last year.
       b.   Production of oranges in Alaska is more systematically this year than last year.

An account of language acquisition that is based solely on imitation would afford no explanation for the judgments concerning these two sentences.

At this point, we might consider a somewhat more sophisticated account, incorporating some of the ideas developed in section 1.1:

(29)   A human being becomes competent in his language by unconscious-ly formulating a system of rules on the basis of his early linguistic experience. This experience yields him a large amount of *basic data* about his language. The greater part of his basic data consists of examples of grammatical sentences. In addition, he may on occasion be corrected after he has uttered an ungrammatical sentence; such occasions provide him with data about which sentences are *not* grammatical.[3] The grammar that he unconsciously formulates is designed to be consistent with his basic data, that is, to generate all of the grammatical sentences in the basic data and none of the ungrammatical sentences. This grammar then forms the foundation for his ability, as a fluent speaker of his language, to produce and

> understand unfamiliar sentences of his language and for his ability to make judgments of grammaticality.

This account, like the preceding one, makes no reference to any innate language capacity. Furthermore, it has the advantage of being consistent with the fact that a fluent speaker can deal quite easily with many more sentences than just those that he has encountered before.

It might seem that we could let matters rest here. But the account in (29) leaves one puzzling question unanswered. Suppose that we were to study some person's basic data, with the aim of constructing a grammar to account for it. If we spent enough time on the project, we would find not just one grammar, but an enormous number of grammars, each of which would be equally in accord with this body of data.[4] Moreover, when we came to check these different grammars to determine what sort of predictions they made about the adult judgments of the person in question, we would find many instances in which the predictions derived from one grammar were in direct conflict with those derived from some other grammar. Moreover, some of the grammars would be markedly more successful than others in the degree to which their predicted judgments coincided with the actual judgments of the adult speaker. The basic question that this account leaves unanswered, then, can be put as follows: If it is possible to develop a wide variety of contradictory sets of rules to account for any person's early linguistic experience, how are we to explain the fact that a human being acquires just one system of rules, and furthermore, one that is very close to the system acquired by others in his linguistic community?[5]

We can get a hint concerning how this question might be answered by looking at a small, informal experiment whose results pose a similar sort of puzzle. In this experiment, a group of English-speaking students, none of whom knew any German, were faced with the task of learning how to form questions in German, with only a very small sample of German sentences as a guide. This sample consisted of three German statements and the question that corresponded to the first statement:

(30)   Er singt.   Singt er?
       'He sings.'   'Does he sing?'

       Hans singt gut.
       'Hans sings well.'

       Der Mann singt gut.
       'The man sings well.'

Having been given this sample of four German sentences, the students were asked to fill in the remaining questions, using as a guide the single one given to them. The responses were divided into two neat groups:

(31)   *Response A*   *Response B*
       Er singt.   Singt er?   Singt er?
       Hans singt gut.   Singt Hans gut?   Singt gut Hans?
       Der Mann singt gut   Singt der Mann gut?   Singt gut der Mann?

The students giving the A responses appear to have formed each question from the corresponding statement by inverting the subject with the verb only. On the other hand, the students giving the B responses appear to have formed each question from the corresponding statement by inverting the subject with the entire predicate. As it happens, the questions given in the A responses are grammatical German questions, whereas the B questions are not. Even though in fact the B response is incorrect, it represents a very good guess: if a similar experiment had been performed with Modern Greek, a response of type B would have turned out to be correct. Considering the smallness of the sample, it is hardly surprising that this problem received two distinct answers.

At first glance, then, there might appear to be nothing in the least puzzling about the results of the experiment. It would seem that we could explain the responses that arose by saying that they are based on the only two rules for question formation that the sample allows. Unfortunately, such an explanation cannot be maintained. There are in fact several other rules that the first statement-question pair might have suggested:

(32)   Interchange the first and last word in the statement to form the corresponding question.

	Response C
Er singt.	Singt er?
Hans singt gut.	Gut singt Hans?
Der Mann singt gut.	Gut Mann singt der?

(33)   Interchange the first and second word in the statement to form the corresponding question.

	Response D
Er singt.	Singt er?
Hans singt gut.	Singt Hans gut?
Der Mann singt gut.	Mann der singt gut?

(34)   Move the last word of the statement to the beginning of the sentence to form the corresponding question.

	Response E
Er singt.	Singt er?
Hans singt gut.	Gut Hans singt?
Der Mann singt gut.	Gut der Mann singt?

(35)   Move the first word of the statement to the end of the sentence.

	Response F
Er singt.	Singt er?
Hans singt gut.	Singt gut Hans?
Der Mann singt gut.	Mann singt gut der?

The puzzling fact, then, is that the students divided their responses between only two out of at least six logically possible rules that would have been consistent with the data that they were given. This fact must go unexplained unless we are willing to assume that the students who came to the experiment were *predisposed* to think of certain kinds of rules to the exclusion of other kinds. Apparently operative in this case was a predisposition, conscious or unconscious, to form rules involving subjects, predicates, and verbs, rather than rules involving first words, last words, second words, or next-to-last words. Whatever the exact nature of the predisposition, it clearly had a beneficial effect in this experiment, since without it we would have expected a much lower proportion of the students to guess the correct German rule.[6]

Let us return now to the much larger puzzle posed by the fact that a human child acquires one particular rule system from basic data that would logically allow a wide variety of conflicting systems. We might take an initial step in the direction of solving this puzzle if we are willing to assume that the child, like the students participating in the experiment, is predisposed to acquire certain very specific kinds of rule systems and not others. If the child were predisposed in this way, then many of the logically possible systems of rules that were consistent with his basic data would be excluded ahead of time as possible rule systems for his language. Moreover, in this situation, as in the small experiment, the exclusion of certain logically possible rule systems would be beneficial to the learner, in that it would narrow down the rule systems under consideration to those that would represent fruitful guesses as to the structure of the language spoken around him. As soon as we begin to investigate the specific nature of such predispositions, we are studying what we must assume to be our innate capacity for language, which we defined as the subject matter of universal grammar.

Having seen some grounds for assuming the existence of innate linguistic predispositions, let us consider how they can be studied. Quite obviously, we would have no luck if we simply asked people what their innate predispositions were. The results would undoubtedly be even less satisfactory than the results of asking people to state the rules underlying their judgments about sentences of their language. Again, as was the case in investigating the rules of individual languages, we must take an indirect approach, in which we try to get at the innate predispositions by looking at their observable effects and trying to formulate a *universal grammar*, an explicit set of universal principles whose logical consequences coincide with the observations. In the present instance, the critical data are much more complex than the data for the grammar of an individual language. The relevant observations would take the form given in (36):

(36)   Persons *X*'s basic data were as follows: (here, a record of his basic data). The following is a list containing some of his adult judgments of sentences: (here, a list of sentences, with his associated judgments of grammaticality).

Correspondingly, we would want our set of universal principles to yield predictions of the following form:

(37)   If a certain person's basic data were as follows: (here, a record of basic data), then we would expect him to make the following judgments as a fluent adult: (here, a list containing some sentences, with associated judgments of grammaticality).

The kind of table that we might construct if we had specific principles to test would thus be of the form given below:

(38)

Records of Basic Data	Lists of Sentences to Be Judged	Predicted Adult Judgments	Actual Adult Judgments

In point of actual fact, we will take a cue from the informal statement in (29), and assume that the task of predicting adult judgments from early experience is not one that is to be accomplished directly, but rather that the predictions are derived in two logical steps. In the first step, the universal principles take a certain record of early linguistic experience and derive from it a *predicted grammar*. In the second step, this grammar yields specific predictions about judgments of sentences. Thus, a clearer picture of how a set of principles might be tested is contained in the following slightly more elaborate table:

(39)

Record of Early Linguistic Experience	Grammar Predicted by Universal Principles	Lists of Sentences to Be Judged	Judgments Predicted from Grammar Predicted by Principles	Actual Adult Judgments

We can now say what counts as support for such a set of universal principles and what counts as an embarrassment. Suppose that we have a record of a given person's basic data. Based on this record, our set of principles leads us to select a certain grammar. From this grammar, we can make a prediction about what his judgment will be on some specific sentence, which we can then check by asking for his judgment. If the predicted judgment and the actual judgment agree, then we have support for the particular grammar that we selected, and thus also for the set of principles that led us to select it. By contrast, if the predicted judgment and actual judgment do not agree, then we have an embarrassment for the selected grammar, and consequently an embarrassment also for the universal principles.

To recapitulate, the central problem that we are trying to solve when we develop a universal grammar (a set of universal principles) can be stated as follows:

(40)   Find a way of making correct predictions about the relationship between early linguistic experience and adult competence, that is, a way of "projecting" from any person's finite and unsystematic basic data to the full and systematic set of his adult judgments.

As we have noted, this problem can be reformulated more specifically as follows:

(41)   Find a way of predicting, from a person's basic data, a grammar that in turn correctly predicts his adult judgments.

For ease of reference, we will refer to this problem in either of the above formulations as the *projection problem*.

Let us turn now to the question of what sorts of universal principles might prove useful in solving the projection problem. An approach that has been followed in much traditional and modern work is to try to develop principles that define a *framework* for grammatical description. Such a framework specifies a basic common outline for grammars of all languages. The framework may include a specification of what kinds of rules are allowed in the grammars of individual languages, and how the rules interact to generate sentences.

As a preliminary example of a grammatical framework, we will look briefly at a simplified sketch of the informal framework that is implicit in much traditional work in syntax. This grammatical framework was inspired in large part by the efforts to construct grammars for Greek and Latin. The task that received the most attention was that of listing the general concepts that were available for use in rules of particular grammars. The following is a brief illustrative list of some of the central concepts:

(42)   a.   *Parts of speech:* nouns, verbs, adjectives, adverbs, conjunctions, prepositions, pronouns, and interjections

       b.   *Categories*, with various *values* that these categories could assume:
          Tense: present, past, future
          Aspect: perfect, progressive
          Mood: indicative, subjunctive, imperative, interrogative
          Voice: passive, active, middle
          Number: singular, plural, dual
          Gender: masculine, feminine, neuter
          Case: nominative, accusative, genitive, dative, ablative, vocative, instrumental

       c.   *Grammatical functions:* subject, direct object, indirect object, object of preposition

These concepts figured in the statement of rules of a variety of types:

(43)   a.   Rules indicating the part-of-speech membership of individual words. For example, "*puer* is a noun" (Latin).

       b.   Rules indicating which parts of speech show differences of form corresponding to different values of certain categories. For example, in Latin "each noun is assigned to one of the three genders, masculine feminine, or neuter; nouns may appear as singular or plural; they are inflected for various cases according to their grammatical function, taking nominative if they are

the subject, accusative if they are part of the direct object, etc.";
and "adjectives agree in gender, number, and case with the
nouns that they modify."

c.   Lists of the various inflectional forms of individual words, as
for example the following chart for the active indicative present-
tense forms of the Latin verb *amāre*, 'to love':

	Singular		*Plural*	
First person	amō	'I love'	amāmus	'we love'
Second person	amās	'you love'	amātis	'you love'
Third person	amat	'he/she/it loves'	amant	'they love'

(Charts such as this are often referred to as *paradigms*. Other
similar charts would be given for the other tenses, and for the
various other voices and moods.)

The examples that we have given of grammatical statements couched
within this traditional framework have been from Latin. Many grammars
based on the same framework were written for languages all over the world
by European scholars, administrators, missionaries, and travelers. Most
of these grammars, whether they were grammars of African, American
Indian, or Asian languages, were organized in much the same fashion as
were the Latin grammars of their day.

In the nineteenth and twentieth centuries, students of language became
increasingly aware of shortcomings in this grammatical framework. In the
first place, they noted that in many instances such a framework would lead
a language-learner or a linguist to expect formal distinctions which simply
did not exist in the language in question. A simple example is provided by
the expectation, based on a prior acquaintance with Latin, that English
nouns should have precisely the cases that Latin nouns have. The unhelp-
fulness of such an expectation, in the learning of English, can be seen by
comparing the singular paradigm for *puella* in Latin and the equivalent
word *girl* in English:

(44)

	Latin	*English*
Nominative	puella	girl
Genitive	puellae	girl's
Dative	puellae	girl
Accusative	puellam	girl
Ablative	puellā	girl

In Latin, the various inflectional forms frequently serve to identify various
grammatical functions. For instance, the subject is generally in the nominative case, the direct object is in the accusative case, and the indirect object in
the dative. Frequently these case inflections provide the only indication of
the function that a certain word plays in a Latin sentence, there being little
other indication in the sentence itself. With Latin grammar made the model
for English grammar, the student of English is certain to be frustrated,
because in place of the large number of case forms for nouns in Latin, he

finds only two in English: the genitive, and the uninflected form used in every construction other than the genitive.

The user of the Classical framework, then, will be disappointed when he looks in English for inflectional distinctions corresponding to those that he has found in Latin. Moreover, his framework will fail to allow the recognition of patterns of quite another type, those involving *word order*. Because of the relatively free word order in the Classical languages, little attention was given to it in traditional grammar.[7] Even in studies of languages such as English and French, word order was discussed quite infrequently. Some authors simply dismissed it by claiming that word order was determined by the order of the speaker's thoughts. (In the absence of any independent indication of the order in which people's thoughts occurred to them, it was of course impossible either to support this view or refute it.) The seriousness of overlooking word order can be seen by considering the following pair of English sentences:

(45) a. The dog bit the man.
      b. The man bit the dog.

It is only the difference in word order that allows us to determine that in the first sentence, the man is the victim, whereas in the second it is the dog. In a language such as Latin, by contrast, this difference could be conveyed entirely by differences in inflection:

(46) a. canis   hominem mordēbat
          dog (nom.) man (acc.) bit   'The dog bit the man.'
      b. canem   homo   mordēbat
          dog (acc.) man (nom.) bit   'The man bit the dog.'

Consequently, a speaker of English who fails to order the parts of his sentence correctly runs the risk of saying virtually the opposite of what he intends. Thus, a novice speaker of English equipped with the Latin-based framework would have no means for organizing information about word order in his grammar of English. This particular traditional framework is thus inadequate, since in at least this one respect it provides no means of organizing one very important type of knowledge which English speakers have of their language.

Many other criticisms against this framework have been advanced in modern times. Nevertheless, many concepts have been carried over virtually intact. Even though many of the traditional definitions of individual parts of speech have been abandoned, the classifications themselves have been maintained. For example, although modern linguists no longer try to maintain the definition of a noun as "the name of a person, place, or thing," they still, for the most part, assume a class of nouns in English, which corresponds very closely to the class of nouns an earlier grammarian might have set up. In particular, the influence of this grammatical tradition will be obvious in the remainder of this book, even though there is much in the book which an earlier grammarian would find unfamiliar.

In succeeding chapters, we will attempt to study a series of increasingly sophisticated syntactic frameworks, giving particular attention to determining how well they fare with English material. If it were feasible, we would test these frameworks by determining what kind of grammars they led us to select for English on the basis of records of the early experience of English-speaking children. As a matter of fact, though, such a strategy is not possible, since we do not possess, and in fact may never possess, a complete record of the early experience of even a single child. In view of these practical limitations, we must evaluate proposed syntactic frameworks somewhat indirectly. Our evaluation will consist chiefly of attempting to answer two questions. The first question can be stated as follows: Can we formulate a descriptively adequate grammar within the terms of this framework, that is, a grammar that generates exactly the sentences that a native speaker would judge grammatical? If the answer to this first question is negative, then we can conclude immediately that the framework under consideration will not allow us to solve the projection problem. The reason is simple: if the framework does not provide a descriptively adequate grammar for English under any circumstances, it certainly will not give us a descriptively adequate grammar on the basis of an English-speaking child's early linguistic experience.

The second question is somewhat more interesting. Within the terms of the framework under consideration, can we formulate a descriptively adequate grammar that has the added virtue of being *revealing*? If the answer to this second question is negative, then we have grounds for suspecting that the framework will not take us as far toward the solution of the projection problem as we might like. Two considerations enter into this general assessment. The first is that, in the absence of any specific knowledge about exactly how much basic data an English-speaking child actually receives, we would do best to seek a framework that allows for the selection of a descriptively adequate grammar *on the basis of the smallest possible body of basic data*. The second consideration is that a smaller body of data is required to arrive at a revealing grammar than is required to arrive at an equivalent grammar that is less revealing. Since this is a difficult point to see in the abstract, we will look again briefly at the two small sets of rules which we compared earlier, one set revealing and the other unrevealing. The first set was written within the traditional framework, in which grammatical rules may make reference to concepts such as *singular* and *plural*. The second set was written within a framework that required all rules to refer solely to features of the outward form of words, features such as the presence or absence of a certain ending.

What basic data would be required to arrive at the first grammar? In other words, what would be the minimum amount required to "motivate" these rules? We would clearly need data to motivate the rules for the regular forms. In addition, we would also require some one piece of evidence for the exceptional nature of *men*. A sentence such as (47) would be sufficient in this regard:

(47)   We saw three men.

This sentence could be most readily accounted for by simply listing *men* as an irregular plural. Once a statement to this effect was made, all of the other respects in which the plural *men* behaves like *dogs* or *books* would be accounted for automatically. All of the rules that apply to such regular plurals as *dogs* and *books* will automatically apply to *men* as well. As a result, this grammar would allow us to predict the correct demonstratives and verb forms for *men*:

(48) a. *We saw that men.
      b. We saw those men.

(49) a. *The men lives here.
      b. The men live here.

The critical point is that these correct predictions could be made even if the basic data contained no sentences illustrating the behavior of *men* with demonstratives or with present-tense verbs. Thus, in listing *men* as an exceptional plural form, we succeeded in killing several birds with one stone, including at least two that we had not even seen before throwing the stone.

When we think about what data would be required to motivate all of the statements in the second, less revealing grammar, we find that the data that sufficed for the first grammar are not enough. The data illustrating the behavior of words such as *dogs* and *books* would serve to motivate the general statements about occurrence with numerals, demonstratives, and present-tense verbs. Sentence (47) would serve to motivate an exceptional statement to the effect that *men*, unlike most other nouns without an *-s* or *-es* suffix, could occur with numerals higher than *one*. But from the general statements and this one exceptional statement, nothing at all would follow concerning the behavior of *men* with demonstratives or present-tense verbs. In this instance, the exceptional statement that we established in order to account for (47) would not have any consequences for (48) and (49). Thus, this particular stone would kill only the bird at which it was thrown. In order to motivate the additional exceptional statements that are necessary in the second grammar, we would have to have a set of basic data that specifically included examples showing the occurrence of demonstratives and present-tense verb forms with *men*. Otherwise, we would have no indication that such statements were necessary.

Let us recapitulate here. When we find that a certain framework does not allow any revealing grammars for English or for some other language, we can conclude that the selection of a descriptively adequate grammar within the terms of the framework would require an unnecessarily large body of basic data. Since we stand a better chance of solving the projection problem with a framework in which descriptive adequacy can be attained on the basis of the smallest possible amount of basic data, we are in such situations compelled to look for an alternative framework that allows more revealing grammars.

Before going on to the next chapter, we might do well to answer one final question about the general procedure to be adopted in the remainder of the book, the question of how we can evaluate various syntactic frameworks by looking only at English. We would certainly be wrong to become complacent about a framework that was successful with English, if we knew nothing about how it fared with other languages. On the other hand, we would know immediately that a certain framework was *not* viable as soon as we succeeded in ascertaining that it did *not* provide a revealing grammar for English. We could be confident in such a negative conclusion even if we had not attempted to apply the framework under consideration to any other languages.

As a matter of fact, the construction of a framework that allows a revealing grammar even for English is a project whose enormous difficulty becomes apparent only as it is actively pursued. Surprising as it may seem, none of the many frameworks that have been proposed over the years appears to be completely successful even with regard to English alone. Thus, when we restrict our discussions primarily to material from English, we do so not out of a belief that a study of English is sufficient to establish a framework, but rather out of the much more modest belief that no framework can be considered viable if it does not give good results for English (or for any other language we care to name). Furthermore, a concerted effort to study the detailed application of various frameworks to material from a single language provides the strongest basis for undertaking the same kind of work with other languages.

Suggestions for Further Reading

There are a number of introductory books that may be of use to readers who desire a wide-ranging introduction to linguistics. These include two justifiably famous works from the first half of this century (Sapir, 1921; Bloomfield 1933) and also a number of more recent works, including Lyons 1968, Winfred P. Lehmann 1972, Langacker 1973, Elgin 1973, and Fromkin and Rodman 1974. The Lyons book is especially helpful in its detailed and clear discussion of the categories of traditional grammar (Chapters 7 and 8). Also useful for readers who would like some help with traditional grammatical terminology is the glossary found in Sledd 1959, Chapter 7.

On the relation between universal grammar and the projection problem, there are no very elementary discussions. Although Chomsky 1965 (Chapter 1) Chomsky 1968, and Peters 1972 will seem difficult to most readers who lack extensive work in syntax, they provide the best existing discussions of this subject.

Notes

1. The term *descriptive adequacy* is often used in a broader sense to include success in predicting other kinds of judgments. An example is afforded by the

following pair of sentences (Chomsky, 1964, p. 34):

(i)   John is eager to please.
(ii) John is easy to please.

Beyond the judgment that the sentences are grammatical, English speakers can also tell that the "understood" relation of *John* to *please* is different in the two examples. In (i), *John* is understood as the subject of *please*, whereas in (ii) the same noun is understood as the object. From time to time as we proceed, we will mention additional types of judgments that we might want a grammar to account for.

Another term that is sometimes used to describe grammars is the term *observationally adequate*. Although occasionally employed in the same way that "descriptively adequate" is employed in the present text, the term *observationally adequate* was introduced in Chomsky 1964 to describe grammars that succeeded in generating the sentences in some fixed, limited body of "observed sentences." Under this interpretation, a certain grammar would be observationally adequate with respect, say, to the set of sentences found in the preface to this book if it simply generated all of them. The same grammar might well turn out not to be *descriptively* adequate, since it might do very poorly in distinguishing grammatical and ungrammatical sentences in the English language as a whole.

2.   In certain respects, even the task of making judgments about sentences involves performance factors. For example, the sentence in (i) below would elicit a favorable judgment from a fluent speaker of English, whereas the one in (ii) would be almost certain to give rise to a strongly negative reaction:

(i)   The man that the dog bit died.
(ii) The man that the dog that the cat scratched bit died.

In this instance, it appears that the negative reaction is not caused by a violation of one or more rules of English syntax, but is caused by the fact that the sentence happens to have a form that puts intolerable burdens on the performance mechanisms involved in comprehending the sentence. For a brief discussion of examples like this, see Chomsky 1965, Chapter 1, pp. 10–15.

3.   Data of these types would be relevant for the acquisition of competence in syntax. Other types of basic data are clearly important for the attainment of semantic competence, i.e., the ability to interpret words and sentences in the language. Here the nonlinguistic contexts in which utterances occur must be of vital importance. It is an interesting open question whether information about the intended meanings of the utterances that the child hears is necessary for the acquisition of syntax.

4.   At this point in the book, it may be difficult to imagine how a fixed body of data from a language could be described in a wide variety of contradictory ways. This possibility will become much easier to envision as we proceed in later chapters to develop sets of rules for English.

5.   A more realistic assumption might be that speakers of a language do not acquire just one set of rules, but several sets that differ slightly in the sentences that they generate. The basic problem is essentially the same if this alternative assumption is made.

6.   For our purposes in this illustration, it makes no difference whether the predisposition at work here is innate or whether instead it has its source in the subjects' previous experiences with their own language. The central purpose is merely to indicate the crucial role that predispositions play in helping us to arrive at fruitful guesses on the basis of fragmentary data.

7. Word order is not completely free in Latin. Furthermore, despite their overall emphasis on parts of speech and syntactic categories, many traditional Latin handbooks contain a few general remarks on "normal" or "preferred" word order. An example of such a discussion is found in Greenough *et al.* 1903, pp. 393–400.

THE DEVELOPMENT OF A SYNTACTIC FRAMEWORK

Our overall aim in Part II of this book will be to provide the outlines of the transformational framework, one particular set of hypotheses concerning universal grammar. As a preliminary matter, we will devote Chapter 2 to a consideration of two frameworks of a more elementary sort. In Chapter 3 we will introduce transformational rules and give an initial sketch of the transformational framework. Chapter 4 will give additional examples of transformational rules for English. The goal of the remainder of Part II (Chapters 5–10) will be to develop a more detailed version of this framework. In the course of developing a general syntactic framework, we will find ourselves giving constant attention to an auxiliary project, that of developing a tentative partial grammar for English.

2

Elementary
Syntactic Frameworks

2.1 WORD CLASS GRAMMARS

The first framework for grammatical description that we will consider is an extremely simple one, which we shall refer to as the *word class framework*.

The major initial attraction of this framework is that it will enable us, indeed force us, to give explicit recognition to the permissible word orders of English. A grammar based on this framework will consist of two parts. The first part is a list of word classes, with the words in each class listed below the name of the class. The second part is a collection of *sentence formulae*; each sentence formula is made up of a sequence of the word class names. The following is very tiny grammar conforming to this model:

(1)   Word Classes:

N	V	*Adj*	*Prep*	Conj	Pro	Det
man	put	large	up	and	we	the
dog	fly	warm	toward	or	he	a
box	stole	tall	below		us	this
birds	vanished	small	into		they	these
bacon	saw		on		him	
count			from		I	
king					me	
pan						
John						

31

Sentence Formulae

```
N   V   Pro
Pro  V   Det  N   Conj  Det  N
Det  Adj  N   V   Det  Adj  N   Prep  Det  Adj  N
```

We will interpret this grammar, and other grammars based on this framework, in the following way:

(2)   A word class grammar generates any sentence that can be derived from some formula by replacing each symbol in the formula by some word from the class which the symbol stands for.

By this interpretation, the word class grammar given above generates each of the following sentences:

(3)   John saw us.   (by substitution in the first sentence formula)

(4)   We saw the count and the king.   (by substitution in the second formula)

(5)   The tall man put the large dog into a large box.   (by substitution in the third formula)

On the other hand, it does not generate the following sentences:

(6)   Bill saw us.

(7)   The birds fly.

The first of these sentences is not generated because *Bill* does not appear in any of the word classes in (1); the second is not generated because this grammar does not contain the necessary formula Det N V.

The grammar that we have presented here for purposes of illustration will of course leave many grammatical English sentences ungenerated. At first glance, this might appear to be a defect that can be repaired merely by listing more words and more sentence formulae, until we reach a point at which every grammatical English sentence is generated. More careful consideration, however, will show that *no word class grammar can generate all of the grammatical sentences of English.* We can demonstrate this by showing that for any particular word class grammar, we can find a grammatical English sentence that is too long to be generated by that grammar.

As a first step in this demonstration, let us note that there are many sequences of successively longer English sentences that can be extended to any length we desire. One such sequence is the following:

(8)   a.   Alice has flat feet.
      b.   Bob knows that Alice has flat feet.
      c.   Bill believes that Bob knows that Alice has flat feet.
      d.   Bob knows that Bill believes that Bob knows that Alice has flat feet.
      e.   Bill believes that Bob knows that Bill believes that Bob knows that Alice has flat feet.

We have just indicated the first five sentences in this sequence. It is easy to see how to proceed from the fifth to the sixth, from the sixth to the seventh, and in general from any sentence in the sequence to the one following. What is important here is that *at no point in the sequence do the sentences cease to be grammatical*. As we proceed in the sequence, we may very well come to a point beyond which no human with an average lifespan would have time to say or listen to the whole sentence. But the fact that these sentences are too long for ordinary human use does not make them any less grammatical than the first few sentences.

Now suppose that someone presents us with a word class grammar which he claims will generate all of the grammatical sentences of English. No matter how many formulae his grammar contains, the list of formulae cannot go on forever. Thus, we can find one formula which is at least as long as any other formula in the grammar. Suppose that this formula contains 300 word class names. Now we can go to our sequence of English sentences indicated in (8), and find a sentence which is more than 300 words long. Although any sentence over 300 words would do, we could settle for the shortest one: the hundredth sentence in our sequence contains 301 words; consequently, this sentence could not possibly be generated by this grammar. Thus, we have found one grammatical sentence of English which the grammar offered to us would not generate. If a word class grammar were proposed to us whose longest formula was much longer than this, all that we would have to do would be to pick out a sentence farther along in our sequence. For any particular word class grammar proposed to us as a grammar of English, we can find grammatical English sentences which this grammar fails to generate. In sum, the word class framework could not possibly provide us with any grammar of English which passes the fundamental test of generating all of the grammatical sentences of English and no ungrammatical ones. It is important to note that this is not merely a defect in one particular grammar based on this framework, but rather a defect in the framework itself.

Even if we were to restrict our attention artificially to English sentences below a certain length (for instance, to sentences less than twenty words long), the word class framework would still have to be judged inadequate. Although it would be possible, given enough time and patience, to construct a word class grammar for this artificially restricted subset of English sentences, any such grammar would necessarily fail the second condition of adequacy for grammars, namely, that the grammar be revealing. Not only would the number of sentence formulae required be immense, but even worse, there would be a wealth of embarrassing coincidences. The most basic type of coincidence is that certain sequences of word classes would occur time after time, both within single formulae and from one formula to another. The following formula will serve to illustrate the point:

(9)   Det Adj N V Det Adj N Prep Det N Prep Det
       Adj N Prep Det N

This formula would be required in a word class grammar of English if that grammar was to generate a sentence such as:

(10)   The large man sent the small dog to the woman in the small house by the ocean.

In this formula, the sequence Det Adj N appears three times, the sequence Det N appears twice, and the sequence Prep Det N appears twice. We find additional instances of all three of these sequences in a formula such as the following:

(11)   Det Adj N Prep Det N V Prep Det N Prep Det N

which would be required by sentences such as:

(12)   The small dog on the mantle belongs to the lady of the house.

What these coincidences suggest is that there are certain fundamental principles of English structure which specify the composition of English sentences not merely as sequences of individual words, but rather as sequences of *phrases*, units larger than individual words. Rather than stating these principles directly, a word class grammar simply gives an extremely cumbersome and unilluminating catalog of the effects of these principles. In the next section, we will develop a more sophisticated framework, one that allows a direct expression for these general principles of English structure.

EXERCISES

1. The word class grammar in the text permits the generation of such ungrammatical sentences as the following:

*John saw he.
*Us saw the count and the king.

In traditional terms, these sentences exhibit incorrect choices of *pronoun case*. How can one revise the word class grammar in the text in such a way as to avoid the generation of these ungrammatical sentences, while still permitting the generation of the sentences below?

John saw us.
We saw the count and the king.

Be sure that the revised grammar that you suggest is still stated within the confines of the word class framework.

2. What other types of ungrammatical English sentences are generated by the word class grammar in (1) in the text? Give examples of each general type that you mention.

3. We say that two grammars (of any kind) are *equivalent* if they generate exactly the same sentences. Below are given two word class grammars that use Roman numerals as class names. The grammars share a common list of word classes, but have different sets of sentence formulae.

GRAMMAR A

Word Classes:

I ✓	II ᴾᴿᴼ	III ᴬᵈʲ	IV ᶜᵒⁿʲ	V ᴰᵉᵗ	VI ᴺ	VII ᴾʳᵉᵖ
put	we	large	and	the	man	up
fly	he	warm	or	a	dog	toward
stole	us	tall		this	box	below
vanished	they	small		these	birds	into
saw	him				bacon	on
	I				count	from
	me				king	
					pan	
					John	

Sentence Formulae:

V III VI I V III VI VII V III VI ᴰᵉᵗ ᴬᵈʲ ᴺ ⱽ ᴰᵉᵗ ᴬᵈʲ ᴺ ᴾʳᵉᵖ

VI I II ᴺ ⱽ ᴾʳᵒ ᴰᵉᵗ ᴬᵈʲ ᴺ

II I V VI IV V VI ᴾʳᵒ ⱽ ᴰᵉᵗ ᴺ ᶜᵒⁿʲ ᴰᵉᵗ ᴺ

GRAMMAR B

Word Classes: Same as in Grammar A

Sentence Formulae:

VI I II ᴺ ⱽ ᴾʳᵒ

V III VI I V III VI VII V III VI

V VI I VII V III VI ᴰᵉᵗ ᴺ ⱽ ᴾʳᵉᵖ ᴰᵉᵗ ᴬᵈʲ ᴺ

Which of these two grammars is *not* equivalent to the grammar given in (1) in this chapter? Support your answer in one of two ways:

A. Give a sentence that is generated by the grammar you picked from the two above but is not generated by the grammar in the text.

B. Give a sentence that is generated by the grammar in the text, but not by the grammar that you picked from the two in this problem.

2.2 THE PHRASE STRUCTURE FRAMEWORK

Traditional grammars generally provide concepts for describing sentences not just as sequences of words, but as sequences of *groups* of words. Among the concepts occasionally used are *noun phrase*, *verb phrase*, and *prepositional phrase*. The beginning of an informal description of English sentences in these terms might contain the following statements:

(13)   A sentence may consist of a noun phrase and a verb phrase. A verb phrase may consist of a verb alone, or a verb and a noun phrase, or a verb and a prepositional phrase, or a verb and a noun phrase and a prepositional phrase. A prepositional phrase may consist of a preposition and a noun phrase. A noun phrase may consist of a noun alone, or an adjective and a noun, or a determiner and a noun, or a determiner and an adjective and a noun.

Descriptive statements of this sort can be formalized in what are known as *phrase structure grammars*.[1] A grammar constructed within the phrase structure framework consists of a set of rules, each rule having a single symbol on the left connected by an arrow to one or more symbols on the right. An example of a grammar based on this framework is given in (14) below. Groups of two or more letters (NP, Adj, etc.) which do not have any spaces between successive letters are to be interpreted as single symbols.

(14) a.　　S → NP　VP
　　　b.　　VP → V
　　　c.　　VP → V　NP
　　　d.　　VP → V　PrepP
　　　e.　　VP → V　NP　PrepP
　　　f.　　PrepP → Prep　NP
　　　g.　　NP → N
　　　h.　　NP → Adj　N
　　　i.　　NP → Det　N
　　　j.　　NP → Det　Adj　N

If the arrow in each rule is interpreted as meaning "may consist of," and if the symbol S is interpreted as standing for sentence, VP for verb phrase, PrepP for prepositional phrase, NP for noun phrase, and the remaining symbols as in the preceding section of this chapter, then this set of rules is exactly equivalent to the set of informal statements preceding it. We might in addition provide a set of rules to specify which English words may be used as nouns, which as verbs, and so forth:

(14)	aa.	N → *man*		nn.	V → *acknowledged*
	bb.	N → *dog*		oo.	Adj → *large*
	cc.	N → *cousin*		pp.	Adj → *warm*
	dd.	N → *birds*		qq.	Adj → *tall*
	ee.	N → *count*		rr.	Adj → *small*
	ff.	N → *king*		ss.	Prep → *up*
	gg.	N → *lake*		tt.	Prep → *into*
	hh.	N → *fact*		uu.	Prep → *of*
	ii.	N → *John*		vv.	Prep → *from*
	jj.	V → *put*		ww.	Det → *the*
	kk.	V → *fly*		xx.	Det → *a*
	ll.	V → *vanished*		yy.	Det → *this*
	mm.	V → *saw*		zz.	Det → *these*

We shall sometimes employ the term *terminal symbol* for items such as *man*, *small*, or *of*, which do not appear on the left-hand side of any rule. Correspondingly, we can use the term *nonterminal symbol* to refer to items such as S, NP, VP, V, Adj, and so forth.

The manner in which phrase structure grammars are interpreted as generating sentences can be illustrated by referring to this sample grammar.

First the symbol S is written; then below that is written the sequence of symbols which appears to the right of S in rule (14a). (If our grammar had contained more than one rule having S as the left-hand symbol, we could have picked any of the rules.) Following this, a third line is formed, which is like the second line except that one of the symbols in the second line is replaced in the third line by a sequence of symbols which appears to the right of the replaced symbol in one of the rules. In the present instance, there are eight possibilities for the third line. If we choose to rewrite the NP in the second line, then the third line will be one of the following:

(15)   N   VP   if we apply rule (14g)
       Adj   N   VP   if we apply rule (14h)
       Det   N   VP   if we apply rule (14i)
       Det   Adj   N   VP   if we apply rule (14j)

On the other hand, we could have chosen to rewrite the VP first; in this case, too, we would have had four possibilities, one for each of the four rules having the symbol VP on the left-hand side. If we had chosen to rewrite the VP first, the four possible third lines would be:

(16)   NP   V   if we apply rule (14b)
       NP   V   NP   if we apply rule (14c)
       NP   V   PrepP   if we apply rule (14d)
       NP   V   NP   PrepP   if we apply rule (14e)

Let us look now at a complete derivation that could be formed in this way:

(17)   S   (Initial Symbol)
       NP   VP   by rule (14a)
       Det   Adj   N   VP   by rule (14j)
       Det   Adj   N   V   PrepP   by rule (14d)
       the   Adj   N   V   PrepP   by rule (14ww)
       the   Adj   N   *vanished*   PrepP   by rule (14ll)
       the   Adj   N   *vanished*   Prep   NP   by rule (14f)
       the   Adj   N   *vanished*   Prep   Det   N by rule (14i)
       the   Adj   N   *vanished*   *from*   Det   N by rule (14vv)
       the   *large*   N   *vanished*   *from*   Det   N by rule (14oo)
       the   *large*   N   *vanished*   *from*   Det   *lake* by rule (14gg)
       the large birds vanished from   Det   *lake* by rule (14dd)
       The large birds vanished from the lake.   by rule (14ww)

We say that a derivation is *terminated* when, as in the last line above, all of the symbols are terminal symbols. Putting it another way, the last line above contains no symbol which is itself eligible for rewriting. Turning now to the interpretation of our original rules as a grammar for generating sentences, we count as generated by this grammar any sentence which is the last line of a terminated derivation constructed according to the rules in this system. The sentence

(18)   The large birds vanished from the lake.

is thus an example of a sentence that is generated by the grammar.

The derivation that we have provided for (18) is only one of a great number that could have been given for this sentence. For instance, instead of going from the second line to the fourth line by first rewriting the NP and then rewriting the VP, we could just as well have rewritten the VP first and then rewritten the NP. We frequently find more than one symbol in a given line that can be rewritten to give the next line. Which symbol we choose to expand in such situations has no effect on the ultimate outcome of a derivation. Such differences in derivations, which arise merely from differences in the order in which various symbols are expanded, have no significance. The only way in which derivations may differ significantly is in the particular choices that are made when there is more than a single rule in the grammar by which a particular symbol can be rewritten. For instance, an entirely different sentence would have resulted if we had used rule (14i) instead of rule (14j) to rewrite the NP in the second line of the derivation. The resulting sentence would have begun with a determiner followed directly by a noun, with no adjective appearing between them.

The essential information in a derivation can be represented in graphic form in a *phrase structure tree* such as the following:

(19)

In fact, phrase structure rules are sometimes thought of as producing phrase structure trees directly: a tree is developed by starting with the initial symbol S, then writing below it a sequence of symbols that appears to the right side of a rule that has S on the left, and continuing in this way to draw branches out of every symbol for which this is possible. A tree is completed when a state is reached in which each branch of the tree ends in a terminal symbol, i.e., in a symbol that cannot be rewritten. We will count a sentence as generated by the grammar if there is some tree in which that sentence appears as the bottom line. Thus, by this alternative definition of how phrase structure rules generate sentences, the rules in the sample grammar still generate sentence (18).

For all practical purposes, the two ways of interpreting phrase structure rules are equivalent; there is no point in this book at which the difference would be in any way significant. For the purposes of exposition, we will assume the latter interpretation; that is, we will assume that the rules are to be interpreted as constructing trees.

Now that we have defined the phrase structure framework and have stated how a grammar constructed on this model is to be interpreted as generating sentences, let us compare it with the word class framework. As we noted in the last section, the word class framework is inadequate in two fundamental respects. First, no grammar constructed within this framework can possibly generate all of the grammatical sentences of English. In the second place, any word class grammar covering even a part of English is bound to be unrevealing.

The phrase structure framework is superior to the word class framework in both of these respects. In the first place, we can write phrase structure grammars which generate an infinite number of English sentences. Let us begin, for example, with the sequence given in (8) of this chapter:

(8) a. Alice has flat feet.

  b. Bob knows that Alice has flat feet.

  c. Bill believes that Bob knows that Alice has flat feet.

  d. Bob knows that Bill believes that Bob knows that Alice has flat feet.

  e. Bill believes that Bob knows that Bill believes that Bob knows that Alice has flat feet.

In order to generate the sentences in this sequence, beginning with the phrase structure rules in our sample grammar, we must of course add rules which allow the introduction of *feet*, *Bob*, *Bill*, and *Alice* under N, and *flat* under Adj, and *knows* and *has* under V. Beyond that, the addition of a single rule to those already given in (14) makes possible the generation of every sentence in this infinite sequence. This rule is the following:

(14) k.   VP → V *that* S

As an example of what this rule does, consider the third sentence in the infinite sequence described above. The tree for this sentence starts out in the usual way:

(19) a.

```
        S
       / \
     NP   VP
```

At this point, we have our choice of five VP rules; we pick the new rule (14k), and the resulting tree is (19b):

(19) b.

```
          S
        /   \
      NP     VP
            / | \
           V that S
```

With the introduction of this second S, we are in effect given the opportunity of starting all over again. We rewrite this S by rule (14a) as NP VP, yielding the following larger tree:

(19) c.

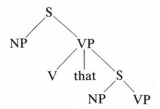

If this bottom VP is now rewritten as V *that* S, and the new S as NP VP, we get the following tree:

(19) d.

Finally, although we could continue in this way for as far as we wish, we now apply rule (14c). After we rewrite the last NP as Adj N and the remaining NP's as N, and then rewrite each of the N's, V's, and Adj's by appropriate rules, we are left at the end with the following tree:

(19) e.

Again, it should be understood that the order in which the rules were applied in forming this tree was chosen entirely for the purpose of making the exposition as simple as possible. Any other order of application would have been just as valid, e.g., rewriting the first NP as N and this N as *Bill* before expanding the VP at all. When we read the sequence of terminal elements from left to right, we see that we have generated (8c), the third sentence in our sequence: *Bill believes that Bob knows that Alice has flat feet.*

It should be clear from this illustration that the phrase structure rules so far given allow the generation of not only this sentence but also the two sentences prior to it in the sequence. More importantly, they allow the generation of *any one of the infinite number of sentences* beyond the third sentence in the sequence. We can go to any length we desire simply by using the new rule (14k) to rewrite a sufficient number of successive VP's as V *that* S.

Have we shown by this demonstration that there must be a grammar based on the phrase structure framework which generates all of the grammatical English sentences and none of the ungrammatical ones? The answer is definitely no. All that we have shown here is that the phrase structure framework passes a fundamental test that the word class framework fails; it allows at least one grammar that generates one particular infinite set of English sentences.

The second inadequacy of the word class framework was that the partial grammars for English based on this framework were quite unrevealing, not taking advantage of certain extremely general regularities in English structure. Specifically, we pointed out that if we were to write down a large set of sentence formulae for English, we would find sequences of the form Det Adj N occurring in many different formulae, and also sometimes more than once within the same formula. Within the word class framework, these recurring sequences must be spelled out anew in every sentence formula in which they occur. If we adopt the phrase structure framework, on the other hand, this particular regularity can be stated just once. Our sample grammar in (14) contains the following rule:

(14) j.   NP → Det   Adj   N

Given the presence of the symbol NP on the right-hand side of each of the four rules (14a, c, e, f), the possibility of Det Adj N sequences in various positions in the sentence is automatically accounted for.

EXERCISES

1.   Find two ungrammatical sentences that are generated by the sample phrase structure grammar in (14).

2.   Suppose that you are told that the following tree has been created using only phrase structure rules:

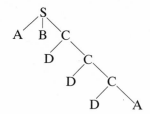

The rules that played a role in the formation of this tree must obviously have mentioned the symbols S, A, B, C, and D. What must the rules have been?

3. Consider the following sequence of sentences:

John saw the king.

John saw the cousin of the king.

John saw the cousin of the cousin of the king.

John saw the cousin of the cousin of the cousin of the king.

State a single phrase structure rule that, together with the rules in (14), will allow the generation of every sentence in this infinite sequence. Show how the third sentence in the sequence is derived. Do this by drawing the tree that the rules would give in the course of generating the sentence. (Note: There is more than one rule that will do the trick. Any rule that works is a satisfactory answer to the question.)

4. Which, if either, of the following sentences is generated by the sample phrase structure grammar in (14), leaving out of consideration the rule that you gave as an answer to Exercise 3?

John saw the cousin of the king.

The cousin of the king saw John.

If you think that the grammar does generate one of the sentences, draw the tree that it assigns. Be sure that it is exactly the tree that the rules as stated actually give.

5. Study the following phrase structure grammars:

GRAMMAR A

    S → NP   V
    S → NP   V   NP
    S → NP   V   PrepP
    PrepP → Prep   NP
    NP → N
    NP → Adj   N
    NP → Det   N
    NP → Det   Adj   N
    NP → Det   N   PrepP
    Rules (14aa–zz)

GRAMMAR B

    S → VP
    S → VP   NP
    S → VP   PrepP
    S → VP   NP   PrepP
    PrepP → Prep   NP
    NP → N
    NP → Adj   N
    NP → Det   N
    NP → Det   Adj   N

VP → N V
VP → Adj N V
VP → Det N V
VP → Det Adj N V
Rules (14aa–zz)

A. What tree would Grammar A assign to the following sentence?

The large birds vanished from the lake.

B. What tree would be assigned to the same sentence by Grammar B?

C. One of these two grammars is not equivalent to the sample phrase structure grammar given in (14) in the text. Which one is it? Support your answer by one or more specific examples. If necessary, review what it means for two grammars to be *equivalent* (Exercise 3 of section 2.1).

2.3 THE CHOICE OF FRAMEWORK AND THE PROJECTION PROBLEM

In the previous section we showed that it is possible to construct a phrase structure grammar for a fragment of English that is much more revealing than any word class grammar for the same fragment. As we mentioned in Chapter 1, the finding that a certain framework does not allow revealing grammars for a language in effect means that the framework would be relatively ineffective as part of a solution to the projection problem, the problem of deriving an adequate adult grammar from childhood basic data.

We can illustrate this point again by looking at a small set of hypothetical basic data, and comparing the results of describing it with a word class grammar and the results of describing it with a phrase structure grammar. (By "hypothetical," we mean that the data were not recorded as part of the linguistic experience of any actual human child.) The body of data can be represented as a list of simple sentences, with a distinction made between those that are grammatical and those that are ungrammatical:

(20) a. The small girl pushed the large dog toward the man.
   b. The tall girl pushed the small dog toward the man.
   c. The small girl pushed the tall dog toward the man.
   d. The large girl pushed the small dog toward the man.
   e. The tall girl pushed the large dog toward the man.
   f. The large girl pushed the tall dog toward the man.
   g. The large girl pushed the tall man toward the dog.
   h. The small man pushed the tall girl toward the dog.
   i. The girl pushed the small dog toward the man.
   j. The man pushed the large dog toward the girl.
   k. The dog pushed the tall girl toward the man.
   l. The tall girl pushed the man toward the dog.

m. The tall man pushed the dog toward the girl.

n. The large man pushed the girl toward the dog.

o. The girl pushed the dog toward the man.

p. The dog bit the large man.

q. The man bit the small dog.

r. The dog bit the man. .

s. *Pushed the small girl the large dog toward the man.

t. *The dog the man large bit.

u. *The girl the small dog the man toward pushed.

v. *The dog toward the tall man bit the girl.

We can suppose that our imaginary child has inferred the well-formedness of sentences (20a–r) by hearing them uttered, and that he has inferred the ill-formedness of sentences (20s–v) by uttering them himself and being corrected by an adult speaker.[2]

If we were to stay within the confines of the word class framework, we would most probably set up the following grammar as an account of these sentences:

(21) Sentence Formulae:

Det	Adj	N	V	Det	Adj	N	Prep	Det	N
Det	N	V	Det	Adj	N	Prep	Det	N	
Det	Adj	N	V	Det	N	Prep	Det	N	
Det	N	V	Det	N	Prep	Det	N		
Det	N	V	Det	Adj	N				
Det	N	V	Det	N					

Word Classes:

Det	N	Adj	V	Prep
the	dog	large	bit	toward
	man	tall	pushed	
	girl	small		

If we were to account for the same data within the confines of the phrase structure framework, we might offer the following grammar:[3]

(22) a. S → NP V NP

b. S → NP V NP Prep NP

c. NP → Det Adj N

d. NP → Det N

e. Det → *the*

f. N → *dog*

g. N → *man*

h. N → *girl*

i. Adj → *large*

j.   Adj → *tall*

k.   Adj → *small*

l.   V → *bit*

m.   V → *pushed*

n.   Prep → *toward*

Having developed a word class grammar and a phrase structure grammar to account for these data, let us now test these two grammars against new data. Suppose, in particular, we check the predictions that the two grammars make with regard to the following four sentences:

(23) a.   The large man pushed the small dog toward the girl.

b.   *The girl the large dog the tall man toward pushed.

c.   The girl pushed the large dog toward the tall man.

d.   The large dog bit the small man.

Not too surprisingly, the word class grammar in (21) generates (23a), which exhibits a sequence of word classes virtually identical to the sequence exhibited in several of the sentences in the basic data. Again not too surprisingly, the grammar does not generate (23b), a clearly ungrammatical sentence. Unfortunately, however, it also fails to generate (23c) and (23d), both of which are perfectly grammatical sentences. It just happened that the basic data in (20) did not include any sentences showing exactly these two sequences of word classes.

Let us see now how well the phrase structure grammar in (22) does with the same set of four sentences. Like the word class grammar in (21), it generates the grammatical sentence (23a) but not the ungrammatical sentence (23b). But unlike the word class grammar, it generates both (23c) and (23d), correctly predicting that they are grammatical. Thus, the phrase structure grammar in (22) comes out ahead of the word class grammar in (21) as soon as we test the two grammars outside of the limited set of hypothetical basic data in (20). In effect, the phrase structure framework has allowed us a certain fruitful idea about the language of which the data in (20) formed a sample, an idea that could not be expressed directly within the word class framework. This idea is simply that both Det–Adj–N sequences and Det–N sequences are instances of a general phrase type (NP), which may occur in several positions (before verbs, after verbs, and after prepositions).

2.4 EVALUATION MEASURES

At this point it might seem that we would be justified in saying that the phrase structure framework enabled us to "predict" the judgments in (23) on the basis of the data in (20), in a way that the word class framework did not. Such a view, though, is not quite tenable as matters now stand. The difficulty is that there are many other phrase structure grammars that we could have devised for the data in (20), some of which would not have fared so well in predicting the judgments in (23). One such grammar is the following:

(24) a.   S → NP V NP Prep Det N
     b.   S → Det N V NP
     c.   NP → Det Adj N
     d.   NP → Det N
     (Also the required rules for expanding N, V, Prep, Adj, Det)

As can be readily verified, this grammar is markedly inferior to the grammar in (22) as regards the predictions that it makes about the judgments of the four sentences in (23). As a matter of fact, it does just as poorly as the word class grammar in (21). Unfortunately, nothing that we have said so far would have led us to favor *in advance* the ultimately more successful grammar in (22). Both grammars clearly satisfy the conditions defining the phrase structure framework, and both are fully compatible with the basic data in (20). Hence, we are not justified in saying that we *predicted* the grammaticality of (23c) and (23d) on the basis of the data in (20).

Before giving up on the phrase structure framework, we might try to find some way of distinguishing superior grammars from inferior grammars in advance of any testing on new data such as the four sentences in (23). Although there are a number of possibilities, we will discuss an approach here that has received a good deal of attention.[4] When we compare the two grammars in (22) and (24), we notice immediately that the grammar in (22) is more concise than the grammar in (24), since the first and second rule in the former have NP occurrences where the corresponding rules in the latter have two-symbol sequences consisting of Det and N:

(22) a.   S → NP V NP Prep *NP*
     b.   S → *NP* V NP

(24) a.   S → NP V NP Prep *Det N*
     b.   S → *Det N* V NP

Suppose, then, that we incorporate the following *evaluation measure* into our universal grammar, alongside the phrase structure framework defined earlier:

(25)   When two or more grammars satisfy the terms of the phrase structure framework, and both are compatible with a certain set of basic data, select the grammar having the smallest number of symbol occurrences as a guide to sentences outside the limited set of basic data.

If we now go back to the task of selecting a grammar on the basis of the data in (20), we see that the evaluation measure in (25) clearly picks the grammar in (22), thus yielding the prediction that (22) will do as well or better outside the basic data than will the competing grammar (24). In this instance, the prediction is correct, so that in this hypothetical situation, the particular evaluation measure in (25) and the phrase structure framework have worked effectively. Together, they have had the effect of determining a grammar that succeeded in filling in some "gaps" in the basic data. These gaps were left by the nonoccurrence in the basic data of any sentences having precisely the form of (23c) and (23d):[5]

(23) c.   The girl pushed the large dog toward the tall man.
            [Det N   V   Det Adj N   Prep DetAdj N]
     d.   The large dog bit the small man.
            [Det Adj   N   V Det Adj   N]

Several points are worth noting about the evaluation measure in (25). The first is that its success is dependent on the framework that is assumed along with it. If we attempt to use a similar symbol-counting procedure in connection with the word class framework, we find that it accomplishes nothing: we still end up with the grammar given in (21), a grammar that proves to be relatively unsuccessful. We will see additional instances later where the effectiveness of a measure of this sort depends on the particular framework assumed.

A second point to note is that other evaluation measures are logically possible; in fact, many could be devised which would not have given us the same results in the test that we have just performed. For example, suppose that we were to adopt the following alternative measure:

(26)   When two or more grammars satisfy the terms of the phrase structure framework, and both are compatible with a certain set of basic data, select the grammar having the smallest number of *rules*.

When we try to use this instruction to choose between the phrase structure grammar in (22) and the one in (24), we find that no definite choice can be made; the two grammars contain exactly the same number of rules. Consequently, the alternative evaluation measure in (26) yields no prediction as to which of these two grammars will yield better results with new sentences. We thus have a straightforward reason for making the measure in (25) a tentative part of our universal grammar rather than the one in (26); the former simply gives better results than the latter.

One last point is important here. In Chapter 1 we began to "evaluate" various rules and sets of rules for English by trying to determine how well their predictions coincided with the judgments of speakers of English. In incorporating into our universal grammar a tentative "evaluation measure" that relies on counting symbol occurrences, we may seem at first to be suggesting an alternative method of carrying out the same task, one which could potentially come into conflict with our first type of evaluation. In point of fact, however, the two types of "evaluation" represent two completely distinct tasks. The type of evaluation introduced in Chapter 1 is evaluation "after the fact": for one reason or another, we have a particular grammar in mind, and are interested in finding out whether in retrospect we would have been wise to choose this grammar. By contrast, in the type of "evaluation" in which an instruction like (25) plays a role, we are interested in making some prediction before the fact as to which one of two or more grammars that are all compatible with a limited set of data will prove to have the best after-the-fact evaluation when new data are considered. Our universal grammar is successful to the extent that the grammar that is picked as most highly valued before the fact turns out to be most highly valued after the fact as well.

An analogy can be drawn here with the person who bets on horses in conformity with some system. For each horse in a certain race, he gathers relevant data concerning the horse's previous record, its ancestry, the jockey's previous record, and any other data that his system calls for. He then deduces from his system a "predicted best horse." This represents his before-the-fact evaluation, on the basis of which he may place a bet. At the end of the race, he is able to evaluate the horses after the fact, that is, the "best horse" now is the one who won the race. He counts his system successful to the extent that the "predicted best horse" before the fact and the "best horse" after the fact are one and the same horse. Even though he always hopes that the results of the two types of evaluation will coincide, he clearly realizes that they are entirely distinct activities and that neither one could possibly serve as a substitute for the other. The two types of "evaluation" of grammars are every bit as distinct.

EXERCISES

1. Describe as concisely as possible the set of sequences that is generated by the following phrase structure grammar:

a.	S → S A
b.	S → A
c.	A → *the*
d.	A → *dog*
e.	A → *man*
f.	A → *girl*
g.	A → *large*
h.	A → *tall*
i.	A → *small*
j.	A → *bit*
k.	A → *pushed*
l.	A → *toward*

Hint: A good way to begin is to go through a number of derivations, beginning with the initial symbol S and proceeding more or less at random. The sequences that result should give some clue as to the nature of the set of sequences generated by these rules.

2. Suppose that we were to apply the phrase structure framework, together with the evaluation measure in (25), to a set of basic data that consisted of (20a–r), that is, a set that consisted of all of the grammatical sentences in (20) but none of the ungrammatical ones. What would be the predicted

[handwritten marginalia] how is this different from the ex. in text?

"best grammar" in that situation, and what predictions would this grammar yield concerning the sentences in (23)?

3. Consider again the set of basic data in (20). Given these data, the evaluation measure stated in (25) led us to select a phrase structure grammar that had the following four nonterminal rules:

   a.   S → NP V NP Prep NP
   b.   S → NP V NP
   c.   NP → Det Adj N
   d.   NP → Det N

No reference is made in these rules to a node VP, dominating V plus any following symbols. Try to find some additional sentences which would lead to the selection of a grammar in which a VP is referred to. Specifically, what you should try to do is to find some sentences that you can add to the set of basic data in (20), so that the most concise phrase structure grammar compatible with this larger set will mention VP. For the purposes of this problem, you should ignore distinctions involving English verb inflection. For example, you need not try to prevent your grammar from generating sentences in which *bit* appears incorrectly where *bite* would be correct, or in which *bite* appears where *bites* would be correct.

4. As a sequel to Exercise 3, try to find some data which, when added to the data already given in (20), would provide motivation for introducing the symbol PrepP into the grammar.

2.5 THE PARENTHESES CONVENTION

In this section we will examine a special convention about how phrase structure rules are to be represented in a grammar. The justification that has been offered for this convention is that it appears to increase the effectiveness of an evaluation measure like (25). We can get an idea of the role that this convention is to play by examining another set of hypothetical basic data, one that happens to include noun phrases of just the three types given in (27a–c):

(27) a.   the seven honorable men
     b.   honorable men
     c.   seven men

Informally speaking, the idea that we might get on the basis of the data in (27a–c) is that an NP consists of an optional determiner, an optional numeral, an optional adjective, and a noun, in that order. Given this idea, we would naturally expect the additional phrases in (27d–h) to be grammatical, an expectation which turns out to be correct.

(27) d.   the seven men
     e.   seven honorable men
     f.   the honorable men
     g.   the men
     h.   men

Unfortunately, when we apply the phrase structure framework as defined so far to the data in (27a–c), we find that the set of rules picked out by the evaluation measure in (25) is just the following:

(28) a.   NP → Det   Num   Adj   N
     b.   NP → Adj   N
     c.   NP → Num   N

Although these rules account for the types of NP's represented in the basic data in (27a–c), they do not generate any of the additional NP's in (27d–h). Thus, the phrase structure framework, in conjunction with the evaluation measure in (25), fails to predict grammaticality for the phrases in (27d–h) on the basis of those in (27a–c).

A greater predictive power can be obtained in this situation if we formulate a convention for writing phrase structure rules which allows us to express the optional status of elements directly. This is the purpose of the following convention:

(29)   If two phrase structure rules are identical except that one contains a symbol or a sequence of symbols that the other does not, we abbreviate the two rules as one by writing out the longer rule and enclosing in parentheses the symbol or sequence of symbols that is missing in the shorter rule.

As an example of how this convention applies, let us look at the following pair of rules:

(30) a.   NP → Det   Adj   N
     b.   NP → Det   N

The first differs from the second only in containing one additional symbol, Adj. Hence, the conditions for applying this new convention are met, and we can "collapse" these two distinct rules into one, indicating the optional status of Adj by putting parentheses around it:

(30) c.   NP → Det (Adj) N

Suppose, further, that our grammar includes the following rules:

(30) d.   NP → Adj   N
     e.   NP → N

These two rules collapse to give (f):

(30) f.   NP → (Adj) N

Furthermore, if we now compare the collapsed rule in (c) with that in (f), we note that the former differs from the latter only in containing the symbol Det, which does not occur in the latter. Consequently, we can collapse these two rules, to give (g):

(30) g.   NP → (Det) (Adj) N

This expression thus abbreviates a total of four separate rules:

(30) a.   NP → Det Adj N
   b.   NP → Det N
   d.   NP → Adj N
   e.   NP → N

With this new convention for stating phrase structure rules, the evaluation measure defined in (25) gives different results than it did earlier. Let us look again at (27a–c): *the seven honorable men, honorable men*, and *seven men*. The parentheses convention allows us several sets of rules for these data that were not available to us before. In fact, one of these rule sets contains only a single rule:

(31)   NP → (Det) (Num) (Adj) N

Among the eight unabbreviated phrase structure rules that are collapsed in this rule are three rules that suffice to generate (27a–c). Furthermore, the set consisting of this one rule contains a smaller number of symbol occurrences than any other set of rules that we could devise for (27a–c), including in particular the set of three rules in (28), which was our "predicted best grammar" before the introduction of the parentheses convention. Thus, the evaluation measure in (25) now leads us to select (31) as our predicted best grammar for describing NP's outside of the original set of three. This time, the evaluation measure appears to be working more effectively, since among the rules abbreviated in (31) are all of those necessary for deriving the additional five NP's in (27d–h): *the seven men, seven honorable men, the honorable men, the men*, and *men*. The argument in favor of the parentheses convention, then, is just that it appears to increase the predictive power of the evaluation measure in (25).[6]

We should note here one side effect of the parentheses convention that will bear watching. When we adopt the rule in (31), we are in effect committing ourselves to a particular tree structure for NP's, one in which all elements mentioned in the rule are equal "daughters" of the NP. For instance, the structure assigned to (27f), *the honorable men*, would be as follows:

(32)

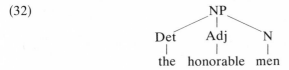

In Chapter 14 we will consider an alternative view as to the tree structures desirable for NP's, namely, that the Adj and the N together make up a constituent of their own within the NP. A structure of this sort is shown below:

(33)

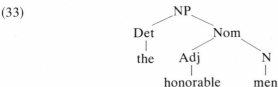

In the event that evidence is found that favors the structure in (33) over the structure in (32), a problem is created for the parentheses convention, since it would favor the selection of the wrong analysis for these NP's. We can see this by comparing the rule in (34) with the set of rules that would be needed to give structures of the alternative sort:

(34)   NP → (Det) (Adj) N

(35) a.   NP → (Det) Nom
     b.   Nom → (Adj) N

The rule in (34) clearly would be selected by the evaluation measure in (25) in preference to the set of two rules in (35). On the other hand, without the parentheses convention, the measure in (25) would favor structures of the second sort, as can be seen by comparing the number of symbol occurrences below:

(36)   NP → Det Adj N   (37)   NP → Det Nom
       NP → Det N   NP → Nom
       NP → Adj N   Nom → Adj N
       NP → N   Nom → N

The rules in (37) contain fewer symbol occurrences than those in (36), and these rules give structures of the type shown in (33). Thus, with the parentheses convention we are pushed toward the structure in (32), whereas without it we are pushed toward (33). If the structure in (33) actually does turn out to be preferable, then we might have reason to count as an argument *against* the parentheses convention the fact that it leads us to select (32).

Another abbreviatory convention that is employed in many works in syntax deserves mention here. This is the convention of using braces to indicate "either-or" options in the selection of elements. The following rule illustrates this convention:

(38)   VP → V NP $\left\{ \begin{matrix} NP \\ PrepP \\ Adj \end{matrix} \right\}$

This rule is informally translated as:

(39)   A VP may consist of a V followed by an NP followed by either an NP or a PrepP or an Adj.

The effect of (38) is thus to abbreviate a total of three individual rules:

(40) a.   VP → V NP NP
     b.   VP → V NP PrepP
     c.   VP → V NP Adj

The justification for this convention takes much the same form as that for the parentheses convention. However, since it is difficult to find convincing examples using material from English, we shall give an imaginary example.

Suppose that we find basic data from a language which indicate that the phrase *G* may take at least the following two forms:

(41) a.   A B C D E

     b.   A F C F E

Without the braces convention, the evaluation measure in (25) would lead to the selection of the following two rules:

(42) a. $G \rightarrow$ A B C D E

     b. $G \rightarrow$ A F C F E

On the other hand, the adoption of the braces convention would lead to the selection of (43) rather than (42):

(43) $G \rightarrow A \begin{Bmatrix} B \\ F \end{Bmatrix} C \begin{Bmatrix} D \\ F \end{Bmatrix} E$

Rule (43) abbreviates a total of four rules:

(44) a. $G \rightarrow$ A B C D E

     b. $G \rightarrow$ A B C F E

     c. $G \rightarrow$ A F C D E

     d. $G \rightarrow$ A F C F E

A grammar containing (43), then, would generate two types of sequences, those in (44b) and (44c), that would not be generated by a grammar that contained the two rules in (42).[7] If (44b) and (44c) turned out to be well-formed sequences in the language, then we would have some tentative support for the braces convention.

Although the arguments that we can make for the value of these two abbreviatory conventions are not terribly strong as matters stand now, we will nevertheless make it a practice to employ them in the rules that we write for English in future sections of this text.

EXERCISES

1. For each of the following expressions, write out the separate phrase structure rules that the expression abbreviates:

    a.   A $\rightarrow$ B (C) D (E)

    b.   A $\rightarrow$ B (C D) E

    c.   A $\rightarrow$ B (C) (D) E

    d. $A \rightarrow B \begin{Bmatrix} C \\ D \end{Bmatrix} E \begin{Bmatrix} F \\ G \\ H \end{Bmatrix}$

    e. $A \rightarrow B (\begin{Bmatrix} C \\ D \end{Bmatrix}) E$

2. Assume the phrase structure framework, the evaluation measure in (25), and the parentheses convention. (Incidentally, in counting symbol

occurrences as dictated in (25), do not count the parentheses themselves.) Show that the parentheses convention does not give a single clear prediction concerning the "best grammar" based on the following set of hypothetical basic data: *the seven honorable men*, *the men*, and *seven honorable men*.

2.6 DETERMINATION OF VERBAL ENVIRONMENTS

The sample phrase structure grammar given in (14), although it did account for many English sentences, failed to make any distinctions in grammaticality of the sort illustrated in the following groups of sentences:

(45) a.   The king captured the duke.
               *The king captured.
       b.   The man vanished.
               The man vanished into the forest.
               *The man vanished the pan.
       c.   The knife belongs on the table.
               *The knife belongs.
               *The knife belongs the man.
       d.   John put the bacon on the table.
               *John put the bacon.
               *John put on the table.

In an informal grammar of English, we might account for these judgments by including statements such as the following:

(46) a.   The verb *captured* requires a following noun phrase.
       b.   The verb *vanished* does not permit a following noun phrase, but allows optionally a following prepositional phrase.
       c.   The verb *belongs* requires a following prepositional phrase.
       d.   The verb *put* requires both a following noun phrase and a following prepositional phrase.

What we will do now is to consider how information of this sort might be built into a formal grammar of the sort that we have been attempting to construct.

Such differences as these can be recognized without going outside the phrase structure framework. This can be done by revising the rules for expanding the symbol VP in such a way that the class of verbs is divided into several subclasses, (47a–d). We then add rules (47e–i) for introducing the actual verbs.

(47) a. $VP \rightarrow V_1$
       b. $VP \rightarrow V_2$ NP
       c. $VP \rightarrow V_3$ PrepP
       d. $VP \rightarrow V_4$ NP PrepP
       e. $V_1 \rightarrow$ *vanished*
       f. $V_2 \rightarrow$ *captured*

g. $V_3 \rightarrow$ *belongs*
h. $V_3 \rightarrow$ *vanished*
i. $V_4 \rightarrow$ *put*

These rules have the effect, for example, of allowing *vanished* to occur either by itself or with a following prepositional phrase, but not with a following NP. Likewise, they allow *put* to appear only in VP's that contain an NP followed by a PrepP.

This treatment is not entirely satisfactory, however, for reasons that we cannot develop fully until the next chapter. For the present, we make the general observation that the phrase structure rules given above for expanding the VP treat the various types of verbs as being entirely unrelated. In this respect, the use of the common symbol V with varying subscripts is deceptive. When we see V_1 in the foregoing rules, this is to be understood as a single symbol, rather than as a sequence of the symbol V plus a subscript. The reason for this is quite simple: if V_1 were understood as two symbols, then rule (47e) would have two symbols on the left-hand side of the arrow, and consequently would no longer satisfy our definition of a phrase structure rule. We would have an entirely equivalent grammar if we were to replace the various types of V's in the rules above by completely unrelated letters of the alphabet:

(48) a.   VP $\rightarrow$ A
      b.   VP $\rightarrow$ B NP
      c.   VP $\rightarrow$ C PrepP
      d.   VP $\rightarrow$ D NP PrepP
      e.   A $\rightarrow$ *vanished*
      f.   B $\rightarrow$ *captured*
      g.   C $\rightarrow$ *belongs*
      h.   C $\rightarrow$ *vanished*
      i.   D $\rightarrow$ *put*

This set of rules would be perfectly adequate if it were never necessary to refer in any descriptive statement to the class of verbs as a whole. Our discussion in the next chapter will show that such a reference to the entire class of verbs is indeed necessary at some points in the grammar of English.

In order to deal with this problem, we will define a slightly revised framework for grammatical description, which we will refer to for convenience as the *extended phrase structure framework.* This framework will allow a grammar of English in which distinctions between various verb subclasses can be recognized without sacrificing the possibility of referring to verbs as a general class. A grammar based on this framework consists of two sets of rules rather than just one. The first set consists of phrase structure rules such as the following:

(49) a.   S $\rightarrow$ NP VP
      b.   VP $\rightarrow$ V (NP) (PrepP)
      c.   PrepP $\rightarrow$ Prep NP
      d.   NP $\rightarrow$ (Det) (Adj) N

These phrase structure rules specify the construction of trees down to but not including the terminal symbols. For convenience, we will refer to such trees as _nonterminal trees._ The particular rules given in (49) would yield nonterminal trees such as the following:

(50) a.

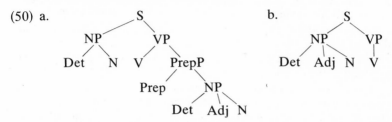

b.

The second set of rules may be referred to as _lexical rules,_ or _lexical entries._ Each lexical rule consists of a word, together with features that indicate the conditions under which that word can be inserted into nonterminal trees.

(51)

a. _man_ ⟨N⟩   n. _captured_ ⟨V⟩, ⟨——— NP⟩
b. _dog_ ⟨N⟩   o. _large_ ⟨Adj⟩
c. _cousin_ ⟨N⟩   p. _warm_ ⟨Adj⟩
d. _birds_ ⟨N⟩   q. _tall_ ⟨Adj⟩
e. _count_ ⟨N⟩   r. _small_ ⟨Adj⟩
f. _king_ ⟨N⟩   s. _up_ ⟨Prep⟩
g. _lake_ ⟨N⟩   t. _into_ ⟨Prep⟩
h. _fact_ ⟨N⟩   u. _on_ ⟨Prep⟩
i. _belief_ ⟨N⟩   v. _from_ ⟨Prep⟩
j. _put_ ⟨V⟩, ⟨——— NP   PrepP⟩   w. _the_ ⟨Det⟩
k. _go_ ⟨V⟩, ⟨——— PrepP⟩   x. _a_ ⟨Det⟩
l. _vanished_ ⟨V⟩, ⟨———(PrepP)⟩   y. _this_ ⟨Det⟩
m. _saw_ ⟨V⟩, ⟨——— NP⟩   z. _these_ ⟨Det⟩

One type of feature will specify what symbol the word can be inserted under. For example, the symbol ⟨N⟩ associated with _man_ will indicate that the word can be inserted into a tree under the symbol N. Likewise, the symbol ⟨Adj⟩ associated with _large_ will indicate that this word can be inserted under the symbol Adj. In addition to these features, which we can refer to as _category features,_ we require a second type of feature for verbs, one which indicates what sort of VP the word can appear in. The latter will be referred to as _subcategory features._ For example, the feature ⟨——— NP PrepP⟩ following _put_ serves to indicate that _put_ can only be inserted into a VP that can be divided up into a V followed by an NP followed by a PrepP. Consequently, this grammar allows the generation of a sentence such as (52a), while excluding (52b) and (52c).

(52) a.   John put the bacon on the table.
     b.   *John put the bacon.
     c.   *John put on the table.

As another example, consider the feature $\langle$——— (PrepP)$\rangle$ associated with *vanished*. This feature indicates that *vanished* can be inserted either into a VP that consists of a V alone, or else into a VP that can be divided up into a V followed by a PrepP. The new sample grammar, then, generates the sentences (53a) and (53b), but excludes (53c):

(53) a.   The man vanished.

     b.   The man vanished into the forest.

     c.   *The man vanished the pan.

At the same time, this grammar has the virtue of identifying both *put* and *vanished* as belonging to a more general class, the class of verbs.

By enlarging our framework to allow category and subcategory features as well as phrase structure rules, we have made it possible to account for differences in the behavior of individual English verbs without complicating our basic phrase structure rules. As we consider an increasingly broad range of data from English, we will find many other instances in which the addition of some new rule type to our descriptive framework allows us to keep our grammar of English as simple and revealing as the language permits.

Suggestions for Further Reading

The phrase structure framework, in the form presented in section 2.2, owes its origin to Noam Chomsky and is discussed in Chomsky 1957, Chapter 4. An introductory discussion of phrase structure rules can be found in Kimball 1973, Chapter 1.

Phrase structure rules were originally developed as a way of expressing the insights found in the "immediate constituent analysis" of pretransformational syntactic studies in the United States. An idea of this kind of analysis may be obtained by looking at Hockett 1958, Chapter 17, and at Gleason 1961, Chapter 10.

There are few satisfactory discussions of the role of evaluation measures and abbreviatory conventions. Chomsky 1965, Chapter 1, summarizes the basic ideas, but the absence of concrete examples makes the discussion a difficult one for beginning students in syntax. An excellent elementary discussion is given in Kimball 1973, pp. 68–75.

Features for the specification of verbal environments are discussed in Chomsky 1965, Chapter 2.

Notes

1. The definition that we will give here is of a limited class of phrase structure grammars known as *context-free* phrase structure grammars. For a discussion of so-called *context-sensitive* phrase structure grammars, see section 18.1. The latter type of rule has been of relatively minor significance in syntactic work since the middle 1960's.

2. In section 17 1, we will examine at some length the interesting question of whether real human children rely on corrections when they learn their native language. In the meantime, it will be necessary to suppose for the sake of discussion that negative evidence provided by corrections is available to children. Exercise 2 at the end of section 2.4 gives an indication of why this supposition is necessary.

3. This grammar is clearly different from the grammar in (14), in that it makes no mention of the symbols VP or PrepP, but instead has V's, NP's, and Prep's sprouting directly out of S. It will become apparent in section 2.4 why the grammar in (22) was selected at this point. See especially Exercises 3 and 4 there.

4. A second, entirely different solution to this problem will emerge from the discussion in section 17.2.

5. Very little is currently known concerning the extent to which the linguistic experience of real human children contains gaps of this sort. Consequently, it is difficult at present to judge the actual usefulness of an evaluation measure like (25) as opposed to its merely potential usefulness.

6. As in the preceding section, the basic data were selected artificially to illustrate a certain kind of argument, in this instance, the kind that would serve to support the parentheses convention. It is an open question whether the sets of basic data available to real human children contain gaps of the sort that the parentheses convention would help to fill in.

7. In order to get this result, we would need to specify that the braces convention take precedence over the parentheses convention. Otherwise, each of the following four alternatives would be equally highly valued by (25):

(i)   G → A (B) (F) C (D) (F) E

(ii)   G → A (F) (B) C (F) (D) E

(iii)   G → A (B) (F) C (F) (D) E

(iv)   G → A (F) (B) C (D) (F) E

Each of these rules accounts for the two types of phrases in (41), and each has the same number of symbol occurrences as the rule in (43). But clearly no one of them is equivalent to (43), and no one of them is equivalent to any of the other three.

3

The Transformational Framework

We began our discussion of phrase structure grammars in the preceding chapter by citing a number of informal statements such as "a sentence consists of a noun phrase and a verb phrase," or "a noun phrase may consist of a determiner and a noun." The phrase structure framework was developed primarily as a means for giving expression to just this kind of statement. Informal remarks of this sort, and the corresponding formal rules, are adequate to give a rough description of a restricted subset of English sentences consisting of simple active declarative sentences.

In this chapter we will consider a number of more complicated English sentences, whose structures cannot be accounted for in a revealing way by stating what they "consist of," or by constructing a grammar whose non-terminal rules are all phrase structure rules. In traditional descriptions of English, these additional sentence types are rarely described from scratch. Instead, they are described by rules that specify a change on some simpler sentence type. The *transformational* framework has been developed primarily as a means of allowing formal expression for this second type of traditional rule. The framework employs phrase structure rules to generate simple structures, and then employs a second set of rules, known as *transformational rules*, to carry out the changes leading to the more complex structures. The nature of this more complicated framework will become clearer in the course of our examination of several areas of English syntax in which phrase structure grammars fail to be revealing. Before we go into any of these problem areas, it will be useful to devote one more section to the development of phrase structure rules for English.[1]

3.1 HELPING VERBS

In the rules of English syntax presented in Chapter 2, no attention was given to the English words traditionally referred to as *auxiliary verbs* or *helping verbs*.[2] These terms are used to refer to words such as the "perfect" verb *have*, the "progressive" verb *be*, and the "modal" verbs *can, could, may, might, will, would, shall, should*, and *must*. What makes these verbs significant is that there are very severe restrictions on the permissible sequences of them. Below are given some grammatical sentences containing helping verbs. Along with each sentence, we list the pattern to which it conforms. (We use the symbol M to stand for "modal.")

(1)							
a.	John could sing.	NP	M				V
b.	John has sung.	NP		have			V
c.	John is singing	NP				be	V
d.	John could have sung.	NP	M	have			V
e.	John could be singing.	NP	M			be	V
f.	John has been singing.	NP		have	be		V
g.	John could have been singing.	NP	M	have	be		V

Let us now list several ungrammatical sentences for the sake of comparison:

(2)					
a.	*John will can sing.	*NP	M	M	V
b.	*John has could sing.	*NP	have	M	V
c.	*John is having sung.	*NP	be	have	V
d.	*John has had sung.	*NP	have	have	V
e.	*John is being singing.	*NP	be	be	V

Let us ignore for the moment the differences of form that each verb shows (e.g., the difference between *is* and *being*), postponing a consideration of these differences until section 3.4. The sequences in the grammatical examples can then be characterized informally as follows: a helping-verb sequence may consist of an optional modal, followed by an optional occurrence of the perfect *have*, followed by an optional occurrence of the progressive *be*. We can translate this characterization into a phrase structure rule that expands a new symbol Aux:

(3)   Aux → (M) (*have*) (*be*)

This new symbol will itself be introduced by a revised version of our phrase structure rule for S's:

(4)   S → NP   Aux   VP

The trees in (5) illustrate the structures that these new rules yield. (We have taken the liberty of putting in the correct inflectional forms.)

(5) a.

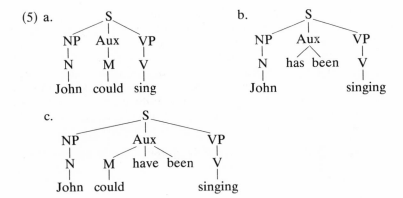

b.

c.

3.2 QUESTIONS

Our first example of a construction in English that provides an argument for a new kind of grammatical rule is the *yes-no question*. In the right-hand column of (6) we give the questions that correspond to the declaratives in (1):

(6) a.   John could sing.   Could John sing?
    b.   John has sung.   Has John sung?
    c.   John is singing.   Is John singing?
    d.   John could have sung.   Could John have sung?
    e.   John could be singing.   Could John be singing?
    f.   John has been singing.   Has John been singing?
    g.   John could have been singing. Could John have been singing?

When these questions are compared one at a time with the corresponding declaratives, it becomes apparent that there is a very simple relation holding in each question-declarative pair. We can express this relation in the following informal rule:

(7)   Given a declarative sentence containing one or more helping verbs, a question can optionally be formed simply by moving the first such verb to the left of the subject.

This rule is quite different from the informal rules in Chapter 2 and in section 3.1. All of those rules took the form of saying that a constituent of a certain kind *consisted of* constituents of other kinds; they translated very readily into phrase structure rules. This new rule, by contrast, says nothing about what a yes-no question consists of. Instead, it describes the formation of questions by making reference to declaratives and then indicating some change that will yield questions. The statement that the rule applies *optionally* is included because we want to generate sentences in which the rule does not apply (declaratives) as well as those in which it does apply (questions).

Let us turn now to the development of a more formal account of these questions, one that follows the spirit of the informal rule (7). Such an account must contain, first, a specification of the sequences of English words that qualify as declaratives, and second, a rule that has the effect of creating questions from the declaratives. The specification of grammatical declaratives we have already: the phrase structure and lexical rules developed in Chapter 2 and in the first section of this chapter fulfill precisely this function. The special rule for questions, however, will be of a distinctly new type that we shall refer to as *transformational*. The rule is as follows:

(8)   Subject-H(elping) V(erb) Inversion   (preliminary version)[3]

$$NP \doteq \begin{Bmatrix} M \\ \text{have} \\ \text{be} \end{Bmatrix} - X$$

$$1 \qquad 2 \qquad 3$$

$$\Rightarrow 2+1, \ 0, \ 3 \quad \text{(Optional)}$$

We interpret this rule in the following way:

(9)   If we are given a tree structure whose terminal sequence can be divided into three parts (the first part an NP, the second either an M or *have* or *be*, and the third anything at all), then a new tree may optionally be formed by copying the second part to the left of the first part, and deleting the original second part.

This new rule clearly has a form that distinguishes it from phrase structure rules. The most obvious departure is that it does not satisfy the stipulation that there be only a single symbol on the left-hand side of the rule. The rule also differs quite markedly in the way in which it is to be interpreted. As a careful reading of (9) will indicate, rule (8) is to be interpreted not as building new branches onto a partially formed tree, but rather as converting one completely formed tree into another.

We can illustrate the operation of this rule by examining its effect on three tree structures that our phrase structure rules give. Consider first the tree in (10a):

(10)   a.

As the underscoring indicates, the terminal sequence of this tree can indeed be divided in the fashion indicated in the rule. Here the NP piece is *John*; the M, *have*, or *be* piece happens to be the modal *could*; and the anything-at-all piece is the verb *sing*. When we make the changes specified in the rule, the tree in (10b) results:

(10) b.

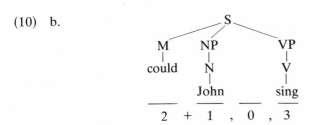

$$\frac{}{2 \;+\; 1} \;,\; 0 \;,\; 3$$

Let us look now at the manner in which rule (8) applies to a tree that contains more than one helping verb:

(11) a.

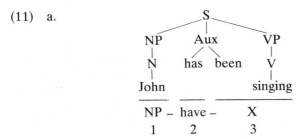

Here the NP piece is again *John*; the **M**, *have*, or *be* piece happens to be *has*; and the anything-at-all piece is the sequence *been singing*. Applying the change specified in the rule, we get:

(11) b.

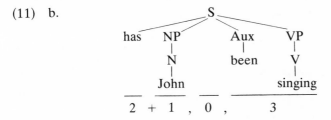

A final illustration of the application of this rule is given in the more complicated trees in (12). Application of the rule to (12a) gives (12b).

(12) a.

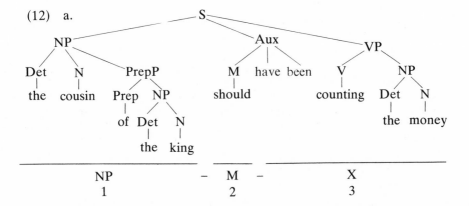

b.

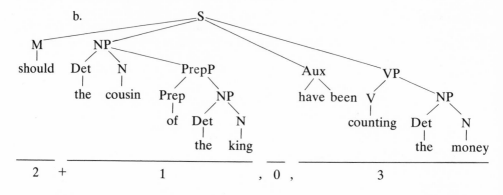

Let us return now to the seven questions given in (6). As can be readily verified, the transformational rule in (8) acts on the trees that arise by the operation of the phrase structure rules already developed for declaratives to give all seven of the questions in (6). One additional point is worth noting. When we adopt this method of dealing with questions, we automatically succeed in avoiding the generation of certain ungrammatical questions:

(13) a.   *Will John can sing?
      b.   *Has John could sing?
      c.   *Is John having sung?
      d.   *Has John had sung?
      e.   *Is John being singing?

The reason for our success is quite simple. In section 3.1 we took care to set up phrase structure rules for helping verbs in such a way as to exclude the following declarative sentences:

(14) a.   *John will can sing.
      b.   *John has could sing.
      c.   *John is having sung.
      d.   *John has had sung.
      e.   *John is being singing.

Since these declarative structures are not generated by the phrase structure rules, they are correspondingly unavailable to be acted on by the transformational rule (8). Consequently, there is no way in which the ungrammatical questions in (13) can arise.

At this point, we have a simple description of questions that includes a transformational rule. Although this account of questions makes use of the phrase structure rules previously developed for declaratives, the description as a whole falls outside the phrase structure framework defined in Chapter 2, by virtue of the presence of the one transformational rule. Thus, if we adopt this analysis of questions, we implicitly commit ourselves to a new and more complex grammatical framework, one that allows rules such as (8).

In order to strengthen the case for moving to a new framework, we would do well to see what sort of description could have been developed for yes-no questions within the confines of the phrase structure framework. In particular, we need to ascertain what new phrase structure rules would be necessary for questions, beyond those already proposed for declaratives. Surprisingly enough, if we wish to generate the grammatical questions in (6) without also generating the ungrammatical ones in (13), we must give not one simple rule, but a rule with three separate, complicated subcases, one for each of the possible types of helping verbs that can introduce a question:[4]

$$(15) \quad S \rightarrow \left\{ \begin{matrix} \left. \begin{matrix} M & NP & (\textit{have}) \\ \textit{have} & NP & \\ \textit{be} & NP & \end{matrix} \right\} & (\textit{be}) \end{matrix} \right\} VP$$

The addition of this phrase structure rule to the phrase structure rules for declaratives gives us a decidedly unrevealing grammar. In particular, the phrase structure rule for questions has to repeat the information concerning permissible helping-verb sequences, information that was provided originally by the phrase structure rules for declaratives. Furthermore, the information is conveyed in a much more fragmentary manner than it was in rule (3), which stated that Aux is rewritten as (M) (*have*) (*be*). In rule (15), *be* has to be mentioned in two places, and so does *have*. Thus, if we were to try to do all of the work of accounting for English yes-no questions by means of phrase structure rules alone, we would be forced to adopt a decidedly unrevealing set of rules.

EXERCISE

1. In the preceding section the claim was made that within the confines of the phrase structure framework, any treatment of yes-no questions in English would be unrevealing, and that the unrevealing rule in (15) was as good as any phrase structure rule or set of such rules that could be developed. At first glance, it might seem that several much simpler phrase structure treatments could be adopted for this construction. For each of the three rules below, show that the rule is inferior to the set of rules given in (15) in the predictions that it makes about grammatical and ungrammatical English questions. (Ignore the problem of verbal inflection.)

(i) $S \rightarrow$ Aux NP VP

(ii) $S \rightarrow \left\{ \begin{matrix} M \\ \textit{have} \\ \textit{be} \end{matrix} \right\}$ NP Aux VP

(iii) $S \rightarrow \left\{ \begin{matrix} M \\ \textit{have} \\ \textit{be} \end{matrix} \right\}$ NP VP

3.3 THE FORM AND INTERPRETATION OF TRANSFORMATIONAL RULES

Before going on to look at other English constructions that warrant a transformational treatment, it will be useful to make some general comments about transformational rules, and to introduce some technical terms. We will use the transformational rule (8), Subject-HV Inversion, as an illustration.

To begin with, we can think of any transformational rule as consisting of two basic parts. The first part, commonly referred to as the *structural description*, serves to indicate what form a tree must have if it is to undergo the rule, and also what divisions of the tree are relevant for the operation of the rule. This structural description indicates the number of pieces (in technical terms, the number of *factors*) into which the terminal sequence of the tree must be divisible. In addition, it lays down the conditions that must be satisfied by each of these factors. For example, the structural description of rule (8) is just the following:

$$(16) \qquad NP - \left\{ \begin{array}{c} M \\ have \\ be \end{array} \right\} - X$$
$$ 1 \qquad\quad 2 \qquad\quad 3$$

This structural description is divided by hyphens into three *terms*. A tree *satisfies* this structural description if its terminal sequence can be divided into three factors in such a way that two conditions are met: 1) the first factor must be an NP; 2) the second factor must be either an M or *have* or *be*. The *variable symbol* X as the third term simply indicates that the third factor of the terminal sequence does not have to meet any special conditions.

The tree given in (17) is an example of a tree that satisfies this structural description.

(17)

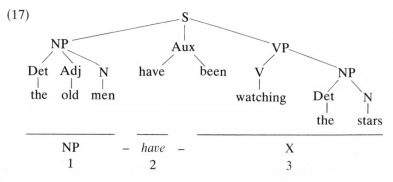

The terminal sequence has been divided into three factors, as indicated by the underscoring. The first is *the old men*, the second is *have*, and the third is *been watching the stars*. The first factor is an NP, and the second factor is *have* (one of the three possibilities allowed by the structural description). As can be seen from this example, the factor of a terminal sequence that is assigned to a variable such as X, Y, or Z does not necessarily have to be a constituent itself. In the tree in (17), the sequence *been watching the stars* does not constitute either a VP or an Aux or any other single constituent, but only part of an Aux plus a VP.

As may have been guessed on the basis of the preceding discussion, a tree does not satisfy a structural description unless each element of the terminal sequence is assigned to exactly one term of the structural description. Thus, a tree may fail to satisfy a structural description by virtue of having one or more elements that cannot be assigned to any term. Following is an example of a structural description (devised solely for purposes of illustration) that fails to be satisfied by the tree considered above.

(18)   NP – *have* – VP
         1   2   3

As is shown by the underscoring in (19), the terminal element *been* cannot be assigned to any of the three terms of the structural description.

(19)

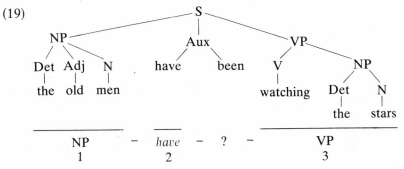

Likewise, a tree fails to satisfy a structural description if it is necessary to assign some terminal element to more than one term. We see a failure of this second sort when we try to divide up the terminal sequence of the example tree in conformity with a second illustrative structural description:

(20)   NP – *have* – Aux – VP
         1   2   3   4

The dilemma that arises here is shown by the underscoring in (21):

(21)

One final point deserves mention. Suppose that we are attempting to divide some terminal sequence in conformity with a structural description, and we encounter some symbol such as NP or Aux as one of the terms in this structural description. In this situation, we must always be able to assign to that term *all* of the terminal elements under some NP or Aux node in the tree. This restriction excludes the following assignment of terminal elements in a tree to terms of a structural description:

(22)

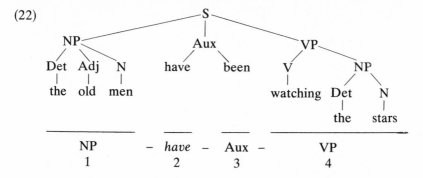

NP	– *have* –	Aux –	VP
1	2	3	4

The difficulty here is that *been* in this tree does not by itself qualify as an Aux, but only as part of one. This means that we are not entitled to let *been* be the entire third factor of the terminal sequence corresponding to the symbol Aux in the structural description.

Before concluding this preliminary discussion of structural descriptions, we should observe that the notation suggested in the preceding paragraphs allows a transformational rule to impose a very limited range of conditions on factors of a terminal sequence. So far, in fact, we have seen only two types of conditions. The first is a requirement that such and such a factor be a constituent of a certain type. The second is a requirement to the effect that such and such a factor be a certain terminal element. We see both types of conditions more clearly when we rephrase the structural description in (16) as the set of conditions in (23):

(16) $\text{NP} - \left\{ \begin{array}{c} \text{M} \\ have \\ be \end{array} \right\} - \text{X}$

   1   2   3

(23)   Number of factors: three.
   Conditions:

   a. The first factor is an NP.

   b. The second factor is an M, or the second factor is *have*, or the second factor is *be*.

At various points in the development of transformational syntax, it has been suggested that structural descriptions should be permitted to contain other sorts of conditions. We will mention several of these later in this book.

Having discussed structural descriptions and the way in which they are interpreted, let us turn our attention to the second part of a transformational rule, the *structural change*. This is an instruction as to how a new tree is to be formed from the original one. The basis for constructing the new tree is provided by the factors into which the old tree was divided by the structural description. For each term in the structural description, the structural change specifies how a corresponding part of the new tree is to be formed. An initial example is provided by the structural change for rule (8), which we repeat in (24a):

(24) a.   2 + 1, 0, 3

The commas indicate a division into three factors corresponding to the three terms in the structural description. The numbers 1, 2, and 3 refer to the factors of the original terminal sequence. This particular structural change, then, provides the following instructions: first, form a new first factor from the old first factor by adjoining the old second factor to the left; second, form the new second factor by deleting the old second factor; third, the new third factor is to be the same as the old third factor. An alternative way of writing this structural change is given in (24b); each old factor is accompanied by an indication of what form its new replacement is to take.

(24) b.   1   2   3
              ⇓   ⇓   ⇓
            2+1   0   3

The effect on the terminal sequence of the tree in (17) is as follows:

(25) a.   Original sequence
           the old men   have   been watching the stars
           _____   ____   _____

              NP   – *have* –   X
               1   2   3

           Transformed sequence
           have   the old men   been watching the stars
           ____   _____   ____ _____

            2 +   1   ,   0 ,

The relation between the original factors and the new factors is summarized in the table below:

(25) b.

	First	*Second*	*Third*
Original Factors	the old men	have	been watching the stars
	1	2	3
New Factors	have the old men		been watching the stars
	2 + 1	0	3

With just this much said, it is possible to determine what the transformed terminal sequence will be when a transformational rule applies to a tree. However, in view of our assertion that transformational rules are to be understood as converting *trees* into *trees*, we need to indicate what shape the new tree takes above a transformed terminal sequence. The tree structures that arise as the result of transformational rules are often called *derived structures* (or *derived constituent structures*). They are distinguished in this way from trees that arise solely by the operation of phrase structure rules and lexical rules. We will give a brief discussion of two basic questions about the assignment of derived structure. How these questions are answered will determine what trees result when we apply a transformational rule.

The first question can be put as follows: when a factor of a terminal sequence is adjoined to an existing factor, which (if any) nodes above it are copied along with it? As a case in point, let us look at the transformational rule (26), a special case of Subject-HV Inversion, and let us suppose that we are asked to apply this rule to the tree in (27).

(26)   NP – M – X
         1   2   3
        ⇒2+1, 0, 3

(27)

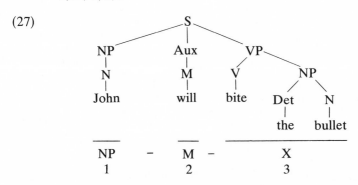

The instruction for forming the new first factor is to copy the second factor on the left of the original first factor. When we carry out this instruction, should we copy the terminal element *will* by itself, or *will* and the M node above it, or *will* and the M node and the Aux node? The three possibilities are shown in (28a–c):

(28)   a.   will   b.   M   c.   Aux
                                | |
                               will   M
                                                  |
                                                 will

In this text, we will adopt the general convention that the node actually mentioned in the relevant term of the structural description will be copied, together with any nodes below it. (For convenience, we shall refer to this as the *Mentioned Node Convention*.) In applying this convention to the specific example at hand, we note that it is the second term in the structural description that corresponds to the factor to be copied, and furthermore that this second term is identified as an M. When we copy this second factor, then, we copy the M above it, without copying the Aux node. This convention thus dictates the second of the three structures in (28) as the structure to be copied.

The second basic question that needs to be raised is the question of precisely how a copied structure is to be connected to a tree in its new location. To make clear what this question means, let us look at the structure that we have developed thus far as the result of applying rule (26) to tree (27).[5]

(29)

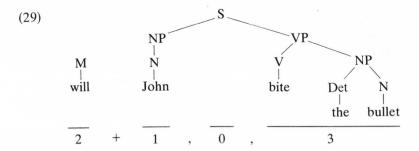

What we need here is some convention that specifies how the M node is to be connected to the remainder of the tree. Let us begin by looking at some of the possibilities that have been discussed in transformational studies.

One straightforward possibility is known as *sister adjunction*. In the present instance, the structural change of our rule specifies that the new first factor is to be formed by adjoining the second factor to the left of the original first. In order to create a sister adjunction, we look at the structural description and note that the original first term is identified as an NP. We look for the corresponding NP node in the tree in question, and plug the new structure into the node *immediately above* this NP. The resulting tree is one in which the copied M node and the subject NP node are "sisters" under a common "parent" node (the S node):

(30)

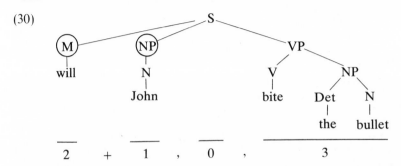

A second possibility would be to incorporate the copy into the NP node itself, as a "daughter" of this NP. The effect of *daughter-adjoining* the copied structure to the left of the first term is shown below :

(31)

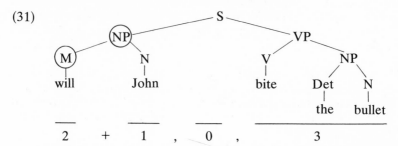

$$2 \quad + \quad 1 \quad , \quad 0 \quad , \quad 3$$

Other possibilities might be considered that are perhaps less obvious. To give just one example, the copied structure might be made an "aunt" of the NP node; a new S node might be created above the S node that is the parent of the NP corresponding to the original first factor, and the copied structure might be plugged into this higher S.[6] This possibility is illustrated below:

(32)

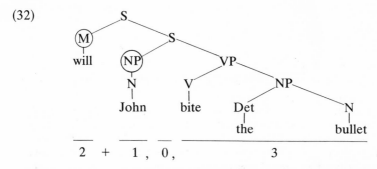

$$2 \quad + \quad 1 \, , \quad 0, \quad 3$$

For the sake of consistency, we will generally adopt the convention that copied structures are to be *sister-adjoined,* the first of the possible conventions mentioned above. This decision dictates the choice of the tree in (30) as the derived structure resulting from the application of rule (26) to the tree in (27). We repeat the rule here for convenience:

(26)   NP – M – X
         1   2   3
       $\Rightarrow 2+1, 0, 3$

Now that the Mentioned Node Convention and the Sister Adjunction Convention have been introduced, a word of caution is in order. At the present stage of research in syntax, our suggestions in the area of derived constituent structure must be considered even more tentative than our suggestions in other areas. The reason is that there is often very little evidence to show that one particular convention is superior to some other one that might have been adopted instead. This arbitrariness can be seen in the decision made above to adopt sister adjunction rather than aunt adjunction. With respect to Subject-HV Inversion, the choice between these two types of adjunction comes down to a comparison of the structures in (33):

(33) a.   b.

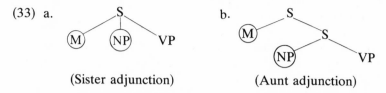

      (Sister adjunction)   (Aunt adjunction)

The basic question here is whether the NP-VP sequence that remains after the modal has been moved is or is not an S in its own right. If we could find some respect in which our grammar worked better if this sequence was not classified as an S, then we would have an argument for the first of these structures. On the other hand, if the classification of the leftover NP-VP sequence as an S in its own right gave better results, we would have an argument in favor of the structure in (33b). Unfortunately, no situations are known at present in which it makes any difference whether or not the NP-VP sequence is analyzed as an S of its own. Later in the book, we will occasionally find instances in which a particular choice of derived constituent structure does seem to have interesting consequences. These discussions will serve to illustrate the way in which the adoption of particular derived structures can be supported.

EXERCISES

1. Study the tree given below and the five structural descriptions that follow it.

#3 NP - V - X
0, 2+1, 3

(i)

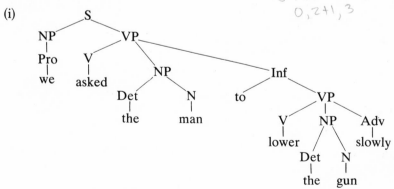

(ii)   NP – VP – Inf
(iii)   X – NP – Inf
(iv)   Pro – X – Inf
(v)   NP – V – NP – X
(vi)   NP – VP – VP

For each of the five structural descriptions, determine whether or not it is satisfied by the tree in (i). If the structural description is satisfied, indicate (by means of underscoring) the way in which the terminal sequence of the tree is divided up.

2. Suppose that the transformational rule below is applied to the tree in Exercise 1.

$$NP - V - X$$
$$1 \quad 2 \quad 3$$
$$\Rightarrow 2+1, 0, 3$$

What is the derived tree that results, assuming the two conventions for derived constituent structure finally adopted in this section? Do not worry if the resulting sequence is ungrammatical.

3. Study the following rule:

$$NP - V - X$$
$$1 \quad 2 \quad 3$$
$$\Rightarrow 0, 2+1, 3$$

This rule has the same structural description as the rule in the preceding problem. Furthermore, the terminal sequences that result when the rules are applied to the tree in Exercise 1 are exactly the same. However, the two derived trees are different. What derived tree arises from applying this rule to the tree in Exercise 1? Hint: It may be helpful to begin by noting that the structural change can be represented in alternative form as follows:

$$1 \qquad 2 \qquad 3$$
$$\Downarrow \qquad \Downarrow \qquad \Downarrow$$
$$0 \qquad 2+1 \qquad 3$$

4. What is the derived tree that results from applying the following transformational rule to the tree in Exercise 1?

$$NP - V - NP - X$$
$$1 \quad 2 \quad 3 \quad 4$$
$$\Rightarrow 3+1, 2, 0, 4$$

5. The following structural description is satisfied in two quite different ways by the tree in Exercise 1.

$$X - V - NP - Y$$

Indicate what the two different divisions are by drawing the tree and providing two separate underscorings for it.

3.4 ENGLISH VERBAL INFLECTION

When we attempt to give a detailed account of the inflection of full verbs and helping verbs in English, we find another instance in which a description that includes a transformational rule is more revealing than one that relies entirely on phrase structure rules and lexical rules. Our first concern here will be to set forth some informal observations on this matter, of the kind that might be found in a traditional grammar of English.

(34)   A verbal element that follows a modal always assumes its uninflected form:

John should $\begin{Bmatrix} \text{sing} \\ \text{*sang} \\ \text{*sung} \\ \text{*singing} \end{Bmatrix}$.

Al could $\begin{Bmatrix} \text{have} \\ \text{*has} \\ \text{*having} \\ \text{*had} \end{Bmatrix}$ gone.

Sharon must $\begin{Bmatrix} \text{be} \\ \text{*been} \\ \text{*was} \\ \text{*is} \\ \text{*being} \end{Bmatrix}$ working.

(35)   The perfect helping verb *have* requires the verbal element following to be in its past participial form:

John has $\begin{Bmatrix} \text{sung} \\ \text{*sing} \\ \text{*singing} \\ \text{been singing} \\ \text{*be singing} \\ \text{*being singing} \end{Bmatrix}$.

(36)   The progressive helping verb (*be* and its associated forms *am*, *is*, etc.) requires that the verb following be in its present participial form:

John is $\begin{Bmatrix} \text{singing} \\ \text{*sung} \\ \text{*sing} \end{Bmatrix}$.

(37)   The verbal element immediately to the right of the subject is inflected for tense and, except for modals, also for the number and person of the subject.[7] (For the time being, we will concern ourselves only with the difference in tense, which is illustrated in the following sentences.)

They *like* music.	(Present)
They *liked* music.	(Past)
We *are* eating breakfast.	(Present)
We *were* eating breakfast.	(Past)
The editors *have* seen the paper.	(Present)
The editors *had* seen the paper.	(Past)
They *can* read it.	(Present)
They *could* read it.	(Past)[8]

Once again, as in section 3.2, we find ourselves with informal rules that do not say anything about what a sentence or a phrase of a certain type "consists of." Instead, each of the rules above states how the form of a verbal element is determined by reference to the verbal element, if any, that happens to come before it.

We would like to incorporate some account of these facts into our description without losing what is already expressed in the phrase structure rule that gives permissible sequences of helping verbs. We can arrive at such a description in the following way. First, information about the appropriate inflectional form will be introduced in the phrase structure rules with the *governing* verb rather than with the *governed* verb. Let us adopt *en* as a convenient marker for the past participial form, and *ing* as a marker for present participial form. Since the perfect *have* determines past participial form, we include *en* as part of the *have* option in the phrase structure rule that expands the Aux node. Likewise, we include the marker *ing* as part of the *be* option. Our basic phrase structure rule is now as follows:

(38)   Aux → (M) (*have en*) (*be ing*)

Finally, we include a tense marker *Tns* as an obligatory first element in the Aux. This element is further expanded by the rule:

(39)   Tns → $\begin{Bmatrix} Pres \\ Past \end{Bmatrix}$

Thus, finally, our phrase structure rule for Aux takes the form:

(40)   Aux → Tns (M) (*have en*) (*be ing*)

This rule gives us a total of eight possible Aux configurations:

(41) a.   Tns   M   have en   be ing
     b.   Tns   M   have en
     c.   Tns   M   be ing
     d.   Tns   M
     e.   Tns   have en   be ing
     f.   Tns   have en
     g.   Tns   be ing
     h.   Tns

As can be seen in (41), the way that we have arranged the parentheses in (40) guarantees that the perfect helping verb *have* will not appear in a tree unless the past participial marker *en* appears also. Likewise, the progressive helping verb *be* cannot appear except in the company of the present participial marker *ing*.

As matters now stand, the inflectional markers are not yet associated with the verbal element whose form they ultimately determine. The phrase structure rules and lexical rules give structures like the following:

(42)

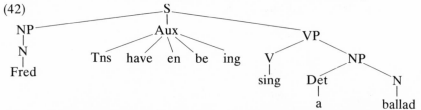

The second step that we require, then, is to associate each of the elements Tns, *en*, and *ing* with the affected verbal element, whether a modal, *have*, *be*, or a V. For this we will employ a rule that "hops" any inflectional marker over the verbal element following it:

(43)   Affix Hopping

$$X - \left\{ \begin{matrix} \text{Tns} \\ en \\ ing \end{matrix} \right\} - \left\{ \begin{matrix} \text{M} \\ have \\ be \\ \text{V} \end{matrix} \right\} - Y$$

$$\begin{matrix} 1 & 2 & 3 & 4 \end{matrix}$$

$$\Rightarrow 1, 0, 3+2, 4 \quad \text{(Obligatory)}$$

The effects of this rule can be stated informally as follows: when we find a tree in which an inflectional marker (Tns, *en*, or *ing*) is followed by a verbal element (an M, *have*, *be*, or a V), then the inflectional element is to be copied to the right of the verbal element, and deleted in its old position.

As a first example, let us consider the application of this rule to the following tree:

(44)   a.

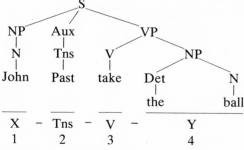

$$\begin{matrix} X & - & \text{Tns} & - & \text{V} & - & Y \\ 1 & & 2 & & 3 & & 4 \end{matrix}$$

When we apply the rule, the resulting tree will be (44b).[9]

(44)   b.

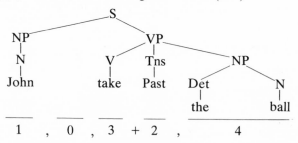

$$\begin{matrix} 1 & , & 0 & , & 3 & + & 2 & , & 4 \end{matrix}$$

The next tree provides a more complicated example; the rule must apply to this tree not once, but three times.

(45) a.

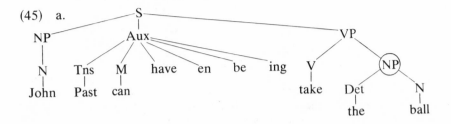

The structural description of the rule is satisfied, first of all, by the following division of the terminal sequence:

(45) b.   John   Past   can   have en be ing take the ball

$$X \;-\; Tns \;-\; M \;-\; \qquad\qquad Y$$
$$1 \qquad 2 \qquad 3 \qquad\qquad\qquad 4$$

A second way in which this tree satisfies the structural description of Affix Hopping is indicated in (45c):

(45) c.   John Past can have   en   be   ing take the ball

$$X \qquad\qquad\quad -\,en\,-\,be\,- \qquad Y$$
$$1 \qquad\qquad\qquad 2 \qquad 3 \qquad\quad 4$$

Finally, the structural description is satisfied in still a third way:

(45) d.   John can Past have en be   ing   take   the ball

$$X \qquad\qquad\qquad -\,ing\,- \;\; V \;-\; Y$$
$$1 \qquad\qquad\qquad\quad 2 \qquad 3 \qquad 4$$

When we carry out the structural change simultaneously in the three places where the structural description is satisfied, we get:

(45) e.   John can Past have be en take ing the ball.

As a final example, let us consider a tree structure that illustrates an important convention concerning the manner in which transformational rules apply:

(46) a.

We would clearly like to have the Affix Hopping rule apply here, to hop *Past* to the right of *leave*. The relevant case of the structural description in (43) is just the following:

(47)   X – Tns – V – Y
         1   2   3   4

The tree in (46a) will satisfy the structural description in (47) only if we allow the variable Y to be associated with nothing at all in the terminal sequence:

(46) b.   Jane   Past   leave
           ___   ___   ___   ___

           X   – Tns –   V   –   Y
           1   2   3   4

Carrying out the structural change here gives us the desired result:

(46) c.   Jane   leave   Past
           ___   ___   ___   ___

            1   ,   0   ,   3 + 2 ,   4

On account of this case and many others that we will see later, we will adopt the convention that a variable term in a structural description may legitimately be associated with nothing at all in the terminal sequence of a tree. The addition of this general convention to our framework in effect makes more precise our definition of what it means for a tree to satisfy a structural description. Although this convention may seem strange or arbitrary at first glance, we will find many other instances in which this interpretation of variables like X and Y is desirable. On the other hand, we will see no instances in which this convention leads to difficulty, that is, in which a transformational rule gives bad results when a variable is interpreted in this way.

With the help of Affix Hopping, we have now obtained the following sequences:

(48) a.   John take Past the ball.
     b.   John can Past have be en take ing the ball.
     c.   Jane leave Past.

All that remains to do is to say what the various inflectional forms actually are. For this we rely on rules of a type commonly referred to as *morphophonemic* rules:[10]

(49) a.   *take Past → took*
     b.   *can Past → could*
     c.   *be en → been*
     d.   *leave Past → left*

With these rules, we finally arrive at finished sentences of English:

(50) a.   John took the ball.
     b.   John could have been taking the ball.
     c.   Jane left.

This more detailed account of auxiliary structure requires a revision in the Subject-HV Inversion rule, so that some reference is made to the symbol Tns. In the questions that this rule is intended to help generate, it is clearly the verbal element *before* the subject noun phrase that is inflected for tense:

(51) a.   Would he go?
   b.   *Will he went?
   c.   Has he been working?
   d.   *Have he was working?

We will account for this fact by revising Subject-HV Inversion as follows:

(52)   Subject-HV Inversion   (second preliminary version)

$$NP - Tns \begin{Bmatrix} M \\ have \\ be \end{Bmatrix} - X$$

$$1 \qquad\qquad 2 \qquad\qquad 3$$

$$\Rightarrow 2 + 1, 0, 3 \quad \text{(Optional)}$$

This rule is designed to apply to trees that have not yet undergone the Affix Hopping rule (for reasons that will be presented in the following section). For example, the rule would apply to the structure given in (53a) below to yield (53b).

(53) a.

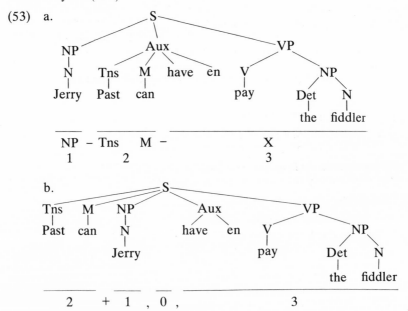

The resulting structure satisfies the structural description of Affix Hopping at two different points:

(53) c.

	Past	can	Jerry	have	en	pay	the fiddler

$$
\begin{array}{ccccc}
X & - \text{Tns} & - \text{M} & - & Y \\
1 & 2 & 3 & & 4
\end{array}
$$

$$
\begin{array}{ccccc}
X & & -en & - V & - & Y \\
1 & & 2 & 3 & & 4
\end{array}
$$

Application of the rule gives:

(53) d.   can Past Jerry have pay en the fiddler.

With the application of the morphophonemic rules that spell out *can Past* as *could* and *pay en* as *paid*, the derivation is complete:

(53) e.   Could Jerry have paid the fiddler?

As a final word on the transformational rule of Affix Hopping, we should note that it differs in one important respect from Subject-HV Inversion. The latter rule, as stated in (52), was *optional*: if it applied, we obtained a well-formed result (a question), whereas if it did not apply, the result was still well-formed (a declarative). However, if Affix Hopping is not applied in cases in which its structural description is met, we generate ill-formed sequences like the following:

(54) a.   *John Past can have en be ing take the ball.
     b.   *Past will you have en finish?

To avoid results like (54), we marked Affix Hopping as an *obligatory* rule. What this means is that it *must* apply in any situation in which its structural description is satisfied.[11]

EXERCISES

1. The phrase structure rules developed so far give the following terminal sequences (among others):

(i)   the fat man Past can have en be ing joke.
(ii)   Al Pres will be ing work.
(iii)   the lights Past have en blink.
(iv)   Fred Past go to the party.

For each of these sequences, write down the declarative sentence that results after all applications of Affix Hopping and the relevant morphophonemic rules.

2. Looking at matters the other way, what structures should we trace the following sentences back to? (Example: *The man will have finished the book* starts out as: *the man Pres will have en finish the book*.)

(i)   The baby may be sleeping.

(ii)   Oscar has been guarding the gate.

(iii)   The doctor was standing in the doorway.

3.   Review the derivation of the question *Could Jerry have paid the fiddler?* (53a–c). Then give a similar derivation for each of the following questions, in each case beginning with the tree that is formed by the phrase structure rules and the lexical rules.

(i)   Had the man been drinking?

(ii)   Will the baby be sleeping?

3.5 THE HELPING VERB *DO*

In our discussion thus far, we have not considered the formation of *yes-no* questions that correspond to declaratives that do not contain helping verbs, such as the following:

(55)   Fred arrived at the party.

We cannot simply shift the verb *arrived* to the left of the subject noun phrase, or else we get an ungrammatical result:

(56)   *Arrived Fred at the party?

What we find in English instead is a structure beginning with some form of the verb *do*:

(57)   Did Fred arrive at the party?

As this question shows, the helping verb *do* takes the inflection for tense (in this case the past tense), whereas the main verb is uninflected.

We can account for questions containing the helping verb *do* by making two revisions in the grammar that we have developed to this point. The first is to specify that the constituent Tns be moved by itself when it is not followed immediately by a modal, *have*, or *be*. This is taken care of by the following restatement of Subject-HV Inversion:[12]

(58)   Subject-HV Inversion

$$NP - Tns \left(\left\{ \begin{array}{l} M \\ have \\ be \end{array} \right\} \right) - X$$

$$1 \qquad\qquad 2 \qquad 3$$

$$\Rightarrow 2 + 1, 0, 3 \quad \text{(Optional)}$$

The revised structural description of this rule abbreviates a total of four specific structural descriptions:

(59) a.   NP – Tns M – X

   b.   NP – Tns *have* – X

   c.   NP – Tns *be* – X

   d.   NP – Tns – X

The last case is the one that is applicable to trees that contain no helping verbs. For example, the rule applies to convert (60a) into (60b).[13]

(60) a.

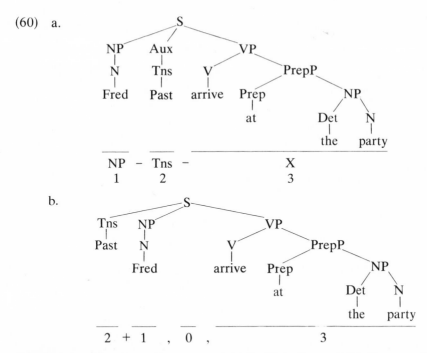

NP – Tns –   X
1   2   3

b.

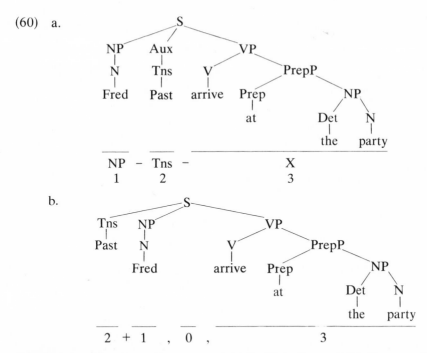

2 + 1 , 0 ,   3

Suppose now that we attempt to apply Affix Hopping to (60b). Because the element *Past* is followed directly by an NP rather than by an M, *have*, *be*, or a V, the structural description of Affix Hopping is not satisfied, and the rule cannot apply. The result is that the tense marker is left stranded.

It is at this point that the second revision becomes necessary. We add to our grammar a new rule that inserts *do* to the left of any Tns that has failed to satisfy the conditions for undergoing Affix Hopping. These occurrences of Tns are just those which happen *not* to be followed directly by any verbal element over which they can hop. We can state the following informal rule:

(61)   *Do* Support

An occurrence of Tns that has not been able to undergo Affix Hopping must have a *do* inserted to the left of it.   (Obligatory)[14]

Since the Tns in (60b) has not satisfied the conditions for Affix Hopping, the rule of *Do* Support is applicable. The result is:

(62)

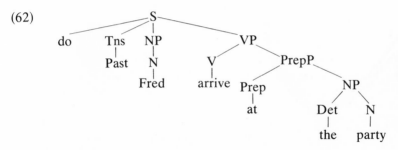

When we apply a morphophonemic rule that converts *do Past* to *did*, we finish the derivation of the question that we set out to derive:

(57)   Did Fred arrive at the party?

At this point, the analysis of *do* just given may seem somewhat arbitrary. We might well ask why we require such an intricate set of rules just to describe English questions. The answer is that this treatment of *do* can be extended so as to account for the appearance of this helping verb in other English constructions.

The first construction that provides further support for this analysis is the type of simple negative sentence illustrated in the right-hand column below:

(63) a.   Al could run.   Al could *not* run.
     b.   Al has run.   Al has *not* run.
     c.   Al is running.   Al is *not* running.
     d.   Al could have run.   Al could *not* have run.
     e.   Al could be running.   Al could *not* be running.
     f.   Al had been running.   Al had *not* been running.
     g.   Al could have been running.   Al could *not* have been running.

The relation between the affirmative sentences on the left and the negative sentences on the right is not hard to see. Each negative sentence is like the corresponding affirmative except for having a *not* after the first helping verb. Since the first helping verb is not the same from one sentence to the next, there is no way of getting *not* into the right place simply by making a revision in our basic phrase-structure rule for Aux. For instance, we cannot simply introduce *not* as an optional element after M:

(64)   Aux → Tns (M) (*not*) (*have en*) (*be ing*)

Although this rule does give us a few of the negative sentences in (63), e.g., *Al could not be running*, it gives the wrong results for negative sentences that do not contain modals, e.g., **Al Pres not have run* instead of *Al has not run*. To generate negative sentences solely by means of phrase structure rules, we must set forth the following cumbersome and unrevealing rule:

$$(65) \quad Aux \rightarrow Tns \begin{Bmatrix} \begin{cases} M \ (not) \ (have \ en) \\ have \ (not) \ en \\ be \ (not) \ ing \end{cases} (be \ ing) \end{Bmatrix}$$

This is the same sort of problem that led us to adopt a transformational rule for *yes-no* questions, the rule of Subject-HV Inversion.

Instead of trying to contrive a set of phrase structure rules that put *not* into the correct place in negative sentences, we might consider a simpler account, which relies on a division of labor between phrase structure rules and transformational rules. First, the phrase structure rule for Aux can be revised in such a way as to introduce *not* as an optional first element:

(66)   Aux → (*not*) Tns (M) (*have en*) (*be ing*)

When the optional *not* is not included, we get affirmative auxiliary structures of the sort that we presented in earlier sections of this chapter. When *not* is included, Aux's such as the following are created:

(67)   a.

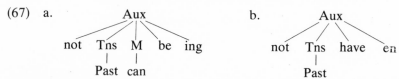

We must now add to our grammar a transformational rule that has the effect of moving the Tns and the immediately following helping verb to the left of the *not*:

(68)   *Not*-HV Inversion   (preliminary version)

$$X - not - Tns \begin{Bmatrix} M \\ have \\ be \end{Bmatrix} - Y$$

1   2   3   4

⇒ 1, 3 + 2, 0, 4   (Obligatory)

To illustrate how this analysis works, let us go through the derivation of the negative sentence *Al had not been running*. To begin with, the phrase structure and lexical rules give the tree:

(69)   a.

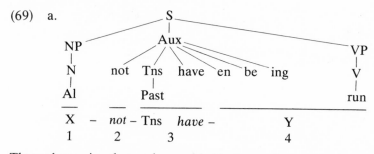

The underscoring that we have added indicates the manner in which the tree satisfies the structural description of *Not*-HV Inversion. The result of carrying out the structural change is shown below:

(69)   b.

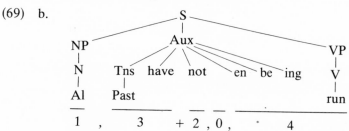

Affix Hopping applies at three points, to give:

(69) c.   Al have Past not be en run ing.

The application of the necessary morphophonemic rules gives the sentence that we set out to derive:

(69) d.   Al had not been running.

Let us look now at how a negative is formed when the corresponding affirmative does not contain a helping verb:

(70)   Al ran.   Al *did not* run.

Just as in *yes-no* questions, we get a helping verb *do* that is marked for tense, and the main verb takes its uninflected form. Thus, it would be reasonable here to give the same kind of analysis for *do* in negatives as we gave for *do* in questions. The crucial transformational rule for questions, Subject-HV Inversion, was formulated in such a way that Tns was moved by itself when no helping verb was present. We now reformulate *Not*-HV Inversion in the same way:

(71)   *Not*-HV Inversion

$$X - not - Tns \; (\left\{\begin{matrix} M \\ have \\ be \end{matrix}\right\}) - Y$$

$$\quad 1 \qquad 2 \qquad\qquad 3 \qquad\qquad 4$$

$$\Rightarrow 1, \; 3 + 2, \; 0, \; 4 \quad \text{(Obligatory)}$$

When an Aux consists of Tns alone, this rule has the effect shown in (72):

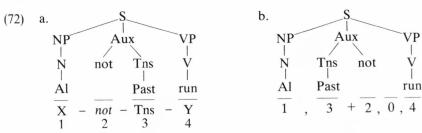

When we try to apply Affix Hopping to the tree in (72b), we find that the rule is not applicable because of the *not* that intervenes between Tns and the verb *run*. This stranded Tns now provides an occasion for the application of the rule of *Do* Support that we formulated originally for questions. After the insertion of *do* to the left of the stranded Tns, we obtain the following result:

(72) c.   Al do Past not run.

The application of one morphophonemic rule (*do Past* → *did*) gives the desired end result:

(72) d.   Al did not run.

We have thus succeeded in finding a second sentence type in the analysis of which it is useful to have the rule of *Do* Support.

Further support for this rule is furnished by an *elliptical* construction found in English, that is, a construction which would traditionally be described as containing some "understood" material:

(73) a.   Fred will sell some cars, and Sam will, too.

b.   The boss has bought a new hat, and his brother has, too.

c.   Mr. Jones is writing a letter, and Mr. Smith is, too.

These sentences are often described by referring to the following fuller sentences, in which the material understood in the sentences above is actually expressed:

(74) a.   Fred will sell some cars, and Sam will *sell some cars,* too

b.   The boss has bought a new hat, and his brother has *bought a new hat,* too.

c.   Mr. Jones is writing a letter, and Mr. Smith is *writing a letter,* too.

For these full sentences, we need a new phrase structure rule:

(75)   S → S *and* S *too*

This rule permits the derivation of structures of the form sketched in (76):

(76)

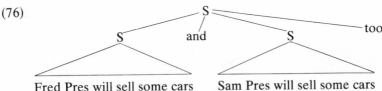

Fred Pres will sell some cars   Sam Pres will sell some cars

Similar structures are provided for the following sequences:

(77)   the boss Pres have en buy a new hat, and his brother Pres have en buy a new hat, too.

(78)   Mr. Jones Pres be ing write a letter, and Mr. Smith Pres be ing write a letter, too.

If no rules except Affix Hopping and morphophonemic rules apply to these structures, the full sentences given in (74) are generated. To account for the elliptical sentences, we add an optional transformational rule:

(79)   *Too* Ellipsis   (preliminary version)

$$NP - Tns \begin{Bmatrix} M \\ have \\ be \end{Bmatrix} - X - and - NP - Tns \begin{Bmatrix} M \\ have \\ be \end{Bmatrix} - Y \quad too$$

1 2   3 4 5   6   7 8

Condition: 3 = 7

⇒ 1, 2, 3, 4, 5, 6, 0, 8   (Optional)

This rule illustrates a new type of condition often found in structural descriptions, a requirement that two particular factors be identical. The rule has the effect of deleting the seventh factor (the second of the two identical factors). The application of this rule is illustrated in the derivation of the third elliptical sentence above. The phrase structure rules and lexical rules give a tree whose terminal sequence is (80a), which is divided for the purposes of *Too* Ellipsis into the factors indicated by the underscoring:

(80) a.

Mr. Jones	Pres be	ing write a letter	and
NP	$-$ Tns *be* $-$	X	$- and -$
1	2	3	4
Mr. Smith	Pres be	ing write a letter	too
NP	$-$ Tns *be* $-$	Y	$- too$
5	6	7	8

Since the structural description of rule (79) is satisfied (including the condition that the third and seventh terms be identical), the rule can apply. The result is:

(80) b.

Mr. Jones	Pres be	ing write a letter	and
1 ,	2 ,	3	, 4 ,
Mr. Smith	Pres be		too
5 ,	6 ,	0 ,	8

Three applications of Affix Hopping and the operation of the required morphophonemic rules give the desired elliptical sentence:

(80) c.   Mr. Jones is writing a letter, and Mr. Smith is, too.

For a full conjoined sentence that contains no helping verbs, the corresponding elliptical sentence contains some form of *do*:

(81)   Bill jumped into the fountain, and Martha jumped into the fountain, too.

(82)   Bill jumped into the fountain, and Martha *did*, too.

This additional elliptical sentence requires only one change in our rules: we put parentheses around the expressions referring to M, *have*, or *be*, just as we did in the previous rules of Subject-HV Inversion and *Not*-HV Inversion. The revised rule is as follows:[15]

(83)   *Too* Ellipsis

$$NP - Tns \; (\begin{Bmatrix} M \\ have \\ be \end{Bmatrix}) - X - and - NP - Tns \; (\begin{Bmatrix} M \\ have \\ be \end{Bmatrix}) - Y - too$$

| 1 | 2 | 3 | 4 | 5 | 6 | 7 | 8 |

Condition: 3 = 7

$\Rightarrow$ 1, 2, 3, 4, 5, 6, 0, 8   (Optional)

Let us see in detail how the revised rule makes possible an account of the elliptical sentence with *do*. We assume, once again, that the full sentence and the elliptical sentence share a common derivation up to the following point:

(84) a.   Bill Past jump into the fountain and Martha Past jump into the fountain too.

If the optional *Too* Ellipsis rule is not applied, we get the full sentence. On the other hand, if the rule is applied, (84a) is transformed into (84b):

(84) a.   Bill   Past   jump into the fountain   and   Martha

        NP – Tns –   X   – and –   NP –
        1   2   3   4   5

        Past   jump into the fountain   too

        Tns –   Y   – too
        6   7   8

   b.   Bill   Past   jump into the fountain   and   Martha

        1 , 2 ,   3   , 4 ,   5   ,

        Past   too

        6 ,   0 ,   8

The first occurrence of *Past* in the transformed sequence in (84b) is eligible for Affix Hopping, since it is followed directly by the verb *jump*. However, the second occurrence of *Past* is not eligible: the application of *Too* Ellipsis has left it stranded. Consequently, the conditions for the application of *Do* Support are satisfied. The result is:

(84) c.   Bill jump Past into the fountain and Martha do Past too.

Two morphophonemic rules now finish the derivation:

(84) d.   Bill jumped into the fountain and Martha did, too.

Thus, the appearance of *do* in this elliptical construction can be accounted for by exactly the same rule that was used to account for its appearance in questions and negatives.

    The main claim of this section, then, is that a transformational rule which inserts *do* as a support for stranded Tns elements has a useful role to play in accounting for several quite different English constructions.

EXERCISES

1. What structures should we trace the following sentences back to? (Example; *The man did not eat the cabbage* starts out as *the man not Past eat the cabbage*.)

(i)   Fred has not finished the painting.

(ii)   Do the students prefer the purple chalk?

(iii)   Maximilian has been sleeping under the stars and Clara has, too.

(iv)   The grocer did not weigh the packages.

(v)   Jones admires Smith and Jackson does, too.

2. In note 13 at the end of this chapter, we propose a convention which is applicable whenever a structural description with parenthesized elements is satisfied both with and without the parenthesized material. This convention was suggested in connection with Subject-HV Inversion:

(i) $$\text{NP} - \text{Tns} \; (\begin{Bmatrix} M \\ have \\ be \end{Bmatrix}) - X$$

$$\qquad 1 \qquad\qquad 2 \qquad\quad 3$$

$$\Rightarrow 2 + 1, 0, 3 \quad \text{(Optional)}$$

The convention dictates that in structures in which both (ii) and (iii) below are satisfied, the structural change can only be carried out in conformity with (ii):

(ii) $$\text{NP} - \text{Tns} \begin{Bmatrix} M \\ have \\ be \end{Bmatrix} - X$$

(iii) $$\text{NP} - \text{Tns} - X$$

Give an example of the kind of ungrammatical English question that this convention serves to prevent. Then do the same for an ungrammatical negative sentence and an ungrammatical elliptical sentence.

3. Imagine that we are given a transformational grammar for English which, among other things, generates all of the well-formed English declaratives. Give several examples of ungrammatical questions that could result from the application of the second case of the Subject-HV Inversion rule, the case that mentions *have*:

$$\text{NP} - \text{Tns} \quad have - X$$

$$\quad 1 \qquad\quad 2 \qquad\quad 3$$

$$\Rightarrow 2 + 1, 0, 3 \quad \text{(Optional)}$$

3.6 THE TRANSFORMATIONAL FRAMEWORK SUMMARIZED

In this chapter we have outlined what may seem to be a bewildering variety of new proposals, both about the grammar of English and about universal grammar. A useful method for reviewing these proposals will be to distinguish carefully between those that are intended as part of English grammar and those that are intended as part of our general descriptive framework, i.e., as part of our universal grammar.

In the first group, we have all of the specific rules that we have suggested for English, including the following rules (among many others):

(85) a.   PrepP → Prep   NP   (a phrase structure rule)

     b.   *put* $\langle V \rangle$, $\langle$_____ NP   PrepP$\rangle$ (a lexical rule)

     c.   NP – Tns $(\left\{\begin{array}{l} M \\ have \\ be \end{array}\right\})$ – X   (a transformational rule)

          1   2   3

        ⇒ 2 + 1, 0, 3   (Optional)

     d.   *do Past* → *did*   (a morphophonemic rule)

By contrast, all of the proposals that concern the form of grammars in general are intended for inclusion in our universal grammar. For instance, we suggested that a grammar of a human language could include four different kinds of rules—phrase structure, lexical, transformational, and morphophonemic—and we gave informal definitions of these general rule types. As one instance of such a definition, we said that a phrase structure rule was any sequence consisting of a single symbol followed by an arrow followed by one or more symbols. Although we have not given equally explicit definitions for the other three rule types, such definitions could be developed. All of these definitions would constitute part of our universal grammar rather than our grammar of English.

Also intended as part of our universal grammar are all of the proposed conventions governing the way in which specific grammars operate to generate sentences. We can give a brief review of these conventions here. First, the phrase structure rules expand the symbol S into a tree that is complete except that it lacks lexical items. Lexical items are inserted into the tree, in accordance with the feature specifications contained in the individual lexical rules. The resulting structure then undergoes the transformational rules in sequence. If the tree at a certain stage satisfies the structural description of some transformational rule, then it *may* undergo the structural change or it *must* undergo it, depending on whether the rule is optional or obligatory. The structure that results from applying the transformational rules then undergoes all of the relevant morphophonemic rules.

In addition to this general outline, we of course require detailed statements about the way to apply each type of rule, in particular, how to apply phrase structure rules to form trees, how to determine whether a lexical item qualifies for insertion into a particular location in a tree, how to determine whether the structural description of a transformational rule is satisfied by a tree, how to determine the new tree that results from the application of a transformational rule, and how to apply morphophonemic rules. If we have a particular grammar that contains rules of just these four types, then it is this body of general conventions on the manner in which rules apply that determines which sentences are generated by the grammar and which ones are not. To put it as briefly as possible, a certain sentence will qualify as being generated by some specific grammar if there is a way to get from the initial symbol S to the sentence in question by applying the rules of that grammar in accordance with the general conventions.

The particular proposals advanced in this chapter about rule types and the way in which rules apply constitute the basic outline of the *transformational framework*. It is important to note that the type of rule from which this framework takes its name is only one of four different rule types that the framework defines. Thus, the transformational framework is not so much a complete replacement for the phrase structure framework as it is an enlargement of it.

It will be helpful now to introduce a number of technical terms for structures that arise in the course of deriving sentences. Trees that result from the application of the phrase structure rules will be termed *prelexical structures*. After lexical items have been inserted, the resulting trees will be referred to as *deep structures*. Application of the transformational rules yields *surface structures*. In a comprehensive universal grammar that dealt with phonological and phonetic structure as well as with syntactic structure, some special term would be reserved for the structures produced by the morphophonemic rules. For our present purposes, however, we can think of the outputs of these rules as being finished sentences. The relation between these structures and the four sets of rules (or *components*, as they are often called) is represented schematically as follows:

(86)

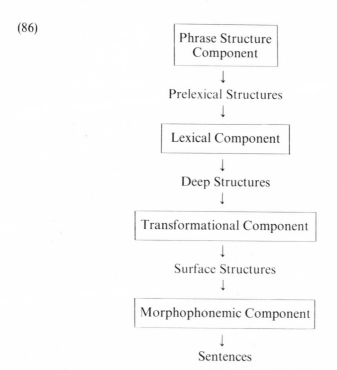

For an actual illustration of a transformational grammar and the way in which it operates, we can use an abridged version of the grammar developed in this chapter:

(87)   Transformational Grammar for a Fragment of English

A. Phrase Structure Component

S → NP   Aux   VP
VP → V (NP) (PrepP)
Aux → (*not*) Tns (M) (*have en*) (*be ing*)
PrepP → Prep   NP
NP → (Det) (Adj) N
Tns → $\left\{ \begin{array}{c} Pres \\ Past \end{array} \right\}$

B. Lexical Component

raven ⟨N⟩
crow ⟨N⟩
object ⟨N⟩
shiny ⟨Adj⟩
steal ⟨V⟩, ⟨———NP (PrepP)⟩
the ⟨Det⟩
from ⟨Prep⟩
can ⟨M⟩

C. Transformational Component

Subject-HV Inversion

NP – Tns ($\left\{ \begin{array}{c} M \\ have \\ be \end{array} \right\}$) – X

1   2   3

⇒ 2 + 1, 0, 3   (Optional)

Not-HV Inversion

NP – *not* – Tns ($\left\{ \begin{array}{c} M \\ have \\ be \end{array} \right\}$) – X

1   2   3   4

⇒ 1, 3 + 2, 0, 4   (Obligatory)

Affix Hopping

X – $\left\{ \begin{array}{c} Tns \\ en \\ ing \end{array} \right\}$ – $\left\{ \begin{array}{c} M \\ have \\ be \\ V \end{array} \right\}$ – Y

1   2   3   4

⇒ 1, 0, 3 + 2, 4   (Obligatory)

Do Support

> An occurrence of Tns that has not been able to undergo Affix Hopping must have *do* inserted to the left of it. (Obligatory)

D. Morphophonemic Component

steal en → *stolen*		*have Pres* → *has*
steal Past → *stole*		*do Past* → *did*
steal Pres → *steals*		*do Pres* → *does*
can Past → *could*		*be en* → *been*
can Pres → *can*		*be Past* → *was*
have Past → *had*		*be Pres* → *is*

Let us now sketch the derivation of one of the sentences that this grammar generates. First of all, one of the prelexical structures created by the phrase structure rules is:

(88)   a.

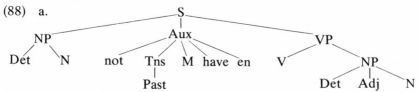

Among the possibilities for inserting lexical items into this tree are those that give the following deep structure:

(88)   b.

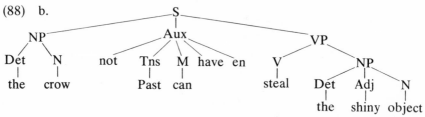

We can now think of this deep structure as "entering" the transformational component. The first transformational rule in the list given in (87) is Subject-HV Inversion. The tree satisfies the structural description for this rule, but since it is marked as an optional rule, the structure may pass on to the next rule. This next rule, *Not*-HV Inversion, is obligatory. It applies, to give a tree whose terminal sequence is:

(88)   c.   the crow Past can not have en steal the shiny object.

The next transformational rule is Affix Hopping, which is also obligatory. In the structure under consideration, the rule applies twice, yielding:

(88)   d.   the crow can Past not have steal en the shiny object.

The last rule on the list, *Do* Support, does not apply here, because no Tns element has been unable to undergo Affix Hopping. Hence, the tree that is assigned to (88d) qualifies as a *surface structure*. This surface structure is given in detail in the following tree:

(88) e.

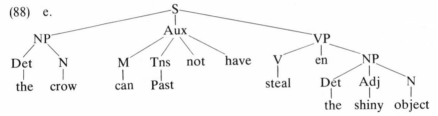

When this structure is modified further by the relevant rules of the morphophonemic component, the result is:

(88) f.   The crow could not have stolen the shiny object.

Sentence (88f), then, is one of the sentences that are generated by the small grammar given in (87).

This small transformational grammar of course generates many other sentences, according to which options are followed in applying the phrase structure rules, inserting lexical items, and applying the optional transformational rules. If we are given a sentence and asked whether this grammar generates it, our task is to determine whether there is a derivation for that sentence that is carried out in conformity with the rules of the specific grammar and our general conventions about how these rules are to be applied. For instance, if we were given the question in (89), we could determine that there is a derivation for this sentence according to these rules.

(89)   Did the crow steal the shiny object?

On the other hand, we could readily calculate that none of the following sentences is generated by this grammar:

(90) a.   The crow stole from the raven.
   b.   Which object did the crow steal?
   c.   The crow stole the small object.

The fact that these sentences are not generated by the rules in (87) does not necessarily indicate a deficiency in the transformational framework itself, since the framework would clearly permit us to construct a much more comprehensive grammar for English, one that contained enough additional rules to generate the sentences in (90).

The major purpose of this chapter has been to outline a new framework for syntactic description, the transformational framework. We have argued that several English constructions can be accounted for in a more revealing manner within this framework than within the phrase structure framework of Chapter 2. In the next chapter we will see three additional English constructions for which an analysis carried out within the transformational framework is superior.

Before we conclude this chapter, a word of caution is in order. The small transformational grammar that we have developed here is only one of a large number that we could have proposed to account for the same English constructions. Furthermore, we have been primarily concerned with arguing in favor of this grammar as compared with its potential phrase structure competitors, and have not attempted to argue that it is superior to all of its transformational competitors. An initial example of a competing transformational grammar is presented in Exercise 3 below. An even more radical alternative transformational description is discussed in Chapter 12, where a large collection of new data from English is presented.

EXERCISES

1. Give derivations for the following sentences, in each instance beginning with the deep structure and then indicating the effects of any relevant transformations:

(i)   The old man had been sleeping.
(ii)   Would Martha have stayed at home?
(iii)   Did the judge know the answer?
(iv)   The men would not have been hiding the still.

2. Study the following pairs of sentences:

(i)   a.   Sam is snoring, and Martha is snoring.
        b.   Sam is snoring, and so is Martha.
(ii)   a.   Sally would be working, and Martin would be working.
        b.   Sally would be working, and so would Martin.
(iii)   a.   Fred saw the movie, and Benny saw the movie.
        b.   Fred saw the movie, and so did Benny.
(iv)   a.   George has been keeping a record, and the man from Tennessee has been keeping a record.
        b.   George has been keeping a record, and so has the man from Tennessee.

We can account for the (a) sentences by means of the following phrase structure rule:

S → S *and* S

How can the (b) sentences be accounted for? Try to write a single transformational rule which, when added to the grammar developed in the body of this chapter, will make it possible to generate the (b) sentences. Be sure to state any identity conditions that you think are necessary. Then give the deep structures and sketch the transformational derivations for (iib) and (iiib).

3. The purpose of this problem is to explore an alternative set of rules for the English sentences considered so far. Like the grammar given in (87), this new set of rules is constructed within the transformational framework.

There are two basic respects in which the new grammar differs from the old. First, instead of having no helping verb *do* in deep structures and having a transformational rule to insert *do* when needed, the new analysis has one occurrence of this helping verb in *every* deep structure and has a transformational rule that deletes this *do* under certain circumstances. Second, the new analysis makes reference to a new constituent, which will be called "Aux_1." This constituent eventually consists of Tns plus whatever shows up as the first helping verb, and figures prominently in the revised versions of several transformational rules.

The phrase structure component of this new grammar differs from that of the grammar in (87) in just one respect. In place of the rule given in (i) below, the new grammar contains the two rules given in (ii):

(i)   Aux → (*not*) Tns (M) (*have en*) (*be ing*)

(ii)   a. Aux → (*not*) Aux_1 (M) (*have en*) (*be ing*)
        b. Aux_1 → Tns *do*

The types of deep structure Aux's to which the rules in (ii) give rise are exemplified in these three sub-trees:

(iii)   a.

b.

c.

It is in the transformational component that this new grammar differs most noticeably from the old one. In (iv) through (viii) are given the transformational rules; the intervening comments indicate the effect of each rule.

(iv)   *Do* Replacement

$$X - do - \begin{Bmatrix} M \\ have \\ be \end{Bmatrix} - Y$$
$$1 \quad 2 \qquad 3 \qquad 4$$

⇒ 1, 3, 0, 4   (Obligatory)

Rule (iv) applies to any deep structure that contains an M, *have*, or *be*. It has the effect of shifting the first such helping verb into the Aux_1 constituent, replacing *do*. After this rule applies, the constituent Aux_1 consists of either Tns plus M, Tns plus *have*, Tns plus *be*, or Tns plus *do*. *isn't do replaced?*

(v)   Subject-Aux_1 Inversion

$$NP - Aux_1 - Y$$
$$1 \quad \; 2 \quad \; 3$$

⇒ 2 + 1, 0, 3   (Optional)

Rule (v) serves the same function within this grammar that Subject-HV Inversion serves in the grammar given in (87).

(vi)   *Not*-Aux$_1$ Inversion

$$X - not - Aux_1 - Y$$
$$1 \quad 2 \quad\quad 3 \quad\quad 4$$
$$\Rightarrow 1, 3 + 2, 0, 4 \quad \text{(Obligatory)}$$

Rule (vi) has the same effect as *Not*-HV Inversion in (87).

(vii)   *Do* Deletion

$$X - Tns - do - V - Y$$
$$1 \quad\quad 2 \quad\quad 3 \quad 4 \quad 5$$
$$\Rightarrow 1, 2, 0, 4, 5 \quad \text{(Obligatory)}$$

Rule (vii) deletes any *do* that has not been replaced by another helping verb and that directly precedes a V. It will not delete a *do* that is followed by something other than a V. When a *do* is deleted by this rule, only Tns remains in Aux$_1$; this Tns is in a position to be hopped over V by the following rule:

(viii)   Affix Hopping

$$X - \begin{Bmatrix} Tns \\ en \\ ing \end{Bmatrix} - \begin{Bmatrix} M \\ have \\ be \\ do \\ V \end{Bmatrix} - Y$$
$$1 \quad\quad 2 \quad\quad\quad\quad 3 \quad\quad\quad 4$$
$$\Rightarrow 1, 0, 3 + 2, 4 \quad \text{(Obligatory)}$$

Rule (viii) has the same function as Affix Hopping in (87). The only difference is that *do* is added to the list of verbal elements over which an affix must hop.

A. Give the derivations that this alternative grammar dictates for the sentences in Exercise 1 above. In each instance, begin with the alternative deep structure, and then indicate the effects of the relevant transformational rules.

B. How would you restate the rule of *Too* Ellipsis in (83) to fit in with the new analysis? Before attempting to answer this question, be sure that you understand the way in which the rules of Subject-HV Inversion and *Not*-HV Inversion have been restated in this exercise.

C. In what respect might this alternative set of rules be judged more revealing than the set of rules developed in the body of this chapter?

Suggestions for Further Reading

The most important supplementary reading for this chapter would be Chomsky 1957, Chapters 5 and 7. The analysis developed there forms the basis for the analysis given in the present chapter. In addition, a number of other transformational rules are proposed for English, several of which will be discussed in later chapters of this book.

For additional discussion of the formulation of transformational rules and conventions for determining derived constituent structure, see Kimball 1973, Chapter 3.

Notes

1. The analysis of English that we will outline in the remainder of this chapter follows very closely the analysis presented in Chapters 5 and 7 of Chomsky 1957.

2. Although the term *auxiliary verb* is more frequently used in current linguistic writing, we will use the term *helping verb*, to avoid the confusion that would result from using the word *auxiliary* in two quite distinct ways. The symbol Aux (for "auxiliary") will be reserved for use in referring to a phrase structure constituent that can include several verbal elements. Rules for this constituent are developed below.

3. In many studies of English syntax, this rule is referred to as *Subject-Auxiliary Inversion*, or *Subject-Aux Inversion*. This customary name for the rule can be misleading, since it is not generally the whole Aux that goes before the subject in questions, but only the first verbal element in the Aux. This is seen clearly in the questions in (6d) through (6g).

4. Exercise 1 at the end of this section offers some simple phrase structure rules for questions which might appear at first glance to be entirely adequate. The point of the exercise is to show that these simple rules are in fact not adequate.

5. We will also make it a practice to delete nonterminal nodes that no longer dominate anything. This is the reason that the Aux node has not been retained in the derived structure in (29).

6. Although the terms *sister* and *daughter* are in standard use, the term *aunt* as used here is not. It is offered merely as an aid in seeing the character of the derived structure in (32).

7. We will postpone until Chapter 5 a discussion of how verbal elements are to be marked for number and person.

8. The classification of *could* as the past form of *can* and *would* as the past form of *will* is supported by the parallel between each of the sentence pairs in (ii) and (iii) and the pair in (i). The (a) sentences are examples of so-called *direct quotation*, whereas the (b) sentences are instances of *indirect quotation*.

(i)   a. John said, "Alice *feels* fine."
        b. John said that Alice *felt* fine.

(ii)   a. Harry said, "Joe *can* swim the English Channel."
        b. Harry said that Joe *could* swim the English Channel.

(iii)   a. Fred said "Clarence *will* come to a bad end."
        b. Fred said that Clarence *would* come to a bad end."

The frequent classification of *might* as the past form of *may* and *should* as the past form of *shall* is not so easy to justify, given the way in which these modals are used in contemporary English.

9. The derived structure here may seem questionable. It is sometimes suggested that a more appropriate derived structure for the VP would be one in which both *take* by itself and *take Past* are classified as V's:

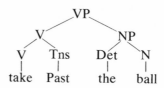

10. These rules clearly do not qualify as phrase structure rules, since two symbols on the left side of each rule are rewritten as a single symbol on the right side.

11. As will be shown in the next section of this chapter and also in Chapter 5, it is necessary to qualify this definition of *obligatory rule*. The basic idea will be that an obligatory rule is one which must be applied if its structural description is satisfied *at a certain point in the derivation*.

12. Although Subject-HV Inversion will be revised again in section 4.3, this is the final version of the rule so far as the present chapter is concerned.

13. Here we require another convention concerning the manner in which transformational rules with parentheses apply. If a tree satisfies a structural description in such a way that part of the terminal sequence is matched up with a parenthesized element of the structural description, then it is only with respect to this division that the structural change can be carried out. To take a concrete example, the structural description in (i) contains an element in parentheses:

(i)   NP – Tns (*be*) – X
         1   2   3

This structural description can be broken down into two more specific ones:

(ii)   NP – Tns *be* – X
         1   2   3

(iii)   NP – Tns – X
         1   2   3

The convention above dictates that when we find a tree that satisfies both (ii) and (iii), we can only carry out the structural change in conformity with (ii), in which the material parenthesized in (i) is present. The reason for this convention is left for Exercise 2 at the end of this section.

14. The precise formulation of *Do* Support given in Chomsky 1957 depends upon the prior application of two rather complicated rules that determine the location of boundaries between words. These rules have the effect of making it possible to distinguish between Tns elements that have undergone Affix Hopping and those that have not. For our present purposes, the informal statement given in (61) will be sufficient.

15. In Chapter 12 we will propose that elliptical sentences of the type considered here are to be accounted for by a rule that is much more general than the rule of *Too* Ellipsis tentatively suggested here.

4

Additional Support
for the
Transformational Framework

In this chapter, we will examine three more English constructions. For each of them, a transformational treatment appears to be more revealing than any treatment that relies solely on phrase structure rules and lexical rules. Besides their value as further illustrations of the new type of rule introduced in Chapter 3, the rules that we will propose here will be important at later points in the book as we attempt to develop a more detailed version of the transformational framework.

4.1 PASSIVE

We have so far made a point of ignoring a very important English helping verb, the *be* that requires a following past participle.

(1) a.   The teacher *was amused* by the small boy.
    b.   The letter had *been sent* to Margaret by John.
    c.   The house is *being watched* by the detective.
    d.   The key might have *been borrowed* by the old man.
    e.   The trunk *was taken* to the station by the porter.

These sentences are traditionally known as *passives*; it is customary to describe them in terms of related *active* sentences:

(2) a.   The small boy amused the teacher.
    b.   John had sent the letter to Margaret.

101

c. The detective is watching the house.

d. The old man might have borrowed the key.

e. The porter took the trunk to the station.

Informally speaking, a passive sentence can be constructed by starting with an active sentence that has a noun phrase following the verb, and then making three changes: first, moving the subject noun phrase to the end of the sentence and inserting *by* before it; second, moving the noun phrase following the verb into subject position; and third, inserting the appropriate form of *be* before the verb and putting the verb in its past participial form. This informal statement can be translated quite readily into a transformational rule:[1]

(3)   Passive

$$NP - Aux - V - NP - X$$
$$ 1 \quad\ \ 2 \quad\ 3 \quad\ 4 \quad 5$$
$$\Rightarrow 4, 2, \ be + en + 3, 0, 5 + by + 1 \quad \text{(Optional)}$$

We can illustrate the operation of this rule by deriving the second sentence given above. We begin the derivation with the deep structure (4a), which we would use in deriving the corresponding active sentence. To this tree we may optionally apply the passive rule, which yields (4b).[2]

(4)   a.

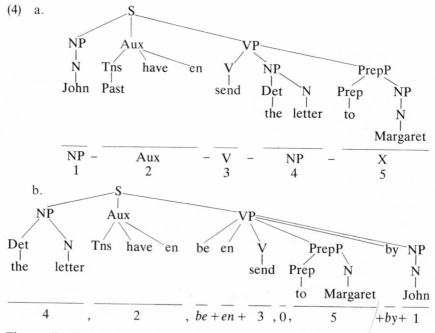

The application of Affix Hopping three times gives

(4)   c.   the letter have Past be en send en to Margaret by John.

All that remains is to apply the relevant morphophonemic rules, which specify *have* Past as *had*, *be en* as *been*, and *send en* as *sent*, yielding:

(4) d.   The letter had been sent to Margaret by John.

This rule works equally well for other types of verbs, as can be seen by the following examples. In each group, the active sentence results if the option of applying the passive rule is not taken, the passive results if the optional passive rule is applied, as follows:

(5) a.   Sally amused the teacher.

b.   The teacher was amused by Sally.

Sally	Past	amuse	the teacher	
NP	– Aux –	V	– NP	– X
1	2	3	4	5

⇒ the teacher	Past	be	en	amuse			by	Sally
4	, 2	, $be + en +$	3	, 0	,	$5 + by +$	1	

(6) a.   Jack called Richard a liar.

b.   Richard was called a liar by Jack.

Jack	Past	call	Richard	a liar
NP	– Aux –	V	– NP	– X
1	2	3	4	5

Richard	Past	be	en	call		a liar	by	Jack
4	, 2	, $be + en +$	3	,	0	, 5	$+ by +$	1

Let us consider how the English passive construction forms the basis for an additional argument in favor of allowing transformational rules in grammars. What we would like to show is that the transformational account just presented is more revealing than any description of active and passive sentences that relies exclusively on phrase structure and lexical rules. We must attempt to devise as good a grammar as we can within the phrase structure framework. If the resulting grammar is still unrevealing, then the argument is successful.

As it happens, there are many fairly simple ways to adapt our existing phrase structure rules so that they will yield passive as well as active structures. One possibility, the one that we shall pursue here, is to set up a special kind of passive phrase (which we can represent by the symbol PassP). This phrase is introduced as an additional option in the rule that rewrites the initial symbol S, as follows:

(7) $S \rightarrow NP \ \ Aux \ \begin{Bmatrix} VP \\ PassP \end{Bmatrix}$

Then the PassP is expanded into the passive helping verb *be en* followed by an ordinary VP followed by the sequence *by NP*:[3]

(8)   PassP → *be en* VP *by* NP

The type of tree that these rules give is illustrated below:

(9)

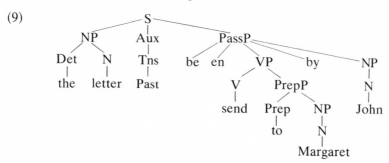

So far, the phrase structure account that we are developing appears to be neither more nor less revealing than the account based on the Passive transformational rule stated as (3). A significant difference shows up, though, as soon as we consider the lexical entries that will be required if we are to make the phrase structure treatment work correctly. Among the judgments that must be accounted for are these:

(10) a.   The small boy amused the teacher.
 b.   The teacher was amused by the small boy.
 c.   *The small boy amused the teacher the principal.
 d.   *The teacher was amused the principal by the small boy.

Given the phrase structure treatment in rules (7) and (8), there is only one way to be sure of generating just the grammatical sentences (10a) and (10b) without also generating the ungrammatical sentences in (10c) and (10d). We must include two separate subcategorization features in the lexical entry for *amuse*, one specifically for active sentences and the other for passives:[4]

(11)   *amuse*, ⟨V⟩, ⟨____ NP⟩, ⟨*be en* ____ *by* NP⟩

Furthermore, in order to give good results with other verbs, we must include corresponding pairs of subcategorization features in the lexical entry of every verb that can occur in passive sentences. To take just one more example, if we are to get the right predictions as regards the sentences (12), we must set up the lexical entry (13) for the verb *paint*:

(12) a.   Jerry painted the car (purple).
 b.   The car was painted (purple) by Jerry.
 c.   *Jerry painted the car the bicycle (purple).
 d.   *The car was painted the bicycle (purple) by Jerry.

(13)   *paint*, ⟨V⟩, ⟨____ NP (Adj)⟩, ⟨*be en* ____ (Adj) *by* NP⟩

It is here that we can charge that the nontransformational description is unrevealing. Even more serious than the fact that each lexical entry requires two subcategorization features is the fact that the relation between the two features is always the same. In every lexical entry, the passive feature is like the active except for having *be en* and *by NP* on the left and right, and having an NP missing after the V position.

Turning back to the transformational treatment of passives, we see that no such unrevealing duplication of subcategorization features is necessary. Because the transformational treatment employs structures with active VP's as one stage in the derivation of passives, we only need to give subcategorization specifications for active structures, and the correct passive forms will be generated automatically. For example, the feature ⟨____NP⟩ in the lexical entry of *amuse* allows this verb to appear in the deep structure VP in (14a) but not in the VP in (14b).

(14) a.   b.

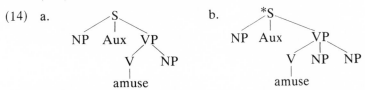

It follows immediately from the way in which the Passive rule is formulated in (3) that *amuse* will appear in the passive structure in (15a), which arises by the application of the Passive rule to the legitimate deep structure in (14a).

(15) a.

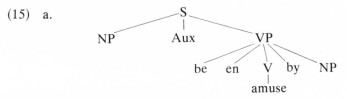

On the other hand, the passive structure in (15b) will never be generated, since it could arise only by the application of the Passive rule to the ill-formed deep structure in (14b).

(15) b.

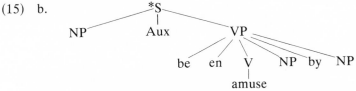

In sum, the description of passive sentences that relies on the transformational rule in (3) is markedly more revealing than the description that relies on the special phrase structure rules in (7) and (8). Although many other phrase structure descriptions of passives can be devised, they all share the weakness of requiring an unrevealing duplication in the lexical entries of individual verbs. We thus have an additional argument in favor of the transformational framework as against the extended phrase structure framework of Chapter 2.

Structures that result from the Passive rule can undergo further rules, including Subject-HV Inversion and *Not*-HV Inversion. For example, the derivation of (16) begins with the tree (17a), the same deep structure tree as that for the corresponding active declarative.

(16)   Was the play panned by the newspaper?

(17) a.

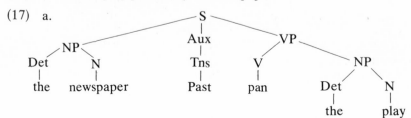

The Passive rule can now apply to this structure, as follows:

(17) b.

the newspaper   Past   pan   the play

$$\underline{\quad\quad} \quad \underline{\quad} \quad \underline{\quad} \quad \underline{\quad\quad}$$

NP   – Aux –   V –   NP   –   X
1   2   3   4   5

⇒ the play   Past   be   en   pan   by   the newspaper

$$\underline{\quad\quad} \quad \underline{\quad} \quad \underline{\quad} \quad \underline{\quad} \quad \underline{\quad} \qquad\qquad \underline{\quad} \quad \underline{\quad\quad}$$

4   ,   2   , *be* +*en*+ 3   ,   0   ,   5 +*by*+   1

At this point, Subject-HV Inversion, which we designed to apply to the *be* of the progressive construction, can apply without any addition or modification:

(17) c.   the play   Past be   en pan by the newspaper

$$\underline{\quad\quad} \quad \underline{\quad\quad} \qquad \underline{\quad\quad\quad\quad\quad}$$

NP   – Tns *be* –   X
1   2   3

⇒ Past be   the play   en pan by the newspaper

$$\underline{\quad\quad} \quad \underline{\quad\quad} \qquad \underline{\quad\quad\quad\quad}$$

2   +   1   ,   0   ,   3

Two applications of Affix Hopping yield:

(17) d.   be Past the play pan en by the newspaper

Morphophonemic rules give the desired end result:

(17) e.   Was the play panned by the newspaper?

Similarly, with no additions or changes in the rules that we already have, we can generate both of the following sentences:

(18)   The play was not panned by the newspaper.

(19)   The play was panned by the newspaper, and the movie was, too.

The latter sentence requires the application of the Passive rule within the individual conjoined sentences, followed by application of *Too* Ellipsis in the conjoined structure as a whole.

We should note a further transformational rule that is needed if we adopt the transformational analysis of passives presented above. The insufficiency of the analysis as it stands now is indicated by the existence in English of perfectly grammatical passive sentences in which there is no final *by* NP, such as:

(20) a.   Jerry was taken to the hospital.

     b.   The painting was sold to a local doctor.

     c.   The house has been watched carefully.

These so-called "agentless passives" may be accounted for by deriving them from deep structures that have an indefinite pronoun *someone* as the subject noun phrase. In this view, the deep structure for the first sentence above would be the following tree:

(21) a.

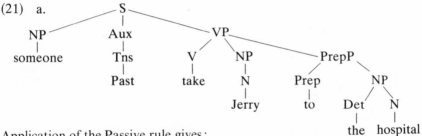

Application of the Passive rule gives:

(21) b.   Jerry Past be en take to the hospital by someone.

To get from this structure to a structure without the *by someone*, we add to the grammar an optional rule:

(22)   Agent Deletion

    X – *by someone*
    1   2
    ⇒ 1, 0   (Optional)

This rule applies to the passive structure given above in the following way:

(21) c.   Jerry Past be en take to the hospital   by someone

                       X   – *by someone*
                       1   2

    ⇒ Jerry Past be en take to the hospital.

                      1   , 0

Affix Hopping and morphophonemic rules finish the derivation.

EXERCISES

1. Give complete derivations for the following sentences:

(i)   The man will not be nominated by the chairman.
(ii)   Was the gun kept in the closet by the housekeeper?
(iii)   The nominee should have been supported by the committee.

(For the third sentence, assume that *should* arises by a morphophonemic rule that converts *shall Past* to *should*.)

2.   In section 2.6, we adopted the use of subcategory features in order to avoid having to use a variety of symbols for the different types of verbs. Suppose that we had not taken this step, that instead we had accounted for different types of verbal environments by rules of the following sort:

$$VP \rightarrow V_1$$
$$VP \rightarrow V_2 \ NP$$
$$VP \rightarrow V_3 \ PrepP$$
$$VP \rightarrow V_4 \ NP \ PrepP$$

How would the Passive rule have to be restated?

3.   Why do sentences (i) and (ii) below create a problem for the analysis of agentless passives proposed in the text?

(i)   The governor general of this colony is universally detested.
(ii)   This view of matters is widely accepted.

Explain your answer briefly but carefully.

4.2 RELATIVE CLAUSES

Another argument in favor of the transformational framework as against the extended phrase structure framework is provided by the relative clause construction in English. The italicized sequences in the following sentences illustrate this construction:

(23) a.   The men *whom we told to come* arrived late.
     b.   The police recovered the car *that Fred stole.*
     c.   The person *to whom Jack addressed the letter* has not come forward to claim it.
     d.   The hat *John was wearing* made Sheila laugh.

In order to simplify the discussion, we will restrict our attention in this section to one particular subclass of relative clauses, namely, those which are introduced by the word *that*. Although it would be necessary to account for other types of relative clauses in a complete grammar of English, the major point to be made here would remain valid if a wider variety of relative clauses were discussed.

Let us begin with an examination of a representative set of these relative clauses:

(24) a.   The sheriff found the man *that took the money from the safe*.

b.   The baby *that the senator kissed* cried.

c.   The sheriff found the safe *that the man took the money from*.

If we were to isolate the part of the relative clause that follows the introductory word *that*, in every case the result would not be grammatical as a sentence in its own right:

(25) a.   *Took the money from the safe.

b.   *The senator kissed.

c.   *The man took the money from.

In all three of these sequences, an identical defect stands in the way of grammaticality: each sequence gives the impression of having an NP missing from it. In the case of (25a), it is a subject NP; in (25b), it is a direct object NP; in (25c) it is an object for the preposition *from*.

Traditional grammars of English commonly take account of this peculiarity of relative clauses by saying that the relative clause in (24a) has an "understood" subject, that in (24b) has an "understood" direct object, and that in (24c) has an "understood" object of the preposition *from*. In developing a transformational description of relative clauses, we will take a cue from this traditional account. We will set up deep structures for these relative clauses that contain full NP's corresponding to those that are missing (or "understood") in the actual surface structure. For example, since the relative clause in (24a) has an understood subject, the deep structure that we assign to it will have a full NP as subject:

(24) a.   The sheriff found the man [that____ took the money from the safe].

Deep structure:

The sheriff found the man [*the man* took the money from the safe].

Similarly, the deep structure for (24b) will contain a full NP as direct object:

(24) b.   The baby [that the senator kissed____] cried.

Deep structure:

The baby [the senator kissed *the baby*] cried.

Finally, in the deep structure for (24c), a full NP will follow the preposition *from*.

(24) c.   The sheriff found the safe [that the man took the money from____].
Deep structure:
The sheriff found the safe [the man took the money from *the safe*].

Having put together deep structures in which the "understood" NP of the relative clause is represented by a full NP, we note that the bracketed portions of the deep structures could qualify as sentences in their own right:

(26) a.   The man took the money from the safe.
     b.   The senator kissed the baby.
     c.   The man took the money from the safe.

As a consequence, we can use exactly the same phrase structure rules to give the deep structures for relative clauses that we have already set up for forming the deep structures of ordinary simple sentences. The only new phrase structure rule that we need is one that creates NP's that contain S's:[5]

(27)   NP → NP S

This rule, acting together with the phrase structure rules already included in our grammar, gives tree (28) as the deep structure for sentence (24a).[6]

(24) a.   The sheriff found the man that took the money from the safe.

(28)

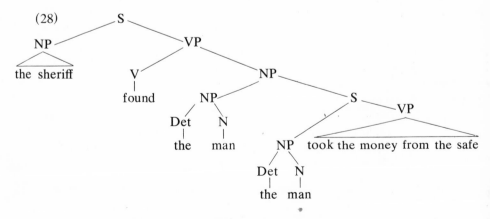

Similarly, the deep structure tree for (24b) will be (29):

(24) b.   The baby that the senator kissed cried.

(29)

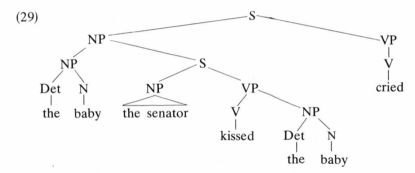

Finally, the deep structure tree for (24c) will be (30).

(24) c.   The sheriff found the safe that the man took the money from.

(30)

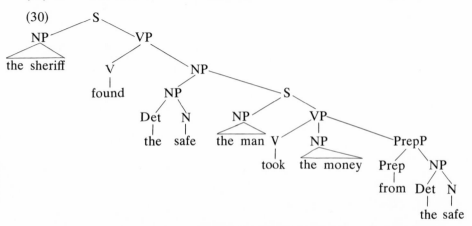

We can now formulate a simple transformational rule to get from the deep structures in (28–30) to the corresponding surface structures. The only transformational changes that need to be made are, first, the insertion of *that* on the left-hand side of the lower S, and second, the deletion of the NP inside the lower S that is identical to the NP to the left of the S. The following transformational rule carries out just these changes:

(31)   Relative Clause Formation

$$X - [_{NP} NP - [_S Y - NP - Z]_S]_{NP} - W$$
$$\quad 1 \qquad 2 \qquad 3 \quad 4 \quad 5 \qquad 6$$

Condition: 2 = 4

⇒1, 2, *that* + 3, 0, 5, 6   (Obligatory)

In this transformational rule, the pairs of brackets labeled NP and S are to be interpreted as follows. If a certain way of dividing the terminal sequence into factors is to qualify as satisfying this structural description, then not only must the second and fourth factors be NP's, but in addition the second through the fifth factors taken together must be an NP, and the third through the fifth must make up an S.

We can illustrate the operation of this rule by looking at the derivation that proceeds from tree (29) to sentence (24b). The manner in which Relative Clause Formation applies is shown below:

(32) a.

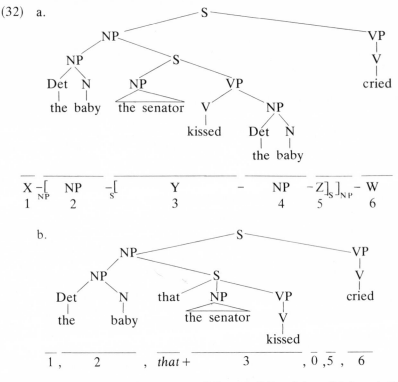

$$X -[_{NP} \; NP \; -[_{S} \quad Y \quad - \quad NP \; -Z]_{S}]_{NP} - W$$
$$1 \qquad 2 \qquad \quad 3 \qquad \quad 4 \qquad 5 \qquad 6$$

b.

$$1, \quad 2 \quad , \; that + \quad 3 \qquad , \; 0, 5, \quad 6$$

The same rule can apply to trees (28) and (30), giving (24a) and (24c), respectively.

The essential character of this transformational analysis can be summarized as follows. Deep structures for relative clauses are created by the same phrase structure and lexical rules that give deep structures for simple sentences. The two major differences between simple sentences and relative clauses are then accounted for by a single transformational rule.

We now have a viable transformational analysis of relative clauses, but this does not in itself provide an argument in favor of the transformational framework as compared with the extended phrase structure framework. It is necessary to ask now whether an equally revealing account can be developed which relies entirely on phrase structure and lexical rules. Among other things, we want to be sure that the set of rules we propose avoids the generation of ungrammatical simple sentences like (33a) and (33b), which lack a necessary NP.

(33) a.   *Took the money from the safe.

b.   *The man took the money from.

On the other hand, the rules should not generate relative clause sentences like (34a) and (34b), which contain one NP too many.

(34) a.   *The sheriff found the man that the man took the money from the safe.

b.   *The sheriff found the safe that the man took the money from the safe.

Let us now look at one particular phrase structure alternative.

In order to distinguish correctly between simple sentences and relative clause sentences without using transformational rules, we will have to introduce several new phrase structure symbols, beginning with a category S′ to designate relative clauses. This symbol S′ will be introduced into trees by the following phrase structure rule:

(35) a.   NP → NP   S′

The rules for expanding S′ will yield sequences consisting of the word *that* followed by what in effect are ordinary sentences with one NP removed:

(35) b.   S′ → *that*   VP   (subject NP missing)

c.   S′ → *that*   NP   VP′   (A VP′ will in effect be a VP with some NP missing from it.)

We now add special rules for VP′:

(35) d.   VP′ → V   (NP)   (Prep)   (NP missing after Prep)

e.   VP′ → V   (PrepP)   (NP missing from direct object position)

These phrase structure rules yield trees such as (36) and (37); the special symbols S′ and VP′ are circled.

(36)

(37)

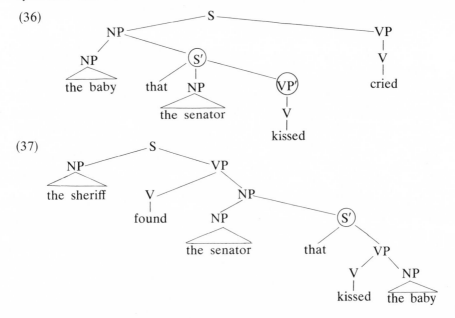

The addition of these extra phrase structure rules clearly represents an unrevealing complication in the grammar. A further undesirable complication is required, this one in the lexicon. In addition to the subcategory features that specify which kinds of VP's an individual verb may appear in, we must add features which do the same for VP′ environments. For instance, the lexical entry for *take* will now require three subcategory features, as follows:

(38) a. $\langle$____ NP   PrepP$\rangle$ (the man *took the money from the*
             VP   VP   *safe*)

 b. $\langle$____ NP   Prep$\rangle$ (the safe that the man *took the money*
             VP′   VP′   *from*)

 c. $\langle$____ PrepP$\rangle$ (the money that the man *took from*
             VP′   VP′   *the safe*)

Without distinct subcategory features for VP and VP′, our rules would generate ungrammatical sentences of both of the types shown below:

(39)   *John took the money from.

(40)   *We found the safe that John took the money from the safe.

Similar unrevealing complications will be required in the feature specifications for other verbs.

There are many other phrase structure descriptions of relative clauses that could be developed. But all of them would necessarily be complicated and unrevealing in much the same way that the present phrase structure grammar is. We thus have another argument for a descriptive framework that allows transformational rules.

One additional point is of interest. The examples of relative clauses that we have discussed up to now all involved the application of Relative Clause Formation to a lower, embedded S that had not undergone any previous transformational rules. Other examples exist, however, in which relativization acts on a lower S that has already undergone a transformational rule in its own right. An example is:

(41)   We arrested the man that John was shot by.

The derivation of this sentence proceeds from the deep structure shown below:

(42) a.

The first transformational rule to apply is Passive. It applies within the lower S, giving (42b) as a result.

(42) b.

Relative Clause Formation now applies to insert *that* and to delete the identical NP in the lower S. The result is the sentence that we set out to derive:

(41)   We arrested the man that John was shot by.

EXERCISES

1.   Give derivations for the following sentences, in each instance starting with the deep structure and then indicating the effects of the relevant transformational rules:

(i)   The clerk put the book that John had bought for Sally on the counter.

(ii)   The man that talked with you has not been found.

(iii)   The librarian found the book that John claimed that Bill had written a note in.

(Note: Only the first of the two occurrences of *that* in (iii) arises from Relative Clause Formation. The second is just the *that* which we find in sentences such as *Bill believes that Alice has flat feet*.)

2.   Study carefully the following extended phrase structure grammar that might be proposed in place of the phrase structure grammar that we examined in this section.

Phrase structure rules:
    S → (that) (NP) VP
    VP → V (NP) (PrepP)
    PrepP → Prep (NP)
    NP → NP   S
    NP → Det   N

Lexical rules:
    took ⟨V⟩, ⟨____ (NP) PrepP⟩
    kissed ⟨V⟩, ⟨____ (NP)⟩
    cried ⟨V⟩, ⟨____⟩
    found ⟨V⟩, ⟨____ (NP)⟩
    disappeared ⟨V⟩, ⟨____⟩
(Also entries for other items: nouns, prepositions, and determiners)

A. Draw the tree that this grammar assigns to the following sentence:

The sheriff found the safe that the man took the money from.

B. Do the same for this sentence:

The sheriff found the man that took the money from the safe.

C. Study the following argument:

Premise 1. This grammar generates all of the grammatical simple sentences and the grammatical relative clause sentences that we have considered in this section.

Premise 2. This grammar does not contain any unrevealing duplications like those in the phrase structure grammar in (35) and (38).

Conclusion. Contrary to what was claimed in the text, the relative clause construction provides no evidence at all in favor of the transformational framework.

Both of the premises in this argument are true as stated, yet the conclusion is false. What is the flaw in the argument?

3. Corresponding to the relative clause sentence in (i) below, there is a sentence that is identical except for the absence of *that*:

(i)   We met the man that John talked with.

(ii)   We met the man John talked with.

Suppose that we wish to account for (ii) by adding an optional transformational rule that has the effect of deleting the *that* which arises through the application of Relative Clause Formation. We are asked to choose one of the following two rules:

(iii) $X - [_{NP} NP - [_S that - Y]_S]_{NP} - Z$
         1   2   3   4   5
         $\Rightarrow$ 1, 2, 0, 4, 5   (Optional)

(iv) $X - [_{NP} NP - [_S that - NP - Y]_S]_{NP} - Z$
         1   2   3   4   5   6
         $\Rightarrow$ 1, 2, 0, 4, 5, 6   (Optional)

Which of these rules should be adopted? Support your answer by providing either grammatical sentences that can be generated only if your choice is adopted, or else ungrammatical sentences that can be avoided only if your choice is adopted.

4. Consider the following informal statement: If, at the end of a transformational derivation, a surface structure tree contains a structure of the form:

to which the relative clause rule has not been able to apply, then the resulting sentence must be marked as ungrammatical.

Although this statement cannot be included in our analysis of English without going beyond the framework adopted thus far, we must include some statement to this effect if we are to maintain the transformational analysis of relative clauses proposed in this section. Otherwise, our grammar will generate an enormous class of ungrammatical sentences. Give an example of an ungrammatical sentence that would be generated without this restriction but would be blocked if such a restriction is invoked.

4.3 A FURTHER LOOK AT QUESTIONS

An additional argument in support of the transformational framework is provided by *constituent questions,* questions that are introduced by a phrase that begins with some interrogative word:

(43)   *What* did you say to John?

(44)   *Whose dog* was the man bitten by?

(45)   *Which policeman* might the killer have recognized?

(46)   *Who* brought the beer?

The relative advantages of a transformational account for constituent questions are much the same as those for a transformational account for relative clauses. We will begin by developing a transformational description; we can then indicate briefly the difficulties of constructing an equally revealing description within the extended phrase structure framework.

As a prelude to a set of transformational rules, let us make a number of informal observations about these questions. The first thing to observe is that many of them show the same type of inverted word order of subject and helping verb that we saw in the *yes-no* questions considered earlier. Compare, for example, the first, second, and third questions above with the following yes-no questions:

(47)   Did you say something to John?

(48)   Was the man bitten by the dog?

(49)   Might the killer have recognized that policeman?

By contrast, if we fail to invert subject and helping verb in these constituent questions, the result is ungrammatical:

(50)   *What you said to John?

(51)   *Whose dog the man was bitten by?

(52)   *Which policeman the killer might have recognized?

The only constituent question in the original set of four that does not have a helping verb preceding the subject is the fourth, in which the subject itself is the questioned constituent.

A second informal observation is of the sort that we might find in traditional school grammars, namely, that the questioned constituent, even though it appears at the beginning of the question, is actually "understood" as fulfilling some function within the sentence. Specifically, *what* would be described as the understood direct object of the verb *say*, *whose dog* as the understood object of the preposition *by*, and *which policeman* as the understood direct object of the verb *recognized*.[7]

Support for this type of description is not difficult to find. If we simply remove the questioned constituents from questions (43–45), the results are ungrammatical:

(53)   *Did you say to John?

(54)   *Was the man bitten by?

(55)   *Might the killer have recognized?

If asked what was wrong with these sentences, most English-speakers would probably say something to the effect that *say* requires an object, *by* requires an object, and *recognized* requires an object. What is especially significant is that they would *not* make similar criticisms about the questions in (43–45), even though neither *say*, *by*, nor *recognized* is directly followed by an NP:

(43)   *What* did you say to John?

(44)   *Whose dog* was the man bitten by?

(45)   *Which policeman* might the killer have recognized?

Let us turn to a description of this construction within the transformational framework. The essential idea will be to derive constituent questions from deep structures that exhibit essentially declarative word order. In particular, questioned constituents that occur in initial position in surface structures of questions will be found in their "understood" position in deep structure.

As a first step, it will prove useful to make a change in the phrase structure rule that rewrites the symbol S, in such a way as to allow a special question symbol Q as an optional element in a deep structure:[8]

(56)   S → (*Q*) NP   Aux   VP

This rule has the following two subcases:

(57) a.   S → NP   Aux   VP
     b.   S → *Q*   NP   Aux   VP

According to which of these subrules is chosen, we can begin the construction of a phrase structure tree in one or the other of the following ways:

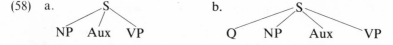

(58) a.   [tree: S branching to NP   Aux   VP]   b.   [tree: S branching to Q   NP   Aux   VP]

Deep structures that are constructed from the left-hand structure will eventually give rise to declaratives; those constructed from the right-hand structure will eventually give rise to questions. The symbol Q will in many instances be realized in an actual question as part of the question-initial interrogative word.

The transformational analysis to be developed here will assign the burden of generating constituent questions to two separate rules. The first of these is a revised version of the Subject-HV Inversion rule proposed in Chapter 3. Instead of stating this as an optional rule, as we did originally, we will state it as an obligatory rule applying to structures that begin with the question symbol Q:

(59)   Subject-HV Inversion   (revised version)

$$Q - NP - Tns \left(\left\{ \begin{matrix} M \\ have \\ be \end{matrix} \right\} \right) - X$$

$$1 \quad 2 \qquad 3 \qquad\qquad 4$$

$$\Rightarrow 1, \; 3 + 2, \; 0, \; 4 \quad \text{(Obligatory)}$$

We can illustrate the operation of this rule by applying it to tree (60a), giving (60b).

(60)   a.

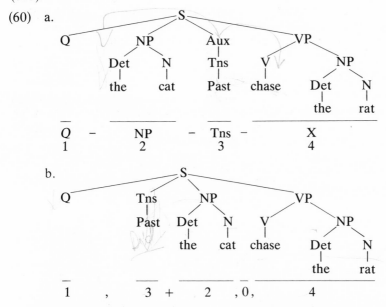

The second rule, the critical one in the derivation of constituent questions, is an optional rule that takes some NP beginning with a determiner from inside the sentence and adjoins it to the Q constituent at the left-hand side of the tree, as follows:

(61)   Question Movement

$$Q - X - [\; Det \quad Y \;]_{NP} - Z$$

$$1 \quad 2 \quad {}_{NP} \quad 3 \quad\quad 4$$

$$\Rightarrow 1 + 3, \; 2, \; 0, \; 4 \quad \text{(Optional)}$$

This rule may apply to tree (60b) in either one of two distinct ways, depending on whether *the cat* or *the rat* is chosen as the representative of the third term in the structural description.

The latter possibility is shown below:

(62)   a.

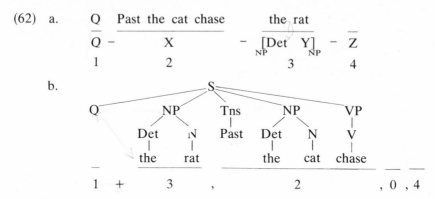

Tree (62b) does not satisfy the structural description of Affix Hopping; consequently, *Do* Support must apply. In addition to the morphophonemic rule that converts *do Past* to *did*, we need a rule which converts the sequence *Q the* to *which*. The resulting question is:

(63)   Which rat did the cat chase?

Suppose, on the other hand, that the subject NP *the cat* is chosen to represent the third term in the structural description of Question Movement. If the tree in (60b) is divided up in this fashion, the subject is moved to the left of the Tns element *Past*. This change is shown below:

(64) a.   Q   Past   the cat   chase the rat

$$Q - X - {}_{NP}[Det \ Y]_{NP} - Z$$
$$1 \quad 2 \quad\quad 3 \quad\quad\quad 4$$

b.

S

Q   NP   Tns   VP
   Det   N   Past   V   NP
   the   cat   chase   Det   N
              the   rat

$$\underline{1 \ + \ 3} \ , \ 2 \ , \ 0 \ , \ 4$$

If we now try to apply Affix Hopping, we find that its structural description is satisfied, because *Past* has become adjacent to the verb *chase*. After application of this rule, and the relevant morphophonemic rules, the following question is generated:

(65)   Which cat chased the rat?

Even though the rule of Subject-HV Inversion yields a tree that looks like an obvious candidate for later application of the rule of *Do* Support, this possibility is not realized in the situation just illustrated, in which the subject NP intervening between Tns and the nearest verbal element is moved out of the way by the rule of Question Movement.

One final possibility for the tree to which Subject-HV Inversion has applied should be discussed. In view of the statement of Question Movement as an optional rule, what will result if this rule does not apply to this tree? We are left with the following structure:

(66)

```
                        S
          _____|_____
         |        |         |          |
         Q       Tns       NP         VP
                  |       /   \      /    \
                Past    Det    N   V      NP
                         |     |   |     /   \
                        the   cat chase Det   N
                                         |    |
                                        the  rat
```

From this structure, we can derive a *yes-no* question by adding a rule to our grammar that simply deletes any occurrence of *Q* that has not had an NP adjoined to it by the optional rule of Question Movement:

(67)   *Q* Deletion

Q – Tns – X
1   2   3
⇒ 0, 2, 3   (Obligatory)

This rule applies to tree (66) to yield the tree below:

(68)

```
                    S
          _____|_____
         |       |         |        |
        Tns     NP        VP
         |     /   \      /    \
        Past  Det   N   V      NP
               |    |   |     /   \
              the  cat chase Det   N
                              |    |
                             the  rat
```

Since the structural description for Affix Hopping is not satisfied, *Do* Support will apply, to give:

(69)   do Past the cat chase the rat.

Application of the morphophonemic rule *do Past* → *did* yields the following question:

(70)   Did the cat chase the rat?

The transformational rules developed in this section allow us to generate a wide range of constituent questions. In particular, the Question Movement rule enables us to account in a simple way for the vast number of possible "understood positions" that a questioned constituent can have. Examples (71–77) give some idea of this wide range.

(71) a.   Henry called *the teacher* a liar.

   b.   *Which teacher* did Henry call _____ a liar?

(72) a.   Alice covered *the table* with the cloth.

   b.   *Which table* did Alice cover _____ with the cloth?

(73) a.   The tourist took a picture of *the cathedral*.

   b.   *Which cathedral* did the tourist take a picture of _____?

(74) a.   Henry sent Alice to *the doctor*.

   b.   *Which doctor* did Henry send Alice to _____?

(75) a.   John told the porter to deliver the trunk to *the hotel*.

   b.   *Which hotel* did John tell the porter to deliver the trunk to_____?

(76) a.   We painted *the car* purple.

   b.   *Which car* did we paint _____ purple?

(77) a.   The boy had *the shirt* on backwards.

   b.   *Which shirt* did the boy have _____ on backwards?

Once we have the rules necessary to generate the declaratives, the related questions are all accounted for uniformly with just the two transformational rules, Subject-HV Inversion and Question Movement.

Within the extended phrase structure framework, we would clearly not fare so well. The difficulties become apparent as soon as we ask how the declaratives and related questions in (71–77) would have to be accounted for. The phrase structure rules needed for the various kinds of VP's found in the declarative sentences would be of no use in generating the corresponding questions. For the questions we would need the same sort of VP′ rules that we found necessary when we tried to describe relative clauses without going outside the extended phrase structure framework. Thus, the constituent question is one more construction for which a transformational description can be developed that is much more revealing than any phrase structure description.

EXERCISES

1.   Give deep structures for each of the following questions, in accordance with the revised analysis of questions presented in this section:

(i)   Has the tenor been practicing the aria?

(ii)   Which aria has the tenor been practicing?

(iii) Has the tenor been practicing?

(iv)   Which dog was John bitten by?

(v)   Which plate did the waiter throw at the manager?

(vi)   Which cup was taken from the shelf?

(vii) Was the cup taken from the shelf?

Note: In order to get a derivation for (iv), (vi), and (vii), it is necessary to assume a slightly revised version of the Passive rule, so as to allow application in a structure in which something precedes the subject NP. One possibility is the following:

$$X - NP - Aux - V - NP - Y$$
$$1 \quad 2 \quad \; 3 \quad \; 4 \quad 5 \quad 6$$
$$\Rightarrow 1, 5, 3, \, be + en + 4, 0, 6 + by + 2 \quad \text{(Optional)}$$

2. In many studies of English questions, some remark such as the following may be found: "The inversion of subject and helping verb does not occur in all questions, but only in *nonsubordinate* questions." Find examples of English subordinate clauses that show why such a restriction on Subject-HV Inversion is necessary in a description of English.

Suggestions for Further Reading

The Passive rule as formulated in this chapter goes back to Chomsky 1957, Chapter 5. A somewhat different analysis is outlined in Chomsky 1965, pp. 103–106. Two treatments that differ even more markedly from the original transformational analysis can be found in Fillmore 1968 and in Hasegawa 1968. A study of the latter could profitably be postponed until after Chapter 6 in the present book.

The first detailed transformational treatment of relative clauses is Smith 1964. Kuroda 1968 is concerned with determining what the deep structure determiners should be for various types of relative clauses. Perlmutter 1972 argues for an analysis of relative clauses in which the relativized NP is a pronoun at an intermediate stage of the transformational derivation. Bach 1965 and Schachter 1974 offer interesting examples of relative clause constructions in other languages.

Constituent questions have been a subject of discussion in a long sequence of works: Chomsky 1957, Chapter 7; Klima 1964; Katz and Postal 1964, pp. 79–117; Baker 1970; Bach 1971; Langacker 1974.

Notes

1. This transformational analysis of passive sentences follows that found in Chomsky 1957, Chapter 5.

2. The derived structure tree (4b) is very close to that which is dictated by the general conventions for derived structure which were proposed tentatively in Chapter 3. The one question for which no answer is provided by the conventions as stated is where precisely to attach the *by NP* on the right-hand side of the fifth factor, since in this instance the fifth term of the structural description is a variable. Thus, the alternative adopted here, attaching it under the domination of the VP, does not follow from the conventions of Chapter 3.

The clearest and most serious problem with the constituent structure in (4b) is that the sequence consisting of *by* and the following NP does not make up a single constituent. There is some evidence that *by* NP actually is a constituent, apparently just a prepositional phrase. The problem is how to ensure that this result is achieved when the transformational rule for forming passive sentences is applied. Several treatments (among them Chomsky 1965, pp. 103–106, and Fillmore 1968) solve the problem ahead of time by assuming that some kind of *by*-phrase is present in the deep structure of passive sentences.

3. We are allowing the nontransformational account of passives to make use of Affix Hopping. We take this liberty in order to make it clear that the basic superiority of a transformational treatment of passives is not merely a special case of the previously noted superiority of a transformational account of verbal inflection.

4. Here again, we are being generous with the phrase structure treatment. In order to be completely sure of preventing bad lexical insertions, we would have to find some clear way of indicating that the subcategorization feature $\langle$____ NP$\rangle$ applied only to active structures. Nothing in the lexical entry as stated in (11) serves to indicate this restriction.

5. An alternative phrase structure rule will be presented and discussed in Chapter 14.

6. We will leave out the Aux's in the trees in this section, since they are of no importance for an understanding of English relative clauses.

7. The reason for this attention to the "understood" position of a questioned element is that an accurate determination in this matter is essential to making the prescriptively correct choice between *who* and *whom*.

8. The account that we shall present here is essentially that suggested in Klima 1964.

5

Order of Application
of Transformational Rules

In the previous two chapters we introduced a number of transformational rules for English and showed how they permit the generation of a variety of English constructions. We interpreted these rules as applying in sequence, starting with a deep structure and ending with a surface structure. The major business of this chapter will be to present two hypotheses about the permissible sequences of rule application. We can best introduce this topic by examining two sequences of rule application that give rise to ungrammatical sentences and that should thus be excluded somehow.

5.1 REFLEXIVIZATION AND *YOU* DELETION

For a first example of a pair of rules that have to be prevented from applying in a certain way, let us consider two rules that we have not yet discussed, which we shall refer to as Reflexivization and *You* Deletion.[1] The first of these is a rule proposed in early transformational work as a means of accounting for the reflexive construction in English:

(1) a.   He talks to himself.
    b.   I shaved myself.
    c.   They looked after themselves.

It is assumed that these sentences with reflexive pronouns are to be derived from deep structures that contain only nonreflexive forms:

(2) a.   He Pres talk to he.

   b.   I Past shave I.

   c.   They Past look after they.

There is then a transformational rule that changes the NP after the verb to reflexive when that form is identical with the subject NP. The following version of this rule is adequate for our present purposes:[2]

(3)   Reflexivization

$$NP - Aux - V - (Prep) - NP$$
$$1 \quad\ \ 2 \quad\ 3 \quad\ \ 4 \quad\ \ \ 5$$

Condition: $1 = 5$

$\Rightarrow 1, 2, 3, 4, 5 + $ *Refl*   (Obligatory)

Later morphophonemic rules will convert *he Refl* to *himself, I Refl* to *myself, they Refl* to *themselves,* and so on.[3] We specify the rule as obligatory in order to avoid the generation of ungrammatical sentences such as these:

(4) a.   *I shaved me.

   b.   *We cared for us.

The condition of identity is necessary to prevent the generation of such ill-formed reflexive sentences as (6a–c) from the deep structures in (5a–c).

(5) a.   He Pres talk to I.

   b.   I Past shave you.

   c.   They Past look after we.

(6) a.   *He talks to myself.

   b.   *I shaved yourself.

   c.   *They looked after ourselves.

The deep structures in (5) should yield the following as surface structures:

(7) a.   He talks to me.

   b.   I shaved you.

   c.   They looked after us.

We can account for the latter sentences by adding to the grammar a rule that assigns an objective case marker to pronouns that follow verbs or prepositions:

(8)   Case Assignment

$$X - \begin{Bmatrix} V \\ Prep \end{Bmatrix} - Pro - Y$$
$$1 \qquad 2 \qquad\quad\ 3 \quad\ \ 4$$

$\Rightarrow 1, 2, 3 + $ *Obj,* 4   (Obligatory)

Morphophonemic rules will convert *I Obj* to *me, you Obj* to *you,* and *we Obj* to *us.*

Let us turn now to the second rule mentioned at the beginning of this section, a rule that we shall refer to as *You* Deletion. This is an optional rule that accounts for the alternation between the (a) and (b) sentences in the following pairs:

(9) a.   You take care of Sally.

    b.   Take care of Sally.

(10) a.   You get that dog out of here.

    b.   Get that dog out of here.

Both sentences in each pair are understood as imperatives; the (b) sentences are described in many traditional school grammars as containing an "understood" subject *you*. We might derive the (b) sentences, then, by assuming that they start out with the same deep structures as the (a) sentences but undergo an optional transformational rule of *You* Deletion:[4]

(11)   *You* Deletion

$$you - Pres - V - X$$
$$\;1 \qquad 2 \qquad 3 \quad 4$$
$$\Rightarrow 0, 2, 3, 4 \quad \text{(Optional)}$$

Let us look at a structure that satisfies the structural description of both of these rules:

(12) a.   you Pres shave you.

If Reflexivization happens to apply first, the resulting structure is:

(12) b.   you Pres shave you Refl.

This structure still satisfies the structural description for *You* Deletion; if the rule is applied, we get:

(12) c.   Pres shave you Refl.

From this structure the morphophonemic rules give:

(12) d.   Shave yourself.

Suppose, on the other hand, that *You* Deletion was allowed to apply to this deep structure ahead of Reflexivization; the result would be:

(13) a.   Pres shave you.

This structure does not satisfy the structural description for Reflexivization; consequently, we would eventually generate the following ungrammatical imperative sentence:[5]

(13) b.   *Shave you.

If the generation of (13b) is to be avoided, we must have some way of ensuring that in structures that satisfy the structural descriptions of both of these rules, *You* Deletion not be allowed to apply before Reflexivization has applied.

There actually is a way of getting around the problem posed above without saying anything about permissible and impermissible sequences of rule applications. This is to add a second rule forming reflexives, a rule designed especially for imperatives in which the subject has already been deleted by *You* Deletion:

(14)   *Pres* – V – (Prep) – *you*
          1   2   3   4

        ⇒ 1, 2, 3, 4 + *Refl*   (Obligatory)

We can illustrate the purpose that this rule would serve by considering again what would happen if *You* Deletion applied before any other rule to the deep structure, as follows:

(15) a.   you Pres shave you. (= 12a)

The result of *You* Deletion would be:

(15) b.   Pres shave you.

This sequence does not satisfy the structural description of our original Reflexivization rule, which was given in (3). But now the second Reflexivization rule comes to the rescue, so to speak, and applies to yield:

(15) c.   Pres shave you Refl.

Application of morphophonemic rules finally yields a grammatical sentence:

(15) d.   Shave yourself.

Although the addition of this second Reflexive rule does enable us to avoid the embarrassment of generating *Shave you, it does absolutely nothing else, and is thus an unwarranted complication in the grammar. We can avoid the use of this extra rule if we can find some way of preventing *You* Deletion from applying until after Reflexivization has had a chance to apply.

5.2 PASSIVE AND NUMBER AGREEMENT

Two more rules that have to be prevented from applying in an incorrect sequence are the Passive rule and a rule that we have not yet discussed, one that helps account for the variation in the form of the first verbal element according to the number of the subject noun phrase:

(16) a.   The dogs eat meat.
     b.   *The dogs eats meat.
     c.   The dog eats meat.
     d.   *The dog eat meat.

(17) a.   The apples are sweet.
     b.   *The apples is sweet.
     c.   The apple is sweet.
     d.   *The apple are sweet.

Although there are many interesting problems yet to be solved in developing a transformational treatment of number agreement, we can make a sufficient first approximation by supposing that the phrase structure rule that forms noun phrases introduces a constituent Nu (for "number") next to the head noun of the noun phrase:

(18)   NP → (Det) (Adj) N   Nu

In addition, another phrase structure rule must be added to expand this new symbol:

(19)   Nu → $\begin{Bmatrix} Sg \\ Plur \end{Bmatrix}$

Given these rules, sentence (20a) would be assigned the deep structure in the tree below:

(20) a.   The boy likes the potatoes.

b.

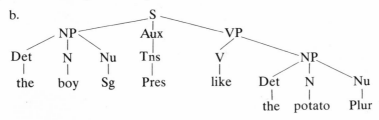

We now set up a transformational rule to copy the number of the head noun of the subject after *Pres* or *Past* below the Tns:[6]

(21)   Number Agreement

$$_{NP}[\; Det \quad N \; - \; Nu \; - \; X \;]_{NP} \quad - \begin{Bmatrix} Pres \\ Past \end{Bmatrix} - \; Y$$
$$\qquad\quad 1 \qquad\quad 2 \quad\;\; 3 \qquad\qquad 4 \qquad\quad 5$$

⇒ 1, 2, 3, 4 + 2, 5.   (Obligatory)

? where

Applied to the tree in (20b), this rule gives the tree below:

(20) c.

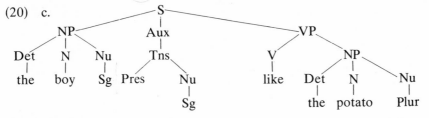

After Affix Hopping applies, the bottom line of the resulting tree is the following:

(20) d.   the boy Sg like Pres Sg the potato Plur.

After *boy Sg* is spelled out as *boy*, *like Pres Sg* as *likes*, and *potato Plur* as *potatoes*, the result is the following sentence:

(20) e.   The boy likes the potatoes.

Let us now examine the interaction of this rule with the Passive. We can start again with the deep structure tree given for the previous example and try out the two possible sequences of Passive and Number Agreement.

Suppose that we apply Passive first. The resulting structure is the following tree:

(21) a.

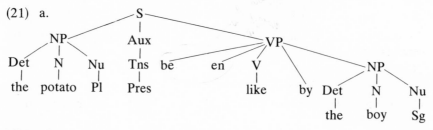

If Number Agreement applies at this point, it will be the number of the new subject noun phrase that is copied to the left of *Pres*, rather than the number of the deep structure subject. The bottom line of the resulting tree is just the following:

(22) b.   The potato Plur Pres Plur be en like by the boy Sg.

Affix Hopping gives:

(22) c.   the potato Plur be Pres Plur like en by the boy Sg.

Finally, morphophonemic rules give the grammatical sentence:

(22) d.   The potatoes are liked by the boy.

Suppose now that these two rules are allowed to apply in the opposite order. Number Agreement, applying to the deep structure tree, yields the following:

(23) a.   the boy Sg Pres Sg like the potato Plur.

Application of the Passive gives:

(23) b.   the potato Plur Pres Sg be en like by the boy Sg.

The morphophonemic rules now yield the following ungrammatical sentence:

(23) c.   *The potatoes is liked by the boy.

If we are to avoid the generation of this last sentence, we must somehow take measures to ensure that no derivations are permitted in which Number Agreement applies before Passive instead of after it.

5.3 THE STRICT ORDER HYPOTHESIS

In order to solve the problem of avoiding impermissible sequences in the application of transformational rules, a hypothesis was set forth in early transformational studies that can be put as follows:

(24)   The grammar of a language must contain not only statements of transformational rules, but also an indication of a *linear ordering* of these rules. That is, for any two rules A and B, the grammar must indicate either that rule A precedes rule B, or else that rule B precedes rule A.

The standard interpretation of such an ordering of rules can be pictured graphically if we imagine a straight conveyor belt with a number of stations alongside it. Each station contains a transformational rule which was assigned to that station by the ordering given as part of the grammar. Deep structures are fed onto the belt at one end, and surface structures are given off at the other end of the belt. The structures being developed go from one station to the next; since the belt only goes forward, it is impossible to take a structure back to a preceding station after the structure has already been moved on to a station nearer the end of the belt.

When a tree arrives at a certain station on the belt, the first question to be asked is whether the structural description of the rule at that station is satisfied by the tree. If the answer is no, the tree is moved on to the next station. If the answer is yes, then another question must be asked. Is the rule optional or obligatory? If it is optional, then two possibilities are allowed. Either the structural change of the rule may be carried out and the rule sent on to the next station, or the tree may be sent on to the next station without undergoing.any change. If the rule is listed as obligatory, on the other hand, the structural change must be carried out before the tree is allowed to go on to the next station.

Suppose that, in keeping with this hypothesis, the transformational rules of English are lined up in a certain order. We can avoid both of the difficulties mentioned in the preceding sections by assigning the relevant rules the proper relative order. In the first instance, we specify that Reflexivization be ordered prior to *You* Deletion, a situation that is represented graphically as follows:

(25)   ... Reflexivization ... *You* Deletion ...
                ("Direction" of Derivation) →

The set of ellipses in the diagram are intended to indicate that other rules may be present, ordered before Reflexivization, between the two rules, or after *You* Deletion. Any such ordering of the total set of rules will avoid the generation of an ungrammatical sentence such as *Shave you*, just so long as Reflexivization is somewhere before *You* Deletion in the order. What any such order ensures is that Reflexivization will always have the first chance in any situation in which the structure in question meets the structural description for both rules.

In the second instance, we can assign Number Agreement a position in the ordering that is later than the position assigned to the Passive:

(26)   ... Passive ... Number Agreement ...
                ("Direction" of Derivation) →

Once we have done this, we can be assured that the grammar will not generate a sentence such as *The potatoes is liked by the boy*. The reason is that if Passive is to apply in a certain derivation, it must apply before Number Agreement is reached. If we take the option of skipping Passive, and go on and apply Number Agreement, we cannot go backwards and have another chance at Passive.

Let us look at the Strict Order Hypothesis from a slightly different point of view and examine the role that it would play in helping to solve the projection problem, i.e., the problem of making predictions of grammaticality on the basis of fixed sets of basic data. Suppose, first, that we have a set of basic data consisting of three groups of sentences: first, sentences providing justification for an obligatory transformational rule of Reflexivization; second, sentences providing justification for an optional transformational rule of *You* Deletion; and third, the following two grammatical sentences, both of which can be accounted for by applying Reflexivization and then *You* Deletion:

(27) a.   Help yourself.
     b.   Shave yourself.

Given the Strict Order Hypothesis, we can now predict that both of the following new sentences are ungrammatical:

(28) a.   *Help you.
     b.   *Shave you.

The reasoning is as follows. First, the grammatical imperatives can be generated by applying Reflexivization and then *You* Deletion, but they cannot be generated by applying *You* Deletion and then Reflexivization. Second, the Reflexive rule can apply first only if it is ordered before *You* Deletion. Third, once this ordering is adopted, there is no way that the grammar in its final form can generate the ungrammatical imperatives without departing from the rule ordering set forth on the basis of the second statement above.

Similar predictions can be made concerning ungrammatical passives. Suppose that we were presented with a set of basic data that included sentences that provided justification for an optional Passive rule and an obligatory Number Agreement rule as well as a sentence that could be generated only by allowing Passive to apply before Number Agreement. The Strict Order Hypothesis would then lead us to predict that any sentence that could be generated only by applying Number Agreement before Passive would be ungrammatical. For example, suppose that sentence (29a) was present in the basic data:

(29) a.   The potatoes are liked by the boy.

We could then conclude (correctly) that the new sentence (29b), which was not present in the basic data, was ungrammatical:

(29) b.   *The potatoes is liked by the boy.

The grammar could generate this sentence only if the rules applied in violation of the order dictated by sentence (29a) in conjunction with the Strict Order Hypothesis.

At first glance, it might appear that we could construct an argument of this sort on the basis of virtually any pair of transformational rules. As an example of where we cannot, let us consider the interaction of two rules already discussed, Passive and Subject-HV Inversion. Suppose that we have sufficient basic data to furnish justification for each of the two rules. Suppose, further, that our basic data include the question:

(30)   Could the books have been read by the librarian?

This sentence can be generated if the Passive is applied, followed by Subject-HV Inversion. It cannot be generated by applying the same rules in the opposite order, for the simple reason that Subject-HV Inversion, by moving part or all of the Aux constituent to the beginning of the tree, creates a structure that does not satisfy the structural description of the Passive rule. In conformity with the Strict Order Hypothesis, then, we specify as part of our grammar that Passive is to be placed earlier in the order of transformational rules than Subject-HV Inversion. So far, we seem to be developing the same sort of argument that we developed earlier. But in the present instance no ungrammatical sentence is blocked by this ordering, since the statement of the rules is sufficient to rule out any derivation in which Subject-HV Inversion and Passive apply in that sequence. Consequently, the Strict Order Hypothesis does nothing here; it does not play a role in making predictions about sentences outside the original set of basic data.

If facts like those considered earlier provide some support for the Strict Order Hypothesis, what kinds of facts (if they could be found) would serve to call this hypothesis into question? The answer is quite simple: the hypothesis would be suspect if we were to find a pair of rules in some language that could apply in either order and give grammatical results in both cases. Very few such pairs of rules have been alleged, and there has sometimes been disagreement as to whether only two rules were involved in the generation of the critical sets of sentences.[7] There is, however, one general class of counterexamples to this hypothesis. This class of counterexamples will be discussed in Chapter 7, and an appropriate qualification on the Strict Order Hypothesis will be suggested.

5.4 THE PARTIAL ORDER HYPOTHESIS

We turn now to a second hypothesis that has sometimes been proposed as an alternative to the Strict Order Hypothesis. This second hypothesis will be referred to as the Partial Order Hypothesis:

(31)   In addition to containing statements of transformational rules, the grammar of a language may also contain one or more statements of the form "Rule A must precede Rule B." Such statements are to be included only when they are required.

In going from the Strict Order Hypothesis to the Partial Order Hypothesis, what we are doing in essence is to *permit* ordering statements in the grammar rather than *requiring* them. This hypothesis still allows us to give an adequate account of the following sentences:

(32) a.   Shave yourself.
     b.   *Shave you.

(33) a.   The potatoes are liked by the boy.
     b.   *The potatoes is liked by the boy.

All we must do is include in our grammar of English the following two statements:

(34) a.   Reflexivization is ordered before *You* deletion.
     b.   Passive is ordered before Number Agreement.

The Partial Order Hypothesis is in one important respect less restrictive than the Strict Order Hypothesis. With the former, it would not be a problem to find an instance in which a transformational rule A preceded another rule B in the generation of one grammatical sentence S_1, but followed the application of the same rule in the generation of another grammatical sentence S_2. This hypothetical situation can be depicted graphically as follows:

(35)   Deep structure$_1$ →   →   → S_1
                           ··· Rule A ··· Rule B ···

        Deep structure$_2$ →   →   → S_2
                           ··· Rule B ··· Rule A ···

These sequences of rule applications could be allowed simply by giving no specification in the grammar about the ordering of A and B. This is precisely the type of situation that is ruled out by the Strict Order Hypothesis. Thus, the Partial Order Hypothesis allows for a wider variety of situations than does the Strict Order Hypothesis. This greater flexibility, however, is not without its price. Specifically, the Partial Order Hypothesis is weaker in the predictions that it affords. For example, if we are once again provided with basic data providing justification for Reflexivization and *You* Deletion, we can no longer conclude from the grammaticality of (36a) that (36b) is ungrammatical:

(36) a.   Shave yourself.
     b.   *Shave you.

We must be provided with some such ungrammatical sentence before we can conclude that there has to be an ordering between Reflexivization and *You* Deletion.

To say that the Partial Order Hypothesis is weaker than the Strict Order Hypothesis is not necessarily to say that the latter is preferable. If we were actually to find convincing cases in which the Strict Order Hypothesis could not be maintained, that is, cases in which a certain pair of rules applied in two different orders, we would be fully justified in retreating to the weaker position. In doing so, we would simply be admitting that rule ordering was not quite as predictable as it was implied to be by the Strict Order Hypothesis.

Until such cases are brought to light, however, the stronger position is preferable.

As a final word, we should note that the hypotheses on rule application that we have examined in this chapter are only two out of a very large number of alternatives that deserve consideration. To take just one more example, we might consider the inclusion in our universal grammar of a convention to the effect that agreement rules invariably apply after any and all rules that create new subjects. From such a convention, it would follow immediately that the Passive rule of English could only apply before Number Agreement. This hypothesis is even stronger than the Strict Order Hypothesis with regard to the two types of rules to which it makes reference. Even without finding either (37a) or (37b) or any sentences like them in our basic data, we could determine in advance that (37a) would be grammatical and that (37b) would not be:

(37) a.   The potatoes are liked by the boy.   (= 29a)
      b.   *The potatoes is liked by the boy.   (= 29b)

Thus, if this hypothesis could be maintained, it would erode one particular kind of argument for the Strict Order Hypothesis, that based on interactions between subject-creating rules and agreement rules.

EXERCISES

1.   In the first section of this chapter, we proposed that objective case pronouns such as *him*, *her*, *me*, *us*, and *them* be derived transformationally from the corresponding nominative pronouns *he*, *she*, *I*, *we*, and *they*, by means of the following transformational rule:

$$X - \begin{Bmatrix} V \\ Prep \end{Bmatrix} - Pro - Y$$
$$1 \qquad 2 \qquad\quad 3 \qquad 4$$
$$\Rightarrow 1, 2, 3 + Obj, 4 \quad \text{(Obligatory)}$$

[handwritten marginal notes: need rule from the potato... to get they from the... the boy to get he... and to g... Passive 1st Case 2nd]

Using this rule and Passive, construct an argument in favor of the Strict Order Hypothesis. Model your argument on the one in the text that was based on the interaction of Passive and Number Agreement.

2.   Study the following two transformational rules:

(i) $X - V - NP - for - NP$
$\qquad 1 \quad 2 \quad 3 \quad\ 4 \quad\ 5$
$\qquad \Rightarrow 1, 2, + 5, 3, 0, 0. \quad \text{(Optional)}$

(ii) $X - V - NP - to - NP$
$\qquad 1 \quad 2 \quad 3 \quad 4 \quad 5$
$\qquad \Rightarrow 1, 2 + 5, 3, 0, 0 \quad \text{(Optional)}$

The following sentences illustrate the interactions of these rules with the Passive rule:

George caught a rabbit for Alice.

A rabbit was caught for Alice by George.

*Alice was caught a rabbit by George.

George caught Alice a rabbit.

John sent the package to Paula.

The package was sent to Paula by John.

Paula was sent the package by John.

John sent Paula the package.

Suppose that we assume the Strict Order Hypothesis. What relative order must be assigned to Passive, rule (i), and rule (ii)? Explain your answer. Suppose, on the other hand, that we do not assume the Strict Order Hypothesis, but assume instead that transformational rules can apply in random order. Which, if any, of the sentences above pose a problem for this hypothesis, assuming that the three transformational rules involved are correct as stated? Explain your answer.

3. In section 5.3, we proposed that the transformational component of a generative grammar should be an *ordered* set of transformational rules. We then suggested how this order should be interpreted in generating sentences. We showed that with this interpretation, certain ungrammatical English sentences could be avoided if we ordered the transformational rules of English in a certain way. Suppose now that someone agrees that the transformational rules in a grammar should be strictly ordered, but suggests that the "conveyor-belt" convention that was given in the text should be replaced by the following alternative convention for the interpretation of this ordering:

> Let the transformational rules apply randomly, but then discard any derivations in which some pair of rules has applied in the relative order opposite to the order which they have in the grammar. In other words, calling the two rules A and B, if their order in the grammar is ...A...B..., then discard any derivation in which B has applied and then at some later point A has applied.

Show that on the basis of the examples discussed thus far in the text, this alternative convention is inferior to the conveyor-belt convention. Do this by finding specific examples of ungrammatical sentences that were excluded by interpreting our rule orderings for English in conformity with the conveyor-belt convention, but that would not be excluded if the same rule orderings were interpreted as dictated by this alternative convention.

Suggestions for Further Reading

There are very few early transformational works directed specifically at the problem of rule ordering. Chomsky 1957, Chapter 5, notes in passing the necessity of specifying a relative order for Passive and Number Agreement. Lees and Klima 1963 make a similar observation with regard to Reflexivization and *You* Deletion.

A great part of the recent syntactic literature on rule ordering has been directed at supporting the contention that language-specific ordering statements are unnecessary, contrary to what is implied by both the Strict Order Hypothesis and the Partial Order Hypothesis. The thesis is that permissible sequences of rule applications are to be taken care of by general conventions of universal grammar. This thesis is defended by Koutsoudas 1971, 1972; Ringen 1972; and Twila Lehmann 1972.

Notes

1. The ordering argument based on these two rules was first set forth in Lees and Klima 1963.

2. In section 6.3, we will see that this rule needs to be made a good deal more general.

3. There are some problems in specifying in detail how the result of the structural change is to acquire its correct final form. For example, *John Refl* must turn out as *himself*, *the woman from Spain Refl* must become *herself*, and *my neighbor Refl* can become either *himself* or *herself*.

4. There is some evidence that all imperatives in English are tenseless, both those that contain *you* and those that do not. The clearest indication is given by the behavior of *be*, which is the only English verb whose imperative form differs from the second-person present-tense form:

> You are quiet.
>
> You be quiet.
>
> *Are quiet.
>
> Be quiet

5. There are a small number of English sentences that superficially resemble imperatives in which the nonreflexive form appears, for example, *Bless you*, *Curse you*, and *Screw you*. However, these special sentences are not understood as commands, and *you* is not understood as the subject. Thus, a different analysis would be required for them.

6. This formulation of the rule does not always have the correct effect. The central difficulty is that the structural description sometimes fails to pick out the head noun of the subject NP, picking out some other noun instead. For instance, in an NP such as *the men's old car*, it is the noun *car* rather than the noun *man* that determines the number marking of the following verb:

> The men's old *car works* well.
>
> *The *men's* old car *work* well.

Yet there is nothing in the statement in (21) that would prevent the plural number of *men* from incorrectly giving the second sentence above. An improved view on agreement rules of this sort will be presented in section 14.2.

7. Analyses in which the Strict Order Hypothesis is violated may be found in Koutsoudas 1971 and Ross 1970.

6

Embedded Sentences

In the preceding chapter we discussed the problem of specifying permissible orders for applying transformational rules. In all of the cases examined there, the rules in question were studied as they interacted in the generation of simple sentences. The major hypothesis presented was the Strict Order Hypothesis. Our discussion in this chapter and the next will focus on the problem of specifying permissible sequences of rule applications in complex sentences. First, it will be useful to develop a treatment of complex structures in English.

6.1 BASIC RULES FOR EMBEDDED CONSTRUCTIONS

In Chapter 2 we discussed very briefly the type of construction illustrated below:

(1)   John believes *that Alice has flat feet*.

Our major concern was to show that phrase structure rules permitted the generation of an infinite sequence of English sentences, each one longer than the one before it. It was sufficient for our purposes at that point to account for these clauses by means of the following phrase structure rule:

(2)   VP → V *that* S

This rule results in the assignment of tree structure (3) to sentence (1).

138

(3)

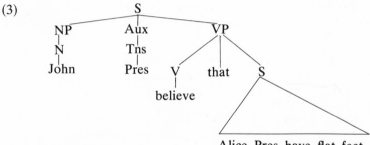

Our first order of business in this section will be to consider some facts about English that appear to justify a more complex phrase structure for this construction. We will refer to sequences of the sort italicized in (1) as *sentential complements,* or simply *complements.* In addition, we will refer to *that* as a *complementizer.*

The first motivation for a change in our treatment becomes apparent when we observe that exactly the same construction can appear in subject position in a sentence:

(4)   *That Alice has flat feet* surprises Bill.

If we were to account for the sentential complement in this sentence in the same manner as the one found in sentence (1), we would have to add to our grammar a new phrase structure rule for expanding the symbol S:

(5)   S → *that* S Aux VP

This rule assigns tree structure (6) to sentence (4):

(6)

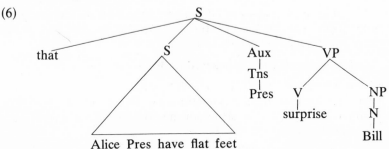

We thus find ourselves in the position of having two distinct phrase structure rules, (2) and (5), that have to mention the sequence *that S.* This is just the sort of situation that led us in earlier chapters to search for a more revealing description.

A simple remedy suggests itself immediately when we observe that for each of the two rules in which *that S* appears, our grammar already contains a parallel rule mentioning NP:

(7) a.   VP → V *that* S (= 2)
    b.   VP → V NP

(8) a.   S → *that* S Aux VP (= 5)
    b.   S → NP Aux VP

All that is required is that we classify the sequence *that* S as an NP. To express this classification, let us tentatively adopt the new phrase structure rule (9).

(9)   NP → *that*   S

The unrevealing rules in (7a) and (8a) can now be eliminated. The tree structures that our revised grammar assigns are illustrated below:

(10)

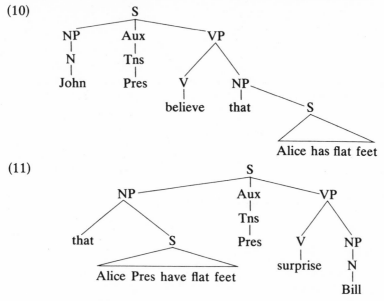

(11)

A second argument in favor of NP status for the sentential complement in our original example (1), *John believes that Alice has flat feet*, rests on the existence of a corresponding passive sentence:

(12)   *That Alice has flat feet* is believed by John.

Suppose that we adopted tree (3) as the deep structure of (1); in this tree the sequence *that Alice has flat feet* is not dominated by an NP. It would then be necessary to complicate the structural description of the Passive rule in the following way:

(13)   NP – Aux – V – $\begin{Bmatrix} \text{NP} \\ \textit{that} \text{ S} \end{Bmatrix}$ – X

On the other hand, if we adopt the structure in (10), in which the complement appears under the domination of NP, then our original Passive rule, with the fourth term simply identified as an NP, will suffice to derive the passive sentence in (12) above. The manner in which the rule applies is indicated below:

(14) a.   John   Pres   believe   that Alice Pres have flat feet

NP	– Aux –	V –		NP	– X
1	2	3		4	5

b.   that Alice Pres have flat feet   Pres   be   en   believe

<u>   4   </u>   ,   <u>2</u>   , be + en +   <u>3</u>   ,

by   John

<u>0</u>   ,   <u>5</u>   + by +   <u>1</u>

Affix Hopping and the relevant morphophonemic rules yield sentence (12).

To summarize our discussion to this point, we have observed that the introduction of sentential complements as NP's makes it possible to describe subject and object complements without unnecessary duplication in the phrase structure rules, and also makes it possible to describe passive sentences containing sentential subjects without complicating the structural description of the Passive rule.

When we examine further data from English, we find evidence in favor of grouping *that S* together into a constituent in its own right under the NP. The following sentences illustrate another environment in which sentential complements appear:

(15)   The claim *that Jack defrauded the public* was made in open court.

(16)   The fact *that all cows eat grass* is irrelevant.

(17)   We reported the allegation *that the candy had been poisoned* to Chief Moles.

Despite their superficial similarities to the relative clauses discussed in Chapter 4, the italicized sequences in (15–17) are not relative clauses, as is shown by the fact that none has an underlying NP missing from it. These sequences are exactly like those that we found in object and subject position in the examples discussed earlier in this section. Unlike the earlier complements, though, these complements could not be plausibly analyzed as complete NP's.

The additional evidence bearing on the analysis of these structures is provided by the fact that we may optionally move these sentential complements to the end of the sentence:

(18)   The claim was made in open court that Jack defrauded the public.

(19)   The fact is irrelevant that all cows eat grass.

(20)   We reported the allegation to Chief Moles that the candy had been poisoned.

A straightforward view concerning these sentences is that they differ from (15–17) only by virtue of having undergone an optional transformational rule that moves the complement out of the NP in which it originates and to the end of the sentence. If we are to state this rule as simply as possible, it will be helpful to have *that S* dominated by some constituent other than NP. If we label such a constituent S̄, then the trees associated with the untransformed sentences (15) and (16) will be (21) and (22), respectively.[1]

(21)

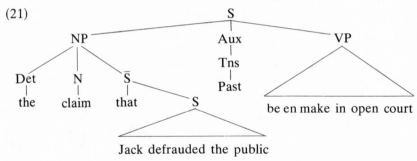

(22)

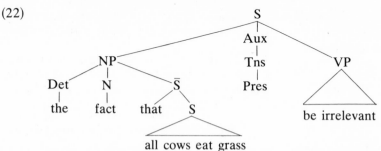

With these structures, the optional rule for forming (18) and (19) can be stated quite simply as follows:

(23)   Extraposition from N

$$X - N - \bar{S} - Y$$
$$1 \quad 2 \quad 3 \quad 4$$
$$\Rightarrow 1, 2, 0, 4 + 3 \quad \text{(Optional)}$$

The application of this rule to (21) is shown below:

(24)

the	claim	that Jack defrauded the public		Past be en make in open court
X –	N –	$\bar{S}$	–	Y
1	2	3		4
⇒ the	claim	Past be en make in open court		that Jack defrauded the public
1 ,	2 ,	0 ,	4	+ 3

If the complement *that S* had not been treated as a constituent in its own right, we would have had to adopt the following, slightly more complicated rule:

(25)   Extraposition from N   (alternative statement)

$$X - N - \textit{that} \ S - Y$$
$$1 \quad 2 \quad 3 \quad 4$$
$$\Rightarrow 1, 2, 0, 4 + 3 \quad \text{(Optional)}$$

In this rule, two elements are required to characterize the third term.

A category S̄ also proves useful in the statement of another rule, which relates the (a) and (b) sentences in the pairs below:

(26) a.   That Fred won a prize amazed me.

b.   It amazed me that Fred won a prize.

(27) a.   That Fred might win was believed by John.

b.   It was believed by John that Fred might win.

These pairs of sentences illustrate a general regularity of English: whenever we have a sentence whose subject is a sentential complement, there is a corresponding sentence in which *it* appears as the subject and the complement appears at the end. The transformational rule for forming the (b) sentences can be stated as follows:

(28)   Extraposition

$$\underset{NP\ NP}{[S]} - X$$
$$\quad 1 \qquad 2$$

$\Rightarrow it, \ 2 + 1$ (Optional)

The common deep structure for (26a) and (26b) is given in (29a), while (29b) shows the result of applying Extraposition:

(29)   a.

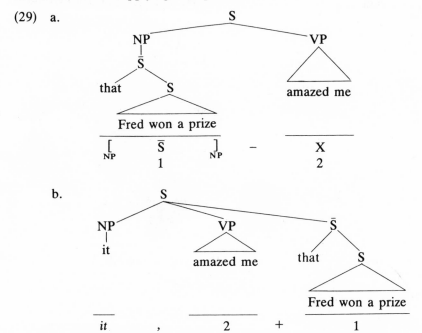

b.

So far we have provided motivation for a category S̄ and for two optional transformational rules that refer to S̄.[2] The analysis just developed is useful in accounting for the behavior of another type of sentential complement in English, illustrated below:

(30)   Fred would like *for the Red Sox to win.*

(31)   *For the Red Sox to lose now* would annoy the reporters.

If we analyze the italicized sequences in (30) and (31) as $\bar{S}$'s, then sentence (32) is automatically accounted for as an optional transformational variant of (31).

(32)   *It* would annoy the reporters *for the Red Sox to lose now.*

For-complements in English show most of the characteristics of ordinary sentences; they contain subjects, perfect and progressive helping verbs, and verb phrases. All of these are seen in the next example:

(33)   Jim wants *the baby to have been sleeping soundly.*[3]

The major difference between *for*-complements and *that*-complements is that in the former the first verbal element is not marked for tense, but instead is preceded by the infinitive marker *to*. In order to make use of the same phrase-structure rules for *for*-complements as for *that*-complements, we will assume that *for*-complements have Tns in their deep structures. The verbal marker *to* will be inserted in deep structure along with *for*, in the same manner that *en* was inserted with *have* and *ing* with *be* in Chapter 3. The relevant case of the $\bar{S}$ rule is given in (34), and a resulting deep structure is shown in (35):[4]

(34) $\bar{S} \rightarrow$ *for   to*   S

(35)

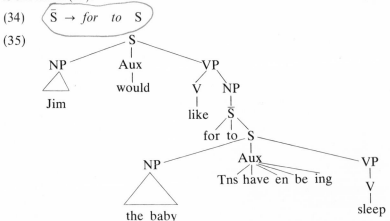

We now need a transformational rule that shifts *to* into the Aux in place of the Tns element:[5]

(36)   *To* Insertion

$$X - to - {}_{\bar{S}}[\ NP - Tns - Y \ ]_{\bar{S}} - Z$$

$$1 \quad 2 \qquad 3 \qquad 4 \quad 5 \qquad 6$$

$$\Rightarrow 1, \ 0, \ 3, \ 2, \ 5, \ 6 \quad \text{(Obligatory)}$$

The application of this rule is illustrated below:

(37) a.   ...for   to   the baby   Pres   have en be ing sleep

$$X \quad - to - \underset{s}{[} \text{ NP} \quad - \text{Tns} - \quad Y \quad \underset{s}{]} - Z$$

1   2   3   4   5   6

b.   ...for   the baby   to   have en be ing sleep

1 ,   0 ,   3   , 2 ,   5   , 6

A final remark on the *for*-complement is in order. In one specific respect, the motivation for classifying this complement as an NP when it occurs after a verb is not as strong as the motivation for an NP classification for the corresponding *that*-complements. As we saw earlier, *that*-complements can be passivized very readily:

(38) a.   John believes that Alice has flat feet.
   b.   That Alice has flat feet is believed by John.
   c.   It is believed by John that Alice has flat feet.

By contrast, the corresponding passives with *want* and *would like* are ungrammatical:

(39) a.   Pete would like for the flowers to bloom.
   b.   *For the flowers to bloom would be liked by Pete.
   c.   *It would be liked by Pete for the flowers to bloom.

(40) a.   Sharon wants for everyone to keep quiet.
   b.   *For everyone to keep quiet is wanted by Sharon.
   c.   *It is wanted by Sharon for everyone to keep quiet.

Before concluding that these *for*-complements are not NP's, we should observe that the ungrammaticality of the (b) and (c) examples above may have nothing to do with the complement. The reason is that passives with *want* and *would like* are not improved significantly when we substitute ordinary NP's for the *for*-complement:

(41) a.   Pete would like the top bunk.
   b.   *The top bunk would be liked by Pete.

(42) a.   Sharon wants the wishbone.
   b.   *The wishbone is wanted by Sharon.

Thus, the ungrammaticality of the passives with *for*-complements does not provide clear evidence against classifying the complements as NP's.

There is one set of data that appears to provide some positive evidence for analyzing these complements as NP's. Like ordinary NP's and *that* clauses, these *for*-complements are allowed in the so-called *pseudo-cleft construction*:

(43)   What John ate ____ was *the pie baked by Freda.*

(44)   What Bill said ____ to Frances was *that all cows eat grass.*

(45)   What Sharon wants ____ is *for everyone to keep quiet.*

On the basis of the evidence provided by this construction, we will tentatively continue to analyze *for*-complements as NP's.

EXERCISES

1.   For each of the following sentences, give the deep structure and sketch the steps in the transformational derivation:

(i)   For John to arrive late would amuse Alice.

(ii)   Was it expected that the cyclist would stay on the pavement?

2.   The sentences in (i) and (ii) below are usually analyzed as relative clauses that lack a head noun.

(i)   John ate what Martha cooked.

(ii)   What Fred did wasn't completely ethical.

At first glance, the following sentences might appear to be of exactly the same type:

(iii)   John knew *what Martha cooked.*

(iv)   *What Fred did* wasn't completely clear.

Give as many arguments as you can think of in favor of the following hypotheses:

(i)   The italicized sequences in (iii) and (iv) above are sentential complements rather than relative clauses.

(ii)   These sequences are in fact subordinate *questions.*

3.   The main purpose of this exercise is to explore one possibility for solving the problem raised by the nonoccurrence of modals in infinitive constructions. (This problem was discussed in note 5 of this chapter.) The problem arose because of our decision to assign a full-S deep structure to *for*-complements, that is, a deep structure identical in all essentials to the deep structures for English sentences that can stand by themselves. Such an analysis has the virtue of revealing the many basic similarities between *for*-complements and ordinary S's. Unfortunately, though, it has the corresponding defect of making it difficult to account for the differences, the most striking being the absence of tenses and modals in infinitives.

The basic idea of the alternative analysis is that finite clauses (including ordinary sentences) and *for*-complements share a common underlying "almost-S" constituent, which will be designated here as S'. This S' has the composition given in the following phrase structure rules:

S' → NP   Pred

Pred → (*have en*) (*be ing*) VP

In order to make a full sentence, we need to combine with S' a constituent F, which consists of Tns and an optional M:

S → F   S'

F → Tns (M)

We can make a complement (S̄) from an S by combining it with *that*:

S̄ → *that*   S

In addition, we can make an S̄ of a different sort by combining an S' with *for* and *to*:

S̄ → *for*   *to*   S'

In place of *To* Insertion, we need a rule that applies to shift F as well as *to*. These elements will be shifted to the right and attached alongside the constituent Predicate:

$$X - \begin{Bmatrix} F \\ to \end{Bmatrix} - _{S'}[\ NP - Pred]_{S'} - Y$$

$$1 \quad 2 \quad\quad 3 \quad\quad 4 \quad\quad 5$$

$$\Rightarrow 1, \ 0, \ 3, \ 2 + 4, \ 5 \quad \text{(Obligatory)}$$

Figure out what deep structure trees this alternative analysis would dictate for the following sentences:

(i)   The apple could have disappeared.

(ii)   Fred would like for the baby to be sleeping.

(iii)   That John swallows goldfish surprises Fred.

6.2 IDENTICAL-NP DELETION

In the previous section we saw some examples of sentences with *for*-complements. In all of the sentences that we examined, the subject NP of the lower sentence was not identical to any NP in the higher sentence. If we attempt to construct an example in which there is such an identity, we find that the result is ungrammatical:

(46)   *I would like for $\begin{Bmatrix} I \\ me \\ myself \end{Bmatrix}$ to finish this book.

What we find in place of this sentence is a sentence in which no subject appears in the complement sentence, and the complementizer *for* is missing:

(47)   I would like to finish this book.

We can account for this sentence by assigning it the same sort of deep structure that we assigned to *for*-complements in which the subject appeared in surface structure. For the sentence above, the deep structure would be as follows:

(48)

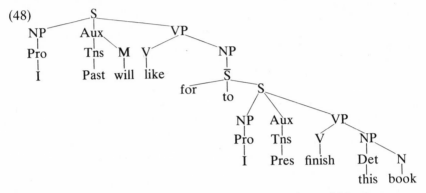

The first transformational rule to apply is *To* Insertion, which gives:

(49)

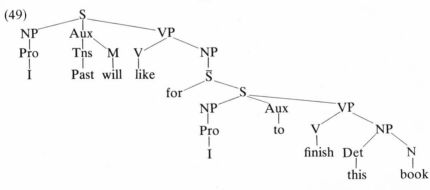

Two additional adjustments must be made by transformational rules if this structure is to result in the correct surface structure. First, the subject NP of the lower sentence must be deleted; this deletion can be accomplished by the following rule:

(50)   Identical-NP Deletion

NP – Aux V – [*for* – [NP – X]]
          $_{\bar{S}}$ $_{S}$ $_{S\bar{S}}$
1   2   3   4   5
Condition: 1 = 4
⇒1, 2, 3, 0, 5 (Obligatory)

Applied to tree (49), this rule gives

(51)

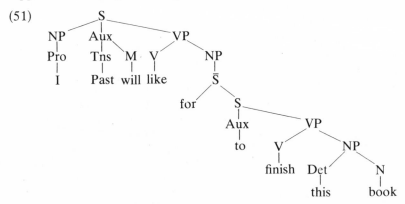

The second adjustment that must be made is that the complementizer *for* must be deleted; otherwise we could get an ungrammatical sentence:

(52)   *I would like for to finish this book.

This deletion can be accomplished by the following rule:

(53)   Complementizer Deletion

X – *for* – Aux – Y
1   2   3   4
⇒ 1, 0, 3, 4   (Obligatory)

This rule applies to the tree in (51) to yield (54):

(54)   I Past will like $[_{\bar{S}}$ $[_{S}$ to finish this book $]_{S}]_{\bar{S}}$

Affix Hopping applies in the main clause of this structure to give:

(55)   I will Past like to finish the book.

A single morphophonemic rule finishes the derivation:

(56)   I would like to finish this book.

There are many other expressions that are similar to the verb *like* in allowing a complement either with or without a subject in surface structure. Others, by contrast, allow only the subjectless infinitive. The verbs *try* and *hope* are examples:

(57) a.   *John tried for Bill to leave.

b.   *John tried for $\left\{ \begin{array}{l} \text{John} \\ \text{him} \\ \text{himself} \end{array} \right\}$ to leave.

c.   John tried to leave.

(58) a.　　*Sally hoped for Bill to leave.

　　　b.　　*Sally hoped for $\begin{Bmatrix} \text{Sally} \\ \text{her} \\ \text{herself} \end{Bmatrix}$ to leave.

　　　c.　　Sally hoped to leave.

Even though *try* and *hope* may never be followed in surface structure by a *for* NP sequence, we will assume that the deep structures of sentences with these verbs contain *for*-complements. However, in one respect the deep structures proposed here will differ from those for sentences with *like*; we will assume that the complement is dominated directly by VP, rather than by an intermediate NP. The reason is that these subjectless infinitive complements have even less in common with ordinary NP's than *for*-complements with *want* and *like* do. They are like the latter in giving bad results when they are passivized:

(59) a.　　Allen tried to write an epic.
　　　b.　　*To write an epic was tried by Allen.
　　　c.　　*It was tried by Allen to write an epic.

(60) a.　　My uncle hopes to buy a spotted hen.
　　　b.　　*To buy a spotted hen is hoped by my uncle.
　　　c.　　*It is hoped by my uncle to buy a spotted hen.

In addition, complements with *try* and *hope* are worse than those with *want* and *would like* in the pseudo-cleft construction:

(61)　　What John wanted was to climb Mt. Whitney.

(62)　　What Max would like would be to get a job at the post office.

(63)　　*What John tried was to climb Mt. Whitney.

(64)　　*What Max hoped was to get a job at the post office.

　　　For sentence (65), then, the deep structure will be tree (66):

(65)　　John tried to leave.

(66)

Exactly the same transformational rules apply here as applied in the derivation of sentence (47), *I would like to finish this book*. The sequence of rules is as follows: 1) *To* Insertion; 2) Identical-NP Deletion; 3) Complementizer Deletion; 4) Affix Hopping; 5) morphophonemic rules.

What justification can be given, in a case like this, for deriving infinitival complements of verbs such as *try* and *hope* from deep-structure *for*-complements? An alternative would be to assign such complements a deep structure that consisted only of a VP, perhaps something such as the following for sentence (65):

(67)

$$S$$

NP   Aux   VP
| | / \
N   Tns   V $\bar{S}$
| | | / \
John Past try to   VP
                   |
                   V
                   |
                   leave

Such a deep structure could result if we added the following phrase structure rule to our grammar:

(68) $\bar{S} \rightarrow to$ VP

The principal obstacle lying in the way of adopting this second analysis (and thus the principal justification for staying with the first) arises from the existence of infinitive phrases such as those italicized in the sentences below:

(69)   Jerry tried *to be liked*.

(70)   George hoped *to be elected by the delegates*.

If we assume that complements that are subjectless in surface structure are also subjectless in deep structure, then we cannot derive the passive infinitives in the preceding sentences by means of the Passive rule as stated in Chapter 4. In fact, we would be forced to adopt an analysis of these passive complements that relied almost entirely on phrase structure rules alone. Specifically, we would have to add special VP rules whose only function would be to allow the generation of passive infinitives. In point of fact, the rules would be exactly those which in Chapter 4 were abandoned in favor of a transformational analysis. If we are to maintain the transformational analysis of the passive construction in simple sentences, then we have every reason to try to maintain the same analysis in infinitive complements.

If complements of *try* and *hope* are assumed to contain full S's in deep structure, then no special problem arises with the passive infinitives in (69) and (70). We simply apply the Passive rule of Chapter 4 within the lower S *before* Identical-NP Deletion removes the subject of the complement. This account can be illustrated by tracing the derivation of *George hoped to be elected by the delegates.* The deep structure tree will be:

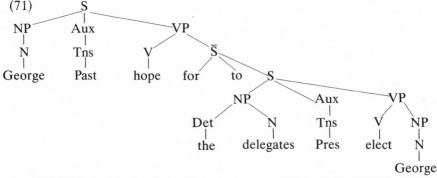

At this initial stage in the derivation, the structural description for Identical-NP Deletion is *not* satisfied, since the subject of the complement S and the subject of the main S are not identical. However, when we apply the Passive rule in the complement S and then apply *To* Insertion, we get:

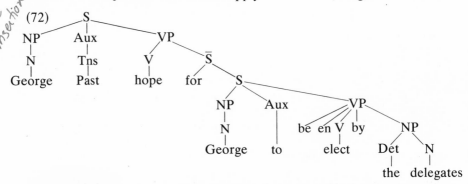

We now have a tree that satisfies the structural description for Identical-NP Deletion, that is, one in which the same NP appears both as subject of the main S and as subject of the complement S. Identical-NP Deletion must apply now, to give:

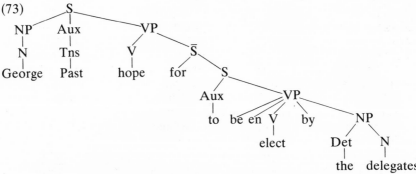

The only remaining rules are Complementizer Deletion and Affix Hopping (two applications). The bottom line of the resulting surface structure is:

(74)   George hope Past to be elect en by the delegates.

The morphophonemic rules then yield the desired sentence.

A transformational rule of Identical-NP Deletion also proves useful in accounting for VP's with verbs like _persuade and urge._ Superficially, these VP's often look very much like those headed by _want_ and _like_:

(75) a.   I wanted Frank to resign.
    b.   I would like Frank to resign.
    c.   I persuaded Frank to resign.

But important differences become apparent when we look at additional data. In the first place, the complementizer _for_, which can appear between _want_ or _like_ and a following NP, is completely impossible after _persuade_;

(76) ?a.   I wanted for Frank to resign.
    b.   I would like for Frank to resign.
    c.   *I persuaded for Frank to resign.

In the second place, whereas the NP's after _want_ and _like_ are deleted when they happen to be identical with the subject of the main S, the NP after _persuade_ may not be deleted:

(77) a.   I wanted _____ to resign.
    b.   I would like _____ to resign.
    c.   *I persuaded _____ to resign.

What we get instead after _persuade_ is a reflexive pronoun:

(77) d.   I persuaded _myself_ to resign.

These differences between _want_ and _persuade_ are accounted for automatically if we assume that the NP which follows _persuade_ is not the subject of a sentential complement but instead is the direct object of the verb _persuade_ itself. Thus, for _persuade_-VP's, we adopt the following phrase structure rule:

(78)   VP → V   NP   S̄

This rule gives us tree (80) as the deep structure of (79):

(79)   I persuaded Frank to resign.

(80)

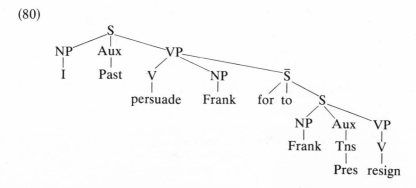

To Insertion applies first, to give:

(81)   I Past persuade Frank $_{\bar{s}}$[for $_s$[Frank to resign]$_s$]$_{\bar{s}}$.

In order to arrive at the desired sentence, the second occurrence of the NP *Frank* must be deleted. The rule of Identical-NP Deletion can apply to carry out this deletion if we add a variable first term and make the term mentioning Aux and V optional:

(82)   Identical-NP Deletion   (revised version)

$$X - NP - (Aux \quad V) - _{\bar{s}}[\ for - _s[\ NP - Y \ ]_s]_{\bar{s}}$$
$$1 \quad 2 \qquad 3 \qquad\qquad 4 \qquad 5 \quad 6$$

Condition: 2 = 5

⇒ 1, 2, 3, 4, 0, 6   (Obligatory)

In this case, this structural description is satisfied as follows:

(83)

I Past persuade	Frank		for	Frank	to resign
X	– NP –		$-_{\bar{s}}[for -$	$_s[NP -$	$Y]_s]_{\bar{s}}$
1	2	3	4	5	6

In this particular instance, the third term is empty, a situation that is allowed by virtue of our having made all the material in the third term optional. The rule applies to give:

(84)   I Past persuade Frank for to resign.

and this is converted by Complementizer Deletion and Affix Hopping into the following surface structure:

(85)   I persuade Past Frank to resign.

By allowing for the suffix *-ing* as a verbal marker for complement sentences, we can account for sentences in which the complement verb shows up in an *-ing* form:

(86)   The car started *rolling down the hill.*

(87)   My dog kept *barking.*

(88)   Fred stopped *talking about his operation.*

The necessary phrase structure rule is:

(89) $S \rightarrow ing \quad S$

This rule, when added to the others currently in our grammar, allows the tree in (90), which serves as the deep structure for (86).

(90)

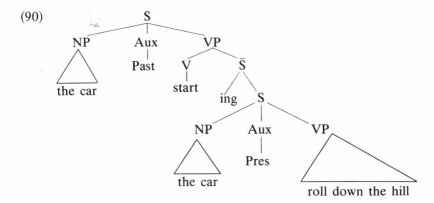

In order to convert this into the desired surface structure, we need only replace the rule of *To* Insertion by a rule that moves *ing* as well. We will dub this new rule Affix Insertion:

(91) Affix Insertion

$$X - \begin{Bmatrix} to \\ ing \end{Bmatrix} - {}_s[\ NP - Tns - Y\ ]_s - Z$$

$$1 \quad\quad 2 \quad\quad\quad 3 \quad\quad 4 \quad\quad 5 \quad\quad 6$$

$$\Rightarrow 1,\ 0,\ 3,\ 2,\ 5,\ 6 \quad \text{(Obligatory)}$$

The application of this rule to the tree in (90) gives (92), a structure to which a slightly revised Identical-NP Deletion can apply:[6]

(92)

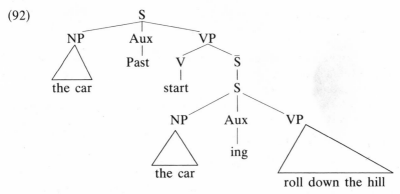

The result is just (93):

(93)   the car Past start ing roll down the hill.

Now the Affix Hopping rule applies, not only to shift *Past* to the right of *start* in the main sentence, but also to hop the *ing* over *roll* in the complement:

(94)   The car start Past roll ing down the hill.

This is just the desired surface structure.

We can account in similar fashion for corresponding *causative* sentences, in which the subject is asserted to have caused the direct object to start or keep doing something:

(95)   Joe started the car rolling down the hill.
         (i.e., Joe caused the car to start rolling down the hill.)

(96)   The full moon kept my dog barking.
         (i.e., The full moon caused my dog to keep barking.)[7]

We already have all the necessary phrase structure and transformational rules. The deep structure of (95), for example, would be (97), a tree very similar to the deep structure proposed for *persuade* sentences.

(97)

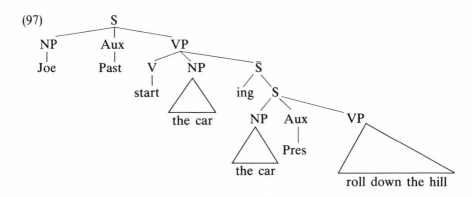

Affix Insertion, Identical-NP Deletion (operating in the same way as with *persuade*), and two applications of Affix Hopping suffice to give the right surface sequence.

Before concluding this section, we should mention one important descriptive problem that we have not dealt with. This is the problem of preventing the generation of ungrammatical sentences with verbs such as *try* and *persuade* that arise when the complement subject fails to be identical with the main-S subject or object.

(98).   *John tried for Alice to leave.

(99)   *The doctor persuaded Frank for Harry to resign.

Nothing in our phrase structure rules or transformational rules as they stand prevents the generation of these sentences, alongside the following perfectly grammatical sentences:

(100)   John tried to leave.

(101)   The doctor persuaded Frank to resign.

Several solutions to this problem have been suggested in transformational studies of English. We will mention one of them in Chapter 10.

EXERCISE

For each of the following sentences, give the deep structure and sketch the transformational derivation:

(i)   John wants to be nominated.
(ii)   We met the girl that John persuaded to drive Bill to Ohio.
(iii) The lawyer is trying to persuade the prisoner to stay in the courtroom.
(iv)   John will urge Bill to try to start playing the bassoon.

6.3 SUBJECT RAISING

In this section, we will examine a complement structure of English that at first glance appears to resemble very closely two of the structures that we discussed in the preceding section. This construction is illustrated by the following sentence:

(102)   Fred believed Alice to be cautious.

Superficially, this sentence bears a close resemblance to these:

(103)   Fred persuaded Alice to be cautious.

(104)   Fred wanted Alice to be cautious.

We might naturally think, then, that determining the correct analysis of sentence (102) with *believe* would simply be a matter of deciding whether to treat it like a *persuade* verb or like a *want* verb, that is, whether to assign it the structure in (105) or the structure in (106):

(105)

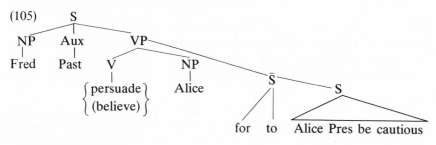

(106)

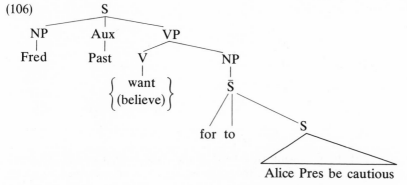

As it happens, however, the evidence that we will examine in studying the *believe* construction will show that it acts sometimes like the *persuade* construction and sometimes like the *want* construction. The major source of this chameleon-like behavior will be the NP that follows *believe*. In one important respect it will act like a complement subject rather than a main-clause direct object, thus making it difficult to assign it the *persuade* structure shown in (105). However, in another respect, it will act more like a main-clause direct object, thus making it difficult to assign it the *want*-type analysis given in (106). First, we will examine the two constructions that appear to give conflicting indications about the status of this NP. We will then propose an analysis of these *believe* complements that resolves the apparent conflict.

Let us begin with a construction that provides evidence against analyzing the critical NP as a direct object of the main clause (and hence against the assignment of a *persuade*-type analysis to the *believe* complement). This is the so-called *existential* construction illustrated in the following examples:[8]

(107)   There is a fly in the soup.

(108)   There is a bat in the belfry.

The word *there* in these sentences occurs in the position in which we find ordinary subject NP's. In addition, it is treated like an NP for the purposes of Subject-HV Inversion:

(109)   Is there a fly in the soup?

Nevertheless, it does not in general occur in other positions where ordinary noun phrases are found, such as in the direct object position or in a prepositional phrase:

(110) a.   *The maid put there into the drawer.
      b.   *The maid put there a spoon into the drawer.
      c.   *We talked about there.
      d.   *We talked about there a book.

We can account for the peculiar distribution of *there* in simple sentences by assuming that it is introduced by a transformational rule. We will assume that the deep structure for the existential sentence in (107) is the following tree:

(111)

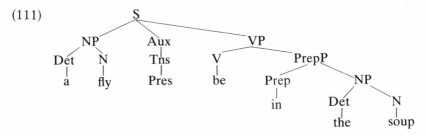

We now add the following transformational rule, which moves the deep-structure subject to the right of the verb and inserts *there* as the new subject:[9]

(112) *There* Insertion

    NP – Aux – *be* – PrepP
     1   2   3   4

    ⇒ *there*, 2, 3 + 1, 4   (Optional)

This rule can apply to tree (111) to give the following derived structure:

(113)

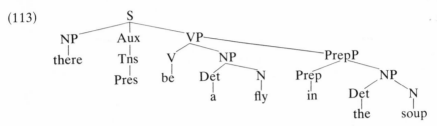

By adopting a treatment in which *there* is inserted transformationally, we ensure that it will not occur as a direct object or object of a preposition in a simple sentence.

Now let us see what this analysis of existential sentences implies for a proposal in which *believe* sentences are derived in the same way as *persuade* sentences. The critical sentences here are the following:

(114)   *John persuaded there to be a bat in the belfry.

(115)   John believed there to be a bat in the belfry.

The ungrammaticality of the first of these sentences is entirely understandable, since it would require a deep structure of the following form:

(116)

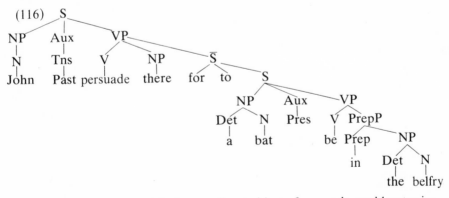

Such a deep structure, with *there* as direct object of *persuade*, could not arise by the phrase structure rules and lexical rules we have proposed, since all occurrences of existential *there* are assumed to arise by being inserted transformationally. Thus, given our analysis of *persuade* sentences, there is no way in which the ungrammatical sentence (114) could be generated. This is of course just what we want.

On the other hand, we do want to generate the grammatical sentence

(115) above, in which *believe* is followed directly by *there*. If we assign the *believe* sentence the same type of deep structure as that assigned to the *persuade* sentence, we make it impossible to generate the *believe* sentence. The reason is that we would have to assume a deep structure in which *there* occurred as direct object of *believe*. This assumption would be inconsistent with our decision not to allow *there* in deep structure, a decision that we found was justified by its effectiveness in helping to avoid the generation of the ungrammatical simple sentences in (110).

By contrast, sentence (115) below is generated with no problem if we analyze the *believe* sentence in the same manner as the *want* sentence, that is, if we assign *believe* sentences the structure in (106). The derivation of (115) will proceed as follows:

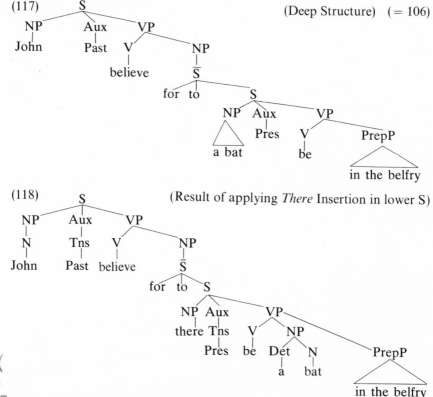

Affix Insertion in the complement and Affix Hopping in the main S yield the desired surface structure:

(119)   John believe Past there to be a bat in the belfry.

We thus have one piece of evidence in favor of analyzing *believe* and *want* in the same way, and against analyzing *believe* and *persuade* in the same way.

Let us turn now to some evidence that appears to dictate just the opposite kind of analysis for *believe* sentences. As was noted in section 6.2, *want* and *persuade* differ in the choice that they make between Identical-NP Deletion and a reflexive pronoun:

(120) a.   *James wants himself to go to bed early.

   b.   James persuaded himself to go to bed early.

(121) a.   James wants ____ to go to bed early.

   b.   *James persuaded ____ to go to bed early.

We accounted for the disappearance of the NP after *want* by analyzing it as the subject of the lower S and postulating a rule of Identical-NP Deletion that removed it when it was identical to the subject of the main S. On the other hand, we accounted for the retention of a reflexive NP following *persuade* by assuming that this NP was the direct object of the main S.

With this as background, let us look at the corresponding examples with *believe*:

(122)   *You believe ____ to be intelligent.

(123)   You believe yourself to be intelligent.

Here the NP following *believe* looks more like a direct object in the main S than like the subject of the complement. These sentences thus appear to favor treating the *believe* construction like the *persuade* construction, that is, assigning the *believe* sentence the structure in (105).

This argument in favor of treating the NP after *believe* as a main-clause direct object can be made even stronger by looking in more detail at the rule of Reflexivization. In section 5.1, we stated the rule in preliminary fashion as follows:

(124)   Reflexivization   (preliminary version)
   NP – Aux – V – (Prep) – NP
   1   2   3   4   5
   Condition: 1 = 5
   ⇒ 1, 2, 3, 4, 5 + *Refl*   (Obligatory)

When we look at a variety of sentences containing reflexives, it becomes apparent that this rule is much too specific as it stands. The following sentences show the kinds of sequences that may intervene between the reflexive and the noun phrase that is understood as its antecedent:

(125) a.   You shaved yourself.

   $\underline{\qquad}$
   V

   b.   You talked about yourself.

   $\underline{\qquad}$ $\underline{\qquad}$
   V   Prep

   c.   You talked to Bill about yourself.

   $\underline{\qquad}$ $\underline{\qquad}$ $\underline{\qquad}$ $\underline{\qquad}$
   V   Prep   NP   Prep

   d.   John talked to us about ourselves.

   $\underline{\qquad}$
   Prep

These sentences can all be accounted for by a revised Reflexivization rule that has a variable first term, a variable final term, and a variable term between the two NP terms:

(126)   X – NP – Y – NP – Z
        1   2   3   4   5
        Condition: 2 = 4
        ⇒ 1, 2, 3, 4 + *Refl*, 5

Having made this change, we find that when we consider complex sentences, the variable third term allows the generation of certain ungrammatical reflexives:

(127)   I   Past will like for the barber to shave   I

        X – NP –   Y   – NP – Z
        *I would like for the barber to shave myself.

(128)   I   Past sue the man that hit   I

        X – NP –   Y   – NP – Z
        *I sued the man that hit myself.

(129)   You Past tell   he   that   he   Past be a genius

                   X   – NP – Y – NP –

        *You told him that himself was a genius.

To avoid the derivation of these ungrammatical sentences, we will propose that a special condition be included in the rule of Reflexivization, namely, that the two identical NP's be *clause mates*. What this means is that the two NP's must be in the same "simple sentence" in the tree: one cannot be within an S that does not include the other. This condition specifically forbids Reflexivization in a situation of the sort represented schematically below:

(130)

As can be readily shown, the trees for (127–129) are all of this disallowed form.

To recapitulate our discussion of the reflexive rule, we began by arguing that the third term in the structural description (the term between the two identical NP's) should be a variable. We then imposed a clause mate condition on these two identical terms, in order to block the generation of ungrammatical sentences in which the reflexive pronoun was in a lower S than its antecedent. It is this condition that we will now use as the basis for strengthening the argument in favor of main-S direct object status for the NP that follows *believe*.

The critical sentence with which we were concerned was (123), *You believe yourself to be intelligent*. Suppose that we were to analyze the second underlying *you* as being the subject of the complement, as in (131):

(131)

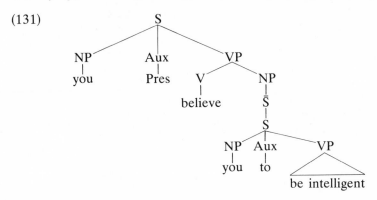

As noted earlier, if Identical-NP Deletion applied here, we would get the following ungrammatical sentence:

(132)   *You believe _____ to be intelligent.

However, even if Identical-NP Deletion were somehow kept from applying here, we would still not derive sentence (123). Since the left-hand *you* and the right-hand *you* in (131) are not clause mates, Reflexivization could not apply. As a consequence, we would generate this ungrammatical sentence:

(133)   *You believe you to be intelligent.

We can finish this argument by looking at what the Reflexive rule will do if the NP after *believe* is analyzed as a main clause direct object:

(134)

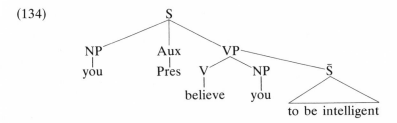

In this tree, the two occurrences of *you* are clause mates. Consequently, Reflexivization applies to give the desired grammatical sentence:

(123)   You believe yourself to be intelligent.

It would appear at this point that we face something of a dilemma. If we analyze the NP after *believe* as a complement subject, then we account easily for the appearance of existential *there*, but we are left without an explanation for the appearance of reflexive pronouns. On the other hand, if we analyze this NP as a main-clause direct object, then it is the appearance of the reflexive pronoun that is expected and the appearance of *there* that remains a puzzle.

A natural way of resolving this apparent conflict is to assume that the NP after *believe* actually has complement-subject status at one point in the derivation and becomes the main-clause direct object at a later stage. An analysis along these lines can be developed in a variety of ways. The specific assumption that we will make here is that the deep structure for the *believe*-construction is like a deep structure of the *persuade* type, except that the direct object NP of the main S starts out as an "empty" NP (which we shall indicate by Δ).[10] The deep structure for (135), modified only by the rule of Affix Insertion, would be tree (136):

(135)   Fred believed Alice to be cautious.   (= 102)

(136)

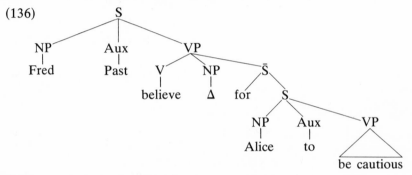

We now need a transformational rule that moves the subject of the complement into the empty direct object NP in the main S:

(137)   Subject Raising   (preliminary version)

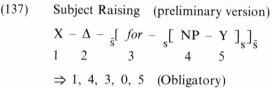

$$X - \Delta - _{\bar{s}}[\; for \; - \; _{s}[\; NP - Y \;]_{s}]_{\bar{s}}$$
$$1 \quad 2 \quad 3 \quad 4 \quad 5$$

$$\Rightarrow 1, \; 4, \; 3, \; 0, \; 5 \quad \text{(Obligatory)}$$

(138)

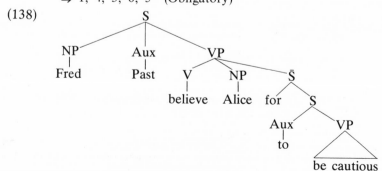

The *for* will be deleted automatically by Complementizer Deletion, and the desired sentence (135) is generated:

(135)   Fred believed Alice to be cautious.

What remains to be done now is to show that this analysis gives correct results as regards the critical existential and reflexive constructions, respectively:

(139)   John believed there to be a bat in the belfry.   (= 115)

(140)   You believe yourself to be intelligent.   (= 123)

The deep structure for (139), on the analysis we are assuming here, would be:

(141)

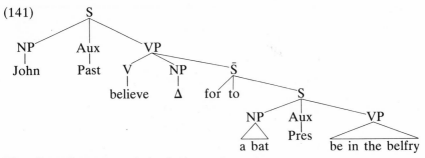

There Insertion can apply in the lower S, to give:

(142)

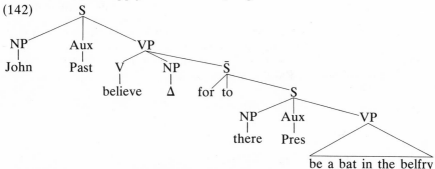

After Affix Insertion, we are ready for Subject Raising. The subject at this stage happens to be the existential marker *there*, which is duly raised into the main-S direct object, to give:

(143)

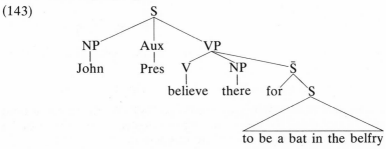

With Complementizer Deletion and Affix Hopping, the derivation arrives at the desired surface structure. Although *there* ends up as the main-clause direct object, it has arrived there in a way that is perfectly consistent with our general analysis of existential sentences, in which *there* can appear in a tree only by virtue of being inserted transformationally into subject position.

Our analysis also affords us a straightforward derivation of (140):

(140)   You believe yourself to be intelligent.

The deep structure for this sentence would be:

(144)

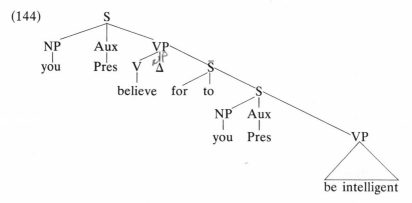

At this early stage in the derivation, the conditions for the application of Reflexivization are not satisfied; the two occurrences of *you* are not clause mates. After Affix Insertion takes place, the conditions are satisfied for the application of Subject Raising, which yields:

(145)

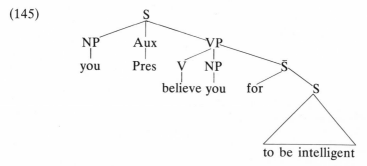

The two occurrences of *you* are now clause mates, so that Reflexivization applies, to give:

(146)   you Pres believe you Refl for to be intelligent.

This derivation thus eventually yields sentence (140). We thus see that both of the critical sentences, the first containing an existential and the second a reflexive pronoun, can be generated with this new analysis.

It will be clear from the preceding discussion that the possibility of deleting the NP immediately after the main verb distinguishes the verbs that take only sentential complements in deep structure from those that take an NP followed by a sentential complement. Thus, the lexical entries of the verbs in (147) all contain the subcategorization feature $\langle$____ *for to* S$\rangle$:

(147)

Jack $\begin{Bmatrix} \text{tried} \\ \text{hoped} \\ \text{intended} \\ \text{managed} \\ \text{forgot} \end{Bmatrix}$ to finish the novel.   *Equi NP deletion*

By contrast, the verbs in (148) all require some kind of NP after the verb in deep structure, either an ordinary NP or one specifically designated as empty:

(148)

*John $\begin{Bmatrix} \text{persuaded} \\ \text{urged} \\ \text{believed} \\ \text{judged} \end{Bmatrix}$ to be careful.

Within the class of verbs that require deep structure NP's following the verb, the possibility of *there* following the verb will serve to distinguish Subject-Raising structures from Identical-NP Deletion structures. Thus, the verbs in (149) are to be treated as Subject Raising verbs, identified as such in the lexicon by the feature $\langle$____ Δ *for to* S$\rangle$:

(149)

I $\begin{Bmatrix} \text{believe} \\ \text{assume} \\ \text{suspect} \\ \text{estimate} \end{Bmatrix}$ there to be over 3,000 beans in this jar.

By contrast, the verbs in (150) warrant an analysis in which Identical-NP Deletion is the critical transformational rule:

(150)

*Jack $\begin{Bmatrix} \text{persuaded} \\ \text{advised} \\ \text{urged} \end{Bmatrix}$ there to be a waiter at every table.

Verbs in the latter class will be marked in the lexicon by the feature $\langle$____ NP *for to* S$\rangle$.[11]

There is a second class of sentences in English for which a Subject Raising analysis seems appropriate:

(151)   Alfred appears to be content.

(152)   Max tends to play it safe.

At first glance, these sentences look no different from the kind described earlier:

(153)   Alfred tries to be content.

(154)   Max hopes to play it safe.

Sentences like (153) and (154) were analyzed in Section 6.2 as having a deep structure complement subject that was removed by Identical-NP Deletion. We might thus be tempted to assign the sentences in (151) and (152) the following deep structures:

(155)   Alfred Pres appear $_\bar{s}$[for to $_s$[Alfred Pres be content]$_s$]$_\bar{s}$.

(156)   Max Pres tend $_\bar{s}$[for to $_s$[Max Pres play it safe]$_s$]$_\bar{s}$.

An argument against an analysis based on Identical-NP Deletion is provided by the occurrence of existential *there* as the surface structure subject of *appear* and *tend*:

(157)   There appeared to be a cellist in the band.

(158)   There tend to be many traffic accidents on national holidays.

Let us focus attention here on the derivation of (157). In light of the argument presented earlier in favor of a transformational derivation of *there*, we cannot adopt either of the following as the deep structure of this sentence:

(159)   there Past appear $_\bar{s}$[for to $_s$[there Pres be a cellist in the band]$_s$]$_\bar{s}$

(160)   there Past appear $_\bar{s}$[for to $_s$[a cellist Pres be in the band]$_s$]$_\bar{s}$.

Suppose instead that we propose a deep structure that has *a cellist* in subject position in both the upper and lower S:

(161)   a cellist Past appear $_\bar{s}$[for to $_s$[a cellist Pres be in the band]$_s$]$_\bar{s}$.

As currently stated, the rule of *There* Insertion can apply only in the complement S. If it applies there, the following tree results:

(162)

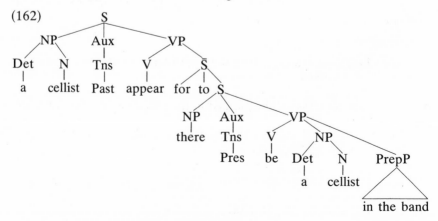

To this structure Identical-NP Deletion is inapplicable, since the subject of the lower sentence (*there*) is not identical with the subject of the higher sentence (*a cellist*). Consequently, we cannot derive sentence (157) by this route, either.

One final suggestion for saving an Identical-NP Deletion analysis might be to modify the *There* Insertion rule in such a way as to allow a variable between the subject noun phrase and *be*:

(163) *There* Insertion   (revised version)

NP – X – *be* – PrepP
1   2   3   4

⇒*there*, 2, 3 + 1, 4   (Optional)

Suppose further that we begin with the deep structure in (164):

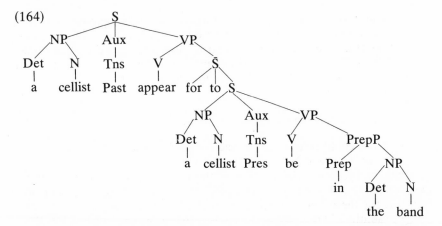

(164)

Application of *To* Insertion, Identical-NP Deletion, and Complementizer Deletion yields the tree below:

(165)

This tree meets the structural description for the revised version of *There* Insertion:

(166) a.   a cellist Past appear to   be   in the band

         NP   –   X   –be–   PrepP
         1   2   3   4

    ⇒

b.   there Past appear to   be   a cellist   in the band

      there ,   2   , 3 + 1 ,   4

Application of Affix Hopping yields the desired sentence:

(167)   There appeared to be a cellist in the band.   (= 157)

    Crucial to the revised analysis of this sentence was the possibility of a revised version of *There* Insertion; with our earlier version, the structural description of the rule would not have been met in the sentence as a whole. But this revised version of *There* Insertion allows the generation of a vast range of ungrammatical sentences. An especially pertinent example is the following:

(168)   *There hoped to be a cellist in the band.

This sentence could be derived in exactly the same way as (167), that is, by first applying Identical-NP Deletion and then applying *There* Insertion in the sentence as a whole. What we have found, then, is that an Identical-NP Deletion analysis is just as unsatisfactory for these *appear* and *tend* sentences as it was for the *believe* sentences studied at the beginning of this section.
    The solution in this case is the same as that proposed earlier for *believe*: we will treat surface structure subjects of verbs such as *appear* and *tend* as originating in complement S's. As before, they will arrive at their surface structure position by replacing an empty NP node.
    This analysis can be illustrated by a derivation of (169), for which the deep structure would be (170).

(169)   Alfred appears to be content.   (= 151)

(170)

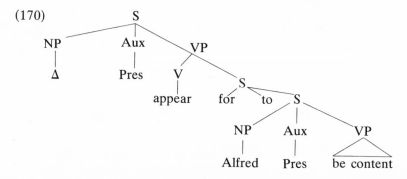

In order to get *Alfred* moved, we need to make only a slight revision in the rule of Subject Raising already developed: we need to allow for an Aux and a V to intervene between the empty NP and the complement. The revised rule thus takes the following form:

(171)   Subject Raising   (revised version)

$$X - \Delta - (\text{Aux} \quad V) - {}_{\bar{S}}[\ for - {}_S[NP - Y\ ]_S]_{\bar{S}}$$
$$1 \quad 2 \quad\quad 3 \quad\quad\quad 4 \quad\quad 5 \quad 6$$
$$\Rightarrow 1,\ 5,\ 3,\ 4,\ 0,\ 6 \quad \text{(Obligatory)}$$

After Affix Insertion applies to (170), the conditions are satisfied for the application of Subject Raising:

(172) a. Δ Pres appear   for   Alfred   to be content

$$X - \Delta - \text{Aux} \quad V \quad - {}_{\bar{S}}[for - {}_S[NP - \quad\quad Y \quad\quad]_S]_{\bar{S}}$$
$$1 \quad 2 \quad\quad 3 \quad\quad\quad 4 \quad\quad 5 \quad\quad\quad 6$$

   b.   Alfred   Pres appear   for   to be content

$$1\ ,\ 5\ ,\ \quad 3 \quad ,\ 4\ ,\ 0\ , \quad 6$$

This derivation eventually yields *Alfred appears to be content*.

For the critical existential sentence (173), we have an equally straightforward derivation.

(173)   There appeared to be a cellist in the band.   (= 157)

The deep structure itself will not contain an occurrence of *there*:

(174)

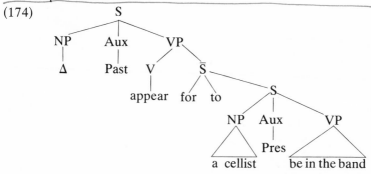

Application of *There* Insertion in the lower S, followed by Affix Insertion, gives:

(175)

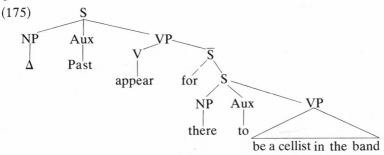

Conditions are now ripe for the application of Subject Raising. The subject of the complement is *there*, so that it is this *there* that gets promoted to subject status in the main S:

(176)

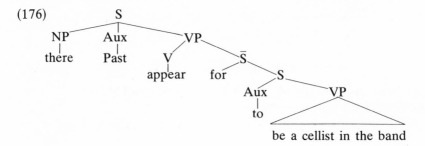

Additional rules give the desired result, *There appeared to be a cellist in the band*. Thus, for a Subject Raising analysis of sentences containing verbs like *appear*, existential sentences do not pose a problem.[12]

We will in general use the possibility of *there* in main-clause subject position to distinguish verbs and adjectives that occur in Subject Raising structures from those that occur in Identical-NP Deletion structures. Thus, all of the verbs and adjectives in (177) belong in the former group, whereas those in (178) belong in the latter:

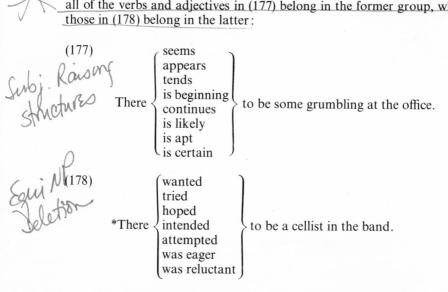

(177)

There
{
seems
appears
tends
is beginning
continues
is likely
is apt
is certain
}
to be some grumbling at the office.

(178)

*There
{
wanted
tried
hoped
intended
attempted
was eager
was reluctant
}
to be a cellist in the band.

One final matter deserves attention in this section. In our analysis of sentences with *believe* and *appear*, we made use of a novel kind of NP, an empty NP signified by Δ. The appearance of this NP in deep structure dictates the addition to our grammar of the following rule:

(179)   NP → Δ

We clearly need to limit the appearance of these empty NP's in some way.

Otherwise, we run the risk of generating a great many ungrammatical sentences, along with perfectly grammatical ones that contain full NP's:

(180) a.   Fred saw the movie.

   b.   *Fred saw Δ

(181) a.   Did John buy the book?

   b.   *Did Δ buy Δ?

In order to have empty NP's in just the proper places in deep structure, we will adopt a convention to the effect that a verb may be inserted into a tree with an empty NP in some position only if it is specifically marked in the lexicon to take such an NP. If we include the feature ⟨____ Δ *for to* S⟩ in the lexical entry of *believe*, then this verb is specifically allowed to appear in a structure with an empty direct object NP and a following *for-to* complement. Similarly, the verb *appear* would be subcategorized with the feature ⟨Δ ____ *for to* S⟩. By contrast, the subcategorization features for *see* and *buy*, the verbs in (180) and (181), would make no reference to empty NP's, but would refer instead simply to ordinary NP's. By the convention suggested above, it would follow that these verbs could not be inserted into prelexical trees in which the subjects or objects were empty NP's. As a consequence, prelexical trees such as (182) and (183) could not be filled out lexically into a well-formed deep structure:

(182)

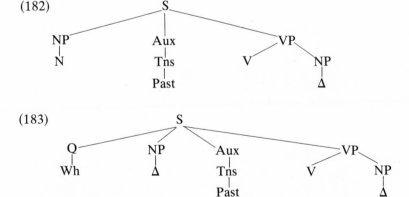

(183)

Hence the ungrammatical (b) sentences in (180) and (181) could not be generated.[13]

EXERCISES

1.   Give the deep structures and sketch the transformational derivations for the following sentences:

(i)   Which book does Alfred believe to be dull?

(ii)   The money appears to have been stolen.

2.   In (112) in the text, the rule of *There* Insertion was formulated in such a way as to apply only when *be* was followed by a prepositional phrase. The following is an alternative formulation of the rule, in which the fourth term is a variable instead of PrepP:

NP – Aux – be – X
1   2   3   4
⇒ *there*, 2, 3 + 1, 4   (Optional)

First, give examples of grammatical sentences that are allowed by the alternative statement of the rule but not by the rule in the text. Next, give an example of an ungrammatical sentence that is allowed by the alternative statement but not by the text statement.

3.   In this section, we presented an analysis of the sentence, *There appears to be a cellist in the band*, in which a revised rule of *There* Insertion was applied in the sentence as a whole. However, we argued against this analysis on the basis of the fact that the proposed revision would allow the generation of a sentence such as **There hoped to be a cellist in the band*, along with the more grammatical sentence, *A cellist hoped to be in the band*. What we proposed instead was that *There* Insertion as originally stated should apply in the lower S.

   In our discussion of these alternatives, no attention was given to the problem of number agreement in existential sentences. Judging by the following sentences of Standard English, which of these two accounts comes out ahead in this area?

There is a fly in the soup.
*There are a fly in the soup.
There are three flies in the soup.
*There is three flies in the soup.
There appears to be a fly in the soup.
*There appear to be a fly in the soup.
There appear to be three flies in the soup.
*There appears to be three flies in the soup.

Explain your answer as carefully as you can.

Suggestions for Further Reading

In Rosenbaum 1967 is the first major attempt to describe English sentential complements within the transformational framework. Kiparsky and Kiparsky 1970 argue that in certain instances the form that a complement takes is dependent on semantic properties of the verb or adjective with which it occurs. Bresnan 1970 suggests a treatment of sentential complements which differs from Rosenbaum's in that complementizers are present in deep structure, rather than being introduced by transformational rules.

The construction illustrated in the sentence *John believes Bill to be intelligent* has been the subject of a good deal of recent controversy. Chomsky 1973 rejects the view that *Bill* is at some point raised into main-clause direct object position. This rejection is tied to the view that the clause-mate condition does not represent the appropriate way of constraining the rule of Reflexivization. Postal 1974 offers a defense of the view that *Bill* does undergo raising into the main clause. Lightfoot 1975 makes some interesting observations on the controversy.

Notes

1. There have been only two instances so far in the book in which a transformational rule has had the effect of moving a nonconstituent. The two rules were Subject-HV Inversion and *Not*-HV Inversion, as they were stated in sections 3.4 and 3.5 and as they applied to the trees resulting from the phrase structure rules proposed in section 3.4. In the alternative analysis developed in Exercise 3 of section 3.6, only single constituents were moved.

2. In many transformational treatments of English syntax, the *it* is made a part of the deep structure of all NP's that consist of sentential complements. When the accompanying complement is extraposed, the *it* is left behind and appears in the surface structure of the sentence. When the option of applying Extraposition is not taken, a special rule of *It* Deletion applies. This analysis is first stated in Rosenbaum 1967 and is incorporated into the transformational grammar for English presented in Burt 1971.

3. When it immediately follows *want* or *like*, the complementizer *for* may optionally be deleted.

4. In Rosenbaum 1967 and also in several other discussions of English complements, the complementizers *that* and *for* are not present in deep structure, but instead are inserted transformationally. Arguments in favor of deep structure complementizers are put forward in Bresnan 1970.

5. One problem with the analysis given here is that it allows two deep structure sources for any *for-to* complement, one in which the underlying Tns is Pres and one in which it is Past. Another embarrassment is that it fails to rule out the appearance of modals in *for-to* complements. The contrast between nonmodals and modals is shown clearly in the following pairs:

(i) a.   We would like for Jack to *be able* to leave.
     b.   *We would like for Jack to *can* leave.

(ii) a.   They do not want for Marsha to *have to* hurry.
     b.   *They do not want for Marsha to *must* hurry.

One solution to this second problem is to reformulate the rule of *To* Insertion so that it replaces not only Tns but also any modal that happens to be present:

(iii) $X - to -_S[\text{ NP} - \text{Tns (M)} - Y]_S - Z$
         1   2   3   4   5   6
         $\Rightarrow$ 1, 0, 3, 2, 5, 6   (Obligatory)

The drawback of this solution is that the first problem becomes even worse than before: there are now approximately twelve deep structure sources for every *for-to* complement. Very little serious attention has been given to these problems in recent syntactic studies. In Exercise 3 at the end of this section, an alternative analysis is outlined which does not show these deficiencies.

6. The rule could be stated as follows:

Identical-NP Deletion   (revised version)

$$X - NP - (Aux \quad V) - _{\bar{S}}[\ (for)\ _S[\ NP - Y\ ]_S]_{\bar{S}}$$
$$1 \quad 2 \qquad 3 \qquad\qquad 4 \qquad 5 \quad 6$$

Condition: $2 = 5$

$\Rightarrow$ 1, 2, 3, 4, 0, 6   (Obligatory)

7. Not all noncausative verbs similar in meaning to *start* and *keep* allow corresponding causatives:

(i) a.   The car began rolling down the hill.

   b.   *Joe began the car rolling down the hill.

(ii) a.   Joe stopped talking about his operation.

   b.   *Bill stopped Joe talking about his operation.

8. This existential use of *there* is to be distinguished from the locative use examplified in the following sentences:

(i)   Thére's my brother, over by the water cooler.

(ii)   Thére goes your investment.

The locative use characteristically receives a greater degree of stress than the existential use.

9. This statement of the rule is too narrow in the requirement that *be* be followed by a prepositional phrase (see Exercise 2 at the end of this section). In another respect, it is less specific than some formulations that have been offered. In these formulations, a condition is imposed to the effect that the NP mentioned in the first term of the structural description must be indefinite. The condition would account for the fact that (ia) is more natural than (ib):

(i) a.   There's a shortage of beer.

   b.   ?There's the shortage of beer.

However, it is not clear that definite existentials like (ib) really should be excluded, since they are completely natural in certain contexts:

(ii)   *Question*: What sources of voter discontent can we exploit in this campaign?

   Answer: Well, there's the shortage of beer. That should be good for something.

One final problem with this rule is that it is not clear how to guarantee NP status for the word *there* in the derived structure. We will simply proceed here as if this had been taken care of.

10. More will be said at the end of this section about the use of this empty NP.

11. Many of the individual verbs mentioned here allow other subcategorizations. For example, *believe* and *urge* also require a feature $\langle \underline{\quad} NP \rangle$:

(i)   We believed his story.

(ii)   The secretary of State urged restraint.

Likewise we need to include the feature $\langle$____*that* S$\rangle$ in the lexical entries for *believe*, *hope*, and *forget*:

(iii)   Bill believes that Alice has flat feet.

(iv)   We hope that the delay was not serious.

(v)   He forgot that the bank would be closed.

12. Number agreement in existential sentences poses a problem for this analysis. See Exercise 3 at the end of this section.

13. To make matters air-tight, we might make explicit the following convention:

Any phrase structure tree that contains unfilled "lexical" nodes (i.e., N, V, Adj, Prep) is discarded as ill-formed.

This convention immediately disqualifies trees (182) and (183).

7

Rule Application
in Complex Sentences

In the preceding chapter we discussed a number of complex constructions in English, and formulated several transformational rules to account
for them. Several of these rules had the property of making reference in
their structural descriptions to material in two separate S's, a higher S and
a lower one. We also saw a number of instances in which the generation of a
sentence required that a rule apply to the lower sentence alone before
another rule applied in the sentence as a whole. For instance, in the derivation of (1a) from the deep structure sketched in (1b), it is necessary to apply
Passive to the lower sentence before the structural description for Identical-
NP Deletion will be met:

(1) a.   The candidate hoped to be nominated by the party.
    b.   the candidate Past hope $_S$[for $_S$[the party Pres nominate
          the candidate]]$_S$ $_S$.

The principal question to be discussed in this chapter can be put as
follows: What convention or conventions govern the order of application of
rules in a tree that contains more than a single S? We will begin by discussing
what appears to be a counterexample to the Strict Order Hypothesis; we
will then suggest a modification in this hypothesis and examine some
additional consequences of adopting this modification.

7.1 AN APPARENT COUNTEREXAMPLE
TO THE STRICT ORDER HYPOTHESIS

In section 6.3 of the previous chapter, arguments were presented in
favor of a rule of Subject Raising, whose effect was to raise the subject of a

lower sentence into either object or subject position in a higher sentence. The basic argument for subject raising into object position hinged on sentences such as the following:

(2) a.   You believe yourself to be intelligent.

Starting with an independently motivated restriction on the application of Reflexivization, we argued that for this rule to apply in the proper way in the derivation of a sentence like (2a), it was necessary that the deep structure subject of the lower S be promoted to object position in the higher S before the application of Reflexivization, The order of application of these two rules in the derivation of (2a), then, is necessarily the following: 1) Subject Raising; 2) Reflexivization.

Let us now turn our attention to another sentence in which both Reflexivization and Subject Raising are involved:

(3) a.   Bill believes you to like yourself.

Under the analysis we have adopted so far, the deep structure of (3a) would be the following:

(3) b.

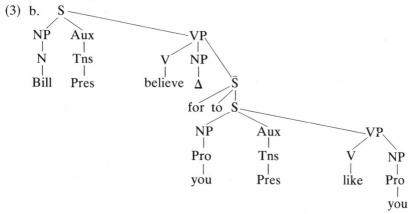

Suppose that we attempt to derive (3a) by applying Reflexivization after Subject Raising, just as we did in deriving (2a). After Affix Insertion, Subject Raising, and Complementizer Deletion, the structure in (3c) results.

(3) c.

When we attempt to apply Reflexivization to this tree, we find that we are prohibited by the clause mate condition, since the second occurrence of the pronoun *you* is found in an S that no longer contains the first occurrence. The best that we can do if Subject Raising is applied before Reflexivization is thus an ungrammatical sentence:

(3) d. *Bill believes you to like you.

On the other hand, suppose that we allow Reflexivization to apply before Subject Raising. The deep structure tree in (3b) satisfied the conditions for Reflexivization; application of the rule gives:

(3) e.

Affix Insertion, Subject Raising, and Complementizer Deletion now give (3f):

(3) f.

Affix Hopping and morphophonemic rules now apply to give (3a), *Bill believes you to like yourself*. We are thus able to generate (3a) only if we allow Reflexivization to apply before Subject Raising.

An apparent difficulty arises at this point. If we allow Reflexivization to apply first in the derivation of (3a) and Subject Raising to apply first in the derivation of (2a), we are forced on the face of it to abandon the Strict Order Hypothesis. It will be recalled that this hypothesis explicitly excludes the following type of situation:

(4)   Sentence (2a)   Sentence (3a)
    (1) Subject Raising   (1) Reflexivization
    (2) Reflexivization   (2) Subject Raising

What we might look for is some modified form of the Strict Order Hypothesis that would be consistent with the examples that we have just considered but would still have the desirable consequences noted in Chapter 5 for the analysis of simple sentences. One thing that we can note immediately is that the application of Reflexivization in the derivation of (2a) occurred in the higher sentence, whereas the application of the same rule in the derivation of (3a) occurred in the lower sentence. If we let S_1 refer to the higher sentence and S_2 refer to the lower sentence, then we can replace (4) by the following more detailed summary:

(5)   Sentence (2a)   Sentence (3a)

	Sentence (2a)	Sentence (3a)
S_1		Reflexivization
S_2	Subject Raising Reflexivization	Subject Raising

It appears that we may get the desired results if we find some way to specify as part of our syntactic theory that rules apply in lower sentences before they apply in higher sentences. Moreover, in the interests of retaining some of the desirable effects of the Strict Order Hypothesis, we might keep intact the part of the hypothesis concerned with the form of grammars. That is, we might maintain as before the following statement as part of our syntactic theory:

(6)   Part of the grammar of any language consists of a strict ordering of the transformational rules.

What we will modify is the convention that dictates how this ordering is to be interpreted in the derivation of sentences.

By way of preparing for the statement of a modified convention on rule application, let us introduce a new term:

(7)   For any S in a tree, the *transformational domain* associated with that S consists of the entire subtree dominated by that S.

For example, in the tree given in (8), there are a total of four transformational domains (see p. 182). The domain associated with S_1, the highest S in the tree, consists of the entire tree and includes all of the lower domains as part of it.

We can now state the modified convention as follows:

(8)

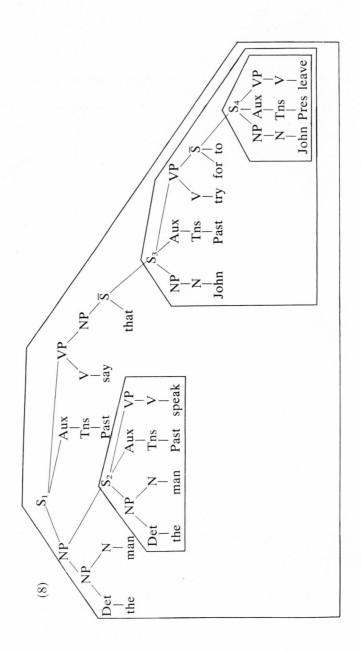

(9)   The Cyclic Convention
      Within each transformational domain in a tree, the transformational
      rules are to be applied according to the order given in the grammar,
      without any regard to material outside the domain in question. The
      rules are not to be applied in a certain transformational domain
      until they have been applied in all lower domains included within it.

   With respect to the tree in (8), this convention dictates that the sequence
of transformational rules must be applied in the S_4 domain before they are
applied in the S_3 domain, and in the S_3 domain before they are applied in the
S_1 domain. In addition, they must apply in the S_2 domain before applying
in the S_1 domain. The convention says nothing, on the other hand, about
whether the rules are to be applied in the S_2 domain before they are applied
in S_4, or vice versa. Silence on this matter is entirely proper, in view of the
fact that no linguistic argument has been found for preferring one of these
possibilities to the other.

   doesn't S_4 does not S_3... before S_3... imply that one only works from lowest S to the highest?

   Let us see what the effect of the Cyclic Convention is with regard to the
two sentences involving Reflexivization and Subject Raising. To begin with,
let us specify as part of our grammar of English that Affix Insertion and
Subject Raising are ordered before Reflexivization. The deep structure for
(3a) is repeated here for convenience.

   *¹ Affix Ins
   ² Subj Raising
   ³ Reflexiviz.*

(3) a.   Bill believes you to like yourself.

(3) b.

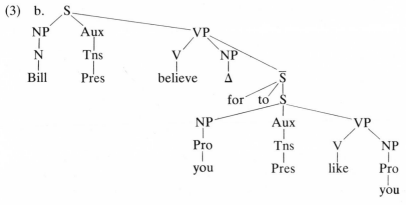

We begin by restricting our attention entirely to the domain of the lower S.
In this domain, the rules of Affix Insertion and Subject Raising cannot apply,
since in each case the structural description makes reference to parts of two
different clauses, one below the other. On the other hand, Reflexivization
does apply, changing the lower S as follows:

(3) g.

```
                    S
          _____/ |  _____
        NP       Aux          VP
         |        |         /  |  \
        Pro      Tns       V      NP
         |        |        |     /  \
        you      Pres     like  Pro   Refl
                                 |
                                you
```

Having run through the rules in the lower domain, we can now proceed to the higher one. The first rule applicable here is Affix Insertion. This rule is followed by Subject Raising, to yield:

(3)   h.

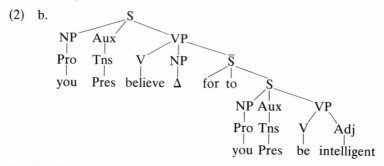

With the application of additional rules, this structure eventuates in the desired sentence (3a).

Turning back now to (2a), *You believe yourself to be intelligent*, we begin with the deep structure:

(2)   b.

Looking first at the lower domain, we see that none of the three rules that we have been concerned with (Affix Insertion, Subject Raising, or Reflexivization) can apply in this S. Proceeding to the higher domain, we now attempt to apply the rules in the order that we have specified in the grammar: 1) Affix Insertion; 2) Subject Raising; 3) Reflexivization. After the first two of these, the resulting structure is:

(2)   c.

This tree satisfies the structural description for Reflexivization; application of the rule gives:

(2) d.   you Pres believe you Refl to be intelligent.

Affix Hopping and morphophonemic rules finally yield (2a), the desired result.

What we have succeeded in showing, then, is that the apparent problem posed for the Strict Order Hypothesis by (2a) and (3a) is resolved by the adoption of the Cyclic Convention. The difference in the order of application of Subject Raising and Reflexivization in these two sentences proves to be a simple consequence of this convention.

7.2 A POSITIVE ARGUMENT FOR THE CYCLIC CONVENTION

In the preceding section we saw an apparent counterexample to the Strict Order Hypothesis, which ceased to be a counterexample when our theory of rule application was augmented by the addition of the Cyclic Convention. This section and the one following are each devoted to the presentation of arguments in support of this convention that are more positive. We will in effect be attempting to answer the question, "What justification is there for the Cyclic Convention beyond the fact that it gets the Strict Order Hypothesis out of trouble?"

The first of these arguments concerns the interaction between Identical-NP Deletion and Reflexivization. Let us suppose that we are provided with basic data that provide us with motivation for each of these rules separately, but that do not give us any indication of how the rules apply in structures in which the structural descriptions for both rules are satisfied. This set of basic data might include sentences such as the following.

(10)   (Providing evidence for Affix Insertion, Identical-NP Deletion, Complementizer Deletion)
  a.   You would like for Bill to leave.
  b.   *I would like for $\left\{ \begin{matrix} \text{me} \\ \text{myself} \end{matrix} \right\}$ to leave.
  c.   I would like to leave.

(11)   (Providing evidence for Reflexivization)
  a.   You shaved yourself.
  b.   *You shaved you.
  c.   You shaved me.
  d.   *You shaved myself.
  e.   I shaved myself.
  f.   *I shaved me.

(12)   (Providing evidence for the clause-mate restriction)
  a.   I would like for the barber to shave me.
  b.   *I would like for the barber to shave myself.
  c.   You know that Bill is avoiding you.
  d.   *You know that Bill is avoiding yourself.

We are now asked to judge the grammaticality of the following two sentences:

(13) a.   You would like to shave yourself.

   b.   You would like to shave you.

The relevant structure for both of these sentences (after the application of Affix Insertion) would be the following:

(13)   c.

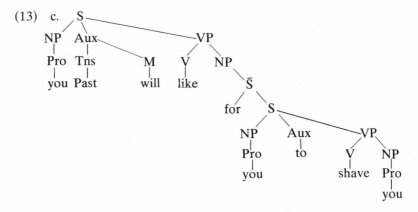

This structure is one that satisfies the structural descriptions of both Identical-NP Deletion (in the higher S) and Reflexivization (in the lower S). As indicated in our basic data, both of these rules are obligatory. If Identical-NP Deletion applies first, then the resulting structure, (13d), does not satisfy the conditions for the application of Reflexivization:

(13)   d.

The only noun phrase that could have triggered the reflexivization of the object of *shave* was the NP that has been deleted. The other NP in the sentence, the subject of the higher sentence, cannot serve to reflexivize the object of the lower S, since the two NP's, although identical, are not clause mates. Consequently, the sentence that results from applying Identical-NP Deletion first is (13b), which is in fact ungrammatical. On the other hand, it is easy to see that if Reflexivization applies first, the grammatical sentence (13a) will result.

We could of course account for the relative grammaticality of the two sentences in (13) by ordering Reflexivization before Identical-NP Deletion in our grammar. The difficulty at this point, however, is that there is absolutely nothing in the basic data given in (10–12) that would provide evidence in favor of this ordering. Even the Strict Order Hypothesis gives us no aid at this point, since it is relevant only in situations in which the basic data include at least one sentence resulting from the operation of both rules in question. Without some outside help, then, we must plead ignorance when asked about the grammaticality of the two new sentences.

Suppose, however, that our universal grammar includes the Cyclic Convention. With regard to the tree in (13c), this hypothesis requires that all relevant transformational rules be applied in the lower S before any are applied in the higher S. So we must apply Reflexivization in the lower S *before* we can apply *any* rule in the higher S, in particular, before we can apply Identical-NP Deletion. Thus, given the Cyclic Convention, we are able to predict that (13a) is grammatical. Likewise, we can predict that (13b) is ungrammatical, since it could be derived only by failing to apply a certain obligatory rule in a structure that satisfied its structural description. In sum, the Cyclic Convention enables us to extract two correct predictions from the basic data in (10) through (12) which we could not extract from the same data without the use of this convention. Consequently, the convention is supported.

7.3 PRONOMINALIZATION AND THE CYCLIC CONVENTION

The second of our positive arguments for the Cyclic Convention is based on pronoun interpretation in English.[1] We should note at the outset that several problems have been found with this argument since its original publication. However, because of its value as an example of the best kind of argument for a linguistic hypothesis, we will present it much as it was originally stated. We will then indicate one of the problems that has been noticed.

The basic transformational rule for our discussion is a rule posited in early transformational studies of English to account for the italicized pronoun in a sentence such as the following:

(14) a.   Jones will go to Paris and *he* will report to the ambassador.

We are interested in the interpretation of this sentence in which *Jones* is interpreted as the antecedent of *he*. The basic assumption in this early analysis is that the pronoun *he* originates in deep structure as a full noun phrase identical to its antecedent. Thus, the deep structure for (14a) would be:

(14) b.   *Jones* will go to Paris and *Jones* will report to the ambassador.

The required transformational rule is one that replaces the second of two identical full NP's by a pronominal NP. This rule may be stated very roughly as follows:[2]

(15)   Pronominalization

X – NP – Y – NP – Z
1   2   3   4   5
Condition: 2 = 4
⇒ 1, 2, 3, *Pro*, 5   (Optional so far)

Applied to the tree for (14b), this rule yields the structure in (14a).

Under certain conditions, the antecedent of a pronoun can be to the right of the pronoun rather than to the left. Consider, for instance, the following sequence:

(16) a.   The girl that *John* dates admires *John*.

If Pronominalization applies, then the resulting sentence is:

(16) b.   The girl that *John* dates admires *him*.

On the other hand, it is also possible in this instance to pronominalize the left-hand occurrence of *John*, giving a different result:

(16) c.   The girl that *he* dates admires *John*.

Roughly speaking, Pronominalization to the left is possible when the left-hand occurrence of the identical NP is found in a subordinate S, more precisely, an S that is subordinate to the lowest S that happens to dominate both of the identical NP's. In (17), which is the tree for (16a), this condition is satisfied.

(17)

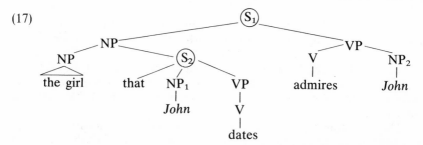

The lowest S that dominates both NP$_1$ and NP$_2$ is in this case just the top S (S$_1$). The left-hand occurrence of *John* (NP$_1$) is dominated by another S (S$_2$) that is subordinate to S$_1$. The following pairs of sentences offer additional illustrations of structures that satisfy the basic condition for leftward Pronominalization:

(18) a.   Whenever *Fred* goes to town, *he* stops to chat with the undertaker.
b.   Whenever *he* goes to town, *Fred* stops to chat with the undertaker.

(19) a.   Before *Jack* died, *he* was awarded a medal.
b.   Before *he* died, *Jack* was awarded a medal.

(20) a.   The girl that *John* dates believes that *he* has flat feet.

     b.   The girl that *he* dates believes that *John* has flat feet.

Let us look now at the Pronominalization possibilities in two structures that do not satisfy this condition:

(21) a.   *Oscar* believes that *Oscar* is unpopular.

(22) a.   *Oscar* wrecked *Oscar's* motorboat.

Forward Pronominalization gives (21b) and (22b):

(21) b.   *Oscar* believes that *he* is unpopular.

(22) b.   *Oscar* wrecked *his* motorboat.

By contrast, Backward Pronominalization cannot apply. Although we do have grammatical English sentences like (21c) and (22c), the pronoun *he* in each sentence must be understood as referring to someone other than Oscar:

(21) c.   *He* believes that *Oscar* is unpopular.   (*He* ≠ *Oscar*)

(22) c.   *He* wrecked *Oscar's* motorboat.   (*He* ≠ *Oscar*)

This fact about the interpretation of (21c) and (22c) follows from our condition on Backward Pronominalization.

Let us now consider the following additional examples of what appears to be Backward Pronominalization:

(23) a.   The fact that *he* is unpopular doesn't bother *Oscar*.

(24) a.   Alice's realizing that *he* is unpopular doesn't bother *Oscar*.

(25) a.   Realizing that *he* is unpopular doesn't bother *Oscar*.

The possibility of Backward Pronominalization in these sentences is not surprising, since each of the three satisfies the conditions for Backward Pronominalization outlined above. A problem becomes apparent, though, when we consider the corresponding possibilities for Forward Pronominalization. Whereas it is possible in the first two structures, it is not possible in the third:

(23) b.   The fact that *Oscar* is unpopular doesn't bother *him*.

(24) b.   Alice's realizing that *Oscar* is unpopular doesn't bother *him*.

(25) b.   *Realizing that *Oscar* is unpopular doesn't bother *him*. *(Oscar ≠ him)*

The last sentence is of course possible, but only if the pronoun *him* is understood as referring to some person other than Oscar. Thus, this sentence is not to be derived by Forward Pronominalization from a structure in which *Oscar* is the original object of *bother*:

(25) c.   Realizing that *Oscar* is unpopular doesn't bother *Oscar*.

At first glance, it might appear necessary to put a special condition on Forward Pronominalization. This condition would necessarily be rather complex, since it would have to prevent Forward Pronominalization from giving (25b), without, however, inhibiting the same rule in the derivation of (23b) and (24b). It would no doubt be possible to formulate such a complex condition and incorporate it into our grammar of English. However, we can explain this apparent peculiarity of English Pronominalization without adding such a condition if we make two additional observations about English and then invoke the Cyclic Convention.

The first additional observation is that Forward Pronominalization is obligatory in certain contexts. One of these contexts is that in which the right-hand NP is contained in a *that*-clause and the left-hand NP is in the immediately higher sentence. The sentences in (26) provide an illustration:

(26) a.   *Oscar* realizes that *Oscar* is unpopular.

b.   *Oscar* realizes that *he* is unpopular.

The second additional observation is that a rule whose effect is like that of Identical-NP Deletion is needed in our grammar to account for sentences such as the following:

(27)   Alice's knowing that Oscar is unpopular doesn't bother Bill.

(28) a.   *Bill's knowing that Oscar is unpopular doesn't bother Bill.

b.   Knowing that Oscar is unpopular doesn't bother Bill.

We can state the observation informally as follows: the subject NP of a gerundial complement in subject position is obligatorily deleted if it is identical with the object of the main verb.

We have now attempted to provide support for the following four statements as part of a grammar of English, independently of the particular problem sentence with which we are primarily concerned:

(29) a.   There is a rule of Forward Pronominalization, which replaces the second of two identical NP's by a pronoun.

b.   There is a rule of Backward Pronominalization, which can replace the first of two identical NP's by a pronoun. This rule may apply only when the left-hand NP is dominated by an S that is subordinate to the lowest S that contains both NP's.

c.   Forward Pronominalization is obligatory if the right-hand noun phrase is contained in a *that*-complement and the left-hand noun phrase is in the immediately higher sentence.

d.   There is a rule that has the effect of deleting noun phrases that are subjects of gerundial complements in subject position when there is an identical noun phrase as object of the main sentence.

Let us now examine the effect of these statements about English, taken together with the Cyclic Convention. The derivation of the pair of sentences in (23a–b) is straightforward. The deep structure would be roughly that given in (23c).

(23) a.   The fact that *he* is unpopular doesn't bother *Oscar*.

b.   The fact that *Oscar* is unpopular doesn't bother *him*.

(17) c.

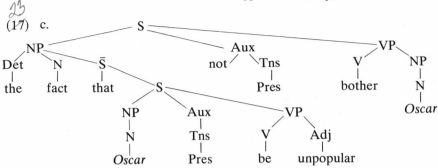

Looking first at the lower S, as the Cyclic Convention requires, we find that neither Pronominalization rule can apply, since this S contains only one occurrence of the NP *Oscar*. Proceeding then to the higher S, we find in this larger domain two occurrences of the NP *Oscar*. We may apply Forward Pronominalization, or, alternatively, we may apply Backward Pronominalization, because of the fact that the left-hand occurrence of *Oscar* is in a subordinate clause. Thus we account for the grammaticality of both (23a) and (23b).

The derivation of the sentences in (24a–b) is equally straightforward.

(24) a.   Alice's realizing that *he* is unpopular doesn't bother *Oscar*.

b.   Alice's realizing that *Oscar* is unpopular doesn't bother *him*.

The deep structure shared by both of these sentences would be essentially that given below:

(24) c.

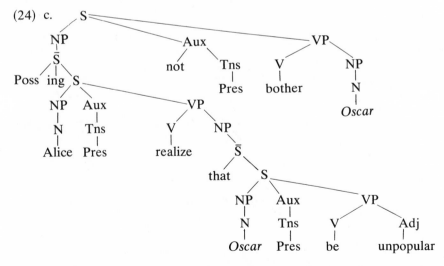

(The complementizer *Poss* will eventually be realized as the possessive ending on the subject NP of the complement, in this case, *Alice*.) Although there are three S's in this tree instead of just two as in (23c), the situation is essentially the same with regard to Pronominalization. Neither Forward nor

Backward Pronominalization can apply in the bottom S or the middle S; it is not until we reach the top S that we have a structure containing two occurrences of the same NP. As in the previous case, the conditions for Backward Pronominalization are satisfied, so that we have a choice concerning which Pronominalization rule to apply. Thus our grammar generates both (24a) and (24b).

The deep structure tree for (25a), that given in (25d) below, differs from the two previous trees in one significant respect: instead of containing only two occurrences of the NP *Oscar*, it contains three.

(25) a.   Realizing that *he* is unpopular does not bother *Oscar*.

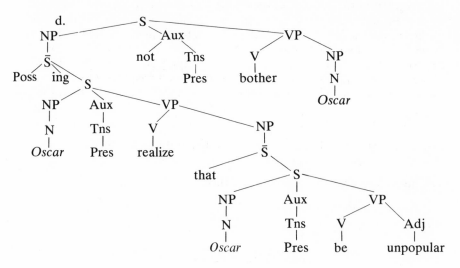

Clearly, neither Pronominalization rule is applicable in the lowest S in the tree. However, when we move to the next higher S, we have a structure containing two occurrences of *Oscar*. Backward Pronominalization is not applicable here, but Forward Pronominalization is not only applicable, but obligatory, by virtue of the third of the four statements concerning English Pronominalization. The resulting structure is given in (25e).

(25) e.

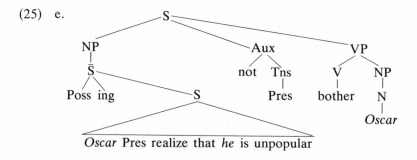

Oscar Pres realize that *he* is unpopular

Moving to the top S, we find that the conditions for the generalized version of Identical-NP Deletion are satisfied here. Application of this rule, plus other rules irrelevant to the present discussion, gives (25a) as a result;

(25) a.   Realizing that *he* is unpopular doesn't bother *Oscar*.

It should be noted that, contrary to first appearances, the derivation of this sentence did not involve Backward Pronominalization at all, but relied on an application of Forward Pronominalization effected by an NP that was then deleted prior to surface structure.

No such derivation is available for (25b):

(25) b.   *Realizing that *Oscar* is unpopular doesn't bother *him*.

There is no way of passing from the deep structure in (25d) to this sentence unless we violate either the condition concerning obligatory Forward Pronominalization or the Cyclic Convention. However, without the Cyclic Convention, the four statements on pronominalization would not block the generation of (25b) from (25d). Specifically, a derivation could be constructed in which Identical-NP Deletion applied at the level of the top S before Forward Pronominalization applied obligatorily in the second S. Such a derivation would have (25f) as an intermediate stage:

(25) f.   Realizing that *Oscar* is unpopular Pres not bother *Oscar*.

From this structure an application of Forward Pronominalization would yield sentence (25b). As a consequence, we would be led to the incorrect prediction that *Oscar* could be interpreted as the antecedent of *him* in this sentence. By contrast, if we adopt the Cyclic Convention as part of our universal grammar, such a derivation as the last is impossible. Thus, this convention provides an explanation for an otherwise puzzling aspect of the interpretation of (25b).

We can rephrase this argument in such a way as to show how, given a certain set of basic data, the Cyclic Convention allows us to make correct predictions about new sentences. We require a set of primary data that includes the following:

(a)   sentences providing evidence for a rule of Forward Pronominalization;

(b)   sentences providing evidence for the obligatory nature of Forward Pronominalization in certain environments;

(c)   sentences providing evidence for a rule deleting subjects of gerunds under identity with main-clause objects.

If we now invoke the Cyclic Convention, as a convention of our general theory that governs the application of transformational rules in all languages, we correctly predict that of the new sentences (25a) and (25b), only the former allows the interpretation in which *Oscar* and the pronoun are understood as referring to the same person.

At the beginning of this section we noted that a rather serious challenge has been raised to the assumption that Pronominalization applies cyclically. Although this assumption enabled us to explain the difference in grammaticality between (25a) and (25b), there are other instances in which it yields predictions that go directly counter to the facts. One such instance can be seen in the following two questions, both of which are grammatical:[3]

(30) a.   How many of the boys that know *her* do you believe that *Alice* likes?

b.   How many of the boys that know *Alice* do you believe that *she* likes?

The common deep structure for these two questions would be:[4]

(30)   c.

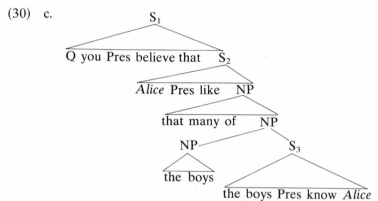

Since the lowest S (S_3) contains only one occurrence of *Alice*, neither Pronominalization rule can apply here. In the next higher domain in the tree, the S_2 domain, the conditions for Forward Pronominalization are met. Furthermore, Forward Pronominalization is apparently obligatory in this situation, as we can see by examining two declarative sentences that have essentially the same structure as the S_2 in (30c):

(31) a.   **Alice likes several of the boys that know *Alice*.

b.   *Alice* likes several of the boys that know *her*.

Application of Forward Pronominalization in S_2 gives (30d).

(30)   d.

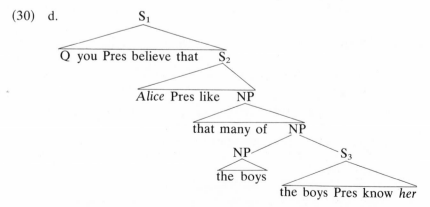

After application of other rules such as Relative Clause Formation on the level of S_2, we move to the top S and apply Subject-HV Inversion and then Question Movement. This last rule moves the object of the verb *like* to the left-hand side of the top S, yielding:

(30) e.

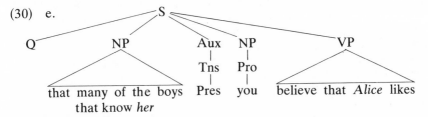

This structure is eventually realized as (30a).

A difficulty arises, however, when we try to construct a derivation for (30b). If we assume that the Pronominalization rules apply cyclically, then there is no way of deriving this question within the analysis of English developed so far. The specific problem is that the Cyclic Convention will dictate that Forward Pronominalization be given a chance to apply in S_2 before Question Movement is allowed to apply in S_1. Consequently, the Cyclic Convention appears to lead to the incorrect prediction that (30b) is ungrammatical.

We can avoid this problem if we abandon the assumption that the Pronominalization rules apply cyclically, and allow them to apply after all of the other rules have applied. The tree that would be relevant for the Pronominalization rules would then be as follows:

(30) f.

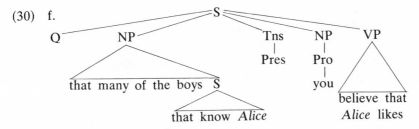

This tree satisfies the conditions for both Forward Pronominalization and Backward Pronominalization, the latter because the left-hand occurrence of *Alice* is contained in the subordinate clause *that know Alice*. Depending on which of these two rules is applied, we get either (30a) or (30b).

Although we can solve the problem posed by (30b) if we abandon the Cyclic Convention, such a step has an obvious cost. If we allow the Pronominalization rules to apply after all other rules have applied, then we must give up our earlier explanation for the impossibility of interpreting *Oscar* and *him* in (25b) as referring to the same person: *Realizing that* Oscar *is unpopular doesn't bother* him. The alternative assumption would lead us to refrain from applying Forward Pronominalization until after the stage shown in (25g) had been reached:

(25) g.   Realizing that *Oscar* is unpopular doesn't bother *Oscar*.

Since Forward Pronominalization could apply here, we would get just the interpretation for (25b) that we had hoped to avoid.

Thus we find ourselves facing a dilemma of a sort frequently encountered in any field of scientific investigation. A certain hypothesis appears to yield correct predictions in one situation while yielding incorrect predictions in another. As with any other dilemma of this sort, there are two basic approaches that can be taken toward resolving it. The first is to abandon the hypothesis in question, in this case the hypothesis that the Pronominalization rules apply cyclically, and then try to formulate an alternative hypothesis that leads to the same correct predictions while avoiding the incorrect ones. The second approach is to attempt to maintain the hypothesis in question by making changes in the other assumptions involved in the incorrect prediction, for example, in the specific formulations of one or more of the other rules that figure in the critical derivations. Both approaches have been taken in recent work; there is as yet no general agreement as to which is likely to prove more fruitful in the long run.

EXERCISES

1. In describing the infinitival construction in English, we postulated a deep structure that contained an underlying Tns. For example, we proposed to derive (i) from the deep structure in (ii):

(i)   John tried to sleep.

(ii)   John Past try $_\text{S}$[for to $_\text{S}$[John Pres sleep] $_\text{S}$] $_\text{S}$.

One of the necessary transformational rules was Affix Insertion, which replaced Tns by the markers *to* or *ing*:

(iii)   Affix Insertion

$$X - \begin{Bmatrix} to \\ ing \end{Bmatrix} - {}_\text{S}[\; NP - Tns - Y \;]_\text{S} - Z$$
$$1 \quad\quad 2 \quad\quad\quad 3 \quad\;\; 4 \quad\; 5 \quad\quad 6$$
$$\Rightarrow 1, 0, 3, 2, 5, 6 \quad \text{(Obligatory)}$$

Show that if this analysis is adopted, then the rule of Affix Hopping must not apply in accordance with the Cyclic Convention.

2. The following groups of sentences illustrate an English construction that has not been discussed in the text:

(i)   a. It is easy for Bill to please Bertha.

        b. Bertha is easy for Bill to please.

(ii)   a. It is tough to play sonatas on this fiddle.

        b. This fiddle is tough to play sonatas on.

        c. Sonatas are tough to play on this fiddle.

Following several current analyses, suppose that we postulate the following transformational rule for English:[5]

(iii)   Object Raising / *Tough Movement*

it – Aux *be* Adj – (*for* NP) – *to* – [X – NP – Y]
                                         VP   VP

    1   2   3   4   5   6   7

⇒ 6, 2, 3, 4, 5, 0, 7   (Optional)

This rule has the effect of taking some NP out of an embedded VP and substituting it for the sentence-initial *it*. We might propose, then, to derive (ib) in the following manner:

(iv)   a.   Deep structure

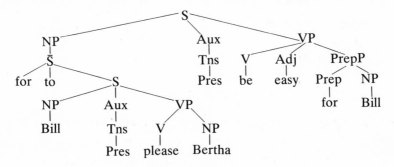

   b.   Extraposition and Affix-Insertion

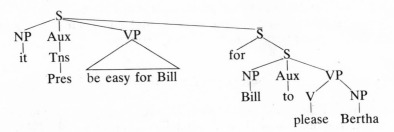

   c.   Identical-NP Deletion, Complementizer Deletion

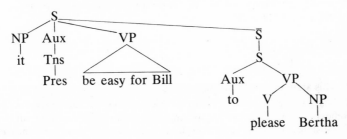

d.   Object Raising

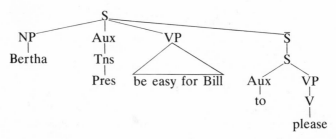

In Chapter 5 we proposed to account for variation in pronoun case in English by assuming that the nominative form was basic, and then introducing an objective case marker by means of the following rule:

(v)   Case Assignment

$$X - \begin{Bmatrix} V \\ Prep \end{Bmatrix} - Pro - Y$$

$$\begin{array}{cccc} 1 & 2 & 3 & 4 \end{array}$$

$$\Rightarrow 1, 2, 3 + Obj, 4 \quad \text{(Obligatory)}$$

Find an ungrammatical English sentence that shows the impossibility of maintaining simultaneously all three of the following propositions:

(vi)   a. Sentences such as (ib), (iib), and (iic) are to be accounted for in part by the Object Raising rule stated above.
   b. The variation in pronoun case is to be accounted for by means of the rule of Case Assignment stated above.
   c. Both Object Raising and Case Assignment are to be applied in accordance with the Cyclic Convention.

Suggestions for Further Reading

The idea of cyclic rule application owes a good deal to Fillmore 1963. The convention is stated in its now-familiar form in Chomsky 1965, Chapter 3. The best-known positive argument for the cycle is the pronominalization argument presented in section 7.3, which is given in Ross 1967b. Major difficulties for the hypothesis of cyclic pronominalization are noted in Postal 1970a, pp. 453–457.

Notes

1. This argument is due to Ross 1967b.
2. Here we encounter a difficulty of the sort that we encountered in stating a Reflexivization rule, that of ensuring that the appropriate pronoun is chosen. For instance, for *John* we want *he*, for *the woman from France* we want *she*, and so

on. Another problem, this one of a more technical sort, is that of ensuring that the pronoun that replaces the full NP is itself classified as an NP in the derived tree. In view of these problems and others, some authors (e.g., Jackendoff 1972 and Wasow 1975) have suggested that pronouns should be present as such in deep structures, and that interpretive rules should be given the burden of determining when two NP's in a sentence could refer to the same person.

3. This argument against the cyclic application of the Pronominalization rules was developed by Postal 1970a.

4. For the purposes of presenting this argument, we will assume that the interrogative word *how* originates in deep structure as the degree determiner *that*.

5. This analysis essentially follows that given in Rosenbaum 1967 (Chapter 6) and Postal 1971 (Chapters 3 and 13). The rule that is referred to in this exercise as Object Raising is frequently called "*Tough* Movement." An alternative analysis will be discussed briefly in section 16.2.

8

Constraints
on the Application
of Transformational
Rules

As we have seen in previous chapters, modifications in our universal grammar may concern not only the form of grammars, but also the manner in which grammars are interpreted. In proposing the Cyclic Convention, for example, we suggested no change in the form of grammar at all: the transformational component of a grammar would, as before, consist of an ordered set of transformational rules. What we suggested was a convention concerning how transformational rules apply in the generation of complex sentences. In the present chapter we will develop arguments for additional conventions governing the application of transformational rules, conventions of a more surprising sort.

8.1 THE COMPLEX-NP CONSTRAINT

In Chapter 4 we developed the following transformational rule for generating constituent questions:

(1)   Question Movement

$$Q - X - [\underset{NP}{} \text{Det} \quad Y \underset{NP}{]} - Z$$

$$1 \quad 2 \qquad 3 \qquad 4$$

$$\Rightarrow 1 + 3, \ 2, \ 0, \ 4 \quad \text{(Optional)}$$

As we saw, the questioned NP can be drawn from many different positions in a tree; this rule allows for these possibilities because the second and fourth terms are variables. However, if we allow this rule to apply without any constraint, we find instances in which it leads to the generation of ungrammatical questions. A first example is provided by tree (2a), which, as the underscoring indicates, satisfies the structural description of the Question Movement rule.

(2) a.

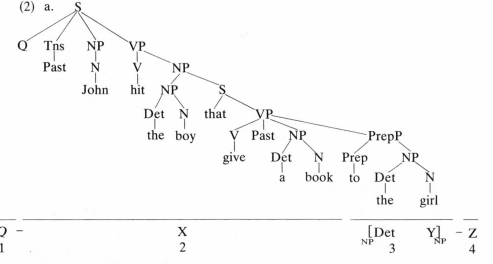

$$Q - \qquad\qquad X \qquad\qquad [_{NP} Det \quad Y]_{NP} - Z$$
$$1 \qquad\qquad\qquad 2 \qquad\qquad\qquad 3 \qquad\qquad 4$$

If Question Movement applies here, we eventually derive the following ungrammatical question:

(2) b.   *Which girl did John hit the boy that gave a book to?

As a first approximation, we might propose to append to the structural description of (1) the following condition:

(3)   The third factor (the NP to be moved) may not be contained in a relative clause.

Although this condition is unlike any that we have made use of previously, it does provide an account for the ungrammaticality of (2b). When we look further, however, we find an additional construction from which an NP may not be moved. This is the construction in which a noun such as *fact* or *claim* is followed by a sentential complement:

(4) a.   Bill acknowledged the fact that John kicked the man.

Suppose now that we begin with the following tree (4)b on the following page. As the underlining indicates, this tree satisfies the structural description for Question Movement. The movement of the NP *the man* is not blocked by the tentative restriction given in (3), since the subordinate structure in this tree is not a relative clause. However, if we allow Question Movement to apply

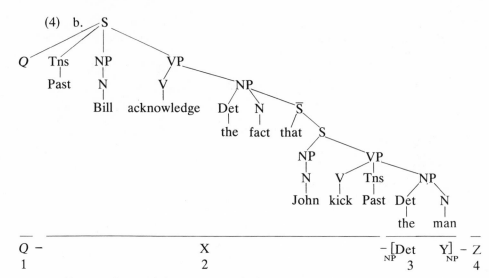

to this tree, the result is ungrammatical:

(4) c.   *Which man did Bill acknowledge the fact that John kicked?

The ungrammaticality of this question does not in itself show that the condition stated in (3) is incorrect. It does suggest, however, that we might attempt to find some property common to the relative clause construction and the sentential complement construction that would allow us to account for both of these instances of ungrammaticality by means of a single restriction. One possibility that might suggest itself immediately is to rephrase the restriction in such a way as to prohibit the rule from applying whenever the NP to be moved is contained in any kind of subordinate S. That this restriction is too strong can be seen by considering the following tree:

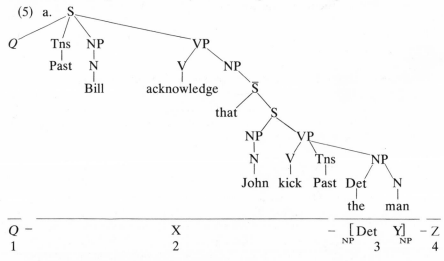

If we apply Question Movement in the manner indicated by the underlining of this tree, we find that the resulting question is grammatical, despite the fact that the NP to be questioned was down inside a subordinate S:

(5) b.   Which man did Bill acknowledge that John kicked?

Thus, we must allow Question Movement to move an NP out of an S in at least some instances.

One possibility that we might consider is that the property shared by the structures in (2a) and (4b) is that in both trees the subordinate clause containing the NP to be moved is dominated by an NP that dominates other material as well.[1] In particular, in both instances the other material in the NP is "lexical" material. In (2a) the additional material is *the boy*; in (4b) it is *the fact*. By contrast, the NP node that dominates the S̄ in (5a) dominates no other material.

Suppose, then, that we replace (3) by the following more general condition on the rule of Question Movement:

(6)   The third factor (the NP to be moved) must not be contained in an S or S̄ dominated by an NP if this NP dominates some lexical material in addition to that found in the S or S̄.

condition on Qstn mvmt

With this condition added, the rule of Question Movement does not yield the ungrammatical questions (2b) and (4c), but does yield the grammatical question (5b). What was true of the condition stated in (3) is also true of (6): incorporation of the condition into the structural description of Question Movement would require a change in the theory assumed to this point, specifically, a change in the types of structural descriptions allowed in individual grammars.

There are other transformational rules of English that would appear to lead to the same type of violation if a condition similar to (6) is not incorporated into their structural description. One of these is Relative Clause Formation, as can be seen from the ungrammatical sentences that result when the identical NP in the subordinate sentence is contained within an S that is dominated by an NP of the appropriate sort.

(7)   a.

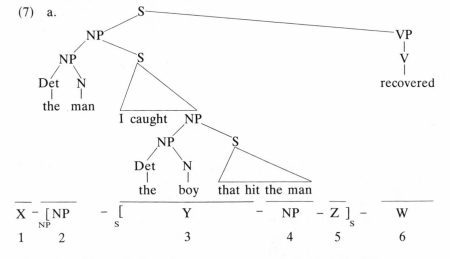

$$X - [NP]_{NP} - [_S \quad Y \quad - \quad NP - Z]_S - W$$
$$1 \quad 2 \quad \quad 3 \quad \quad 4 \quad 5 \quad \quad 6$$

(7) b.   *The man that I caught the boy that hit will recover.

(8) a.

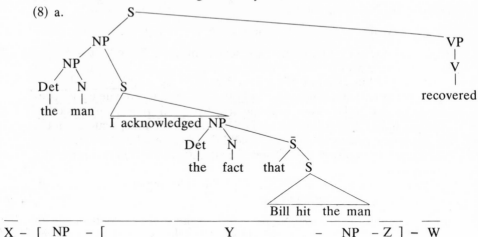

$$X - \underset{NP}{[} \text{ NP } - \underset{S}{[} \qquad\qquad Y \qquad\qquad - \text{ NP } - \text{ Z } \underset{S}{]} - \text{ W}$$

1   2   3   4   5   6

(8) b.   *The man that I acknowledged the fact that Bill hit will recover.

In order to prevent the generation of these sentences in the same way as we prevented the ungrammatical questions, we would require a special condition on Relative Clause Formation, of roughly the following form:

(9)   The fourth factor (the identical NP) must not be contained in an $\bar{S}$ dominated by an NP if this NP dominates some lexical material in addition to that found in the $\bar{S}$, and if this $\bar{S}$ is contained in the part of the tree assigned to terms 3, 4, and 5.

A similar sort of condition would also be required for a rule that we have not mentioned heretofore:

(10)   Topicalization

X – NP – Y
1   2   3
⇒ 2 + 1, 0, 3   (Optional)

This rule accounts for such optional variants as the following:

(11) a.   I like this picture.
     b.   This picture, I like.

(12) a.   No one is likely to buy that picture from you.
     b.   That picture, no one is likely to buy from you.

However, when we attempt to form topicalized sentences from the sorts of structures considered above, we find that the results are again ungrammatical:

(13) a.   I caught the boy that hit that man.
     b.   *That man, I caught the boy that hit.

(14) a.   Bill acknowledged the fact that John kicked that man.

　　 b.   *That man, Bill acknowledged the fact that John kicked.

For this rule, then, the following condition appears to be necessary:

(15)   The second factor (the NP to be topicalized) must not be contained in an $\bar{\text{S}}$ dominated by an NP if this NP dominates some lexical material in addition to that found in the S.

Instead of building a special condition into each new rule that appears to require it, as we did above, we might take a different approach to the problem and assume that sentences of the sort that we have been considering are ungrammatical by virtue of violating a general convention governing the application of transformational rules.[2]

(16)   Complex-NP Constraint

No transformational rule may apply in a derivation in such a way as to move a constituent out of an S contained in a complex NP, even though the structure satisfies the structural description of the rule.

With (16) proposed as a general constraint, that is, as a part of our universal grammar, we need to include no special conditions in our statements of the rules of Question Formation, Relativization, and Topicalization, but instead can leave them as originally stated. The explanation for the ungrammaticality of the six examples discussed above is then very simple. We need only observe that with the phrase structure and transformational rules that we have developed for English, there is no way of deriving any of the above sentences without violating the convention stated in (16).

Let us look in more detail at the role that this convention would play in explaining adult judgments on the basis of basic data. Suppose that we are provided with a large set of basic data from English, consisting of simple declaratives, constituent questions, and relative clauses. The simplest transformational grammar compatible with this set of basic data would contain phrase structure rules that assign a complex NP structure to a sequence such as *the boy that gave a book to the girl*. This grammar would also contain a rule something like (1) for the generation of constituent questions:

(1) $Q - X - [\text{ Det } Y]_{NP} - Z$

　　　　 1   2   3   4

　　 $\Rightarrow 1 + 3, 2, 0, 4$ (Optional)

Now suppose that we are presented with a question that does not appear in the set of basic data:

(17)   Which girl did John hit the boy that gave a book to?

Upon examination, we find that the rules of our transformational grammar do not yield for this new question any derivation that does not violate the Complex-NP Constraint. Therefore, this sentence is predicted to be ungrammatical, a prediction that turns out to be correct.

At this point, let us consider again the approach with which we began this discussion, in which we attempted to account for the ungrammaticality of (2b) by building a special condition of a novel sort into the structural description of the rule of Question Movement. Although this move would permit us to account for an adult English speaker's judgment that (2b) is ungrammatical, we would be left with a rather disturbing problem, namely that of finding something in the previous linguistic experience of the speaker of English that would force him to learn such a complicated condition. In point of fact, it would appear that no such evidence exists; specifically, (2b) is not the kind of question that a child might mistakenly utter and that a parent might then correct. Hence, the simplest grammar consistent with the child's basic data would almost certainly be one that did *not* contain such a condition on Question Movement. We would thus be left with no explanation for the fact that English speakers reject questions in which the questioned constituent is moved out of a complex NP.

By contrast, no such problem arises if we include the Complex-NP Constraint in our universal grammar as a general restriction on the application of transformational rules. By doing this, we assert in effect that this constraint represents part of the innate capacity common to all human beings, and thus that speakers of English show the effects of this constraint in the judgments that they make, without ever having had to learn it from the basic data provided by their environment. In proposing to include this constraint in our universal grammar, we also commit ourselves to the proposition that similar transformational rules in other human languages will be constrained in the same fashion. The studies that have been made to date appear to afford no reason for doubting the truth of this proposition: in every language investigated so far, the predictions derivable from the Complex-NP Constraint appear to be correct.

8.2 THE RIGHTWARD MOVEMENT CONSTRAINT

In Chapter 6 we introduced the transformational rule of Extraposition, which we formulated as follows:

(18) $[_{NP} \bar{S}\ ]_{NP} - X$
         $\quad\ 1 \qquad\quad 2$

   $\Rightarrow it,\ 2\ +\ 1$ (Optional)

This rule would account for (19b) as an optional variant of (19a):

(19) a.   That John is a scholar is obvious.
     b.   It is obvious that John is a scholar.

Additional sentences can be found that appear to support a slight generalization of this rule. These are sentences in which the *it* of Extraposition appears in object position rather than in subject position:

(20) a.   Arthur made *it* clear *that he would resign.*

(21) a.   I find *it* amusing *to listen to his stories.*

These sentences can be analyzed as arising from the following structures:[3]

(20) b.   Arthur made $\begin{bmatrix} & [\text{that he would resign}] & \end{bmatrix}$ clear.
$\qquad\qquad$ NP $\bar{\text{S}}$ $\qquad\qquad\qquad\qquad$ $\bar{\text{S}}$ NP

(21) b.   I find $\begin{bmatrix} & [\text{to listen to his stories}] & \end{bmatrix}$ amusing.
$\qquad\quad$ NP $\bar{\text{S}}$ $\qquad\qquad\qquad\qquad$ $\bar{\text{S}}$ NP

The only change that is required in the Extraposition rule is to add a variable first term:

(22)   Extraposition   (revised version)

$$X - \underset{NP}{[} \overline{S} \underset{NP}{]} - Y$$
$$1 \qquad 2 \qquad 3$$
$$\Rightarrow 1, \; it, \; 3 + 2 \quad \text{(Optional)}$$

Reformulated in this way, the rule can apply to (20b) and (21b) to give the corresponding (a) sentences.

Suppose now that we are given the task of determining the ways in which this rule could apply to the following tree:

(23)   a.

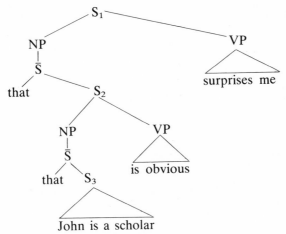

The structural description of the rule is clearly not met in the S_3 domain. In the S_2 domain, on the other hand, it is satisfied:

(23)   b.

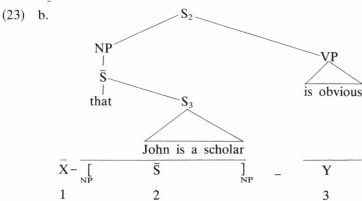

If the rule is applied, the following is the new structure for S_2:

(23)   c.

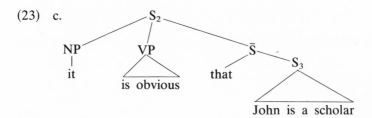

When we reach the S_1 domain, we find that the structural description for Extraposition is again satisfied:

(23)   d.

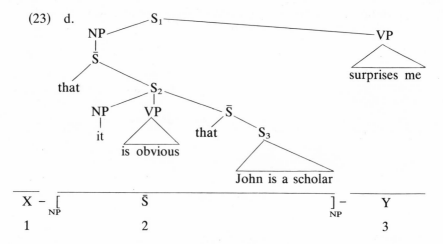

If the rule applies here, we eventually get:

(23)   e.   It surprises me that it is obvious that John is a scholar.

If the rule is not applied, the derivation yields a different result:

(23)   f.   That it is obvious that John is a scholar surprises me.

Both of these sentences are perfectly grammatical.

There is another, less obvious way in which the structural description of this rule could be satisfied. Suppose that we do not take the option of applying Extraposition in the S_2 domain, but instead proceed to apply the rules in the S_1 domain. As we saw before, the rule can apply in the S_1 domain in such a way as to move S_2 and its associated complementizer. But we can also divide up the tree in such a way that the $\bar{S}$ in the structural description corresponds to the lower $\bar{S}$ in the tree:

(23) g.

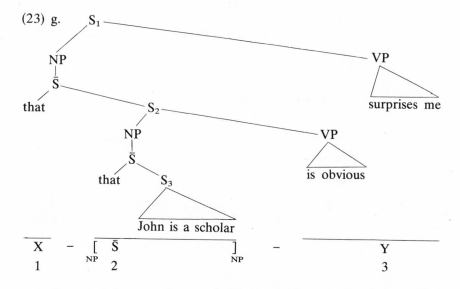

$$X \quad - \quad [\quad \bar{S} \quad]_{NP} \quad - \quad Y$$
$$1 \quad _{NP} \quad 2 \quad \quad 3$$

If Extraposition is applied in accordance with this division in the tree, the sentence that eventually results is ungrammatical:

(23) h.   *That it is obvious surprises me that John is a scholar.

Here, as with our discussion in the previous section, we might at first be tempted to incorporate some special condition into the rule of Extraposition. Instead of doing this, however, we might propose the following as another general convention:

(24)   Rightward Movement Constraint[4]
        No constituent may be moved to the right outside of the S most immediately above it.

In the derivation of the ungrammatical sentence (23h) we have violated this constraint: the lower $\bar{S}$ is moved to the end of S_1, and thus is taken outside of S_2, the S that was most immediately above it.

    In formulating this constraint as a general convention rather than as a special condition on the Extraposition rule, we would expect to find other rules that are constrained in their application by the same convention. Another rule of English that has to be constrained in the same fashion is a rule that we have not yet discussed, which we will refer to as *Relative Clause Extraposition*. This rule accounts for the (b) sentences below as optional variants of the (a) sentences:

(25) a.   The man left the stew that he had cooked there.
     b.   The man left the stew there that he had cooked.

(26) a.   The letter that Bob sent finally arrived.

b.   The letter finally arrived that Bob sent.

We may state this rule as follows:

(27)   (Relative Clause Extraposition)

$$X - [\underset{NP}{NP} - \underset{NP}{S}] - Y$$
$$1 \quad 2 \quad 3 \quad 4$$
$$\Rightarrow 1, 2, 0, 4 + 3 \quad \text{(Optional)}$$

The necessity for constraining the application of Relative Clause Extraposition can be seen by examining a larger structure such as the following:

(28)   a.

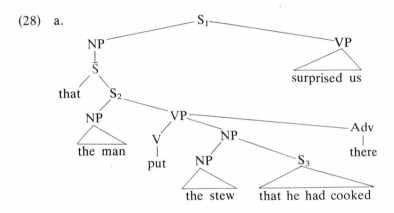

If we do not apply the rule of Relative Clause Extraposition, we simply derive:

(28) b.   That [the man put the stew *that he had cooked* there] surprised us.
           S_2 S_2

If we take the option of applying the rule in the S_2 domain, then the result is to move the relative clause to the end of S_2:

(28) c.   That [the man put the stew there *that he had cooked*] surprised us.
           S_2 S_2

Both of these results are grammatical.

Suppose now that we had not exercised the option of applying the rule on the S_2 cycle. Going to the S_1 domain, we find that the structural description is met again, in the manner indicated below:

(28) d.

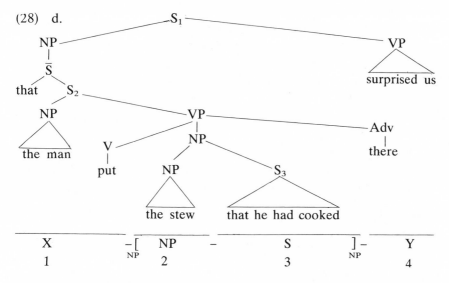

If the structural change is now carried out in accordance with this division of the tree, the relative clause is moved all the way to the end of S_1, giving an ill-formed result:

(28) e.   *That the man put the stew there surprised us *that he had cooked*.

An explanation for this negative judgment is provided by the Rightward Movement Constraint. In moving S_3 to the end of S_1, in conformity with the division of the tree given in (28d), we had to move S_3 to the right out of S_2, the S most immediately above S_3. This movement violated the Rightward Movement Constraint. Since there is no way of deriving (28e) that does not involve a violation of this constraint, the sentence is correctly predicted to be ill-formed. Thus we have found additional support for the constraint in the behavior of Relative Clause Extraposition.

Again, as with the Complex-NP Constraint, it appears that speakers of English are never confronted with any evidence, in the course of their acquisition of their language, that would provide a reason for incorporating the Rightward Movement Constraint into their system of rules for English. This fact gives us good reason to propose that this constraint belongs in our universal grammar rather than in our description of English proper. We are thus proposing that the constraint forms part of the general language faculty common to all humans, no matter what their native language happens to be. In making such a proposal, we naturally commit ourselves to the proposition that the constraint is operative in any language whose grammar contains rules that move constituents to the right. The research carried out to date has revealed few potential counterexamples.[5]

EXERCISES

1.   In the text, we noted that the ungrammatical sentence (i) below provides support for the Rightward Movement Constraint, assuming that Extraposition is reformulated as in (ii):

(i)   *That it is obvious surprises me that John is a scholar.   (= 23h)

(ii) $X - \begin{bmatrix} \bar{S} \end{bmatrix}_{NP} - Y$
       $\quad _{NP}\quad 1 \quad 2 \quad\quad 3$

$\Rightarrow$ 1, *it*, 3 + 2   (Optional)

Would sentence (i) have provided support for the Rightward-Movement Constraint if we had kept our original statement of Extraposition, that repeated in (iii)?

(iii) $\begin{bmatrix} \bar{S} \end{bmatrix}_{NP} - X$
        $_{NP}\quad 1 \quad\quad 2$

$\Rightarrow$ *it*, 2 + 1   (Optional)

Explain your answer in detail.

2.   When Relative Clause Extraposition applies to (i) in the manner indicated by the underscoring, it gives the ungrammatical result in (ii):

(i)

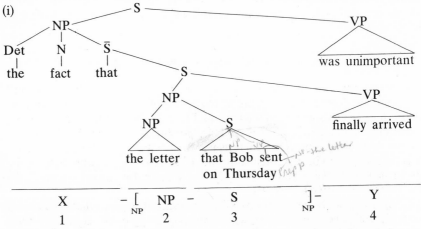

X	$-\begin{bmatrix}$ NP $-$	S	$\end{bmatrix}-$	Y
1	$_{NP}$ 2	3	$_{NP}$	4

(ii)   *The fact that the letter finally arrived was unimportant that Bob sent on Thursday.

This application of Relative Clause Extraposition clearly violates the Rightward Movement Constraint. Thus, the constraint yields the correct prediction that (ii) is ungrammatical. Nevertheless, this argument in support of the Rightward Movement Constraint is not as strong as the argument based on the ungrammatical sentence given as (28e) in the text:

(iii)   *That the man put the stew there surprised me that he had cooked.
        (= 28e)

What is the problem with arguing for the Rightward Movement Constraint on the basis of (ii) above? (Hint: Review section 8.1.)

8.3 THE LEFT-BRANCHING CONSTRAINT

An additional example of a situation in which a general convention may be called for is provided by a type of constituent question that we have not yet discussed:

(29) a.   Which senator's car did Bob steal?

We might assume roughly the following as the deep structure of this sentence:

(29) b.

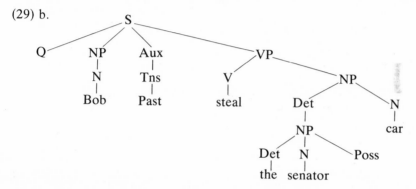

Application of Subject-HV Inversion would give the tree in (29c), a tree that satisfies the structural description of Question Movement:

(29) c.

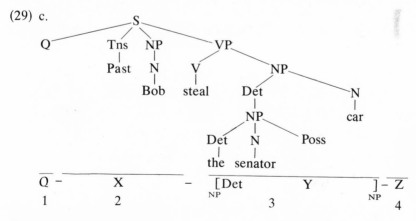

Application of Question Movement in accordance with the division of the tree eventually yields the grammatical question (29a) above.

Unfortunately, as Question Movement is now stated, there is a way of dividing the tree that leads to an ungrammatical sentence when the rule is applied:

(29) d.

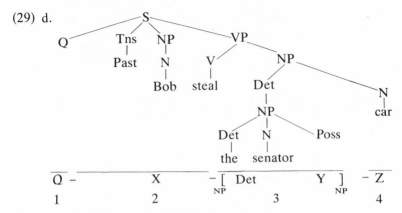

$$\overline{Q} - \qquad X \qquad - [\; Det \qquad\qquad Y\;]_{NP} \quad - Z$$
$$\qquad\;\; 1 \qquad\quad 2 \qquad\qquad {}_{NP}\; 3 \qquad\qquad\qquad 4$$

(29) e.   *Which senator's did Bob steal car?

In deriving this ungrammatical sentence, we moved only the possessive NP modifying the noun *car*, instead of moving the larger NP of which it was a part.

As a first attempt at solving the problem posed by (29e), we might propose to revise the rule of Question Movement as follows:

(30) a. $Q - X - [\; Det\; (N\; Poss)\; Y\;]_{NP} - Z$
$\qquad\quad 1 \quad 2 \quad {}_{NP} \qquad\qquad 3 \qquad\quad 4$
$\qquad \Rightarrow 1 + 3,\; 2,\; 0,\; 4$

The structural description for this rule breaks down into two cases:

(30) b. $Q - X - [\; Det\; N\; Poss\; Y\;]_{NP} - Z$
$\qquad\qquad\quad {}_{NP}$

    c. $Q - X - [\; Det\; Y\;]_{NP} - Z$
$\qquad\qquad\quad {}_{NP}$

We might again adopt the convention first mentioned in Chapter 3, which specifies that when both cases of a transformational rule containing parentheses are satisfied by a certain tree, then the rule must be applied in accordance with the division imposed by the longer case. In the present instance, this would force us to divide the relevant tree as follows:

(29) f.

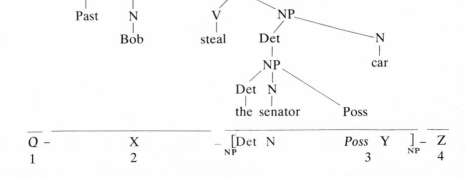

$$\overline{Q} - \qquad\qquad X \qquad\qquad - [Det\; N \qquad\qquad Poss\; Y\;]_{NP} - Z$$
$$\qquad\; 1 \qquad\qquad\qquad 2 \qquad\qquad {}_{NP} \qquad\qquad\qquad 3 \qquad\qquad 4$$

Application in this fashion would give the grammatical question with which we began this discussion: *Which senator's car did Bob steal?*

When we attempt to question an NP with a longer string of possessives, we find that even this reformulation of Question Movement is not adequate to prevent the generation of ungrammatical questions. For instance, let us attempt to derive constituent questions from the following tree:

(31) a.

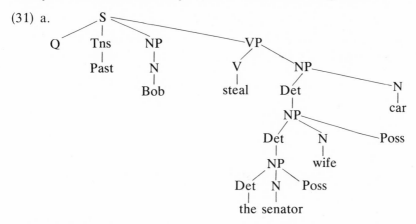

Since the longer of the two formulae in (30b–c) is satisfied by this tree, we must apply that subcase:

(31) b.   Q   Past Bob steal   the senator Poss wife Poss car

$$Q - \quad X \quad -[\underset{NP}{} Det \; N \; Poss \quad\quad Y \underset{NP}{}]- \quad Z$$
$$1 \quad\quad 2 \quad\quad\quad\quad 3 \quad\quad\quad\quad\quad 4$$

Application of the rule according to this division yields a grammatical question:

(31) c.   Which senator's wife's car did Bob steal?

But the same structure may be divided in a different way in conformity with the same subcase of the alternatively formulated rule:

(31) d.   Q   Past Bob steal   the senator Poss wife Poss   car

$$Q - \quad X \quad -[\underset{NP}{}Det \; N \quad Poss \quad Y \underset{NP}{}]- \quad Z$$
$$1 \quad\quad 2 \quad\quad\quad\quad\quad 3 \quad\quad\quad\quad 4$$

Application in accordance with this division again gives an ungrammatical question:

(31) e.   *Which senator's wife's did Bob steal car?

We are thus exactly where we started, again deriving an ungrammatical sentence by applying our rule in such a way as to move only part of the direct object NP. We could of course make the structural description for Question Movement even longer and more complicated, but no matter how complicated we made it, there would be some string of possessives long enough to create exactly the same sort of problem that we have seen already.

Let us investigate a different possibility, namely, that our Question Movement rule should be left as originally stated and that the burden of accounting for the ungrammaticality of sentences such as (29e) and (31e) should be shifted to some general convention on the application of transformational rules. As a first guess, we might propose the following convention:

(32)   No transformational rule may apply in such a way as to move one NP out of another NP.

Given a structure such as (31a), repeated below, this convention would prevent the rule of Question Movement from moving any NP except the entire direct object NP, the top node of which is circled:

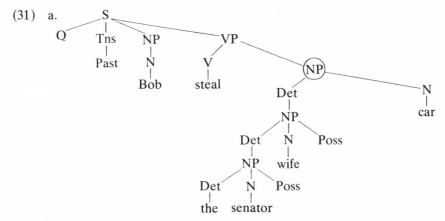

(31) a.

Movement of either of the two lower NP's, even though not forbidden by the structural description of Question Movement, would be blocked by the convention stated in (32).

As it stands, however, this convention is too strong. For instance, it would prevent Question Movement from applying to the following tree according to the division indicated, since this application of the rule would move the smaller NP, *the singer*, out of the larger NP, *a picture of the singer*:

(33) a.

It would thus incorrectly predict the following fully grammatical question to be ungrammatical:

(32) b.   Which singer did Shirley buy a picture of?

Exactly the right distinction for these examples is provided by the following constraint:[6]

(34)   The Left Branching Constraint
       No transformational rule may apply in such a way as to move the left-hand branch of an NP out of that NP.

This constraint prohibits the movement of either NP_2 or NP_3 in the tree on the left, but allows the movement of NP_2 in the tree on the right:

(35) a.   ...NP_1...   b.   ...NP_1...

It thus explains the ungrammaticality of (29e) and (31e) without interfering with the derivation of the grammatical question (33b).

At present, it is not clear whether or not the Left-Branching Constraint can be maintained as a general convention on the application of trans-formational rules. In particular, sentences have been found in Russian and Latin which are grammatical despite the fact that a questioned possessive is separated from the noun that it modifies.[7] It should be remarked, though, that both of these languages allow considerable freedom of word order, so that it is possible that the constraint applies even in these languages, with the separation of possessive and following noun being effected by a transform-ational rule, ordered after Question Movement, that produces certain optional word orders. Until the facts of these languages are studied more closely, the status of this constraint will not be clear. If further study of these or other languages showed that the constraint could not be maintained, its effects would have to be built specifically into the grammar of English. This would apparently require the addition of new types of rules or conditions to the specification of the form of grammar that we have developed in this text.

EXERCISES

1.   For each of the following ungrammatical sentences, indicate which of the constraints proposed in this chapter would explain the ungrammaticality:

(i)   *The fact that John told a story to Bill amused us that he hadn't read in the paper.

(ii)   *The man whose we found car was very grateful to us for filling the gas tank.

(iii)   *Which one of those books did Sheila marry the fellow who wrote?

(iv)   *The allegation that Bill sent the girl whose sister's Fred used to know husband to the company shocked us which Sheila married the man who owned.

2.   The ungrammatical (b) sentence below is not blocked by any of the constraints presented in this chapter:

(i)   a. John can ride a tricycle faster than Bill can ride that bicycle.
       b.*Which bicycle can John ride a tricycle faster than Bill can ride?

How might the Complex-NP Constraint be generalized so as to provide an explanation for the ungrammaticality of this question?

3.   Compare the following pairs of grammatical and ungrammatical sentences, and then suggest a single constraint that might account for the instances of ungrammaticality.

(i)   a. John went to town with Alfred and Bill.
       b.*Who did John go to town with Alfred and?

(ii)   a. We sent the man and the woman to City Hall.
       b.*The man that we sent and the woman to City Hall has disappeared.

(Sentences of this sort are discussed in Ross 1967a, Chapter 4.)

4.   In each of the following pairs of questions, the first is much better than the second:

(i)   a. Which movie star did Bill buy several pictures of?
       b.*Which movie star did several pictures of arrive in the mail?

(ii)   a. Which chest did the movers scratch the front of?
       b.*Which chest did the front of get scratched?

(iii)   a. Which friend was Martha upset at not seeing?
       b.*Which friend did not seeing upset Martha?

None of the constraints suggested in this chapter would lead us to predict that the (b) sentences above were less well-formed than the corresponding (a) sentences. Try to develop a constraint that would account for this difference.

Suggestions for Further Reading

The necessity of constraining the application of transformational rules was first pointed out in Chomsky 1964. The most influential single work in this area has been Ross 1967a. Chomsky 1973 develops an alternative body of constraints. Bresnan 1975 refines some of the constraints in order to solve problems posed by the English comparative construction. Several articles on particular constraints are worth reading. They include Kuno 1973, Grosu 1973 and 1974, Kaufman 1974, Kohrt 1975. An interesting alternative explanation for the impossibility of moving possessive NP's is given in Bresnan 1976.

Postal 1971 suggests a different sort of restriction on transformational rule application.

Notes

1. This suggestion is made in Ross 1967a, Chapter 4.

2. Minor details aside, this convention is essentially that proposed by Ross 1967a, Chapter 4.

3. It might appear at first glance that an analysis for (20a) and (21a) that relies on an optional Extraposition rule would be undesirable, in view of the ill-formedness of the sentences that arise from the structures in (20b) and (21b) when the option of applying Extraposition is not taken:

(i)   *Arthur made *that he would resign* clear.

(ii)   *I find *to listen to his stories* amusing.

But there are instances in which the failure to extrapose from subject position also gives bad results:

(iii)   a. *Why does *that the moon is made of green cheese* surprise you?
         b. Why does *it* surprise you *that the moon is made of green cheese*?

(iv)   a. *Ruth doesn't understand why *for him to go to Australia* would be undesirable.
         b. Ruth doesn't understand why *it* would be undesirable *for him to go to Australia*.

One account of the ungrammatical (a) sentences in (iii) and (iv) is to say that there is a *surface structure constraint* in English to the effect that sentential complements reduce the grammaticality of a sentence if they happen to be found in some "clause-internal" position at the end of a transformational derivation (Ross 1967a, Chapter 3). This constraint would account not only for (iiia) and (iva), but also for (i) and (ii), the ill-formed sentences with which we are primarily concerned.

4. This constraint is also due to Ross 1967a, Chapter 5.

5. Possible counterexamples are discussed in Kaufman 1974 and in Kohrt 1975. The first of these is based on Navajo, the second on German.

6. First proposed in Ross 1967a, Chapter 4.

7. Ross 1967a, Chapter 4.

9

Syntax and Semantics

So far in this book, the data that we have tried to account for in our description of English have been mostly of a single sort: a sequence of English words, with an associated judgment as to whether the sequence is or is not grammatical.[1] The following pairs of sentences with their associated judgments are typical of those that we have used as data for our syntactic description of English:

(1) a.   Are you working?
    b.   *Do you be working?

(2) a.   Jack should be able to go.
    b.   *Jack should can go.

(3) a.   The child seems hungry.
    b.   *The child seems sleeping.

(4) a.   John can't remember where he stayed.
    b.   *John can't remember where did he stay.

We have judged our syntactic description successful to the extent that it generates grammatical sentences such as the (a) sentences above, without generating ungrammatical sentences such as the (b) sentences.

During the first few years of work in generative-transformational grammar, it was primarily with this type of data that linguists concerned themselves. Within more recent years, attempts have been made to broaden generative descriptions of English in such a way as to account not only for judgments about the form of sentences, but also judgments having to do with their meaning and use. Judgments of this latter type are usually referred to as *semantic judgments*. We begin this chapter by cataloguing some of the semantic judgments that native speakers of English can make.

9.1 TYPES OF SEMANTIC JUDGMENTS

A first type of judgment that speakers of English can make is to decide whether or not two sentences presented to them are *synonymous*, that is, whether they "mean the same thing" or "convey the same message." A speaker of English can tell, for instance, that (5) and (6) mean the same thing, whereas (7) means something different from either (5) or (6):

(5)   John bought a book from Bill.

(6)   Bill sold a book to John.

(7)   John sold a book to Bill.

Similarly, he can recognize that (8) and (9) are synonymous, but that neither has the same meaning as (10):

(8)   John is a bachelor.

(9)   John is a man who has never married.

(10)   John is a widower.

A second type of judgment that a speaker of English can make concerns the number of possible interpretations a given sentence can have. For example, he can recognize that whereas (11) and (12) have only one interpretation each, (13) admits of two possible interpretations:[2]

(11)   Flying planes is dangerous.

(12)   Flying planes are dangerous.

(13)   Flying planes can be dangerous.

One interpretation of (13) is identical with that of (14):

(14)   It can be dangerous to fly planes.

The other interpretation is that associated with (15):

(15)   Planes that are flying can be dangerous.

In similar fashion, he can recognize that the first and second sentences below are unambiguous, whereas the third permits two interpretations:

(16)   The gift shop is near the river bank.

(17)   The gift shop is near the savings bank.

(18)   The gift shop is near the bank.

A third type of judgment concerns whether two sentences are or are not contradictory. We can illustrate this type of judgment by referring to the following three sentences:

(19)   John killed Bill.

(20)   John wasn't caught.

(21)   Bill didn't die.

The first two of these sentences are judged to be logically compatible with each other, whereas the first and third are felt to be contradictory. Related to this type of judgment is a judgment concerning what we might call "internal contradiction," contradiction within a single sentence. For example, whereas (22a) is a perfectly normal sentence semantically, (22b) is definitely not:

(22) a.   The man who killed Bill wasn't caught.
    b.   The man who John killed didn't die.

The judgment that (22b) contains an internal contradiction clearly has the same basis as the judgment that the separate sentences (19) and (21) are contradictory. We find a similar internal contradiction in (23b), as compared with the perfectly normal (23a):

(23) a.   That man has never been married.
    b.   That widower has never been married.

More subtle violations are illustrated in the following pairs of sentences:[3]

(24) a.   John kicked Harold in the arm with both feet.
    b.   John kicked Harold in the foot with both arms.

(25) a.   We bent the sheet metal.
    b.   We bent the blanket.

(26) a.   John is coming here to meet us right now.
    b.   John is going here to meet us right now.

Just as we require of a syntactic description of English that it generate precisely the grammatical sentences of a language, we will require of a semantic description that it account for judgments concerning synonymy, ambiguity, and contradiction. Many different proposals have been made in recent years concerning just how such a description should be framed. It would be impossible in a book of this sort even to give a brief survey of these different positions. Here we will simply sketch a general organizational scheme, and indicate how data of the sort illustrated above might be accounted for by a semantic description carried out within the terms of this scheme. The framework of assumptions that will be developed here can be summarized as follows:

1. Corresponding to each sentence of English, there are one or more *semantic representations*.
2. There is a set of *rules of inference* that operate on the semantic representations to yield predictions concerning actual semantic

judgments. These rules are a part of general linguistic theory, rather than belonging to one particular language.

3. There is a set of rules, *the semantic interpretive rules,* that associates the syntactic structure of each sentence with its semantic representation(s). These rules are in large part language-particular.

In the following sections, we will take up each of these three statements in turn.

9.2 SEMANTIC REPRESENTATIONS

The type of format that we will assume for semantic representations is that found in the logical notations developed in this century by philosophers and logicians. In using this notation, it is necessary to analyze English simple sentences into a *predicate* and one or more associated *arguments*. For example, in sentence (27a), the verb *kill* stands for the predicate, and the words *John* and *Bill* stand for the two arguments:

(27) a.   John killed Bill.

In translating a simple sentence of this sort into logical notation, we first write the predicate and then follow the predicate with the two arguments:

(27) b.   Kill (John, Bill)

Predicates that are like *Kill* in taking two arguments are often referred to as *two-place predicates.* As with many other two-place predicates, the order of the two arguments in a representation containing *Kill* is very important. Representation (28), in which the order is the opposite of that in (27), is to be interpreted as a translation of (29):

(28)   Kill (Bill, John)

(29)   Bill killed John.

A similar treatment can be given to simple sentences in which the most important element in the VP is an adjective, preposition, or noun. The following pairings of English sentences with corresponding logical representations illustrate the manner in which this is done:

(30) a.   Albert is fond of Victoria.
     b.   fond (Albert, Victoria)

(31) a.   Albert is in London.
     b.   In (Albert, London)

(32) a.   Albert is Edward's father.
     b.   Father (Albert, Edward)

The above sentences all involve two-place predicates. We also find

English words that designate one-place predicates (*die, tall, dunce*) or three-place predicates (*blame, between*):

(33) a.   Joe died.
     b.   Die (Joe)

(34) a.   Emily is tall.
     b.   Tall (Emily)

(35) a.   Horace is a dunce.
     b.   Dunce (Horace)

(36) a.   Jack blamed the accident on Sarah.
     b.   Blame (Jack, the accident, Sarah)

(37) a.   Chicago is between New York and Seattle.
     b.   Between (Chicago, New York, Seattle)

Following a well-established tradition, we shall refer to a predicate together with its associated arguments as a *proposition.*

So far, we have only attempted to deal with simple sentences. We must now decide what sort of logical representation to provide for syntactically complex sentences, for example:

(38) a.   John tried to kill Bill.

One possibility would be to analyze the proposition as consisting of a complex two-place predicate "try-to-kill":

(38) b.   Try-to-kill (John, Bill)

But this approach would commit us to setting up a vast number of additional complex predicates, one for every verb that can be embedded under *try*. It would be necessary to postulate *try-to-eat, try-to-prove, try-to-win, try-to-escape*, to mention only a few examples. An alternative possibility, the one most widely adopted in attempts to represent the logical properties of natural languages, is to say that certain predicates take propositions as one of their arguments. Under this approach, the verb *try* would still be analyzed as expressing a two-place predicate. However, the second argument, instead of being an individual such as *Bill*, would itself be a proposition in its own right:

(38) c.   Try (John, Kill (John, Bill))

A similar logical treatment is often proposed for certain English sentences that have been traditionally analyzed as simple sentences. For example, the logical structure of this negative sentence:

(39) a.   John didn't kill Bill.

might be analyzed as consisting of a one-place predicate *Not*, which takes the entire proposition *Kill (John, Bill)* as its single argument:

(39) b.   Not (Kill (John, Bill))

A similar analysis might be proposed for sentences containing certain adverbs:

(40) a.   John probably killed Bill.

    b.   Probable (Kill (John, Bill))

In fact, the logical structure just given is the same one that might be offered for the syntactically complex sentences (41) and (42):

(41)   It is probable that John killed Bill.

(42)   That John killed Bill is probable.[4]

In illustrating the kind of format that we will assume in attempting to represent the semantic structure of sentences from English, we have not given any particular attention to the predicates that appeared in the logical representations. In setting up a level of semantic representation for English, though, we will want to avoid using as our basic predicates just a large set of English nouns, verbs, adjectives, and prepositions. What we will propose instead is that the predicates appearing in these semantic representations must be drawn from a universal stock of *primitive predicates*, which, when combined in various ways, can serve to represent the semantic structure of any sentence in any language. In what follows, we will distinguish these primitive predicates by putting them in capital letters.

In some cases, there will be a close correspondence between the sense of a particular English word and the sense of one of the primitive predicates. For instance, a very likely candidate for a primitive predicate would be one that we can represent as NOT, a predicate that would appear in the semantic representation of most English sentences containing the English word *not*, and also in many sentences in which the idea of negation was expressed in some other way. On the other hand, there are other English words that should arguably be analyzed as corresponding to a rather complex structure composed of several primitive predicates. One such word is *kill*, which can be paraphrased roughly (and clumsily) by "cause to become not alive." Let us assume that our stock of primitive predicates includes elements such as CAUSE, BECOME, and ALIVE, in addition to the predicate NOT mentioned above. Then we can represent sentence (27a) by the formula given in (27c):

(27) a.   John killed Bill.

    c.   CAUSE (John, BECOME (NOT (ALIVE (Bill))))

In similar fashion, sentence (43a) can be given the representation in (43b):

(43) a.   Bill died.

    b.   BECOME (NOT (ALIVE (Bill)))

We can now make use of such representations to predict the first two types of semantic judgments that speakers of English can make. The actual conventions might be as follows:

(44)   Two sentences S_1 and S_2 are predicted to be synonymous if they share a semantic representation.

(45)   A sentence is predicted to be ambiguous if it has associated with it more than one semantic representation.

9.3 RULES OF INFERENCE

When we come to accounting for judgments of semantic anomaly and contradiction, however, we find that the representations by themselves are not enough. For purposes of illustration, we will attempt to give an account of the contradiction that speakers of English perceive in the following pair of sentences:

(46) a.   John killed Bill.   (= 27a)

(47) a.   Bill didn't die.

The semantic representations that we would assign to the two simple sentences are as follows:

(46) b.   CAUSE (John, BECOME (NOT (ALIVE (Bill))))

(47) b.   NOT (BECOME (NOT (ALIVE (Bill))))

It may appear that these representations are in themselves sufficient to account for the contradiction between (46a) and (47a). We look at the representations and immediately detect a contradiction.

But such an account is seriously deficient in one critical respect: it requires us to use our knowledge of the meaning of the English words *cause*, *become*, and *not* to interpret the primitive predicates CAUSE, BECOME, and NOT. Thus this account requires implicit use of the very kind of semantic knowledge that it purports to be characterizing.

What we must have, if we are to arrive at a fully explicit account of the contradiction between (46a) and (47a), is a set of *rules of inference*, universal rules that spell out the logical properties of the various primitive predicates. One of the rules of inference that we would want to have with CAUSE is a rule that expresses our informal intuition that if we are told that someone caused a certain state of affairs to come into being, then we are entitled to conclude that the state of affairs actually did come into being. We can translate this informal rule into the following rule of inference:

(48)   Let x stand for any argument, and let R stand for any proposition. Then the proposition CAUSE (x, R) entails R.

Another rule of inference that we will require here is one that tells us something about the primitive predicate NOT:

(49)   Let R_1 and R_2 be propositions. Suppose that there is some proposition R_3 such that R_1 entails R_3 and R_2 entails NOT (R_3). Then R_1 and R_2 are contradictory.

In order to make this definition work as generally as possible, we need one trivial rule of inference:

(50)   Let R be any proposition. Then R entails R.

We now have enough machinery to give a demonstration that the proposition represented in (46b) and the one represented in (47b) are contradictory:

(46) b.   CAUSE (John, BECOME (NOT (ALIVE (Bill))))

(47) b.   NOT (BECOME (NOT (ALIVE (Bill))))

First of all, we apply the rule of inference (48) to (46b) and get:

(51)   (46b) entails BECOME (NOT (ALIVE (Bill))).

Then we apply the trivial rule (50) to (47b), and get (52):

(52)   (47b) entails NOT (BECOME (NOT (ALIVE (Bill)))).

Now we have satisfied the conditions for applying the rule of inference (49), where we let R_3 be BECOME (NOT (ALIVE (Bill))). One of the two propositions with which we began, (46b), entails R_3, whereas the other proposition, (47b), entails NOT (R_3). Hence, by rule (49), we infer that (46b) and (47b) are contradictory.

We should note here in passing that both our semantic representations and our rules of inference are much too simple to give a fully adequate account of the semantic properties of sentences (46a) and (47a). A more accurate set of representations would for one thing require some sort of representation of the times of the events referred to in the two sentences, as reflected in the verb tenses. In addition, the one rule of inference that we have given for the concept of CAUSE is clearly not sufficient to characterize this predicate. A more complete account would include, among other rules of inference, one that would allow us to deduce from *John killed Bill* that some action of John's was a necessary condition for Bill's dying at the time he did, i.e., that without some specific action of John's, Bill would not have died when he did. To describe CAUSE and BECOME, then, as "primitive predicates" is not in the least to imply that it is a simple matter to state the rules of inference that should be associated with them. What we mean instead is that these predicates, with their associated sets of rules of inference, are available as units for the semantic representation and interpretation of sentences in all human languages.

9.4 SEMANTIC INTERPRETIVE RULES

Although we have succeeded in devising rules of inference that mark the propositions (46b) and (47b) as being contradictory, we have not yet succeeded in giving a full account of the contradiction felt by speakers of English between the corresponding plain English sentences (46a) and (47a). For this we need an additional set of rules, which we will refer to as *semantic interpretive rules*. The function of these rules is to provide a link between ordinary sentences and their semantic representations. In order to account for the present examples, we must establish a rule that associates any sentence containing *kill* with a corresponding semantic representation:

(53)   With a structure of the form
          NP$_1$ *kill* NP$_2$,
          associate a semantic representation of the form
          CAUSE (NP$_1$, BECOME (NOT (ALIVE (NP$_2$)))).

Similarly, we need semantic interpretive rules that assign representations to structures containing the word *die* and the word *not*. These rules operate to match sentences (46a) and (47a) with their respective semantic representations (46b) and (47b). The rules of inference now come into play, yielding the desired prediction that the two sentences are contradictory.

9.5 THE INTERACTION OF SYNTAX AND SEMANTICS: AN EARLY PROSPECT

In the foregoing discussion of the form that a semantic description might take, we have given a much-simplified picture of both the semantic interpretive rules required to match sentences with their semantic representations and the semantic representations themselves. This brief sketch, however, is sufficient to permit us to discuss a question that has received a great deal of attention ever since the beginning of generative studies of syntax and semantics. The question can be put as follows: On what types of structures do semantic interpretive rules operate? Early investigators noted that there were a number of logical possibilities: they could operate on deep structures, on surface structures, on structures intermediate between deep and surface structures, or on some combination of different levels. In addition, certain semantic rules might be associated with specific optional transformations, so that the semantic representation of a sentence would be altered in some way if a certain transformational rule was applied in the course of its derivation.

It became clear very soon that some interpretive rules can apply most effectively if they apply to deep structures. Rule (53), which plays a role in the interpretation of sentences containing the verb *kill*, is one such rule. To see this, we need only examine the variety of different surface forms found in the following sentences:

(54)   Bill killed the man.

(55)   The man was killed by Bill.

(56)   The man that Bill killed was a resident of Tennessee.

(57)   The man was hard for Bill to kill.

Despite the fact that the same activity is involved in each of these sentences, sentence (54) is the only one whose surface structure permits application of rule (53). If we were to insist on making semantic interpretive rules operate exclusively on surface structure, we would find it necessary to devise additional rules for specifying the semantic structure of the verb *kill*. In fact, each

of the three additional sentences would almost certainly require an interpretive rule of its own.

On the other hand, suppose that rule (53) is understood as operating
at the level of deep structure. According to the analysis developed in previous
chapters, sentences (54) and (55) share a common deep structure:

(58)

```
                        S
              /         |         \
            NP         Aux        VP
            |           |        /    \
            N          Tns      V      NP
            |           |       |    /    \
           Bill        Past    kill Det    N
                                    |      |
                                   the    man
```

In addition, essentially the same structure is to be found as part of the deep
structure of the complex sentences (56) and (57). Rule (53) can thus apply
in the interpretation of every one of these sentences, if it is allowed to apply
at the level of deep structure.

It would appear, then, that at least some aspects of semantic interpretation are best accounted for by having interpretive rules apply to deep
structures. We might now ask whether we can account for *all* semantic
properties of English sentences by interpretive rules that apply to deep
structures. The answer to this question clearly depends on the particular
proposals that we make in the syntactic analysis of English. Given the
analysis developed in the early chapters of this book, the answer must be
negative. The reason is that the treatment of questions proposed in Chapter
4 requires a semantic rule that is sensitive to the application of an optional
rule. In the analysis proposed there, all three of the following semantically
distinct questions share the deep structure given in (62):

(59)   Which man sank the boat?

(60)   Which boat did the man sink?

(61)   Did the man sink the boat?

(62)

```
                        S
         /        /      |        \
        Q        NP     Aux        VP
              /    \     |        /    \
            Det     N   Tns      V      NP
            |       |    |       |    /    \
           the     man  Past    sink Det    N
                                    |      |
                                   the    boat
```

In order for an adequate semantic description to be built on this syntactic
analysis, it would be necessary to set up an interpretive rule that was sensitive
to whether the rule of Question Movement was applied, and, if the rule was
applied, which NP in the tree was moved.

The form of linguistic description required by our original analysis,
including our analysis of questions, can thus be represented schematically

as in (63). For convenience, we shall refer to this as the "multiple input framework."

(63)   Multiple Input Framework

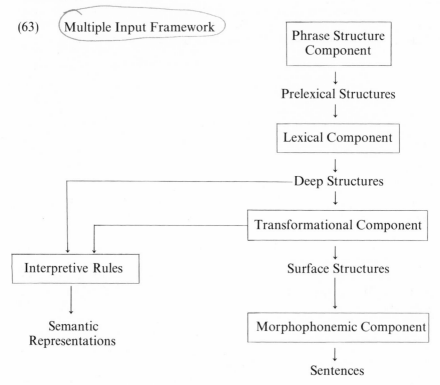

In a work that made a very deep impression on generative descriptive practice in the ensuing years, Katz and Postal (1964) proposed that the operation of the transformational component should have no effect on the semantic interpretation of sentences. What they proposed was a descriptive framework in which the set of interpretive rules requires no information other than that found in deep structure. Their proposed framework is represented schematically in (64) on the following page. For convenience, we will refer to it as the "deep structure framework." As the diagram indicates, their framework was distinguished by the fact that it did not allow any description to contain an interpretive rule whose operation depended in any way on the workings of the transformational rules.

As we have already noted, our original description of questions does not satisfy the requirements of this more restricted framework. It will be instructive at this point to see what changes are necessary in our analysis if we are to arrive at a description in conformity with the deep structure framework. The new analysis that we will suggest here is similar in all essentials to the one that Katz and Postal proposed themselves.

(64)   Deep Structure Framework

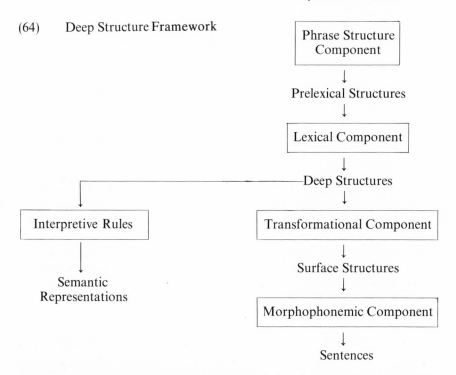

We will attempt to develop an analysis in which the following three questions have distinct deep structures:

(65)   a.   Which man sank the boat?

(66)   a.   Which boat did the man sink?

(67)   a.   Did the man sink the boat?

One such analysis is obtained by allowing *which* as a possible deep-structure determiner, along with *the*, *that*, etc. In this analysis, the respective deep structures of the three sentences above would be as follows:

(65)   b.

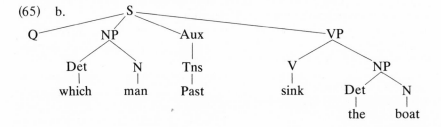

(66) b.

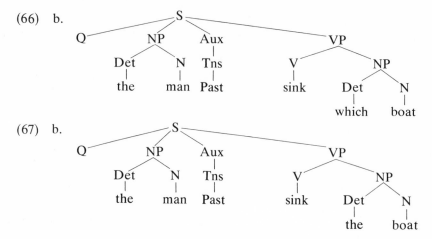

(67) b.

The differing interpretations of the three questions can now be accounted for by an interpretive rule that is sensitive to which NP, if any, in a sentence contains an interrogative word such as *which*.

This new proposal concerning the deep structure of questions requires a revision in the rule of Question Movement. The rule as originally stated was optional; it moved a random NP to initial position in a tree containing the question-marker *Q*. The new version of the rule will be stated in such a way that it can move a constituent only if the constituent contains an underlying *which*; moreover, the rule must apply obligatorily to any structure that does contain such an NP.

(68) $Q - X - [\ which\ Y\ ] - Z$
        $_{NP}_{NP}$
        1   2   3   4
        $\Rightarrow$ 3, 2, 0, 4   (Obligatory)

The only constituent in (65b) that rule (68) can move is the subject NP. It cannot move the object NP because this NP does not contain the determiner *which*. In (66b) just the reverse is true: only the object NP can be fronted. Finally, in (67b) neither NP can be fronted, and we get a simple yes-no question as a result. At least as regards these three sentences, then, the new analysis, unlike the old, is consistent with the deep structure framework.

So far, we have not said anything about the significance of adopting the deep structure framework instead of the multiple input framework. The first thing that we should take note of is that the former is *more restrictive* than the latter. In other words, for any body of data that we might try to describe, the multiple input framework will allow at least as many descriptions, and usually more, than the deep structure framework. As a concrete example, both our old analysis of questions and our new analysis are permitted in the multiple input framework, whereas only the new analysis is permitted within the deep structure framework.

Should this greater restrictiveness of the deep structure framework be counted as an advantage or a disadvantage? The only way to give even a tentative answer to this question is to compare the descriptions that the more restrictive framework allows with the descriptions that it excludes. In the present context, we are naturally led to compare the new analysis of questions, which is permitted by the deep structure framework, with the Chapter 4 analysis, which is excluded. If the new analysis emerges as the stronger of the two, then we would have one piece of evidence that the restriction is a healthy one, since the analysis that we would in effect be "throwing away" in advance would apparently be one that we would be better off without. On the other hand, suppose that the Chapter 4 analysis were to emerge as the stronger of the two. Then we would have reason to view the restriction as a harmful one, in that it would force us to throw away in advance the better analysis and allow an inferior one.

Both analyses are consistent with all of the data on questions that we have considered so far. However, there is one important group of grammatical English questions that are accounted for automatically in the new analysis but not in the original. These are questions in which more than a single noun phrase is questioned:

(69) a.   Which man sank which boat?

(70) a.   Which book did John give to which policeman?

In the new analysis, the element *which* may be inserted by the phrase structure rules as the determiner into noun phrases in any position, and into any number of noun phrases within a single sentence. Consequently, questions such as (69a) and (70a) will automatically be generated, by way of the deep structures in (69b) and (70b):

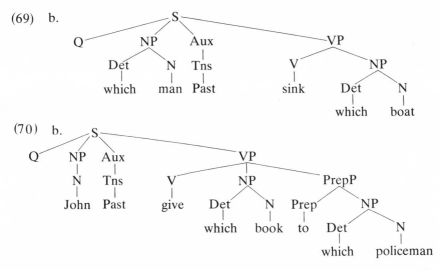

In the old analysis, by contrast, questions (69a) and (70a) are not generated. This analysis allows for at most one questioned constituent per sentence, namely, the constituent that happens to be moved to the front and incorporated into the Q constituent. Thus, of the two descriptions that we have considered here, the one that the more restrictive framework allows appears in fact to be superior to the one that it does not allow. Consequently, the adoption of this more restrictive framework has found some small measure of support in that the specific direction in which it forces the analysis of English questions appears to be a beneficial one.

In studying other constructions, we may find little difference in the adequacy of descriptions that satisfy the restrictions of the deep structure framework and descriptions that do not. Such constructions would provide no evidence in favor of either framework as against the other. We may also, however, find data from English or from some other language that are best accounted for by a description that is inconsistent with the more restricted framework. Such data, which force the deep structure framework in its strict form to be abandoned, have in fact been found in English. We will discuss these data, and the difficulty that they pose for the narrow framework, in Chapter 15.

EXERCISES

1. Describe as fully as you can the differences between the verb *kill* and the verb *murder*. In particular, try to describe as carefully and generally as possible the much more restricted conditions in which *murder* can be used correctly.

2. Suppose that LIQUID is one of our primitive predicates, and suppose that we represent the sense of the intransitive use of *melt* in the following interpretive rule:

NP *melt* → BECOME (LIQUID (NP))

How is this rule as it stands insufficient to account for our interpretation of English intransitive sentences with *melt*?

3. Study the following two informal definitions of the intransitive verb *soften*:

(i)   become soft
(ii)   become softer

Which of these is a more accurate paraphrase? Support your answer with examples.

4. Suppose that an objection were raised to our use of English words spelled in capital letters to designate the primitive predicates that are by assumption drawn from a universal stock of such predicates. Show that this objection is baseless, by showing that we could get exactly the same consequences as we obtained in sections 2, 3, and 4 if we were to replace CAUSE, BECOME, NOT, and ALIVE, wherever they occur, by $P_1, P_2, P_3,$ and P_4, respectively. What are the new semantic representations for the sentences *John killed Bill* and *Bill didn't die*? What are the revised rules of inference? What is the semantic interpretive rule that replaces (53)?

Suggestions for Further Reading

Katz and Fodor 1963 was the first work to address itself to the problem of developing a semantic framework that would interact with a generative-transformational syntactic framework. Katz and Postal 1964 elaborated this framework further. As noted in the text, they gave special attention to the possibility of having all semantic interpretation done at the level of deep structure. Criticisms of these early efforts are given in Bolinger 1965 and in Weinreich 1966.

The type of semantic representation sketched in the present chapter is close to that found in Reichenbach 1947 and McCawley 1968a. Interesting discussions of primitive predicates are found in Zwicky 1973 and Jackendoff 1976.

A sizable number of informal works in the semantics of English have appeared in recent years. Examples of the best work of this type are provided by Fillmore 1966, 1970, 1971; and Karttunen 1971.

Notes

1. The major exception was our attempt in Chapter 7 to account for possibilities of identical reference between pronouns and full NP's.

2. In early works in generative syntax, judgments about ambiguities of this type were cited as evidence in favor of the transformational framework. See, for example, Chomsky 1957, Chapter 8, and Chomsky 1964.

3. For detailed discussions of these three pairs of sentences, see McCawley 1970b, Fillmore 1970, and Fillmore 1966, respectively.

4. The words *probably* and *probable* furnish an example of a pair of words that represent the same predicate despite a difference in the part-of-speech class to which they belong. There is no significance in the fact that we used *Probable* to designate this predicate in (40b) rather than *Probably* or some other symbol.

10

Further Uses of Features

In Chapter 2 we made some initial suggestions concerning the manner of representing information about the syntactic behavior of individual words. We adopted the view that there is a distinct component of a generative grammar, the *lexical component*, in which are found the words of a language, each word accompanied by a set of features indicating the types of tree environments into which it may be inserted. In this chapter we discuss several other types of information about individual words, information that must be included if certain types of ungrammatical sentences are to be avoided. We also discuss some revisions in the type of treatment proposed in the earlier chapters for the categories of number and case.

10.1 INHERENT FEATURES: THE COUNT-MASS DISTINCTION

A great many types of lexical features find a clear motivation when we attempt to determine the role or roles that certain distinctions of traditional grammatical theory play in the grammar of English and the grammars of other languages. As a first example, let us consider the distinction traditionally made between *count nouns* and *mass nouns*. One basic reason for distinguishing these two classes is implied by the term "count": count nouns such as *book* and *spoon* can occur with numerals such as *one*, *two*, and *thirty-six* and with other special quantity words such as *several*, *many*, and *every*:

(1)   John read $\left\{\begin{array}{l}\text{one}\\\text{every}\end{array}\right\}$ book.

(2)   John read $\left\{\begin{array}{l}\text{two}\\\text{many}\\\text{several}\end{array}\right\}$ books.

On the other hand, a mass noun such as *sand* or *water* cannot occur in these environments:[1]

(3)   *Bob spilled $\left\{\begin{array}{l}\text{one}\\\text{every}\end{array}\right\} \left\{\begin{array}{l}\text{sand}\\\text{water}\end{array}\right\}$.

(4)   *Bob spilled $\left\{\begin{array}{l}\text{three}\\\text{many}\\\text{several}\end{array}\right\} \left\{\begin{array}{l}\text{sands}\\\text{waters}\end{array}\right\}$.

Certain other quantity words, including *much* and *little*, show exactly the opposite distribution:

(5)   *John didn't spill much $\left\{\begin{array}{l}\text{book}\\\text{books}\end{array}\right\}$.

(6)   John didn't spill much $\left\{\begin{array}{l}\text{sand}\\\text{water}\end{array}\right\}$.

We can represent this distinction by including a feature ⟨count⟩ in the lexical entries of English nouns, assigning the value ⟨+count⟩ to *book* and *spoon* and ⟨−count⟩ to *sand* and *water*. We now include contextual features in the lexical entries of quantity words. For example, with *one*, *three*, *many*, and *several* we include the feature ⟨——⟨+count⟩⟩. This feature will be interpreted as indicating that these words can be inserted only into an NP in front of a noun that carries the feature ⟨+count⟩. On the other hand, a quantity-word such as *much* will have associated with it the feature ⟨——⟨−count⟩⟩, indicating that it can be inserted only before a mass noun.

Another part of English grammar in which the count-mass distinction is significant concerns the distribution of the word *one* in its use as an optional noun-replacement.[2] This use is exemplified below:

(7) a.   Fred owns an old *car* and a new *car*.

   b.   Fred owns an old *car* and a new *one*.

Let us propose, as a first approximation, the following transformational rule:

(8)   *One* Substitution   (preliminary version)

   X – N – Y – N – Z
   1   2   3   4   5
   Condition : 2 = 4
   ⇒ 1, 2, 3, *one*, 5   (Optional)

This first approximation is too general in one important respect: in addition to yielding the grammatical sentence (7b) above, it also allows the derivation of the ungrammatical sentences (9b) and (10b):

(9) a.   The *mud* on his boot was darker than the *mud* on his coat.

     b.   *The *mud* on his boot was darker than the *one* on his coat.

(10) a.   We'll finish using this *stuff* before we start using that *stuff*.

     b.   *We'll finish using this *stuff* before we start using that *one*.

Let us add to the rule the requirement that the replaced noun be a count noun:

(11)   *One* Substitution   (preliminary version)

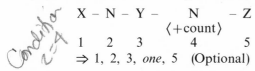

$$X - N - Y - \quad N \quad - Z$$
$$\langle +\text{count} \rangle$$
$$1 \quad 2 \quad 3 \quad \quad 4 \quad \quad 5$$
$$\Rightarrow 1, \ 2, \ 3, \ one, \ 5 \quad \text{(Optional)}$$

Revised in this way, the rule still allows us to derive (7b), but blocks the derivation of (9b) and (10b). Thus, the count-mass distinction plays an essential role in a second area of English grammar.

EXERCISES

1.   Show that the words *trousers* and *clothes* pose difficulties for the analysis suggested in the preceding section, whether they are marked with the feature ⟨+count⟩ or with the feature ⟨−count⟩. How might one revise and/ or expand the analysis in order to avoid these difficulties?

2.   Think of as many examples as you can of English nouns that may be used either as mass nouns or count nouns. Then look in Jespersen 1965, pp. 198–201, and compare your list with the one that appears there.

10.2 INHERENT FEATURES: GENDER DISTINCTIONS

A second example of a traditional category that might be incorporated into generative grammar by means of lexical features is the category of "gender" in nouns. In many modern European languages, as in older stages of English, adjectives, demonstratives, and articles do not have a single invariable form as in Modern English. Instead, the form that they take is determined in part by the particular noun with which they are associated. For example, in French we can find many pairs such as *crime* ('crime') vs. *rime* ('rhyme'), which despite their similarity in form require entirely different sets of modifying words:

(12)   *Ce* crime était *ingénieux*.   'That crime was ingenious.'

(13)   *Cette* rime était *ingénieuse*.   'That rhyme was ingenious.'

These sentences illustrate the difference in form of a demonstrative (*ce* vs.

cette) and an adjectival modifier (*ingénieux* vs. *ingénieuse*). We also find differences in the definite article (*le crime* vs. *la rime*), the indefinite article (*un crime* vs. *une rime*), and possessive modifiers (*son crime* ['his/her crime'] vs. *sa rime* ['his/her rhyme']). In standard descriptions of French, a noun like *crime* is assigned to the so-called *masculine* gender, whereas *rime* is assigned to the *feminine* gender.

In other European languages, including Greek, Latin, and Modern German, there are not two gender classes, but three, the third class being traditionally referred to as *neuter*. In these languages, a word modifying a noun in a certain position in the sentence can frequently have any of three forms, depending on the gender class of the particular noun that it happens to modify. In still other languages, one can find an even larger variety of gender classes; Swahili, for example, is frequently analyzed as having a total of nine different noun classes, each one requiring a distinct system of agreement prefixes attached to other words in the sentence.

What sorts of lexical entries might we establish for nouns in languages in which the general class of nouns is divided into two or more gender classes? In order to make an analysis available to languages in which the traditional Indo-European terms *masculine*, *feminine*, and *neuter* would not be appropriate, we will use numbers to represent gender classes. In French, we will require just the numbers 1 and 2; in German, we need 1, 2, and 3; and in Swahili, we must use the numbers from 1 through 9. In French, for example, every noun that is inserted into a deep structure tree must carry either the feature ⟨1 gender⟩ (if it is a member of the traditional "masculine" class) or the feature ⟨2 gender⟩ (if it is "feminine"). Leaving aside irrelevant details, the deep-structure tree for (13) would be:

(14)

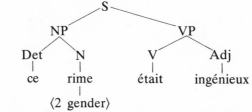

Transformational rules must then apply to copy the gender feature of the noun onto both the preceding demonstrative determiner *ce*, and the predicate adjective *ingénieux*. These rules can be formulated roughly as follows:[3]

$$(15) \quad X - [\underset{NP}{\ } Det - Y - \underset{\langle \alpha\ gender \rangle}{N}]_{NP} - Z$$

$$\quad\quad\quad 1 \quad\quad 2 \quad 3 \quad\quad 4 \quad\quad\quad 5$$

$$\quad\quad \Rightarrow 1, \quad\quad 2 \quad , \quad 3, 4, 5$$

$$\quad\quad\quad\quad \langle \alpha\ gender \rangle$$

$$(16) \quad X - \underset{\langle \alpha\ gender \rangle}{N} - V - Adj - Y$$

$$\quad\quad\quad 1 \quad\quad 2 \quad\quad 3 \quad 4 \quad 5$$

$$\quad\quad \Rightarrow 1, 2, 3, \quad 4 \quad , 5$$

$$\quad\quad\quad\quad\quad \langle \alpha\ gender \rangle$$

The first rule above is to be interpreted as saying that in any noun phrase, whatever gender feature is found with the noun is to be copied onto the determiner. If the noun has the feature ⟨1 gender⟩ then the feature ⟨1 gender⟩ is to be copied onto the determiner. Correspondingly, the feature ⟨2 gender⟩ on the noun gives ⟨2 gender⟩ on the determiner. Rule (16) does a similar copying job from the head noun of the subject onto a predicate adjective. These two rules apply to the tree in (14) to give:

(17)

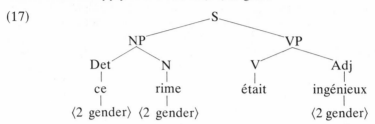

Morphophonemic rules now apply to give the correct surface forms:

(18)   a.   *ce*   →   *cette*   b. *ingénieux*   →   *ingénieuse*
                | |
          ⟨2 gender⟩   ⟨2 gender⟩

The resulting sentence is just (13):

(13)   Cette rime était ingénieuse.

10.3 AN EARLIER APPROACH

An alternative approach to the representation of the traditional category distinctions is worth mentioning here, if for no other reason than that it can be found in many early generative grammars.[4] We can illustrate this older approach by showing how the count-mass distinction might be represented. In this approach no inherent features would appear. Instead, there would be additional phrase structure rules expanding the symbol N:

(19) $N \rightarrow \begin{Bmatrix} N_c \\ N_m \end{Bmatrix}$ (N_c = "count noun")
                                 (N_m = "mass noun")

Instead of including in the lexical entry of a word such as *sand* the two features ⟨N⟩ and ⟨−count⟩, we merely include the single feature ⟨N_m⟩. The noun phrase *the sand* would be assigned the following constituent structure:

```
        NP
       /  \
     Det    N
      |     |
     the    N_m
            |
           sand
```

We might adopt a similar approach to the treatment of gender in a language such as French. In the first place, phrase structure rules are added that rewrite the symbol N in one of two ways:

(21) $N \rightarrow \left\{ \begin{array}{l} N_{masc} \\ N_{fem} \end{array} \right\}$

Now each noun, instead of being provided with two features (one indicating that it is a noun and one indicating its gender), needs only to be provided with a single feature, either $\langle N_{masc} \rangle$ or $\langle N_{fem} \rangle$. The agreement rules that we formulated earlier could be quite simply reformulated in such a way as to refer to the symbols N_{masc} or N_{fem} appearing in the tree.

At first glance, this approach may seem to be in no way inferior to the feature approach. But a serious problem arises as soon as we attempt to describe more than one kind of distinction in the same language. For instance, suppose that we attempt to construct a grammar of French that takes account of the count-mass distinction as well as the masculine-feminine distinction. We should note at the outset that the count-mass distinction is important in French, just as in English, in determining where various quantity words can appear. Given the rules in (21), we must now provide additional phrase structure rules:

(22) a. $N_{masc} \rightarrow \left\{ \begin{array}{l} N_{masc,c} \\ N_{masc,m} \end{array} \right\}$ (masculine count noun) (masculine mass noun)

b. $N_{fem} \rightarrow \left\{ \begin{array}{l} N_{fem,c} \\ N_{fem,m} \end{array} \right\}$ (feminine count noun) (feminine mass noun)

The lexical representations of nouns can now be exemplified as follows:

(23) a.   *crayon* $\langle N_{masc,c} \rangle$ 'pencil'

b.   *sable* $\langle N_{masc,m} \rangle$ 'sand'

c.   *chemise* $\langle N_{fem,c} \rangle$ 'shirt'

d.   *bière* $\langle N_{fem,m} \rangle$ 'beer'

Noun phrases containing these words would be as follows:

(24)   a.   NP   b.   NP   c.   NP   d.   NP

Det   N   Det   N   Det   N   Det   N

N_{masc} N_{masc} N_{fem} N_{fem}

$N_{masc,c}$ $N_{masc,m}$ $N_{fem,c}$ $N_{fem,m}$

crayon   sable   chemise   bière

As before, we have little difficulty in writing rules that account for gender agreement. But the features that we set up to provide for the correct insertion of quantity words will have to be complicated in a most unrevealing manner. In informal terms, we can say that the numeral *trois* ('three') can appear in an NP only if the following noun is a count noun. But with the rules that we have set up, there is no way to refer to count nouns as a general class. What we are forced to do instead is to refer to two separate classes: masculine count nouns and feminine count nouns, represented by the symbols $N_{masc,c}$ and $N_{fem,c}$. The lexical entry for *trois* must thus contain the following rather complicated expression:

$$(25) \quad \left\langle \underline{} \quad \begin{Bmatrix} N_{masc,c} \\ N_{fem,c} \end{Bmatrix} \right\rangle$$

A similar complex feature would have to be included in the lexical entry of every other quantity word that could be followed only by count nouns. The difficulty is that the gender of the noun in question is completely irrelevant to the choice of quantity words, yet there is no way, given the phrase structure rules above, that we can avoid mentioning this irrelevant distinction.

Matters are not helped any if we decide to make the gender distinction more fundamental than the count-mass distinction. We can do this by replacing the phrase structure rules in (21) and (22) by the following rules:

$$(26)\ a. \quad N \rightarrow \begin{Bmatrix} N_c \\ N_m \end{Bmatrix}$$

$$b. \quad N_c \rightarrow \begin{Bmatrix} N_{c,masc} \\ N_{c,fem} \end{Bmatrix}$$

$$c. \quad N_m \rightarrow \begin{Bmatrix} N_{m,masc} \\ N_{m,fem} \end{Bmatrix}$$

We are able in this way to avoid including irrelevant information about gender in the lexical entries of quantity words. However, rather than solving the problem, we have simply shifted it to another area: there is now no straightforward way of stating the gender agreement rules. Whereas originally we had a single class of masculine nouns, represented by the symbol N_{masc}, we now have two classes, represented by the distinct symbols $N_{c,masc}$ and $N_{m,masc}$. Consequently, whenever we want to set up a gender agreement rule, we are forced to mention the count-mass distinction, even though this distinction is completely irrelevant for the rules governing gender agreement.

The difficulty that arises when we adopt this approach can be summarized as follows: if we decide to make it easy to refer to one distinction, we necessarily make it difficult to refer to any other distinctions. For example, if we desire easy reference to the masculine-feminine distinction, we must be prepared to sacrifice any possibility of equally easy reference to the count-mass distinction. This is precisely the type of dilemma that we avoid by adopting the feature approach presented earlier. Within the feature approach, we are not forced into an arbitrary choice as to which of two distinctions we wish to treat as "more important" in situations in which this choice does not make sense. Instead, we are given the possibility of referring to the gender distinction in a simple way whenever this distinction is "more important," and to the count-mass distinction in an equally simple way in those rules in which that is "more important." Many additional arguments of this sort in favor of a feature treatment arise as attempts are made to construct more detailed grammars for various languages.

10.4 A FEATURE TREATMENT OF NUMBER

As indicated in the previous sections regarding the traditional gender distinctions in nouns, the major role is that of making it possible to determine the correct forms of various sorts of other elements in the sentence, in particular, of elements that modify the noun in question. In our actual examples, we have not mentioned several other distinctions that, depending on the particular language involved, may be just as important as gender class for the determination of the correct form of modifiers. Unlike the gender distinctions, however, these distinctions are not generally inherent in the noun in question, but rather are introduced in the course of a derivation, either by the rules that yield the prelexical trees, or else by transformational rules. The first of these distinctions is that between singular and plural.

In Chapter 5 we sketched an analysis of number agreement based on the treatments found in early transformational studies of English. In this analysis there is a special number-carrying element *Nu*, which is introduced into noun phrases by a phrase structure rule and which may be rewritten as either Sg (singular) or Plur (plural). We then proposed a transformational rule of Number Agreement, which placed in the Tns node a copy of the Nu constituent found in the subject.

In more recent studies of English grammar, number is sometimes not analyzed as a separate constituent within the noun phrase, but instead is generated as a feature of the N node in deep structure, along with other features such as ⟨count⟩. The rules in question would be the following:

(27) $N \rightarrow \langle \pm count \rangle$

(28) $\langle +count \rangle \rightarrow \langle \pm plural \rangle$

(29) $\langle -count \rangle \rightarrow \langle -plural \rangle$

(The reason for this last rule will become clear immediately.) These rules are to be interpreted as yielding the following three structures:

(30)   a.
```
        NP
       /  \
     Dét    N
            |
       ⟨+count⟩
            |
       ⟨+plural⟩
```
b.
```
        NP
       /  \
     Dét    N
            |
       ⟨+count⟩
            |
       ⟨-plural⟩
```
c.
```
        NP
       /  \
     Dét    N
            |
       ⟨-count⟩
            |
       ⟨-plural⟩
```

We now adopt the convention that a noun in the lexicon can be inserted into a structure of this sort just as long as the lexical entry contains no features that disagree with the features already in the tree. For example, suppose that the lexical entry for *coat* is the following:

(31)   *coat* ⟨N⟩, ⟨+count⟩

This noun qualifies for insertion into either the (30a) structure or the (30b) structure. The fact that the lexical entry contains no specification for the feature ⟨plural⟩ does not prevent it from being inserted. On the other hand, the noun *coat* cannot be inserted into the (30c) structure, since the feature $\langle +\text{count} \rangle$ in its lexical entry conflicts with the feature $\langle -\text{count} \rangle$ found in the tree. In similar fashion, a noun such as *gravel*, with a feature specification $\langle -\text{count} \rangle$ in its lexical entry, would be eligible for insertion only into the (30c) structure.

Given this way of dealing with number in deep structures, we must make some modifications in our account of number agreement. Instead of copying a separate node, the rule of Number Agreement must copy a feature of the noun. We might in fact go one step further and propose that *Pres* and *Past* be represented as features under the node Tns, perhaps as $\langle -\text{Past} \rangle$ and $\langle +\text{Past} \rangle$. Our rule of Number Agreement can then be formulated so as to copy the number feature of the subject noun below the node Tns and the feature $\langle \pm \text{ Past} \rangle$:[5]

(32)   Number Agreement (revised version)

$$\underset{NP}{[} \text{ Det } - \underset{\langle \alpha \text{ plural} \rangle}{N} - X \underset{NP}{]} - \text{ Tns } - Y$$

$$\quad\quad 1 \quad\quad\quad 2 \quad\quad\quad 3 \quad\quad\quad 4 \quad\quad 5$$

$$\Rightarrow 1, \; 2, \; 3, \quad\;\; \underset{\langle \alpha \text{ plural} \rangle}{4} \quad , \; 5 \quad \text{(Obligatory)}$$

Again, as in the rules given above for gender agreement in French, the alpha notation is interpreted as specifying that whatever value for the feature $\langle \text{plural} \rangle$ is found in the subject noun, this same value is to be copied below the node Tns. One reason for including rule (29) is now apparent: for the purposes of number agreement in English, a mass noun requires exactly the same verb form as a nonplural count noun:

(33)   The potato chip $\left\{ \begin{array}{l} \text{tastes} \\ \text{*taste} \end{array} \right\}$ salty.

(34)   The milk $\left\{ \begin{array}{l} \text{tastes} \\ \text{*taste} \end{array} \right\}$ sour.

(35)   The potato chips $\left\{ \begin{array}{l} \text{*tastes} \\ \text{taste} \end{array} \right\}$ salty.

English demonstratives also show number agreement with their nouns, as the following sentences show:

(36)   John wants to eat $\left\{ \begin{array}{l} \text{this} \\ \text{*these} \end{array} \right\}$ potato chip.

(37)   John wants to drink $\left\{ \begin{array}{l} \text{this} \\ \text{*these} \end{array} \right\}$ milk.

(38)   John wants to eat $\left\{ \begin{array}{l} \text{*this} \\ \text{these} \end{array} \right\}$ potato chips.

As with verbal number agreement, the demonstratives that go with mass nouns are the same as those that go with singular count nouns. This fact provides us with a second justification for rule (29), which ensures that mass nouns are assigned the feature specification $\langle -\text{plural} \rangle$ when they are inserted into trees. The alternation between *this* and *these*, and the corresponding alternation between *that* and *those*, can be accounted for now by adding the following transformational rule to the grammar of English:

(39)   Demonstrative-Noun Agreement

$$X - \underset{NP}{[} \text{Det} - \underset{\langle \alpha \text{ plural} \rangle}{N} - Y \underset{NP}{]} - Z$$

$$1 \qquad 2 \qquad 3 \qquad 4 \qquad 5$$

$$\Rightarrow 1, \quad 2 \quad , 3, 4, 5 \quad \text{(Obligatory)}$$
$$\langle \alpha \text{ plural} \rangle$$

We will then require special morphophonemic rules to give the plural forms:

(40) a.   *this*   →   *these*
$$\langle +\text{plural} \rangle$$

    b.   *that*   →   *those*
$$\langle +\text{plural} \rangle$$

By omitting any special rule for the feature $\langle -\text{plural} \rangle$, we ensure that the final form of *this* and *that* will simply be identical with the underlying form. In addition, the absence of any rule at all for the definite determiner *the* means that its form will not be affected by the number feature copied onto it.

Thus, what we have seen in this section is an example of a feature that is introduced into a prelexical tree. It may then be copied onto other elements in the sentence: in English, onto demonstratives and the Tns element in the auxiliary. In many other languages, a variety of other modifiers, including ordinary adjectives and participles, are made to agree in number with the noun that they modify.

EXERCISE

1. Assuming the analysis adopted in the preceding section, what would be the lexical specifications for the features of plurality and countability for the noun *people*, in the sense that it has in a sentence such as, *The people that attended your party obviously didn't realize that you were the host*? What would be the feature specification for the word *news*?

10.5 A FEATURE TREATMENT OF CASE

Formal distinctions of another type that we have seen earlier are also amenable to a feature treatment. These are distinctions of *case*, distinctions in form that are determined by grammatical function in a sentence. In English, the major case distinction for nouns is that of possessive versus nonpossessive. A second case distinction is found in the pronoun system: the so-called "objective" or "accusative" pronouns are used as direct objects and as objects of prepositions, whereas the "subjective" or "nominative" forms are used as subjects. In Chapter 5 we accounted for this case variation in English pronouns by adopting the following rule:

(41)   Case Assignment

$$X - \left\{ \begin{array}{l} V \\ Prep \end{array} \right\} - Pro - Y$$
$$1 \quad\quad 2 \quad\quad 3 \quad 4$$
$$\Rightarrow 1, 2, 3 + Obj, 4 \quad \text{(Obligatory)}$$

If we take the alternative approach of representing cases by features rather than by special segments, then the above rule would be reformulated as follows:

(42)   Case Assignment   (revised version)

$$X - \left\{ \begin{array}{l} V \\ Prep \end{array} \right\} - Pro - Y$$
$$1 \quad\quad 2 \quad\quad 3 \quad 4$$
$$\Rightarrow 1, 2, \underset{\langle Obj \rangle}{3}, 4 \quad \text{(Obligatory)}$$

We would assume as before that only the nominative forms are listed in the lexicon. In a structure such as the following, Case Assignment will not apply:

(43)   we Past eat the sandwich.   *structural description doesn't fit anyway*

Here the surface pronoun will be identical with the underlying pronoun. By contrast, Case Assignment will apply in structures such as:

(44)   John Past see we.

(45)   Oscar Past speak to we.

In each of these structures, the feature Obj will be assigned to the pronoun *we*. The pronoun will then be converted to the objective form *us* by the following morphophonemic rule:

(46) $\underset{\langle Obj \rangle}{we} \quad \rightarrow \quad us$

Similar morphophonemic rules will be required for the other nonnominative pronouns.

In many languages, the case of a noun is carried over to other words by rules of agreement that are very similar in character to the rules that determine agreement in number and gender. In Classical Arabic, for example, adjectival modifiers within an NP agree in case with the noun that they modify. This agreement is illustrated in the examples in (47); the two cases shown are *nominative* (the case of the subject, marked by the suffix -*u*-), and *accusative* (the case of the direct object, marked by -*a*-).

(47) a.   Maata kalb-[u]-n kabiir-[u]-n.

died dog-nom.-indefinite large-nom.-indefinite
'A large dog died.'

b.   Wajad-tu kalb-[a]-n kabiir-[a]-n.

found-I dog-acc.-indefinite large-acc.-indefinite
'I found a large dog.'

In Latin and Greek, agreement in case is extended even further, to include predicate modifiers. In Latin, for example, the subject of a simple sentence is in the nominative case, and a predicate adjective that modifies it is likewise nominative:

(48)   [Puella] est [bona].

girl (nom.) is good (nom.)
'The girl is good.'

When a sentence of this sort is embedded as a complement with a verb such as *dicit* ('he says'), the subject takes the accusative case and the verb is shifted to its infinitival form. As a consequence, the predicate adjective now is assigned the accusative case:

(49)   Dicit [puellam] esse [bonam].

he-says girl (acc.) to-be good (acc.)
'He says that the girl is good.'

In Latin, then, agreement of adjectives for case appears to be just as extensive as agreement for number and gender.[6]

10.6 RULE FEATURES

In the preceding chapters we have had occasion to propose many transformational rules in the course of attempting to develop a maximally revealing account of English syntactic structure. Many of the rules, although they apply quite widely, have a number of apparent exceptions.[7] A first example is provided by the Passive rule, which we stated as follows:

(50)   Passive

NP – Aux – V – NP – X
1   2   3   4   5
⇒ 4, 2, *be* + *en* + 3, 0, 5 + *by* + 1   (Optional)

A thoroughgoing examination of English verbs that may be followed by noun phrases reveals a few that are ungrammatical in passive sentences, among them the following:

(51) a.   This newspaper costs a dollar.

   b.   *A dollar is cost by this newspaper.

(52) a.   John resembles Fred's cousin.

   b.   *Fred's cousin is resembled by John.

One way of accounting for the absence of passive sentences with these verbs is to propose that the lexical entries for any verb that may not undergo the Passive rule contain a rule feature ⟨−Passive⟩, the minus indicating that the Passive rule is not to apply even in structures in which the structural description for the Passive rule is otherwise met. When a verb is inserted into a tree, any feature of this type that appears in its lexical entry will go along with it. A verb such as *take* or *hit* will not have such a feature associated with it, and thus the Passive rule will be free to apply to any tree that contains either of these verbs and has the structure specified in (50). On the other hand, the deep structure for sentence (51a) will contain the feature ⟨−Passive⟩:

(53)

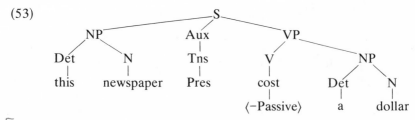

It would be a general convention on the application of any transformational rule that the rule could not apply in any structure in which the lexical item corresponding to one of the nonvariable nodes mentioned in the structural description is marked negatively for that rule.

   Another transformational rule found in some treatments of English would appear to require a similar treatment. This rule, which we will refer to as Dative Movement, can be formulated as follows:[8]

(54)   Dative Movement

   X − V − NP − *to* − NP
   1   2   3   4   5
   ⇒ 1, 2 + 5, 3, 0, 0   (Optional)

It is designed to apply to the deep structure of a sentence such as (55a), changing it to a form that is eventually realized as (55b):

(55) a.   Alice sent a book to Alfred.

   b.   Alice sent Alfred a book.

As the following sentences show, there are many other verbs that appear in both types of structures:

(56) a.   Alice gave a book to Alfred.

   b.   Alice gave Alfred a book.

(57) a.   The cook tossed a sandwich to Jimmy.
     b.   The cook tossed Jimmy a sandwich.

(58) a.   We mailed a postcard to your daughter.
     b.   We mailed your daughter a postcard.

(59) a.   The sitter told a story to the child.
     b.   The sitter told the child a story.

However, we also find verbs that may appear only in structures of the first type:

(60) a.   Joe reported the crime to the authorities.
     b.   *Joe reported the authorities the crime.

(61) a.   Jack conveyed the news to his parents.
     b.   *Jack conveyed his parents the news.

(62) a.   Joe said something to his uncle.
     b.   *Joe said his uncle something.

Here again, we can block the ungrammatical (b) sentences above if we include the rule feature ⟨−Dative Movement⟩ in the lexical entries of the verbs *report, convey* and *say*. As a consequence of these feature specifications, a structure such as that underlying (60a) above cannot undergo Dative Movement, since the verb corresponding to the V term in the structural description will have associated with it a negative rule feature corresponding to this transformational rule.

A second type of exception feature is suggested by a residual problem in the analysis of English developed in the preceding chapters. The problem is readily apparent when we examine one of the trees that can be derived by the operation of the phrase structure rules followed by lexical insertion:

(63)

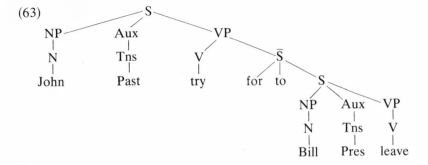

After Affix Insertion applies, we must ask whether this tree satisfies the structural description of Identical-NP Deletion. Since the subject of the lower sentence is not identical with the subject of the higher sentence, the structural description is not satisfied, and the rule cannot apply. What our rules leave us with, then, is an ungrammatical sentence:

(64)   *John tried for Bill to leave.

It should be noted that marking Identical-NP Deletion as an obligatory rule does not enable us to avoid generating this sentence. What we have meant so far by the phrase "obligatory rule" is a rule that must apply *when its structural description is satisfied*. In this instance, the structural description is not satisfied, by virtue of the lack of identity between the main-clause subject and the subordinate subject. Our analysis in its current form thus generates the ungrammatical sentence (64).

The ungrammaticality of such sentences can be accounted for by including in the lexical entry of the verb *try* a feature ⟨+Identical-NP Deletion⟩. We will interpret this feature as follows: when a deep structure tree contains a verb that has this feature as part of its lexical entry, then the resulting sentence is grammatical *only if*, first, the structural description for Identical-NP Deletion is met on the cycle of the S that has the verb in question as its main verb, and second, the rule of Identical-NP Deletion actually applies. For example, the tree given above in (63) contains an occurrence of *try*, which would carry with it the feature ⟨+Identical-NP Deletion⟩. However, the structural description of this rule fails to be met on the cycle of the top S, and the sentence resulting from this tree is consequently predicted to be ungrammatical.

This treatment does not prevent us from generating certain sentences whose deep structures do not satisfy the structural description of Identical-NP Deletion, for example:

(65) a.   John tried to be arrested by a Texas Ranger.

In the deep structure for this sentence, the subject of the lower S is not identical with the subject of the higher S, and thus the structural description of Identical-NP Deletion is not satisfied:

(65) b.

However, if we take the option of applying the Passive rule in the lower S, then *John* becomes the new subject. Now when we go to the cycle of the higher S, the structural description for Identical-NP Deletion is satisfied, and the rule applies. Consequently, the requirement imposed by the positive rule-feature with *try* has been satisfied, and we correctly predict that the resulting sentence will be grammatical.

A similar situation arises with certain verbs that may appear only in passive sentences. One example is the verb *rumor*:

(66) a.   It was rumored that the police were hunting for John.

     b.   *Someone rumored that the police were hunting for John.

Just as we listed *try* with a positive rule feature for Identical-NP Deletion, we can list *rumor* with a positive rule feature for Passive. The ungrammaticality of a sentence such as (66b) will then be accounted for, by virtue of the fact that the Passive rule was not applied in a structure containing a verb that is positively marked for the rule.

Having briefly examined the kinds of rule features that are assumed in many syntactic descriptions, we should note that the use of features of these types is not without serious problems. These problems will become apparent in Chapter 17, where a more concerted effort will be made to determine the effect of various syntactic devices in moving us toward or away from a solution to the projection problem.

10.7 LEXICAL REDUNDANCY RULES

A final question to which we will turn our attention is one that has always been of interest to grammarians: to what extent are various *syntactic* properties of words predictable from semantic and morphological properties? In this section, we will take up this question first with regard to the category of gender, and second with regard to the count-mass distinction.

Again restricting ourselves for purposes of illustration to gender in French, the question can be rephrased in a form familiar to every teacher of elementary French: are there any general rules by which the gender of French nouns can be predicted? For many words, including *crime* and *rime*, it appears that no such rules exist. In such cases, gender membership must be learned on a word-by-word basis. For some other words, however, the gender can be predicted by a general rule that applies to a great many different nouns.

An initial rule is suggested by the names traditionally given to the two genders. Words that refer by definition to male beings (e.g., *mari*, 'husband'; *garcon*, 'boy'; and *fils*, 'son') are always assigned to the masculine gender, what we have referred to above by the more neutral designation "1 gender." On the other hand, words that refer to feminine beings (e.g., *femme*, 'woman, wife'; *fille*, 'daughter, girl'; and *tante*, 'aunt') always belong to the feminine gender, i.e., to "2 gender." These informal rules serve to predict a syntactic property of certain words on the basis of key semantic properties. Another oft-cited rule of traditional French grammar takes the same form: it states that names of species of trees (e.g., *chene*, 'oak'; *peuplier*, 'poplar'; and *orme*, 'elm') are generally assigned to the masculine gender.

A regularity of an entirely different sort is expressed in another traditional remark: all nouns ending in *-sion* or *-tion* (e.g., *décision, attention,* and *présentation*) are feminine. In this instance, gender membership can be predicted on the basis of a *morphological* property of certain nouns, a property of their form rather than of their meaning. A second traditional rule of the same type states that nouns ending in the suffix *-té* (e.g., *beauté*, 'beauty'; *santé*, 'health'; and *volonté*, 'will') are also feminine.

Turning now to the count-mass distinction, we might at first expect to find that the syntactic behavior of a given noun in this regard was entirely predictable on the basis of its semantic properties. Following many traditional rules of thumb, we might state simply that a noun that refers by definition to individual *things* will be a count noun, whereas one that refers to undifferentiated *substances* will be a mass noun. However, a close examination of the distinction as it is manifested in English affords some reason for not placing too much faith in this statement. We will consider here only a small number of the instances in which this statement is of doubtful benefit.

A simple initial example is afforded by a comparison of the word *cookie* and the word *candy*. As the following sentences show, they pattern in completely dissimilar fashion:

(67)   Alice ate too many $\left\{ \begin{array}{l} \text{cookies} \\ \text{*candies} \end{array} \right\}$.

(68)   Alice ate too much $\left\{ \begin{array}{l} \text{*cookie} \\ \text{candy} \end{array} \right\}$.

(69)   Alice ate seventeen pieces of $\left\{ \begin{array}{l} \text{*cookie} \\ \text{candy} \end{array} \right\}$.

Other similar examples are not difficult to find. For instance, *cabbage* can be either a mass noun or a count noun:

(70)   Jill put too much cabbage into the cole slaw.

(71)   Jill bought too many cabbages.

The word *lettuce*, on the other hand, can occur only as a mass noun, unless it is preceded by the word *head*:

(72)   Jill put too much lettuce into the salad.

(73)   *Jill bought too many lettuces.[9]

(74)   Jill bought too many heads of lettuce.

Even more surprising examples come to light when we look at certain more abstract nouns that appear to refer neither to "things" nor to "substances." The contrasting behavior of *suggestion* and *advice* is instructive in this regard. *Suggestion* is very clearly a count noun in its most important use:

(75)   The lawyer gave me three very useful suggestions.

From the similarity in meaning of the related verbs *suggest* and *advise*, we might expect that we could construct a sentence corresponding to (75) using the word *advice*, an expectation that is in fact frustrated:

(76)   *The lawyer gave me three very useful advices.

Advice, like *candy*, can only be counted in *pieces*:

(77)   The lawyer gave me three very useful pieces of advice.

In this connection, it is also worth noting that different languages may classify words for some one concept in entirely different ways. For example, the noun *hair* in English may be used as either a count noun or a mass noun:

(78)   The two hairs were both black.

(79)   Not much of John's hair is still brown.

In French, by contrast, the corresponding word *cheveu* is invariably a count noun, so that a speaker of French would always use the plural form *cheveux* and a plural verb form in translating an English sentence such as *His hair is long*.

Despite the frequently capricious manner in which this distinction is made in English, there do seem to be a few general rules. For instance, within the domain of vegetables, those which consist of leaves or stalks of plants are generally analyzed as mass nouns (e.g., *asparagus*, *rhubarb*, *celery*, *broccoli*, *spinach*, *cauliflower*). We also find that nouns denoting various types of grain tend to be mass nouns (*barley*, *wheat*, *rye*, *corn*). By contrast, legumes are generally treated as count nouns in English (e.g., *beans*, *peas*, *lentils*, *peanuts*), as are roots (e.g., *carrots*, *radishes*, *turnips*).

We have given some examples here of rules that allow for the prediction of syntactic properties of certain words on the basis of their semantic or phonological properties. Rules of this type are sometimes referred to as *lexical redundancy rules.* We can conceive of these rules as making up a subcomponent of the lexical component, whose purpose is to express the relative degree of regularity that exists in the feature specifications in the lexicon. We could in fact design an evaluation measure in such a way as to make the "predicted best grammar" for a set of primary data the grammar whose individual lexical entries contained the smallest number of non-redundant features, that is, the smallest number of features that did not follow from some lexical redundancy rule. The consequences of this general proposal for the projection problem may be illustrated with an example from French.

Let us imagine that we are presented with a set of basic data from French. These data may serve to motivate a redundancy rule to the effect that nouns ending in *-ion* are to be assigned to the feminine gender (the "2 gender"). The basic data also include a few instances of the noun *impression*, without, however, any clear indication of its gender class. (This is not as unimaginable as it sounds, since the gender distinctions normally found in the singular definite article and demonstrative are lost when the following word begins with a vowel.) With no direct evidence concerning the gender of *impression*, what gender feature does our universal grammar assign as part of its lexical entry? Because of the lexical redundancy rule for *-ion* nouns, a feminine marking for *impression* is in effect free of charge. In other words, such a marking does not count as contributing to the complexity of the lexicon. By contrast, a masculine marking would not follow from this redundancy rule, and it would thus be counted as increasing the complexity of the lexicon. If, as suggested above, we specify that our evaluation measure select the lexical component that contains the smallest number of non-redundant features, then a lexicon with a feminine feature specification for *impression* comes out ahead of one with a masculine marking. In this hypothetical situation and in others like it, this would be just the desired result.

Suggestions for Further Reading

Chomsky 1965, Chapter 2, is the first work to propose features as the appropriate mechanism for representing many properties of individual English words. Rule features in particular are the basic subject matter of Lakoff 1970a. A description of English that makes extensive use of features of all kinds is developed in Jacobs and Rosenbaum 1968.

Notes

1. In some instances, nouns that are fundamentally mass nouns may be used as count nouns, with special interpretations. One common special interpretation is that N stands for 'kinds of N':

(i)   We tasted twenty-five wines (kinds of wine) last night.

Another common interpretation is that the N stands for some standard portion of N:

(ii)   John bought a beer (glass of beer, can of beer, or single-serving bottle of beer, but not quart-bottle or keg).

(iii)   Get a milk for Fred (glass of milk or single-serving carton of milk).

2. Actually, *one* may substitute for more than just a noun alone. We will give this construction a more comprehensive treatment in section 14.2.

3. The rules as formulated here are not entirely satisfactory. In NP's that contain more than a single N, these rules will frequently pick the wrong N as the basis for determining agreement. This problem is discussed in detail in section 14.2, and a solution is proposed.

4. See, for example, Lees 1960 and Chomsky 1962.

5. This rule, like the one stated earlier for French gender agreement, does not work adequately with any but the simplest sorts of subject NP's. Once again, a more adequate treatment is proposed in section 14.2.

6. Although case agreement rules of this type are not difficult to state informally, some interesting problems arise when an attempt is made to obtain the effect of such rules within the transformational framework. The fundamental difficulty is that the transformational framework does not allow the traditional term *modifies* as one of the concepts that may appear in the statement of grammatical rules. This problem is discussed in Andrews 1971 and Quicoli 1972.

7. The approach presented in this section is essentially that developed in detail in Lakoff 1970a.

8. This rule was mentioned in Exercise 2, section 5.4.

9. There is apparently some dialectal variation here. In contrast to the author's dialect, the British dialect in which Beatrix Potter's stories for children are written appears to allow *lettuce* as a count noun.

Part III

SOME ALTERNATIVES FOR THE ANALYSIS OF ENGLISH

One of our projects in this book has been to develop a partial grammar of English in order to illustrate the grammatical framework being developed and also to provide some evidence as to what form a general framework should take. Although we have at several points considered two or more alternative transformational treatments of some single English construction, a choice between alternative sets of rules has never formed the primary focus of our discussion.

In the following four chapters, the primary objective will shift temporarily from the development of a general syntactic framework to the evaluation of alternative sets of rules within a more-or-less fixed framework, that developed in Part II. On a few occasions, we will find it useful even here to consider revisions in the general framework, in the interests of doing an adequate job of dealing with certain specific English constructions. But the major aim will be to illustrate the kinds of considerations that lead us to prefer one grammar to another, in cases in which both are allowed by some single general framework.

11

The Basic Structure
of Simple Sentences

We have been assuming an analysis of English in which the rules have the effect of grouping the verb and object together in a constituent separate from the subject:

(1) a.   S → NP   Aux   VP
    b.   VP → V (NP) (PrepP)

These rules yield trees of the general form below:

(2)

```
              S
          /   |   \
        NP   Aux   VP
                  / | \
                 V (NP) (PrepP)
```

Our aim in this chapter will be to compare the "VP analysis" with an alternative analysis, one in which <u>subject, verb, object, and following prepositional phrase are coequal partners under S, with no intervening VP</u> node. Such an analysis, which we will refer to as the "<u>non-VP analysis</u>," is represented in the following phrase structure rule:

(3)   S → NP   Aux   V (NP) (PrepP)

The constituent structure developed by the operation of this new rule is:

(4)

```
                   S
          /   /   |   \    \
        NP  Aux   V  (NP)  (PrepP)
```

259

It might seem "intuitively clear" at this point that the VP analysis is correct. Such an assertion presupposes that native speakers of a language are able to make reliable judgments not only about the grammaticalness of a sentence presented to them, but also about the correct constituent structure of a sentence. However, a brief survey of the wide variety of constituent structures proposed in previous generative studies of English syntax affords little reason for confidence in such judgments. The preference for the VP structure as opposed to the non-VP structure can arguably be explained by the fact that the former is much more in keeping with the traditional division of the English sentence into a subject and a predicate. As such, this preference deserves the same critical scrutiny that we would want to give to a widely accepted idea in any field of study.

11.1 SOME INITIAL OBSERVATIONS

We begin here by noting some arguments for the VP analysis that do *not* work. In the first place, given the general outline of the transformational analysis that we have adopted so far, the replacement of the two phrase structure rules in (1) by the single rule in (3) does not require any complication of the remaining phrase structure rules. The balance would tip in favor of the VP analysis if we could find another phrase structure rule in which the symbol VP appeared as part of the right-hand side. However, in the analysis of English that we have developed so far, there is only one, namely the rule that rewrites the initial symbol S. In certain instances, we have in surface structure what appear to be VP's that would not be generated by this one phrase structure rule:

(5)   John tried to *throw the ball.*

(6)   Charlie seems to *keep his savings in a mattress.*

However, it will be recalled that in the analysis of complement sentences developed in Chapter 6, the italicized VP's in both of the preceding sentences originated in deep structure as VP's in full S's, developed by exactly the same phrase structure rule as that used for developing simple sentences. It seems, then, that we are not forced into any appreciable loss of generality in the phrase structure component if we replace the two rules in (1) by the single rule in (3).

We might now ask if any of the transformational rules proposed thus far would work any less well if we were to adopt the non-VP analysis. The answer appears to be negative. There are many rules that refer to NP, and also several that refer to V (Passive, for instance, refers to both). There are also some that contain a variable standing for everything after the first auxiliary verb (e.g., Subject-HV Inversion), and others in which one of the variables refers to everything after the subject (e.g., Subject Raising). But there has been none so far that has had to make reference specifically to our VP, that is, to a unit consisting of a transitive verb and its object, or a verb and its locative prepositional phrase, or some other similar sequence.

Surprising as it might seem, then, the syntactic phenomena we have studied up to this point appear to provide us with no reason for preferring the VP structure to the alternative non-VP structure.

11.2 *DO SO*

A phenomenon that is sometimes cited as providing an argument in favor of the VP analysis is the optional appearance of *do so* as a replacement for a sequence consisting of a verb and following elements when there is an identical sequence preceding it.[1] This optional construction is illustrated in the following examples:

(7)   John threw the ball, because not to $\left\{\begin{array}{l}\text{throw the ball}\\ \text{do so}\end{array}\right\}$ would have lost

the game.

(8)   Alfred signed a confession, but Bill refused to $\left\{\begin{array}{l}\text{sign a confession}\\ \text{do so}\end{array}\right\}$.

(9)   John put a nickel in the plate, and Sarah $\left\{\begin{array}{l}\text{put a nickel in the plate}\\ \text{did so}\end{array}\right\}$,

too.

Given our original analysis, the replaced constituents *throw the ball, sign a confession*, and *put a nickel in the plate* would all be VP's. Consequently, we could account for this alternation by adding to our grammar the following optional transformational rule:

(10)   *Do-So* Substitution   w/ VP analysis

X – VP – Y – VP – Z
1   2   3   4   5
Condition: 2 = 4
⇒ 1, 2, 3, *do so*, 5   (Optional)

Let us see now how the same construction could be described if we were to assume the non-VP analysis. An informal rule might be framed: when we have an S in which the verb and everything after it is identical to a similar sequence occurring earlier, then we can optionally replace the second of the two identical sequences by *do so*. This rule can be stated formally as follows:

(11)   *Do-So* Substitution   (non-VP form)

T – [X – V   Y] – U – [Z – V   W] – R
1 $_S$ 2   3 $_S$ 4 $_S$ 5   6 $_S$ 7
Condition: 3 = 6
⇒ 1, 2, 3, 4, 5, *do so*, 7   (Optional)

We can illustrate the operation of this rule by showing how it would apply in the derivation of (8). The rule applies as follows:

(12)

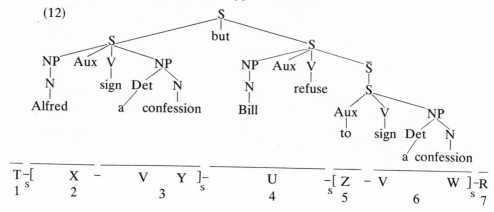

$$T\underset{1}{-}[\underset{s}{}\quad \underset{2}{X}\quad -\quad \underset{3}{V}\quad \underset{s}{Y}\underset{s}{]-}\quad \underset{4}{U}\quad \underset{s}{-[}\underset{5}{Z}\quad -\quad \underset{6}{V}\quad \underset{7}{W}\underset{s}{]-R}$$

Alfred Aux sign a confession but Bill Aux refuse to do so

$$1\ ,\quad 2\quad ,\quad 3\quad ,\quad 4\quad ,5\ ,do\ so,\ 7$$

An apparent problem for both analyses is raised by the fact that the phrase *do so* does not always replace everything after the verb. The following two sentences show that the sequences *take a walk after dinner* and *practice law in California* both qualify for replacement by *do so*:

(13)   Alice takes a walk after dinner, and John $\left\{\begin{array}{l}\text{takes a walk after dinner}\\ \text{does so}\end{array}\right\}$, too.

(14)   Horace refuses to practice law in California, because to $\left\{\begin{array}{l}\text{practice law in California}\\ \text{do so}\end{array}\right\}$ would be much too expensive.

In the next two sentences, by contrast, we can see that the shorter sequences *take a walk* and *practice law* can also be replaced, even though they occur as part of a larger sequence:

(15)   Alice takes a walk before dinner, and John $\left\{\begin{array}{l}\text{takes a walk}\\ \text{does so}\end{array}\right\}$ after dinner.

(16)   Horace practices law in Arkansas, because to $\left\{\begin{array}{l}\text{practice law}\\ \text{do so}\end{array}\right\}$ in California would be too expensive.

In (15), the temporal phrase *after dinner* has been left behind by the rule; in (16), it is a locative phrase that has not been included in the replaced material. It should be observed here that not just any locative phrase can be left behind, as the following sentences show:

(17)   Ben put the money in the desk drawer, because to

$\left\{\begin{array}{l}\text{put the money} \\ \text{*do so}\end{array}\right\}$ in the safe would have been too risky.

(18)   Bill resides in southern California; he used to $\left\{\begin{array}{l}\text{reside} \\ \text{*do so}\end{array}\right\}$ in Okla-

homa.

How might we account for these facts within a VP analysis? One possibility (the one that we will actually pursue here) is to leave the *do-so* rule exactly as it is stated in (10), and try to arrange the constituent structure of the sentences with which we are concerned in such a way that the correct result will be given when the rule applies in its present form. What this amounts to, essentially, is that we will try to arrange things so that every replaceable sequence is a VP. Let us begin with the sentence *John takes a walk after dinner*. As we saw in (13) and (15), there are two sub-sequences of this sentence that are potential candidates for replacement by *do so*. The first is the sequence *takes a walk*; the second is the larger sequence *takes a walk after dinner*. The way to create a tree in which both of these sequences are VP's is to set up the smaller sequence as a VP within the larger one:

(19)

```
                        S
          _____/ _____
        NP                          VP
         |              _____/ _____
         N            VP                      PrepP
         |        __/ \__              ____/  \____
       John     V         NP         Prep         NP
         |      |       _/ \_          |           |
       takes    |     Det    N       after         N
              takes    |     |                      |
                       a    walk                  dinner
```

In a sentence such as (13), in which the larger VP is identical to some preceding VP, we can replace this larger structure. On the other hand, when only the smaller VP is identical to a preceding VP, as in (15), only this smaller VP can be replaced.

What constituent structure might we assign to the sequence *put the money in the safe*? In order to avoid replacing the sub-sequence *put the money*, giving the ungrammatical form of (17), we must set up the constituent structure of this phrase so that *put the money* is not a VP. A structure that satisfies this condition is the following:

(20)

```
                    VP
          _____/   |   _____
        V          NP          PrepP
        |        _/ \_        __/  \__
       put     Det    N     Prep     NP
               |      |      |      _/ \_
              the   money    in   Det    N
                                  |      |
                                 the   safe
```

Given this constituent structure, only the entire sequence *put the money in the safe* can possibly qualify for replacement by the *do-so* rule. Any smaller sub-sequence will fail to be a VP.

As a general rule, a given prepositional phrase will be part of a "minimal" VP for the purposes of *Do-So* Substitution whenever the particular verb is subcategorized for such a prepositional phrase. For example, the verb *put* must be marked in the lexicon with the feature ⟨____NP PrepP⟩, so as to prevent sentences such as **Ben put the money*. Correspondingly, the single possibility for *Do-So* Substitution indicates that this prepositional phrase should be contained in the lowest VP. By contrast, the sentence *Horace practices law* shows that the verb *practice* should not be subcategorized to require a prepositional phrase. Correspondingly, the dual possibilities for the appearance of *do so* seem to indicate that the prepositional phrase in the sequence *practice law in California* should not be included in the minimal VP, but should instead be introduced under the domination of a higher VP.

Let us see now how these facts might be accounted for in the non-VP analysis. At first glance, it may appear completely impossible to distinguish the structure of the sentence *Horace practices law in Arkansas* from the structure of the sentence *Ben put the money in the safe*. Both, it would appear, would have to be assigned trees of the following form:

(21)

Rule (11) as it stands will generate those sentences in which everything after the V is replaced by *do so*, that is, sentences like (13) and (14). However, it will not allow the generation of the grammatical (16), in which the prepositional phrase *in California* is left unreplaced. If we set out to change rule (11) in such a way as to allow the generation of (16), then we are faced with the opposite difficulty: how can we prevent it from replacing the sequence *put the money* within the larger sequence *put the money in the safe*, to give the ungrammatical form of (17)? Thus, when we apply rule (11) to the constituent structure in (21), we encounter a serious dilemma.

However, rather than admitting defeat, a resourceful defender of the non-VP analysis might counter with an alternative view of the constituent structure of sentences containing prepositional phrases. He would still assign *Ben put the money in the safe* a tree structure in which all of the major parts of the sentence were immediately dominated by a single S:

(22)

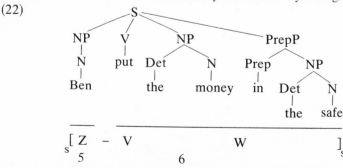

The only way of dividing up this clause in the way indicated in the second half of the structural description of (11) is indicated by the above underlining. Consequently, the only sequence eligible for deletion in this tree will be the sequence *put the money in the safe.*

For the sentence *Horace practices law in Arkansas*, he would suggest an entirely different tree structure, one in which the prepositional phrase is dominated by a higher S, which is different from the one that contains the sequence *Horace practices law*:

(23)

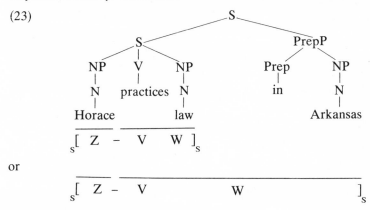

or

As the underlining indicates, there are now two sequences that potentially qualify for replacement by *do so*, subject only to the additional condition that there be some identical sequence in the preceding material. The sequence *practices law* is the verb-plus-everything-else in the lower S, and the sequence *practices law in Arkansas* is the verb-plus-everything-else in the larger S. In sum, we can make the same sorts of distinctions in the non-VP analysis by allowing lower and higher S's as we made in the VP analysis by allowing lower and higher VP's. Hence, the VP analysis, contrary to what appeared at first, does not come out clearly ahead of the non-VP analysis in its capacity to account for the sentences discussed so far.

There are two problems for the rule in (11) that are not so easy to solve. The first problem is that in more complicated structures, the variables X and Z allow the rule to apply in such a way as to give grossly ungrammatical results. An example is provided by the tree in (24) on the following page. When rule (11) applies to this tree in accordance with the divisions indicated by the above underscoring, then the eventual result is ungrammatical:

(25)   *The woman that left broke a jar and the man that did so.   *argument*
0 ≠ VP

This is of course not the only way to apply rule (11) to this tree, but the fact that it *can* be applied in this undesirable way must be counted as a shortcoming in this analysis. By contrast, no such unfortunate result can be obtained with the VP analysis and the *Do-So* Substitution rule (10), which mentions VP in its structural description. In this analysis, we would have tree (26) on page 266 as an input to *Do-So* Substitution, instead of the one given in (24). In this tree, the sequence *left broke a jar* is not a VP, and the *Do-So* rule (10), which specifically mentions VP, cannot apply. Thus, if we

(24)

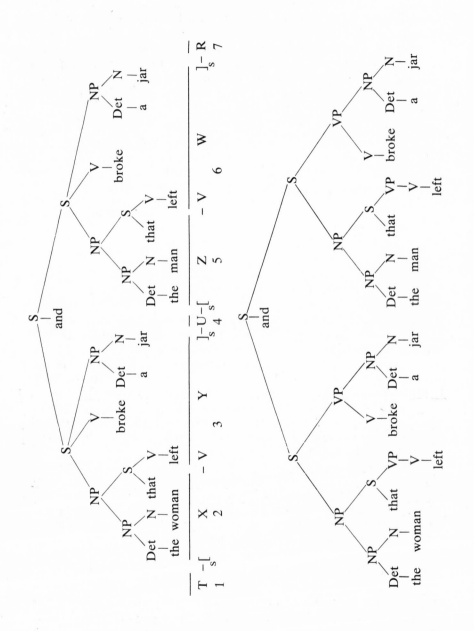

(26)

266

adopt the VP analysis and the original *Do-So* rule given in (10), the un-grammatical sentence (25) poses no problems.

The second problem for the alternative *Do-So* rule given in (11) is provided by sentences such as the following:[2]

(27)   The man who always wanted to ride a camel finally $\begin{Bmatrix} \text{rode a camel} \\ \text{did so} \end{Bmatrix}$.

On the non-VP analysis, the full version of (27) would have roughly the structure given below.

(28)

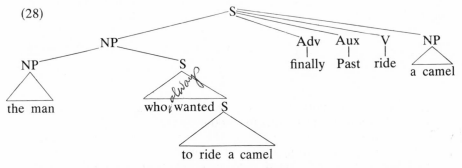

Rule (11) as stated cannot apply to this structure, since the structural description has S-brackets around terms 5 and 6. In order to substitute *do so* for the right-hand occurrence of *ride a camel* in (28), we would need to add to our grammar a second rule of *Do-So* Substitution:

(29) $\text{T} - {}_{\text{S}}[\ \text{X} - \text{V}\ \ \text{Y}\ ]_{\text{S}} - \text{Z} - \text{V}\ \ \text{W}$
        $\quad\ 1 \qquad 2 \qquad 3 \qquad\ 4 \qquad 5$

Condition: 3 = 5
⇒ 1, 2, 3, 4, *do so*   (Optional)

This additional rule allows us to substitute *do so* for the second occurrence of *ride a camel* in (28). However, the resulting grammar, which contains two separate *Do-So* Substitution rules, is clearly unrevealing.

If we assume the VP-analysis, and with it the *Do-So* Substitution rule given in (10), no problems arise in the generation of the second version of (27).

(10)   *Do-So* Substitution   (VP form)

        X – VP – Y – VP – Z
        1   2   3   4   5
        Condition: 2 = 4
        ⇒ 1, 2, 3, *do so*, 5   (Optional)

The structure available for *Do-So* Substitution would be that shown in (30); the underscoring indicates how the structural description would be satisfied. When the structural change is carried out, the result is the second version of (27). Thus, if we adopt the VP form of *Do-So* Substitution for the sentences

(30)

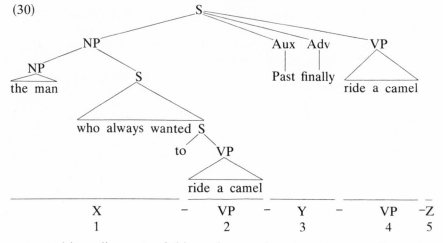

X	–	VP	–	Y	–	VP	–Z
1		2		3		4	5

presented in earlier parts of this section, we do not need to complicate the rule or add another rule in order to account for the *did so* in (27).

To summarize the discussion in this section, the VP analysis makes possible a simple and straightforward account of the appearance of *do so* in English. On the other hand, the non-VP analysis requires us to set up complicated and unrevealing rules for this construction. Consequently, the *do-so* construction provides evidence in favor of the VP analysis as against the non-VP analysis.

EXERCISE

1. The non-VP version of *Do-So* Substitution given in (11) in the text specified that the two identical terms each had to be the right-hand portion of some S:

$$T - [\; X - V \; Y \;]_S - U - [\; Z - V \; W \;]_S - R$$
$$1 \quad\; 2 \quad\; 3 \qquad 4 \quad\; 5 \quad\; 6 \qquad 7$$

Condition: 3 = 6
⇒ 1, 2, 3, 4, 5, *do so*, 7   (Optional)   (= 11)

A simpler alternative might have seemed possible here:

$$X - V \; Y - Z - V \; W - R$$
$$1 \quad\; 2 \quad\; 3 \quad 4 \quad\; 5$$

Condition: 2 = 4
⇒ 1, 2, 3, *do so*, 5   (Optional)

Show that the S-bracketing in the first rule above is necessary. Do this by finding several examples of ungrammatical sentences which arise if the second rule is assumed but do not arise with the first.

11.3 CONJOINED STRUCTURES

A second argument for the VP analysis is based on the relative grammaticality of conjoined structures in English such as the following:[3]

(31)   John cooked the supper and washed the dishes.

(32)   ?John cooked and Alice ate the supper.

(The question mark prefixed to sentence (32) indicates a slightly lower degree of grammaticality.) The basic assumption underlying this argument is that conjoined sentences such as (31) and (32) are to be derived from sentences (33) and (34):

(33)   John cooked the supper and John washed the dishes.

(34)   John cooked the supper and Alice ate the supper.

The critical rule can be stated as in (35):

(35)   Conjunction Reduction

$$[\underset{1}{X} - \underset{2}{Y} - \underset{3}{Z}]_s - \text{and} - [\underset{5}{U} - \underset{6}{W} - \underset{7}{R}]_s$$

Conditions: $1 = 5$ and $3 = 7$

$\Rightarrow 1, 2 + 4 + 6, 3, 0, 0, 0, 0$ (Optional)

What this rule says, in effect, is that when we have two sentences joined by the word *and*, and the two sentences are identical except for some single sub-sequence in each, we can optionally form a new sentence in which the *unlike* portions of the original sentences are joined by *and*, and identical parts of the second of the two sentences are deleted. By way of illustration, this rule gets us from the full conjoined sentences above to the corresponding reduced sentences as follows:

(36)

John	cooked the supper		and	John	washed the dishes	
$[\underset{1}{X} -$	$\underset{2}{Y}$	$- \underset{3}{Z}]_s -$ and $-[\underset{4}{\ } \underset{5}{U} -$			$\underset{6}{W}$	$- \underset{7}{R}]_s$
John	cooked the supper	and	washed the dishes			
$\Rightarrow \underset{1}{\ }$,	$\underset{2}{\ }$	$+ 4 +$	$\underset{6}{\ }$	$\underset{3}{\ }$, 0 , 0 , 0 , 0		

(37)

	John cooked	the supper	and		Alice ate	the supper
$[\underset{1}{X} -$	$\underset{2}{Y}$	$- \underset{3}{Z}$	$]_s -$ and $-[\underset{4}{\ } \underset{5}{U} -$	$\underset{6}{W}$	$- \underset{7}{R}]_s$	
	John cooked	and	Alice ate	the supper		
$\Rightarrow \underset{1}{\ }$,	$\underset{2}{\ }$	$+ 4 +$	$\underset{6}{\ }$,	$\underset{3}{\ }$, 0 , 0 , 0 , 0		

As it now stands, rule (35) allows the generation of both (31) and (32), without in any way accounting for the fact that the former is more fully grammatical than the latter. What we must attempt to do is to formulate some principle that will enable us to distinguish those instances of reduced conjoined sentences which are completely well-formed from those that are not.

By way of preparing to set forth a statement, let us examine other cases in which the free application of Conjunction Reduction, as stated in (35), gives conjoined sentences of differing degrees of well-formedness. The following are some relevant examples:

(38) a.

Calvin sent letters	to the President		and	Calvin sent letters
[X	Y	Z]–and–[		U
s 1	2	3 s 4 s		5

to his congressman	
W	R]
6	7 s

   b.   Calvin sent letters to the President and to his congressman.

(39) a.

John	threw a stone at	his host	and	John	rolled a boulder toward	his host
[X	Y	Z]–and–[U			W	R]
s 1	2	3 s 4 s 5			6	7 s

   b.   ?John threw a stone at and rolled a boulder towards his host.

(40) a.

Fred knew	that Bill attended the lecture		and	Fred knew
[X	Y	Z]–and–[		U
s 1	2	3 s 4 s		5

that Suzie appeared at the rally	
W	R]
6	7 s

   b.   Fred knew that Bill attended the lecture and that Suzie appeared at the rally.

(41) a.

Fred   knew that Bill   attended the lecture   and   Fred   assumed that Suzie

$$_s[\text{ X } - \quad \text{Y} \quad - \quad \text{Z} \quad]_s - \text{and} -_s[\text{ U } - \quad \text{W} \quad -$$
$$\quad 1 \qquad\qquad 2 \qquad\qquad 3 \qquad\qquad 4 \qquad 5 \qquad\qquad 6$$

attended the lecture

$$\qquad\qquad \text{R} \qquad]_s$$
$$\qquad\qquad 7$$

b.   ?Fred knew that Bill and assumed that Suzie attended the lecture.

One possible generalization that we might draw from the examples above is the following:[4]   *John cooked – S ?*   *Alice ate – S .*

(42)   Constituency Condition
      A reduced conjoined sentence will be fully grammatical only if the factors corresponding to terms 2 and 6 of the structural description of rule (35) are *single constituents* (i.e., only if these factors are analyzable as NP's, PrepP's, S's, or N's, etc.).

An illustration of the effects of this statement is provided by (38b) and (39b). In the derivation of (38b) from its underlying source, term 2 corresponded to the sequence *to the President*, and term 6 to the sequence *to his congressman*. Since both of these sequences are constituents (in this case, prepositional phrases), we predict correctly that Conjunction Reduction will give perfectly good results here. In the derivation of (39b), by contrast, the terms being joined together are *throw a stone at* and *roll a boulder toward*, neither of which is a constituent. We thus predict (again correctly) that (39b) will not be entirely well-formed. It is worth noting here that what we have said in this paragraph holds true whether we adopt the VP-analysis or the non-VP analysis. In other words, we can assume that proponents of both of these competing views could agree that *to the President* is a single constituent whereas *throw a stone at* is not.

    A similar explanation is available for the difference in grammaticality of (40b) and (41b). The sequence *that Bill attended the lecture* is a constituent (in this case, an S̄), and thus we correctly predict that (40b) is fully well-formed. On the other hand, the sequence *knew that Bill* is not a constituent, and sentence (41b) is consequently predicted to be not fully well-formed. To use a common phrase, the Constituency Condition *is supported by* the data in (40) and (41); that is, the condition proves useful in accounting for the judgments represented there.

    At this point, it is natural to ask whether the same condition on Conjunction Reduction might also help us to account for the difference in grammaticality that we were originally concerned with, that existing between *John cooked the supper and washed the dishes,* and *?John cooked and Alice ate the supper.* With this pair of sentences, as opposed to those just considered, the impact of this condition depends critically on whether we adopt the VP analysis or the non-VP analysis. If we take the former course, then the sequence *cooked the supper* will be a constituent (a VP), but the sequence *John cooked* will not be. This situation is shown as follows:

(43)

(is a constituent)

(is not a constituent)

It follows from the Constituency Condition that (31) should be fully grammatical whereas (32) should not be, as is indeed the case.

Suppose now that we were to adopt the non-VP analysis. Then neither the sequence *cooked the supper* nor the sequence *John cooked* would be a constituent, as we can see below:

(44)

(is not a constituent)

(is not a constituent)

Consequently, we predict that neither (31) nor (32) will be fully well-formed, a prediction that is not consistent with the data.

Let us pause at this point to recapitulate the steps in this argument. As a first step, we attempted to provide justification for the Constituency Condition, a condition whose purpose was to account for differences in relative grammaticality of reduced conjoined sentences. In particular, we tried to demonstrate its usefulness for situations in which the choice between the VP analysis and the non-VP analysis was irrelevant. We then showed that with a VP analysis, the same statement sufficed to yield correct predictions about sentences (31) and (32), whereas with the non-VP analysis, the same condition did not give the correct results. We are now justified in asserting that, assuming the Constituency Condition to be correct, the difference in relative grammaticality of (31) and (32) *provides support for the VP analysis as against the non-VP analysis*.

How might a defender of the non-VP analysis try to counter this argument? It might at first glance seem that his best hope would lie in simply adding an extra clause to the Constituency Condition:

(42′)   A reduced conjoined sentence will be fully grammatical only if the factors corresponding to terms 2 and 6 of the structural description of rule (35) are single constituents, *or* if these factors are each of the form V NP.

This extra clause, however, is to all appearances completely *ad hoc*; that is, its sole function is to avoid embarrassment for the non-VP analysis. Such an extra clause is completely unnecessary if we opt for the VP analysis.

A more promising possibility for the defender of the non-VP analysis would be to look critically at the Constituency Condition. His aim would be to arrive at an alternative condition that works just as well as (42) and further-more fits in as nicely with the non-VP analysis as with the VP analysis. He would be in an especially strong position were he to find new examples for which his condition actually came out ahead of the Constituency Condition.

With all of this at the back of his mind, he might notice that all of the fully grammatical reduced conjoined sentences discussed so far had nothing at all to the right of the nonidentical material joined by *and*, whereas just the opposite was true for the sentences that failed to be fully grammatical:

(31)   John *cooked the supper* and *washed the dishes*.

(32)   ?*John cooked* and *Alice ate* the supper.

(38) b.   Calvin sent letters *to the President* and *to his congressman*.

(39) b.   ?John *threw a stone at* and *rolled a boulder toward* his host.

(40) b.   Fred knew *that Bill attended the lecture* and *that Suzie appeared at the rally*.

       b.   ?Fred *knew that Bill* and *assumed that Suzie* attended the lecture.

He now proposes (45) as a substitute for (42) as a condition on rule (35),

(35)   Conjunction Reduction

$$_s[\ X - Y - Z \ ]_s \ - \ \text{and} \ - \ _s[\ U - W - R \ ]_s$$
$$\quad \ 1 \quad 2 \quad 3 \qquad\qquad\quad 4 \quad 5 \quad 6 \quad 7$$

Condition: 1 = 5 and 3 = 7

$\Rightarrow$ 1, 2 + 4 + 6, 0, 0, 0, 0   (Optional)

argument for non VP analysis

(45)   Conjunct-on-Right Condition
A reduced conjoined sentence will be fully grammatical only if term 3 (likewise term 7) is empty, i.e., has no material from the tree assigned to it.

This new condition, like the old one, accounts for all of the data given above. However, unlike the old one, it makes no reference at all to the constituent structure of the two underlying sentences. In other words, when we wish to apply the principle, we do not need to know anything about the shape of the trees associated with the two underlying S's. Consequently, and this is what is important in the present context, the difference between our original sentences (31) and (32) is accounted for equally well whether we adopt the VP analysis or the non-VP analysis. Thus, if the new condition is assumed to be correct, sentences (31) and (32) no longer provide any evidence in favor of the VP analysis.

Having shown that the Conjunct-on-Right Condition is just as effective as the Constituency Condition in accounting for the data considered so far, the non-VP defender might seek to strengthen his position by citing examples with respect to which his condition would come out ahead of the original. One example that he might give is the following:

(46)   John goes to Boston three times a week and to New York three times a year.

The full conjoined source for (46) would be (47), and the structural description for Conjunction Reduction would be satisfied in the manner indicated:

(47)   John goes   to Boston three times a week   and

$$\underset{S}{[} \quad \underset{1}{X} \quad - \quad \underset{2}{Y} \quad - \quad \underset{3}{Z} \underset{S}{]}- \underset{4}{and}$$

John goes   to New York three times a year

$$\underset{S}{[} \quad \underset{5}{U} \quad - \quad \underset{6}{W} \quad - \quad \underset{7}{R} \underset{S}{]}$$

Given the Conjunct-on-Right Condition, the fact that (46) is perfectly grammatical is just what we should expect, since terms 3 and 7 are both empty.

For our original statement based on constituency, by contrast, sentence (46) proves to be embarrassing. This sentence should be good only if the sequence *to New York three times a year* is a single constituent:

(48)

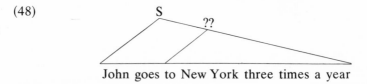

John goes to New York three times a year

But to regard this sequence as a single constituent leads to a serious inconsistency with the description of the *do-so* construction developed earlier in this chapter. The following examples illustrate the *do-so* possibilities for the first half of (47):

(49)   John goes to Boston three times a week, and Bill

$\left\{ \begin{array}{l} \text{goes to Boston three times a week} \\ \text{does so} \end{array} \right\}$ too.

(50)   John goes to Boston three times a week, and Bill $\left\{ \begin{array}{l} \text{goes to Boston} \\ \text{does so} \end{array} \right\}$

three times a year.

(51)   John goes to Boston three times a week, and Bill $\begin{Bmatrix} \text{goes} \\ \text{*does so} \end{Bmatrix}$ to
New York three times a year.

On the basis of these sentences and the VP analysis of the *do-so* construction, the VP proponent would have to accept essentially the tree below as the deep structure for the first half of (47):

(52)

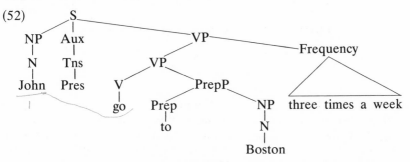

In this tree, the sequence *to Boston three times a week* does not make up a single constituent. Thus, if the VP proponent is to maintain his analysis of the *do-so* construction, he must apparently give up or modify his condition that Conjunction Reduction gives fully grammatical results only when the second and sixth terms are single constituents.

While the Conjunct-on-Right Condition thus enjoys at least one advantage as compared with the Constituency Condition, it is not without some disadvantages. In the first place, there are certain sentences that are correctly predicted to be fully grammatical if we assume the earlier condition but not if we assume the later one. One such sentence is:

(53)   We sanded and painted the chairs.   *ambiguous DO of sanded*

This sentence would have the following underlying source, with Conjunction Reduction applying as indicated by the underlining:

(54)   We   sanded   the chairs   and   we   painted   the chairs

$$\underset{S}{[}\underset{1}{X} - \underset{2}{Y} - \underset{3}{Z} \underset{S}{]} - \text{and} - \underset{S}{[}\underset{5}{U} - \underset{6}{W} - \underset{7}{R} \underset{S}{]}$$

Since terms 3 and 7 are not empty, the Conjunct-on-Right Condition is not satisfied. On the other hand, the Constituency Condition *is* satisfied: both term 2 and term 6 are constituents (in this case, V's). Consequently, with the Constituency Condition, we get a correct prediction of full grammaticality for sentence (53).

A problem for the Conjunct-on-Right Condition of precisely the opposite sort is posed by the sentence:

(55)   *Photographs of movie stars cost a dollar and of baseball players cost a penny.

This sentence could arise by the application of Conjunction Reduction to the following structure:

(56)   photographs   of movie stars cost a dollar   and

$$_S[\quad X \quad - \quad \quad Y \quad \quad - \quad Z \;]_S - and -$$

       1   2   3   4

       photographs   of baseball players cost a penny

$$_S[\quad U \quad - \quad \quad W \quad \quad - \quad R \;]_S$$

       5   6   7

Since terms 3 and 7 are empty, the Conjunct-on-Right Condition will not account for the ungrammaticality of the resulting sentence (55). By contrast, the ungrammaticality of (55) poses no problem for the Constituency Condition: it is just what we should expect, given that the sequence *of movie stars cost a dollar* is not a single constituent.

Let us summarize the discussion to this point. We have been studying two competing views of the structure of simple sentences, which we have referred to as the VP analysis and the non-VP analysis. In the course of this discussion, we were led to examine two competing descriptions of reduced conjoined sentences, those expressed in the Constituency Condition and in the Conjunct-on-Right Condition. We observed that the Constituency Condition accounted for the difference between (31) and (32), our original pair of sentences, only if we assumed the VP analysis. With the Conjunct-on-Right Condition, on the other hand, we arrived at the correct results with either of the two analyses, and thus had no grounds for preferring the VP analysis. In this situation, it became of the utmost importance to ask which (if either) of the two conditions was superior to the other. What we discovered was that neither enjoyed a distinct overall advantage, in that each had particular strengths and weaknesses as compared with the other.

If we were to continue the investigation here, a natural next step would be to try to find another condition on Conjunction Reduction, one that would avoid the respective pitfalls of the two conditions examined thus far. We would then want to determine whether this third condition worked more effectively with the VP analysis than with the non-VP analysis, or whether it worked equally well with either. In the former case, we would once again be in possession of an argument for the VP analysis based on sentences (31) and (32); in the latter case, no such argument would be viable.

EXERCISES

1.   Suppose that we are asked to evaluate an entirely different analysis of reduced conjoined sentences. In this analysis, there is no rule of Conjunction

Reduction. Instead, conjoined struc.ures are generated directly in deep structure by the addition of the following phrase structure rules to the rules developed in earlier chapters:

S → S *and* S
NP → NP *and* NP
VP → VP *and* VP
N → N *and* N
PrepP → PrepP *and* PrepP
S̄ → S̄ *and* S̄

A. Which of the fully acceptable sentences discussed in section 11.3 would not have a derivation by these rules?

B. Assuming again for the moment the rule of Conjunction Reduction, give an example of a grammatical sentence that could be obtained only if Conjunction Reduction was allowed to apply *after* one of the transformational rules discussed in the earlier chapters. Why would this sentence pose a problem for the alternative analysis suggested in this problem?

2. Consider the following condition on Conjunction Reduction, intended as an alternative to the Constituency Condition and the Conjunct-on-Right Condition:

A reduced conjoined sentence will not be fully grammatical if either (a) the second factor (and likewise the sixth factor) can be analyzed as one or more constituents <u>followed by a subpart of a following constituent</u>, *or* (b) the second factor (and likewise the sixth factor) can be analyzed as one or more constituents <u>preceded by a subpart of a preceding NP or S constituent</u>.

[handwritten: which is/are]

[margin handwritten: Rule is okay except that it's cumbersome + having a or b — it's not revealing]

A. Show that with this condition we correctly predict less than full grammaticality for the following sentences from the text:

?John threw a stone at and rolled a boulder toward his host.
?Fred knew that Bill and assumed that Suzie attended the lecture.

B. It will be recalled that the first sentence below posed a problem for the Constituency Condition, and that the other two sentences posed problems for the Conjunct-on-Right Condition:

[margin handwritten: for non-VP analysis]

John goes to Boston three times a week and to New York three times a year.

[margin handwritten: a + b are satisfied but 2nd factor c) made up of a partial VP (see S2)]

We sanded and painted the chairs. *[handwritten: ok for VP analysis]*
?Photographs of movie stars cost a dollar and of baseball players cost a penny.

[margin handwritten: a + b are satisfied but 2nd factor c) made up of a partial VP (see S2)]
[handwritten: doesn't work; part (b) not satisfied - "of the ___" is part of preceding NP]

How does the alternative condition fare with these sentences?

C. Assuming the alternative condition, determine whether or not the following sentences from the text provide a basis for an argument in favor of the VP analysis:

John cooked the supper and washed the dishes.

?John cooked and Alice ate the supper.

3.   In Chomsky 1957, an additional condition is placed on Conjunction Reduction: not only must the sequences joined by *and* be constituents; in addition, they must be constituents *of the same type*. See if you can construct any ungrammatical reduced conjoined sentences that would provide justification for setting up this additional constraint.

11.4 SUMMATION

Before concluding, we should take note of several general points that are illustrated by this discussion. In the first place, our framework for linguistic description frequently confronts us with what seem at first to be rather straightforward choices, like the choice between two different tree structures for simple sentences. Despite our eagerness to make a definite decision, it may turn out to be anything but straightforward to find convincing grounds for electing one of the alternatives over the other.

In the second place, our search for arguments will typically involve us in a detailed examination of one or more specific constructions whose relevance for the question at hand we may have been completely unaware of at the outset of the investigation. The two constructions whose relevance we evaluated in this chapter were the *do-so* construction and the reduced conjunction construction. We have actually seen several similar arguments in previous chapters. One was in section 6.3, when the point at issue concerned the proper surface structure for sentences such as *John believes Alice to be nice*. In that case, the critical argument in favor of viewing *Alice* as a surface-structure direct object in the main clause depended critically on our acceptance of the clause-mate condition as a restriction governing the rule of Reflexivization.

A related observation should perhaps be made here. Our arguments in favor of a linguistic hypothesis such as the VP analysis typically depend very critically on other assumptions, in the present instance, assumptions about the *do-so* construction and the reduced conjunction construction. Whenever, as often happens, new data arise that force the revision of these "background assumptions," then we are obligated to see whether the *new* assumptions permit a similar argument, or whether, on the contrary, they do not.

One final point deserves mention here, so that the preceding discussion can be seen in proper perspective. The efforts made on behalf of the non-VP analysis have been purely defensive in nature. At no point has the imaginary supporter of the non-VP analysis been able to point to any positive advantages for his analysis. All of his efforts have instead been aimed at reducing the effectiveness of the positive arguments of the opposition. In future chapters we will examine some controversies in which the positive advantages are divided more equitably between the two competing analyses.

Suggestions for Further Reading

Conjoined constructions are discussed briefly in Chomsky 1957, Chapter 5, and in more detail in Gleitman 1965. Arguments in favor of analyzing at least some conjoined NP's as conjoined NP's in deep structure are given in Lakoff and Peters 1966.

The *do-so* construction in English is treated in Lakoff and Ross 1966.

In a few descriptions of English, the deep structure order of English is taken to be Verb-Subject-Object, and the VP is viewed as being the result of a transformation that moves an NP into subject position to the left of the verb (Fillmore 1968; McCawley 1970a). Berman 1974b is a critique of the latter paper.

Notes

1. The relevance of the *do-so* construction for arguments about constituent structure was first noticed by Lakoff and Ross 1966.

2. The problem that this sentence poses for (11) was pointed out to the author by Tom Wasow.

3. This argument was presented by Chomsky 1957, Chapter 5.

4. This is essentially the condition proposed by Chomsky.

12

Helping Verbs

In this chapter we will again be comparing an analysis developed in a previous chapter with a new one. The old analysis will be the analysis of the helping verbs presented in Chapter 3. It will be recalled that in this analysis there was a separate auxiliary constituent containing all of the helping verbs; the two phrase structure rules that were central in setting up this constituent were the following:

(1) a. $\quad$ S → NP Aux VP

   b. $\quad$ Aux → Tns (M) (*have en*) (*be ing*)

These phrase structure rules resulted in the assignment of the tree in (3) as as the deep structure of sentence (2):

(2) $\quad$ John may have been shining the doorknob.

(3)

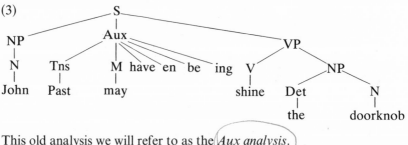

This old analysis we will refer to as the *Aux analysis*.

12.1 AN ALTERNATIVE ANALYSIS OF HELPING VERBS

In a number of more recent studies, an alternative view of helping verbs is developed.[1] This new analysis can perhaps best be characterized by the emphasis that it gives to the "verbal" character of helping verbs, as opposed to their "helping" character. Although we will arrive at a more detailed picture as we go along, some idea of the general outlines of this new analysis can be gained from the following tree, which is roughly the surface structure that would be assigned to sentence (2) in the new analysis:

(4)

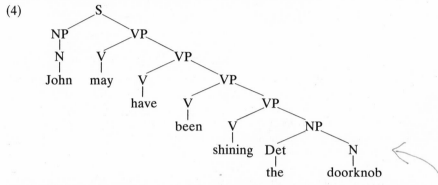

Each of the words *may*, *have*, and *been* here functions as the head of its own VP constituent. Consequently, we will refer to this analysis as the *main verb analysis*.

Before saying anything about the deep structure proposed for this sentence in the Main Verb Analysis, we must review briefly some of the ideas developed in Chapter 6. There we argued in favor of deriving apparently subjectless infinitive phrases such as the following from deep structures containing embedded full sentences.

(5)   Cornelia tried to enjoy the concert.

(6)   Cornelia appeared to enjoy the concert.

Furthermore, we argued that different deep structures were appropriate for these two sentences. For (5), we proposed:

(7)

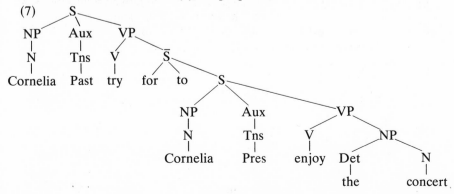

The critical rule in the derivation of (5) from this deep structure was the rule of Identical-NP Deletion, which deleted the lower occurrence of *Cornelia* under identity with the occurrence of the identical NP in the main clause. For sentence (6), on the other hand, we proposed a deep structure in which the subject of the main S was initially empty:

(8)

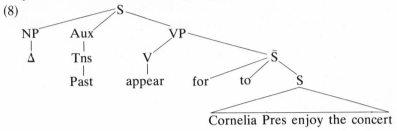

In the derivation of this sentence, the critical rule is Subject Raising, which replaces the empty subject of the higher S by the subject of the lower S.

Within the main verb analysis, every occurrence of a helping verb is assumed to occur in at least one of these two deep structure configurations, and some are assumed to occur in both. For instance, the progressive helping verb *be* in a sentence such as (9) below would be analyzed as the main verb of a sentence with an empty subject. The *ing* which in the Aux analysis was introduced as part of the Aux constituent would in this analysis be introduced under S.

(9)   John is undergoing an appendectomy.

(10)

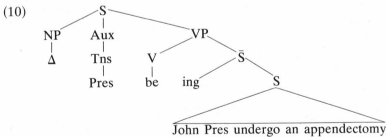

First, the Affix Insertion rule of Chapter 6 applies to move *ing* into the Aux of the lower S, replacing the Tns. Then Subject Raising applies to this tree in exactly the same fashion as it applied to the tree in (8). *John* is promoted to subject position in the main clause, yielding:

(11)

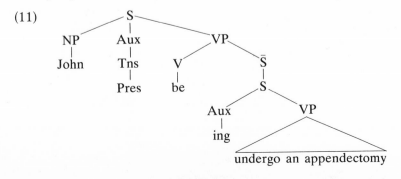

Affix-Hopping applies twice, and the correct surface-structure sequence is obtained.

By contrast, the occurrence of *will* found in the *if* clause of (12), a use known by traditional grammarians as the "volitional *will*," is analyzed as arising by Identical-NP Deletion from the deep structure given in (13).[2]

(12)   If you will sweep the porch, I will wash the dishes.

(13)

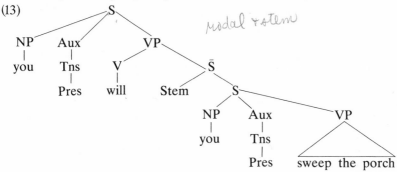

The element *Stem* present in the complementizer will, like *to* and *ing*, replace the Tns constituent in the Aux. However, unlike them, it will be phonologically null. Its purpose will be precisely to indicate that the form of the verb used in a complement of *will* is just the bare verb stem.

The derivation from (13) to (12) now proceeds as follows. First, by a revision of Affix Insertion that moves *Stem* into the Aux position in the same manner as *to* and *ing* are moved, we get the structure:

(14)

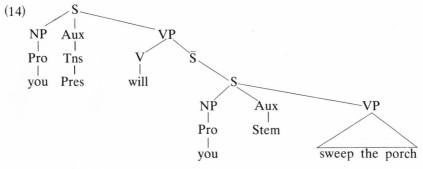

Identical-NP Deletion applies, yielding:

(15)

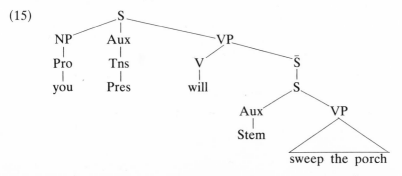

With Affix Hopping in both clauses, we arrive at the desired surface structure sequence.

For the use of *will* as a simple future, we will assume a deep structure like that for the progressive *be*, in which the subject of the top S is initially empty. Sentence (16) provides an illustration; its deep structure would be the tree in (17).

(16)   The tree will fall into the lake.

(17)

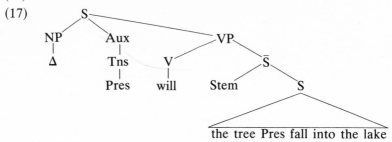

The derivation in this case proceeds in the same fashion as in the derivation of (9). The first rule to apply is Affix Insertion, which replaces the Tns in the lower Aux by *Stem*. Next, Subject Raising moves the lower-S subject, *the tree*, into subject position in the higher S, yielding:

(18)

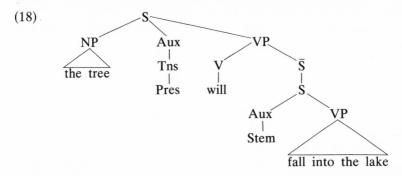

Two applications of Affix Hopping finish the derivation.

Let us pause now to answer a question that might be raised at this point. Within the Aux analysis, we could derive the passive member of an active-passive pair such as that in (19) below by means of the transformational rule stated in (20):

(19) a.   The police may have arrested Sam.

   b.   Sam may have been arrested by the police.

(20)   Passive

   NP – Aux – V – NP – X
   1   2   3   4   5

   $\Rightarrow$ 4, 2, *be* + *en* + 3, 0, 5 + *by* + 1   (Optional)

Given the main verb analysis, however, we have a structure for (19a) that does not satisfy the structural description of (20). This structure is given in (21).

(21)

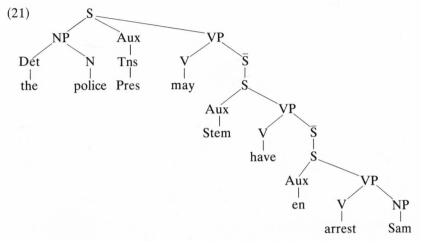

The material found between the subject NP and the verb *arrest* is now no longer analyzable as a single constituent Aux. Consequently, the structural description for the Passive rule must apparently be made much more complicated:

(22)   NP – Aux (V) (Aux) (V) (Aux) – V – NP – X
         1   2   3   4   5

However, if we review briefly the analysis of passive infinitives in sentences containing verbs such as *appear* and *seem*, we will see that there is really no problem at all. Let us consider first the derivation of a sentence such as the following:

(23)   Teddy seems to be admired by the public.

In the deep structure of this sentence, *Teddy* will appear as the direct object of the verb *admire* in the lower sentence:

(24)

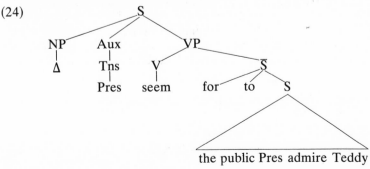

Passivization is taken care of immediately, on the cycle of the lower S, giving:

(25)

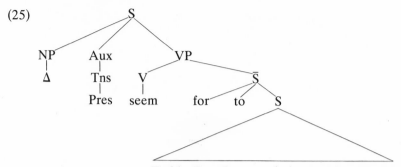

Teddy Pres be en admire by the public

Now that *Teddy* has been made the subject of the lower S, the application of Subject Raising in the domain of the higher S has the effect of moving *Teddy* into the empty subject NP. The ultimate result is just the desired passive sentence (23).

Turning back now to helping verbs, the same treatment makes it possible to derive (19b) without recourse to the more complicated Passive rule given in (22). We start with the following tree:

(26)

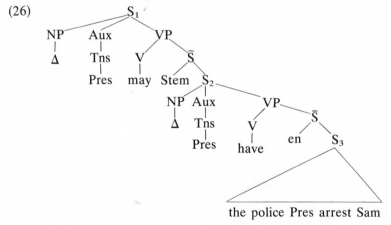

the police Pres arrest Sam

The basic idea is to do just what we did in deriving sentence (23) with *seem*: we apply Passive in the lowest S, before any complicated intervening sequence of verbal elements has a chance to build up between the NP *the police* and the verb *arrest*. For passivization in this lowest S, the structural description of our original Passive rule is satisfied. Application of the rule gives:

(27)

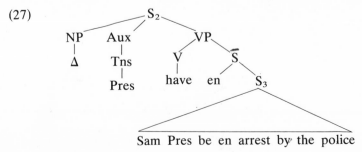

Sam Pres be en arrest by the police

From this point on, the derivation is straightforward. In the S_2 cycle, after Affix Insertion applies, the NP *Sam* gets promoted into subject position by Subject Raising, giving:

(28)

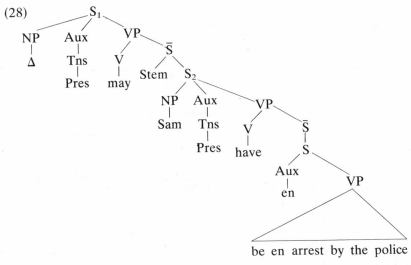

Going now to the S_1 cycle, after Affix Insertion applies, we are in a position to apply Subject Raising again. *Sam* now becomes the subject of S_1, giving the following structure:

(29)

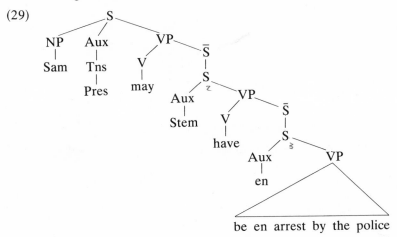

With three applications of Affix Hopping, we succeed in obtaining the surface structure for (19b). Thus we see that the main verb analysis does not in fact require any revision in the Passive rule as it was stated in Chapter 4.

The major features of the main verb analysis, then, can be summarized as follows:

(a) The Aux constituent in each sentence contains only the Tns node, optionally preceded by *not*.

(b) All other elements that appeared in the Aux constituent in the old analysis now appear either as head verbs of VP's (the modals, perfect *have*, and progressive *be*), or under the domination of S (*en*, *ing*).

(c) The basic rules in deriving structures containing helping verbs are the same as those involved in the derivation of sentences with embedding verbs; they include Affix Insertion, Subject Raising, and Identical-NP Deletion.

Seem
appear

(d) Rules such as Passive which have an Aux as part of their structural description can still apply, with the difference that now they apply in the lowest S possible.

Before proceeding to the arguments that might be put forward in favor of one or the other of the two analyses, we should point out a slight modification that will be made in the Aux analysis. Instead of assuming that modals occur in deep structure Aux's without any associated inflectional marker, we will assume that they have the marker *Stem* associated with them. The basic rule for expanding the Aux constituent will thus take the following form:

(30)   Aux → (*not*) Tns (M *Stem*) (*have en*) (*be ing*)

This element *Stem* will be attached to following verbal elements by Affix Hopping in exactly the same manner as Tns, *en*, and *ing* are attached. This revision will make it somewhat easier to compare the main verb analysis and the Aux analysis. Moreover, we will see later that this element *Stem* proves useful in at least one transformational rule that is designed specifically to work with the Aux analysis.

EXERCISES

1.   Give the deep structure that would be assigned to the following sentence in the main verb analysis:

Jack could have been reading the book.

Assume that all of the helping verbs in this sentence occur in the same type of structures as *seem* and *appear* do.

2.   Give the deep structure that would be assigned to the following sentence in the main verb analysis:

The baby wouldn't eat the spinach.

Assume that the helping verb here takes a nonempty subject and a postverbal complement, just as *try* does.

3.   Give the deep structure that would be assigned to the following sentence in the main verb analysis:

There may have been a fly in the soup.

Assume that both *may* and *have* in this sentence are like *seem* and *appear*.

Be sure to review the discussion of *There* Insertion in section 6.3. The rule was stated there as follows:

There Insertion

NP – Aux – *be* – PrepP
1   2   3   4

⇒ *there*, 2, 3 + 1, 4   (Optional)

Why must the rule as stated apply in the lowest S of the deep structure for the above sentence, if that sentence is to be derived?

4.) Suppose that the charge is made that the main verb analysis does not interact correctly with the clause mate condition on the rule of Reflexivization. Specifically, it is alleged that sentence (i) below could not be generated, since in (ii), which is the constituent structure tree assigned to this sentence, the two NP's are not clause mates.

(i)   He has been talking to himself.

(ii)

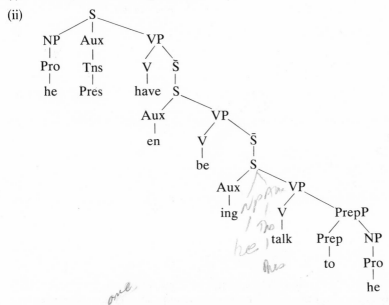

Even granting, as he is indeed forced to, that Reflexivization could not apply in this structure if it was subject to the clause mate condition, the main verb proponent still has a reply. What is it?

12.2 AN ENGLISH ELLIPTICAL CONSTRUCTION

The argument that we will present and discuss in this section is one that is frequently advanced in support of the main verb analysis.[3] It is based on elliptical sentences of a type illustrated in the following examples:

(31) a.   Paul is studying French and Marsha is (studying French), too.

(32) a.   Bill told us that he would have worked on the letter, and I am sure that he would have (worked on the letter).

(33) a.   Jack won't keep quiet about it, but George will (keep quiet about it).

(34) a.   Morton likes loud parties, and Ike does (like loud parties), too.[4]

(35) a.   Jocko will break all the furniture, unless you can persuade him not to (break all the furniture).

In all of the above examples, the deleted material qualifies, under either the original analysis or our new one, as a VP plus (in three of the five cases) a preceding affix (ing, en, and Stem, respectively):

(31) b.   ...Marsha Pres be *ing study French*

(32) b.   ...he Past will Stem have *en work on the letter*

(33) b.   ...George Pres will Stem *keep quiet about it*

(34) b.   ...Ike Pres *like loud parties*

(35) b.   ...unless you Pres can Stem persuade him not to *break all the furniture*

We might account for these examples by adding to our grammar an optional transformational rule that has the effect of deleting a VP (and also a preceding *ing* or *en* or *Stem*) when there is an identical VP earlier in the sentence:

(36)   (VP Deletion)

$$X - VP - Y - \left(\begin{matrix} en \\ ing \\ Stem \end{matrix} \right) - VP - Z$$

$$1 \quad 2 \quad 3 \quad 4 \quad 5 \quad 6$$

Condition: $2 = 5$

$\Rightarrow 1, 2, 3, 0, 0, 6$ (Optional)

With regard to the four example sentences that we have considered so far, it clearly makes no difference whether we adopt the Aux analysis developed in Chapter 3 or the main verb analysis outlined in this chapter. Rule (36) works equally well either way.

In other sentences, however, where we observe what would appear to be the same type of ellipsis, only one of the two analyses would permit the application of VP Deletion as stated above:

(37)   George may have been sleeping, and the sentry may have (been sleeping), too.

(38)   Ronald won't have finished, but Donald will (have finished).

In the Aux analysis, each of the deleted sequences includes one verbal element on the right-hand side of the Aux constituent in addition to a VP:

(39)

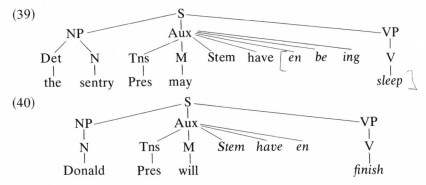

(40)

Thus, if we assume the tree structures in (39) and (40), the VP Deletion rule will not account for the elliptical versions of (37) and (38).

Given the main verb analysis, however, we would postulate (41) and (42) on the following page as the structures of the full versions of the second clauses in (37) and (38). In these trees, the sequences *be ing sleep* and *have en finish* do qualify as VP's, so that rule (36) can apply, deleting these sequences plus in each case the preceding affix. Thus, if the main verb analysis is adopted, a very simple transformational rule accounts for all the elliptical sentences that we have considered so far.

It is now appropriate to ask what kind of transformational rule is required for these elliptical sentences if we assume the Aux analysis. We saw above that in the Aux analysis the deleted material frequently does not make up a single constituent. Consequently, the only possibility for identifying deletable sequences would seem to lie in identifying the elements to the left of the sequences. One of the simplest rules of this sort that we could state can be put informally as follows: optionally delete a sequence following a helping verb, Tns, or *to*, when there is an identical sequence earlier in the sentence. (As before, we need to allow for the presence of affix-markers before the identical material; any such marker will be deleted along with the material that is identical.) In formalizing this alternative statement, we represent the deleted material by a variable (the variable "X_9") instead of by the nonvariable symbol VP:

(43)   Post-H(elping) V(erb) Deletion

$$X_1 - {}_S[\ X_2 - X_3\ ]_S - X_4 -$$
$$1234$$

$$_S[\ X_5 - \begin{Bmatrix} Tns \\ en \\ to \\ Stem \end{Bmatrix} - (\begin{Bmatrix} M \\ have \\ be \end{Bmatrix}) - (\begin{Bmatrix} Stem \\ en \\ ing \end{Bmatrix}) - X_9\ ]_S - X_{10}$$
$$5678910$$

Condition: 3 = 9

$\Rightarrow$ 1, 2, 3, 4, 5, 6, 7, 0, 0, 10   (Optional)

(41)

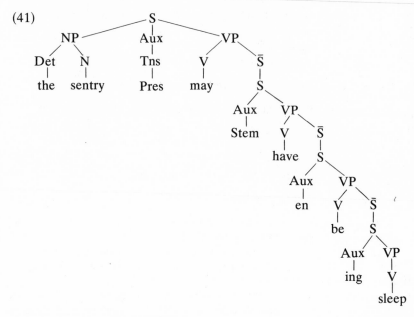

(42)

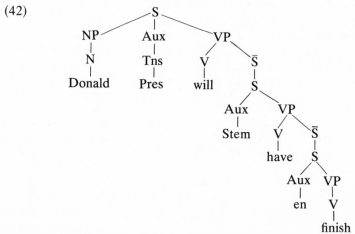

Since (43) is a complicated rule, it will be helpful to illustrate the manner in which its structural description is satisfied in the derivations of four of the sentences considered above:

(31) c.   Paul Pres be ing   study French   and   Marsha

$$X_1 - {}_S[\quad X_2 \quad - \quad X_3 \quad]_S - X_4 - {}_S[\; X_5 \quad -$$

     1   2   3   4   5

     Pres   be   ing   study French   too

$$Tns - be - ing - \quad X_9 \quad]_S - X_{10}$$

     6   7   8   9   10

(34) c.

| Morton Pres | like loud parties | and | Ike |

$$X_1 - {}_S[\quad X_2 \quad - \quad X_3 \quad]_S - X_4 - [X_5 -$$
$$1 \qquad 2 \qquad\qquad 3 \qquad 4 \qquad 5$$

| Pres | like loud parties | too |

$$\text{Tns} - \quad - \quad - \quad X_9 \quad]_S - X_{10}$$
$$6 \quad 7 \quad 8 \qquad 9 \qquad 10$$

(35) c.

| Jocko Pres will Stem | break all the furniture |

$$X_1 - {}_S[\quad X_2 \quad - \quad X_3 \quad]_S \quad -$$
$$1 \qquad 2 \qquad\qquad 3$$

unless you can persuade him   not   to

$$X_4 \qquad\qquad - {}_S[X_5 - to - \quad - \quad -$$
$$4 \qquad\qquad\qquad 5 \quad 6 \quad 7 \quad 8$$

break all the furniture

$$X_9 \qquad]_S - X_{10}$$
$$9 \qquad 10$$

(37) c.

| George Pres may Stem have en | be ing sleep |

$$X_1 - {}_S[\qquad X_2 \qquad - \quad X_3 \quad]_S -$$
$$1 \qquad\qquad 2 \qquad\qquad 3$$

and   the sentry Pres may   Stem have en

$$X_4 - {}_S[\quad X_5 \qquad - \text{Stem} - \text{have} - \text{en} -$$
$$4 \qquad 5 \qquad\qquad {}^- 6 \qquad 7 \qquad 8$$

be ing sleep   too

$$X_9 \quad]_S - X_{10}$$
$$9 \qquad 10$$

The argument for the main verb analysis can now be put as follows: if we assume this analysis, then a wide range of elliptical sentences can be accounted for by a very simple transformational rule, the rule of VP Deletion given in (36). On the other hand, if we assume the Aux analysis, then the best that we can do is the quite complex rule of Post-HV Deletion stated in (43). Thus, the charge that the main verb proponent brings against the Aux analysis is that this original analysis makes a quite simple process appear much more complicated than it really is.

At this point, the logical tack for the defender of the Aux analysis to take is to try to show that even with the main verb analysis, the elliptical construction under consideration is more accurately described by the complicated rule of Post-HV Deletion than it is by the simple rule of VP Deletion. In particular, he might search for instances in which VP Deletion fails to apply when it should apply, or else applies when it should not. As it happens, cases of both types exist.

We can begin by considering some cases in which material that is in fact readily deletable might fail to qualify as a VP, and hence would be ineligible for removal by VP Deletion. Examples of this type are provided by the deletion of various predicate elements after the copula *be*:

(44)   John is angry, and his sister is (angry), too.

(45)   Fred is a burglar, but no one will admit that he is (a burglar).

(46)   Fred may not be the man who robbed the Gulf station, but then again he may be (the man who robbed the Gulf station).

By contrast, Post-HV Deletion applies with no problem in structures of these types. Each of the structures contains some form of *be*, with the material immediately following it automatically qualifying for deletion, just as did the material in (31) that followed *be* in its progressive use. On the other hand, the rule of VP Deletion can apply to these structures only if the sequences *angry*, *a burglar*, and *the man who robbed the Gulf station* are all VP's in the trees in which they appear.

We must count it as a mild objection that we have not previously encountered any evidence in favor of analyzing these sequences as VP's. A more serious objection is that in other environments the same sequences are not deletable:

(47)   *John became *angry*, and his sister became _____, too.

(48)   *Fred looks like *a burglar*, and his brother looks like_____, too.

(49)   *We can't be sure that Fred isn't *the man who robbed the Gulf station*, even though the owner tentatively identified Jack as_____.

Unless the main verb proponent can find some independent reason to analyze these sequences as VP's when they occur with the copula, but as something else when they occur in other environments, his claim that it is precisely VP's that are eligible for deletion must be considered somewhat suspect. For the rule of Post-HV Deletion, the ungrammatical sentences above pose no problem, since they are not preceded on the left by the required kind of material, essentially a helping verb or *to*.

Problems of the opposite sort also arise, in which the deletion of clear VP's gives bad results. An initial example is provided by structures in which the entire largest VP of the main verb analysis is identical with some preceding VP:

(50)   John Pres *have en be ing work* and Sally Pres *have en be ing work*, too.

If we take the option of not applying VP Deletion, or of applying it in lower VP's, we get good results:

(51)   John has been working, and Sally has been working, too.

(52)   John has been working, and Sally has been, too.

(53)   John has been working, and Sally has, too.

On the other hand, if we apply VP Deletion to delete what is presumably the largest VP (*have en be ing work*), then *Do* Support will apply on account of the Tns element left stranded by the deletion, and we eventually generate an ungrammatical result:

(54)   *John has been working, and Sally does, too.

We should note here that this problem cannot be solved by ordering Affix Hopping and *Do* Support earlier than VP Deletion. If we were to do this, we might avoid the generation of the ungrammatical (54), but we would no longer be able to generate the elliptical version of (34), which we repeat here:

(34)   Morton likes loud parties, and Ike does, too.

In order to be able to get *does* in the second clause of (34), the Tns element must not yet have been joined to the verb *like* by the rule of Affix Hopping, as would have been the case if Affix Hopping applied before VP Deletion. To summarize the problem posed by (54), then, the rule of VP Deletion gives bad results when it applies to the highest VP in a clause, whenever the highest VP happens to be headed by a helping verb.

Again, as before, sentence (54) poses no problem for Post-HV Deletion. We first recall the convention introduced in Chapter 3: whenever we have a choice between assigning material in a tree to a variable in a structural description and assigning the same material to one or more optional non-variable terms, we must always take the latter alternative. What this convention entails in the present instance is that the division shown in (55a) below, in which *have* and *en* are assigned to the variable term X_9, is strictly prohibited:

(55) a.   Sally   Pres   have en be ing work

$$X_5 \;-\; \text{Tns} \;-\; \quad - \quad - \qquad X_9$$
$$5 \qquad 6 \quad\; 7 \quad 8 \qquad\quad 9$$

This prohibition rests on the existence of the alternative division shown in (55b), which is the same as (55a) except that *have* and *en* are assigned to the optional seventh and eighth terms of the structural description:

(55) b.   Sally   Pres   have   en   be ing work

$$X_5 \;-\; \text{Tns} \;-\; \text{have} \;-\; \text{en} \;-\; \quad X_9$$
$$5 \qquad 6 \qquad 7 \qquad 8 \qquad 9$$

We could have generated the ungrammatical (54) only by applying Post-HV Deletion in the prohibited manner indicated by the underscoring in (55a). The sentence that we get from the legal application of the rule indicated in (55b) is just the grammatical sentence (53): *John has been working, and Sally has, too.*

An additional difficulty for the VP Deletion rule is posed by certain

VP's in complement structures that are in fact undeletable:

(56)   Harry insisted on *singing the Marseillaise*, but Sue tried to

$$\begin{cases} \text{keep him from } singing\ the\ Marseillaise \\ \text{*keep him from _____} \end{cases}.$$

(57)   Horace regretted *taking the subway*, and Alice

$$\begin{cases} \text{regretted } taking\ the\ subway \\ \text{*regretted _____} \end{cases}, \text{too.}$$

It will not do here to attach some sort of condition on VP Deletion to the effect that deletion of *ing* forms is prohibited, since such forms are clearly deletable when the preceding verb is the progressive *be*:

(58)   Harry is *singing the Marseillaise*, and Sally

$$\begin{cases} \text{is } singing\ the\ Marseillaise \\ \text{is _____} \end{cases}, \text{too.}$$

With the Post-HV Deletion rule, on the other hand, the ill-formed elliptical sentences in (56) and (57) pose no problem. In neither case does the second of the two identical sequences satisfy the requirement of being preceded by a helping verb, Tns, or *to*.

One final difficulty for VP Deletion is posed by sentences in which the verbal element preceding the deleted material ends up in an *ing* form:

(59)   Bill is being nasty, and Jack $\begin{cases} \text{is being nasty} \\ \text{*is being _____} \\ \text{is _____} \end{cases}, \text{too.}$

(60)   The conspirators have kept quiet, and $\begin{cases} \text{having kept quiet} \\ \text{*having _____} \end{cases}, \text{they}$
feel that the President owes them something.

In the Post-HV Deletion rule, the ungrammatical variants in (59) and (60) are excluded by the nonappearance of *ing* in the sixth term of the structural description. What this absence guarantees is that Post-HV Deletion will not take place after a helping verb that is preceded by the *ing* suffix, i.e., a helping verb that will eventually end up (after Affix Hopping) as *having* or *being*. The rule as stated allows deletion only after helping verbs that will eventually show either a tense form (Tns), the past participial form (*en*), or the bare uninflected form (*Stem*). Incidentally, it is this need to differentiate the helping verb forms that do not allow a following deletion from those that do that justifies the use of the marker *Stem* in the Aux analysis.

Let us recapitulate the course of the debate to this point. The proponent of the main verb analysis began by noting that if the main verb analysis was assumed, then all of the elliptical sentences originally considered could be accounted for by means of the very simple VP Deletion rule given in (36). On the other hand, if the Aux Analysis was adopted, this simple rule would no longer account for (37) and (38). A more complex deletion rule would be required, namely, the rule of Post-HV Deletion given in (43).

The Aux defender's reply at this point was to try to show that the rule of Post-HV Deletion, despite its initial appearance of undesirability, was actually a better rule on several scores than the rule of VP Deletion. If this point was conceded, it then followed that no argument for the main verb analysis could be constructed on the basis of the sentences in (31) through (35), and (37) and (38), for the simple reason that Post-HV Deletion worked equally well with either of the two competing constituent structures.

There are at least two types of responses that the main verb proponent might make in attempting to re-establish an advantage for his analysis. The first would be to try to overcome the objections raised against the rule of VP Deletion. He might begin by trying to find some independent evidence that such phrases as *angry*, *a burglar*, and *the man who robbed the Gulf station* really are VP's when they occur after the copula *be*, but not when they occur in other environments. He might also try to find some independently just-ified restrictions that would account for the bad elliptical sentences in (54) through (60), so that the ungrammaticality of these sentences would not have to be counted an embarrassment for the VP Deletion rule. To say that he might attempt to carry out these projects is of course not to guarantee in advance that he would succeed.

The second type of response offers a more immediate prospect of gain. In taking this tack, the main verb proponent actually begins by acknowledg-ing the general superiority of the Post-HV Deletion rule. However, he then notes a hitherto unmentioned embarrassment for this rule: in certain instan-ces, the variables X_3 and X_9 can cover far too much ground. For example, (62) below would be allowed as an elliptical variant of (61):

(61)   If the fact that Jack is moody annoys Sally, then the fact that George is moody annoys Sally, too.

(62)   *If the fact that Jack is moody annoys Sally, then the fact that George is, too.

The faulty application of the rule is just that which would result from the division given below:

(63)   if   the fact that Jack Pres be   moody Pres annoy Sally

$$X_1 - [_s \quad\quad X_2 \quad\quad - \quad\quad X_3 \quad\quad]_s$$
$$1 \quad\quad\quad 2 \quad\quad\quad\quad 3$$

then   the fact that George   Pres   be

$$X_4 - [_s \quad\quad X_5 \quad\quad - Tns - be - \quad -$$
$$4 \quad\quad\quad 5 \quad\quad\quad 6 \quad 7 \quad 8$$

moody Pres annoy Sally   too

$$X_9 \quad\quad]_s - X_{10}$$
$$9 \quad\quad\quad\quad 10$$

The problem here is very similar to that which we found in the preceding chapter in the discussion of the *do-so* construction. The main verb proponent now offers a straightforward solution to the problem raised by sentence (62): just require that the optional modal, *have*, or *be*, plus the optional affix, plus the following variable term, all go together to make up a VP. After we have made a similar change in the first half of the structural description, we arrive at the following restatement:

(64)   Post-HV Deletion   (revised version)

$$X_1 - [\ X_2 - X_3\ ]_{VP} - X_4 - \begin{Bmatrix} Tns \\ en \\ Stem \\ to \end{Bmatrix} - [\ (\begin{Bmatrix} M \\ have \\ be \end{Bmatrix})_{VP} -$$

$$\quad 1 \qquad 2 \quad\; 3 \qquad\quad 4 \qquad\;\; 5 \qquad\qquad\quad 6$$

$$(\begin{Bmatrix} Stem \\ en \\ ing \end{Bmatrix}) - X_8]_{VP} - X_9$$

$$\quad\; 7 \qquad\; 8 \qquad 9$$

Condition: $3 = 8$

$\Rightarrow$ 1, 2, 3, 4, 5, 6, 0, 0, 9   (Optional)

This revised rule, just like the original Post-HV Deletion rule, avoids the difficulties raised for the VP Deletion rule by the sentences in (44) through (54). It also avoids the difficulty raised for the original Post-HV Deletion rule by the ungrammatical sentence (62). The reason for this is simple: the sequence *be moody Pres annoy Sally* is not a VP, and thus the sub-sequence *moody Pres annoy Sally* does not qualify for deletion by the revised rule.

Although the difference between the new version and the old version of Post-HV Deletion may appear small, the adoption of the revised version is of the utmost significance for the contest between the main verb analysis and the Aux analysis. In the revised version of Post-HV Deletion, we once again have a rule which, like VP Deletion, works more effectively in the main verb analysis. A second look at a sentence such as (37) will show why this is so:

(37)   George may have been sleeping, and the sentry may have (been sleeping), too

In the main verb analysis, the structure of the second clause at the point at which the revised Post-HV Deletion rule applies is that given in (65), with the relevant division indicated by the underscoring. Because of the fact that the entire sequence *have en be ing sleep* qualifies as a VP, the revised Post-HV Deletion can apply to delete everything after *have*.

(65)

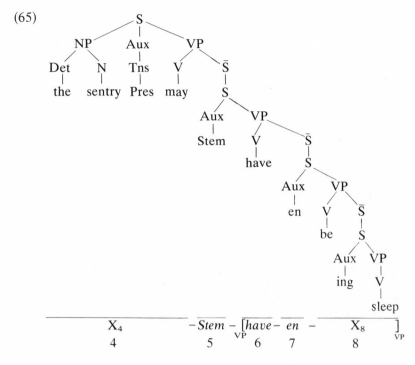

In the Aux analysis, the same second clause would be assigned the following tree:

(66)

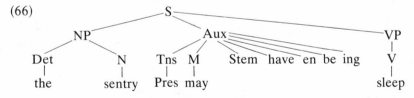

In this tree, the sequence *have en be ing sleep* is not a VP, and thus the material after *have* fails to qualify for deletion by the revised Post-HV Deletion rule (64). Thus, given the Aux analysis, we cannot derive (37) by means of the rule that at this point appears to have come out ahead of both of the rules proposed earlier.

We will arbitrarily close off debate for the time being, with the verdict that the main verb analysis now holds a slight advantage, based on the general effectiveness of the revised Post-HV Deletion rule, and on the fact that this rule works better with the main verb analysis than with the Aux analysis. It should not be thought, however, that this advantage is necessarily secure. In fact, Exercise 6 at the end of this section will give the reader an opportunity to construct a possible reply for the Aux analysis which, if successful, would again leave the Aux analysis equal to the main verb analysis with respect to the elliptical sentences discussed in this section.

EXERCISES

1. For the purposes of this problem, assume the main verb analysis. Then, for each of the following elliptical sentences in turn, determine two things: (a) whether the sentence is an embarrassment for the rule of VP Deletion (36); (b) whether the sentence is an embarrassment for the revised rule of Post-HV Deletion (64).

(i)   I don't know whether John is tall, but he $\left\{ \begin{array}{l} \text{may be tall} \\ \text{*may} \end{array} \right\}$.

(ii)   I can't guarantee that Jack is working right this minute, but he seems

$\left\{ \begin{array}{l} \text{to be working right this minute} \\ \text{to be} \\ \text{*to} \end{array} \right\}$.

(iii)   George has decided not to run again, because $\left\{ \begin{array}{l} \text{to run again} \\ \text{*to} \end{array} \right\}$

would create a great deal of resentment.

2. What kind of derived constituent structure would be dictated for passive sentences, if we were to assume the rule of VP Deletion as stated in (36)? What kind of difficulty would we encounter with the derived constituent structure assigned to passives in Chapter 4? Support your answers with relevant elliptical sentences.

3. Study the following sentence:

Some of the people who were *playing tennis* shouldn't have

$\left\{ \begin{array}{l} \text{been } playing\ tennis \\ \text{been} \underline{\hspace{2cm}} \end{array} \right\}$.

Determine whether the elliptical version of this sentence is generated by the first rule of Post-HV Deletion (43) in conjunction with the Aux analysis. Then decide whether matters are better, worse, or unchanged if we assume the revised rule of Post-HV Deletion in conjunction with the main verb analysis. Justify your answers as clearly as you can.

4. In the course of generative studies of English syntax, a number of conflicting proposals have been made about the tree structure of the following sentence:

(i)   John seems to me to be healthy.

Three of these proposed structures are shown here:

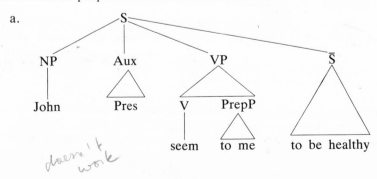

b.

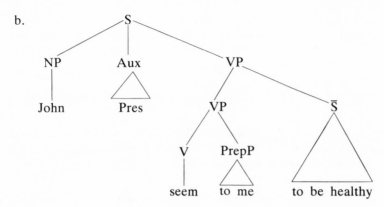

c.

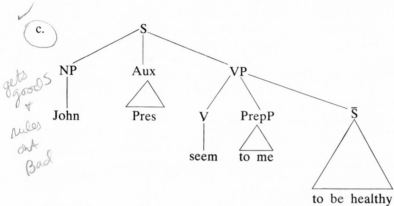

Suppose that we assume the rule of VP Deletion given in (36), which we repeat here:

(ii) $X - VP - Y - (\begin{Bmatrix} en \\ ing \\ Stem \end{Bmatrix}) - VP - Z$
         1   2   3   4   5   6

Condition: $2 = 5$
$\Rightarrow$ 1, 2, 3, 0, 0, 6 (Optional)

Given this rule, which of the above tree structures yields the best results with respect to the following data?

(iii)   George seems to me to be healthy, and John does, too.

(iv)   *George seems to me to be sick, but John does to be healthy.

Explain your answer briefly but clearly.

5. In this section we have considered several proposals concerning elliptical sentences such as (i) below and their relation to full sentences such as (ii):

(i)   John has disappeared completely, and his wife has, too.

(ii)   John has disappeared completely, and his wife has disappeared completely, too.

One might attempt to find fault with the discussion in this section, however, on the grounds that none of the alternative proposals as regards constituent structure or elliptical rules would permit the generation of a second elliptical variant:

(iii)   John has disappeared completely, and his wife, too.

Show that this objection cannot be sustained. Do this by finding sentences that show that the type of ellipsis exhibited in (iii) is possible in a much more limited range of environments than is the type illustrated in (i). What such a finding would suggest is that the type shown in (iii) is to be described by an entirely different rule.

6.   In Chapter 8 we studied a number of universal constraints on movement rules. In each case, the adoption of the constraint in question allows us to leave the statement of individual transformational rules fairly simple. For example, once we adopt the Complex-NP Constraint as part of our theory of grammar, it is not necessary to incorporate any *specific* restriction into the statement of Question-Movement. We simply leave Question-Movement as stated in Chapter 4, and leave it to the Complex-NP Constraint to explain the ungrammaticality of a sentence such as (i):

(i)   *Which girl did John chase the man who threw a snowball at?

Suppose now that we were to find some justification for including in our grammatical theory the following constraint on *deletion* rules:

(ii)   If a certain term in the structural description of a transformational rule undergoes deletion in the structural change, then the rule may not apply in such a way that this term is assigned a proper subpart of some S, plus part of a higher S.

Two examples of sequences which could not be deleted, given this convention, are shown below:

(iii)   The boy $[$that talked to Minnie$]_s$ got on the train.

(iv)   I told you that $[$Bill$]_s$ was right$]_s$.

Note that the convention in (ii) would block the deletion of these sequences even if they satisfied the structural description of some deletion rule.

A. How does the adoption of this convention affect the outcome of the debate between the main verb analysis and the Aux analysis of helping verbs? You will recall that the main verb proponent in the end based his alleged advantage on the superiority of rule (64), a version of Post-HV Deletion that specifically mentioned VP. The evidence cited in support of this version of the rule was the following ungrammatical sentence:

(v)   *If the fact that Jack is moody annoys Sally, then the fact that George is _____, too.

This sentence was a problem for rule (43), the original version of Post-HV Deletion, the structural description of which did not contain any reference to VP.

    B. How, if at all, does the adoption of convention (ii) affect the success of the *do-so* argument (Chapter 11) in favor of the VP analysis as against the Non-VP analysis? (Be careful with this one!)

12.3 PERMISSIBLE SEQUENCES OF HELPING VERBS

    We will now look at an argument that might be put forward in favor of the Aux analysis, and at the type of defense that might be offered for the main verb analysis. An objection that could be raised immediately against the main verb analysis is that there are certain restrictions on permissible sequences of helping verbs that are not accounted for:

(67)   *The captain *will can* take the call.   (Sequence of two modals)

(68)   *The old man *has could* fly a plane.   (Perfect *have* followed by a modal)

(69)   *John *was having* finished the book.   (Progressive *be* followed by perfect *have*)

(70)   *Alfred *is being* cleaning the carburetor.   (Sequence of two progressive *be*'s)

(71)   *Several of the people *have had* finished.   (Sequence of two perfect *have*'s)

There is nothing in the main verb analysis as we have developed it thus far that would have the effect of blocking these impermissible combinations. In the Aux analysis, on the other hand, these impermissible combinations are not generated. Indeed, the avoidance of sequences of just these types was one of the main justifications for setting up the Aux analysis in Chapter 3 in just the way we did. So far, then, these ungrammatical sentences appear to be an embarrassment for the main verb analysis, thus giving an apparent advantage to the Aux analysis.

    A logical defensive tactic for the main verb proponent at this point would be to argue, for as many of the above cases as possible, that the sentences in question are ungrammatical by virtue of violating general prohibitions in the grammar of English that have some independent use beyond simply restricting the occurrences of helping verbs with one another. As it happens, such defenses actually have been proposed for the main verb analysis.

To begin with, let us consider the restriction against more than a single modal in succession. It has frequently been noted that English modals may not occur in infinitival and gerundial constructions. This general rule is illustrated below for the modal *can*; the sentences with the approximately synonymous *be able* are provided for the purpose of contrast:

(72)   *The watchman seems to can talk.

(73)   The watchman seems to be able to talk.

(74)   *The watchman's canning talk surprised us.

(75)   The watchman's being able to talk surprised us.

Within the analysis of complex sentences outlined in Chapter 6 (a treatment that incorporated the Aux analysis of helping verbs), no provision was made for excluding ungrammatical sentences of these types. For instance, the deep structure given in (76) is allowed by the phrase structure rules and lexical rules assumed in that chapter.

(76)

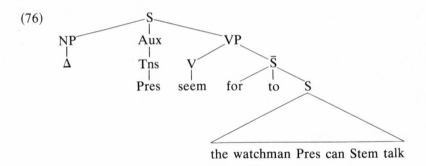

the watchman Pres can Stem talk

Affix Insertion replaces the Tns in the lower S by *to*, and the derivation proceeds automatically to give the ungrammatical (72) above. Similarly, there is nothing to stop the derivation of (74).

What even the Aux proponent must do, then, is to make some adjustments in his grammar so that it will not generate (72) and (74). Although there are many possibilities that might be explored, we will mention just one proposal here, which is along the lines of several mentioned in recent works:[5]

(77)   If a surface structure contains a modal that is not directly followed by a Tns element (either Pres or Past), then the resulting sentence is ungrammatical.

In proposing this statement as part of our grammar of English, we are in effect proposing a new type of rule for inclusion in our general framework, a type which is frequently referred to as a *surface structure constraint*.[6] We interpret this constraint in the following manner. Our phrase structure rules are allowed to operate freely as before, generating deep structure trees such as (76) as well as others. The various transformational rules apply in just the usual way. In particular, the surface structure that results from the application of the relevant transformational rules to (76) will be:

(78)   the watchman seem Pres to can talk Stem.

At this point in the derivation, any surface structure constraints listed in the grammar come into play. A check must be made to see if this surface structure violates any such constraint. Since (78) clearly does violate the constraint stated in (77), we predict correctly that the sentence is ungrammatical.

Clearly, then, this restriction gives an account of (72) and (74), and thus solves the problem raised for the Aux analysis by these sentences. But in solving this problem for the Aux analysis, we also solve the problem posed for the main verb analysis by the ungrammatical sentences that contain two successive modals. Sentence (67), which we repeat here, will correctly be predicted to be ungrammatical by constraint (77) because of the fact that in its surface structure, the second modal will not be followed by a Tns element:

(67)   *The captain *will can* take the call.

(79)   the captain will Pres can Stem take Stem the call

In addition, ungrammatical sentences in which perfect *have* is followed by a modal are not a problem for the main verb analysis any longer. Sentence (68) for instance, is ruled out because its surface structure contains a modal that is followed by the past participial marker *en* instead of by a Tns element:

(68)   *The old man *has could* fly a plane.

(80)   the old man have Pres can en fly Stem a plane.

Thus if we add constraint (77) to our grammar in order to account for certain sentences that were previously embarrassments for both analyses, then the ungrammatical double-modal and perfect-plus-modal sentences are no longer embarrassing for the main verb analysis. In other words, sentences like (67) and (68) no longer provide us with any argument for preferring the Aux analysis to the main verb analysis.

Let us turn now to the impossibility of progressive *be* followed by perfect *have* or a second progressive *be*:[7]

(69)   *John *was having* finished the book.

(70)   *Alfred *is being* cleaning the carburetor.

In order to solve the problem posed for the main verb analysis by these sentences, we must look briefly at a small class of English verbs that are frequently referred to as "verbs of temporal aspect":

(81)   John $\begin{Bmatrix} \text{began} \\ \text{continued} \\ \text{kept on} \\ \text{stopped} \end{Bmatrix}$ studying French.

We can immediately observe one favorable consequence if we were to classify the progressive *be* with these verbs: the fact that the verb after the progressive *be* occurs in the *ing* form would follow immediately from the more general principle that all verbs of temporal aspect allow the *ing* form in the verb of their complements.

When we look at other properties of these verbs of temporal aspect, we find that the inclusion of the progressive *be* in this verb class has further favorable consequences. In the first place, we can state as a general rule that verbs of temporal aspect prohibit the perfect *have* as the following verb:

$$(82) \quad *\text{John} \begin{Bmatrix} \text{began} \\ \text{continued} \\ \text{kept on} \\ \text{stopped} \end{Bmatrix} \text{having studied French.}$$

In the second place, we can state that verbs of temporal aspect prohibit the progressive *be* as the following verb:

$$(83) \quad *\text{John} \begin{Bmatrix} \text{began} \\ \text{continued} \\ \text{kept on} \\ \text{stopped} \end{Bmatrix} \text{being studying French.}$$

With *be* classified as a verb of temporal aspect, the ungrammaticality of (69) follows immediately from the first statement given above:

(69)   *John *was having* finished the book.

Likewise, it follows from the second statement that a sentence in which progressive *be* is followed by another progressive *be* will be ungrammatical:

(70)   *Alfred *is being* cleaning the carburetor.

Thus, the ungrammaticality of these two sentences, which originally appeared to be a serious embarrassment for the main verb analysis, is now accounted for by two constraints that play a role in describing the behavior of an entire class of verbs. All that is necessary is to include progressive *be* in this class, a classification that receives independent support from the fact that *be*, like the nonhelping verbs in this class, allows the present participial form for whatever verb follows it.

At this point, only one of the ungrammatical sentences mentioned at the beginning of this section still poses a problem for the main verb analysis, namely, sentence (71), which contains a sequence of two perfect *have*'s:

(71)   *Several of the people have had finished.

At the present time, no general restriction is known which would have as one of its effects that of accounting for the ungrammaticality of this sentence. In this one type of impermissible sequence, then, the Aux analysis still appears to hold a slight advantage.

Suggestions for Further Reading

Ross 1969 sketches the basic outlines of the main verb analysis of helping verbs. The analysis is developed in the direction of greater abstractness in McCawley 1971, where tenses are treated as deep-structure verbs in their own right.

Detailed discussions of the ellipsis phenomena treated here by VP Deletion or Post-HV Deletion are given in Kuno 1975 and in Akmajian and Wasow 1975. Emonds 1969 suggests independent motivations for some restrictions that would have the effect of ruling out certain ungrammatical combinations of helping verbs.

Notes

1. The first statement of this view is to be found in Ross 1969. The analysis is elaborated further in McCawley 1971.

2. The term *volitional* is used to describe this *will* because it is interpreted as indicating willingness or agreement to do something. This interpretation is seen clearly in the fact that (12) can be paraphrased by:

(i)   If you would be willing to sweep the porch, I will mow the lawn.

As a consequence of its interpretation, this *will* is distinctly out of place in the *if* clause of a conditional sentence that expresses a threat:

(ii)   ?If you'll take Harry's daughter to the movies tomorrow, you'll be lucky to get out of town alive.

Here an *if* clause without *will* is more appropriate:

(iii)   If you take Harry's daughter to the movies tomorrow, you'll be lucky to get out of town alive.

3. This argument is presented very briefly in Ross 1969.

4. We discussed sentences like (31) and (34) in Chapter 3, and proposed a transformational rule of *Too* Ellipsis in order to account for them. In this section we attempt to develop much more general rules, which will account for all of the examples that *Too* Ellipsis accounted for, and many more in addition.

5. Essentially this suggestion is made at the conclusion of Langendoen 1970. An alternative account was offered in Exercise 3, section 6.1. This latter account is incompatible with the view that modals are main verbs of VP's.

6. For a general discussion of surface structure constraints in syntax, see Perlmutter 1971, Chapter 2.

7. The discussion here follows Emonds 1969 very closely.

13

Prenominal Modifiers

We have accounted for the adjectives in noun phrases such as *the red hat* and *an old house* by means of the following phrase structure rule:

(1)   NP → (Det) (Adj) N

In this chapter we will develop an alternative analysis of these NP's, in which they share the same deep structure as the NP's *the hat that is red* and *a house that is old*, respectively. Before we discuss this new analysis, it will be useful to make some simple elaborations in the original analysis (section 1), and also to make some observations about postnominal modifiers (section 2). We will then examine a problem posed for the original analysis by certain ungrammatical postnominal modifiers (section 3), and then introduce the new analysis as a way of solving this problem (section 4). Finally, in section 5 we will turn to some problems that the new analysis encounters, and suggest how they might be resolved within the original analysis.

13.1 SOME ADDITIONAL PHRASE STRUCTURE RULES FOR ADJECTIVES

The only adjective positions that we have accounted for thus far are the two positions that arise by the operation of the following phrase structure rules:

(1)   NP → (Det) (Adj) N
(2)   VP → V   Adj

The first rule allowed us to generate sequences such as *the old man*, and the second gave us sentences such as *Alfred is old* and *John became sleepy*. As a matter of fact, what occurs in the position taken up by the symbol *Adj* in the above rules is in neither instance necessarily a simple adjective.

In the case of the VP rule, the necessity for introducing some larger unit becomes apparent when we consider examples such as the following:

(3)   Felix is *fond of country hams.*

(4)   Florence became *angry at the fry cook.*

(5)   Alfred is *eager to graduate.*

In these sentences, the adjectives are followed by sequences much like those that follow verbs within verb phrases. Let us refer, then, to sequences of the type seen above as *adjective phrases*, which we will abbreviate as *AdjP* for the purpose of writing the required phrase structure rules. Our first step will be to replace the rule in (2) above by the following rule:

(6)   VP → V   AdjP

We then introduce rules for the various types of phrases that we have encountered so far:

(7)   AdjP → Adj   (*old*)

(8)   AdjP → Adj   PrepP   (*fond of country hams, angry at the fry cook*)

(9)   AdjP → Adj   S̄   (*eager to graduate*)

Furthermore, just as we marked individual verbs for the types of VP environments in which they could occur, we must mark each adjective for the appropriate AdjP environments. For example, *old* must be marked with the feature ⟨____⟩, *fond* with the feature ⟨ ____ of NP⟩, *angry* with the feature ⟨ ____ (at NP)⟩, and *eager* with the feature ⟨ ____ (S)⟩. With these feature specifications, we avoid the generation of such ungrammatical sentences as the following:

(10)   *Alfred is old of country hams.

(11)   *Felix is fond.

(12)   *Alfred was angry to graduate.

(13)   *Florence was eager at the fry cook.

Still another modification must be made in our rules for adjectives and adjective phrases, if we are to account for sentences such as the following:

(14)   The man is *very old.*

(15)   Felix is *extremely fond of country hams.*

(16)   Florence was *awfully angry at the fry cook.*

(17)   Alfred is *quite eager to graduate.*

In order to account for these additional sentences, we will have to assume a somewhat more complicated structure for adjectival phrases. In the first place, we will assume that such phrases as *old, fond of country hams, angry at the fry cook*, and *eager to graduate* are dominated most immediately by an intermediate node labeled *Adjectival*, rather than by AdjP. Concomitantly, we introduce the new symbol *Deg* for "degree adverb," and we establish the following rule for the expansion of AdjP:

(18)   AdjP → (Deg) Adjectival

The rules in (7) through (9) are now replaced by rules in which Adjectival appears as the left-hand symbol:

(19)   Adjectival → Adj

(20)   Adjectival → Adj   PrepP

(21)   Adjectival → Adj   S̄

The operation of these rules is exemplified in the following three trees:

(22)
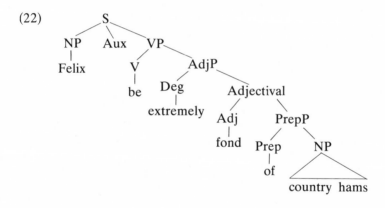

(23)
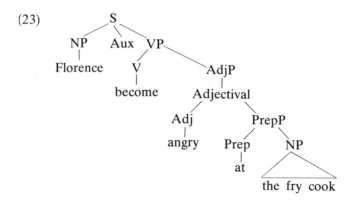

(24)

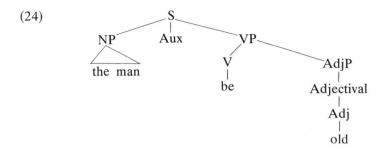

When we turn our attention to prenominal adjectives, we might at first consider revising rule (1) above in such a way as to allow an AdjP between determiner and noun:

(25)   NP → (Det) (AdjP) N

Such a rule has one significant advantage over its predecessor: it allows for the generation of such noun phrases as *a very old man*, in which the adjective is preceded by a degree modifier. On the other hand, the new rule has a significant drawback: it permits phrases such as **a fond of country hams fellow*, and **an eager to graduate student*. In view of the ungrammaticality of these noun phrases, we might analyze prenominal adjectives or adverb-plus-adjective sequences as instances of a special constituent which we will refer to by the special symbol *Prenom*. The rules that we require are then the following:

(26)   NP → (Det) (Prenom) N

(27)   Prenom → (Deg) Adj

These give us noun phrase structures of the type illustrated below:

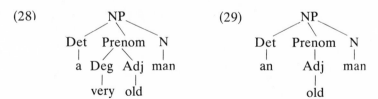

13.2 POSTNOMINAL MODIFIERS

We begin this discussion with a consideration of some types of English modifiers that we have not yet considered:

(30)   A man *anxious to please his employers* should shine his shoes frequently.

(31)   The cake *on the kitchen table* was eaten by the maid.

(32)   The fellow *tapping his foot to the music* is Ivan's brother-in-law.

In each of these sentences, we have a noun phrase in which the head noun is followed by a phrase of a type that we have already studied in other contexts. In the first sentence, the modifying construction is an adjective phrase, in the second it is a prepositional phrase, and in the third it is an ordinary verb phrase, with the verb taking its present participial form. A plausible first analysis for these sentences might be one in which the phrases in question are introduced by the phrase structure rules that expand the NP node:

(33)   NP → Det   N $\left\{ \begin{array}{l} \text{AdjP} \\ \text{PrepP} \\ \textit{ing}\ \text{VP} \end{array} \right\}$

There is an additional type of postnominal modifying construction, however, which is not easy to account for in this manner:

(34)   The burglar *arrested by the sheriff last night* has a record as long as your arm.

In this instance, the italicized sequence is one that we would not want to account for solely by means of a phrase structure rule. The reason is simple: the phrase has all the earmarks of a passive construction, except for the absence of an initial occurrence of the verb *be*. In Chapter 6, the existence of passive infinitives was used to argue for a sentential source for apparently subjectless complements of verbs such as *want* and *try*. Here, just as there, we cannot make use of our Chapter 4 analysis of passives unless we assume some kind of full-sentence deep structure source for the modifying phrase in (34). As a matter of fact, one that lies ready at hand is the deep structure that we would assume for the corresponding NP with a full relative clause:

(35)   The burglar *that was arrested by the sheriff last night* has a record as long as your arm.

Suppose, then, that we begin the derivation of (34) as follows:

(36)   The burglar $_S$[the sheriff Past arrest the burglar]$_S$ Pres have a record as long as your arm.

Application of Passive in the subordinate S gives:

(37)   The burglar $_S$[the burglar Past be en arrest by the sheriff]$_S$ Pres have a record as long as your arm.

We now apply Relative Clause Formation:

(38)   The burglar $_S$[that Past be en arrest by the sheriff]$_S$ Pres have a record as long as your arm.

If left essentially in this form, the structure would eventually yield the grammatical sentence below:

(39)   The burglar that was arrested by the sheriff has a record as long as your arm.

To derive (34), the sentence in which we are most interested, we require an optional transformational rule that deletes the relative pronoun, the Tns element, and *be*, when these are followed by a passive VP:

(40)   X – $\underset{NP}{[}$NP – $\underset{S}{[}$*that* Tns *be* – *en* VP]$\underset{S}{]}\underset{NP}{]}$ – Y
         1   2   3   4   5
         $\Rightarrow$ 1, 2, 0, 4, 5   (Optional)

Applied to the structure sketched in (38), this rule gives:

(41)   the burglar $_S$[en arrest by the sheriff]$_S$ Pres have a record as long
         as your arm.

With the application of Affix Hopping and the relevant morphophonemic
rules, this structure is converted into sentence (34), the sentence with which
we were concerned.
    Instead of letting matters rest here, we might notice that a similar
derivation is possible for the original three sentences mentioned in this
section:

(30)   A man *anxious to please his employers* should shine his shoes
         frequently.

(31)   The cake *on the kitchen table* was eaten by the maid.

(32)   The fellow *tapping his foot to the music* is Ivan's brother-in-law.

This possibility becomes apparent when we note the existence of corresponding sentences containing ordinary relative clauses:

(42)   A man *that is anxious to please his employers* should shine his shoes
         frequently.

(43)   The cake *that was on the kitchen table* was eaten by the maid.

(44)   The fellow *that is tapping his foot to the music* is Ivan's brother-in-
         law.

Instead of accounting for (30) through (32) by means of a phrase structure
rule, as we suggested at first, we can account for them by generalizing the
structural description of Relative Clause Reduction in such a way as to
allow the deletion of relative pronoun, tense, and *be* before these other types
of phrases as well as before a passive VP:

(45)   Relative Clause Reduction

         X – $\underset{NP}{[}$NP – $\underset{S}{[}$*that* Tns *be* – Y]$\underset{S}{]}\underset{NP}{]}$ – Z
         1   2   3   4   5
         $\Rightarrow$ 1, 2, 0, 4, 5   (Optional)

In effect, this rule just deletes material which, if left intact, would end up as a
relative pronoun followed by *is* or *was*.

EXERCISES

1. Explain why the analysis of reduced modifiers developed thus far is not sufficient to provide a satisfactory account of the modifying phrase in the following sentence:

(i)   Any person *knowing anything about Smith's current plans* should telephone the state police.

2. The rule of Relative Clause Reduction stated in (45) is clearly insufficient to derive the phrase *with a straw hat* in an NP such as *the man with a straw hat*, since the necessary source is ungrammatical:

(i)   *the man that is with a straw hat.

There are two approaches that might be taken to account for noun phrases of this sort. The first would be to treat *with a straw hat* as a nonsentential modifier in deep structure, i.e., to assign the NP *the man with a straw hat* a deep structure identical with its surface structure. The second would be to derive it from some sort of underlying relative clause by means of a different reduction rule. Which of these two approaches is favored by the ungrammaticality of the following sentence?

(ii)   *Alice has taken a fancy to the straw hat that George likes the girl with.

In answering this question, it may prove helpful to compare the above sentence with the following two:

(iii)   Alice has taken a fancy to the chocolates that George lured the girl with.

(iv)   Alice spilled a drink on the table that George just finished polishing the top of.

Explain your answer as clearly as you can.

13.3 A PROBLEM FOR RELATIVE CLAUSE REDUCTION

In all of the modifying sequences discussed above, which we are now analyzing as arising by way of Relative Clause Reduction, the material following the underlying *be* consisted of more than just a single word: *anxious to please his employers, on the kitchen table, tapping his foot to the music,* and *arrested by the sheriff last night.* However, the structural description of Relative Clause Reduction as stated in (45) will also be satisfied in cases in which the *be* is followed by an AdjP or a VP that does not contain any material after the Adj or V:

(46)   We talked with a man *that was very sick.*

(47)   The police found the car belonging to the man *that was murdered.*

(48)   A baby *that is soundly sleeping* often sucks its thumb.

Application of Relative Clause Reduction in these cases, however, gives bad results:

(49)   *We talked with a man *very sick.*

(50)   *The police found the car belonging to the man *murdered.*

(51)   *A baby *soundly sleeping* often sucks its thumb.

As a first stop-gap measure to prevent these ungrammatical reductions, we might append a special negative condition to Relative Clause Reduction:

(52) $\text{X} - [\text{NP} - [that \quad \text{Tns} \quad be - \text{Y}]] - \text{Z}$
$\qquad \quad \text{1} \quad \text{2} \quad \text{3} \quad \text{4} \quad \text{5}$

Condition: Term 4 must not be analyzable as $\text{W} \left\{ \begin{array}{c} \text{Adj} \\ \text{V} \end{array} \right\}$ (where

W is a variable).

$\Rightarrow$ 1, 2, 0, 4, 5   (Optional)

With this condition, the ungrammatical sentences in (49) through (51) are not generated.

However, if we turn our attention to NP's based on single-word indefinite expressions such as *someone, something,* and *somewhere,* it becomes apparent that matters are even more complicated than the rule in (52) would lead us to expect. These words can be followed by single-word modifiers as well as by multiple-word modifiers:

(53)   *Something ridiculous* happened to me on the way to this meeting.

(54)   I hope that this time you hire *someone competent.*

(55)   *Anyone murdered* will be given a very nice funeral.

(56)   *Everyone sleeping* must be awakened.

If we are to allow the italicized NP's in (53) through (56) to be derived by Relative Clause Reduction, we must relax the special condition stated in (52) above. One possibility is as follows:

(57)   Unless term 2 is $\left\{ \begin{array}{c} some \\ any \\ no \\ every \end{array} \right\} \left\{ \begin{array}{c} one \\ body \\ thing \\ where \end{array} \right\}$, term 4 must not be

analyzable as $\text{W} \left\{ \begin{array}{c} \text{Adj} \\ \text{V} \end{array} \right\}$.

This condition, although it allows us to account for the data discussed thus far, is quite complex. Consequently, we should welcome the chance to consider any new descriptive proposal that would allow us to simplify this condition.

EXERCISES

1. Show that the rule of Relative Clause Reduction stated in (52), in which the fourth term is a variable, is still too general, even with the condition given as part of the rule. Do this by giving an example of an important type of constituent which occurs quite generally after the copula *be*, but which cannot occur as a reduced postnominal modifier, not even after *someone* or *something*.

2. Give an example to show that the condition included in rule (52) is actually too strong, quite apart from the fact (noted in the text) that it would block certain permissible reductions after single-word indefinites such as *someone*. (Hint: Look for situations in which the variable W in the condition could cover too much territory.)

13.4 A SOLUTION TO THE PROBLEM

Let us return now to our consideration of prenominal modifiers, our main topic of discussion in this chapter. In particular, let us see which of the grammatical postnominal modifiers mentioned in section 2 and the ungrammatical postnominal modifiers mentioned in section 3 can be used as prenominal modifiers:

(58) $\left\{\begin{array}{l}\text{A man anxious to please his employers}\\ \text{*An anxious to please his employers man}\end{array}\right\}$ should shine his shoes frequently.

(59) $\left\{\begin{array}{l}\text{The cake on the kitchen table}\\ \text{*The on the kitchen table cake}\end{array}\right\}$ was eaten by the maid.

(60) $\left\{\begin{array}{l}\text{The fellow tapping his foot to the music}\\ \text{*The tapping his foot to the music fellow}\end{array}\right\}$ is Ivan's brother-in-law.

(61) $\left\{\begin{array}{l}\text{The burglar arrested by the sheriff}\\ \text{*The arrested by the sheriff burglar}\end{array}\right\}$ has a record as long as your arm.

(62)   We talked with $\left\{\begin{array}{l}\text{*a man very sick}\\ \text{a very sick man}\end{array}\right\}$.

(63)   The police found the car belonging to $\left\{\begin{array}{l}\text{*the man murdered}\\ \text{the murdered man}\end{array}\right\}$.

(64) $\left\{\begin{array}{l}\text{*A baby soundly sleeping}\\ \text{A soundly sleeping baby}\end{array}\right\}$ often sucks his thumb.

We might tentatively describe the general situation here in the following terms: those modifiers that can occur grammatically after a noun cannot occur before a noun, whereas those that cannot occur after a noun do occur without loss of grammaticality in prenominal position. Under these circumstances, we can remove the condition on Relative Clause Reduction, provided that we set up an obligatory transformational rule that converts the ungrammatical postnominal modifiers in (62) through (64) into grammatical sequences. But the prenominal versions of (62) through (64) provide just the desired target for our transformational change. In other words, we can let Relative Clause Reduction apply without any condition, and then set up a transformational rule that makes the conversions sketched below:

(65)   a man very sick → a very sick man

    the man murdered → the murdered man

    a baby soundly sleeping → a soundly sleeping baby

This rule can be stated as follows:[1]

(66)   Modifier Shift

$$X - N - [\,[\, Y \begin{Bmatrix} Adj \\ V \end{Bmatrix}]\,] - Z$$
$$\quad\;_{S\;VP}\qquad\qquad _{VP\;S}$$
$$1 \quad 2 \qquad\qquad 3 \qquad\qquad 4$$
$$\Rightarrow 1,\; 3 + 2,\; 0,\; 4 \quad \text{(Obligatory)}$$

The following trees illustrate the successive operation of Relative Clause Reduction and Modifier Shift:

(67) a.

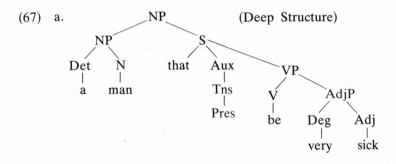

(Deep Structure)

   b.

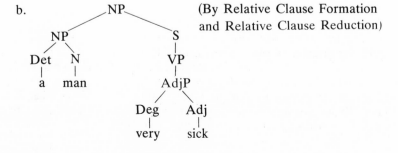

(By Relative Clause Formation and Relative Clause Reduction)

c.   (By Modifier Shift)

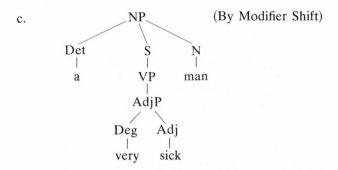

Thus far, there is little reason to favor this new analysis over the original. Although we have succeeded in eliminating a quite complicated negative condition from the rule of Relative Clause Reduction, it might appear that we have done so at the cost of adding to the grammar a new transformational rule with a correspondingly complicated structural description. However, when we re-examine the behavior of words like *somebody* and *something* with the new analysis in mind, we find that the peculiar behavior of these words falls into place.

As a preliminary matter, let us note that there is some reason to analyze these words as indivisible NP's, rather than as sequences of Determiner plus Noun. A treatment along these lines draws its support from the fact that *-body* (in the sense of "person") and *-where* (in the sense of "place") may be preceded only by *some, any, no,* and *every,* and not by the host of other words that ordinary nouns allow:

(68)   Let's talk with $\begin{Bmatrix} \text{somebody} \\ \text{everybody} \\ \text{*thatbody} \\ \text{*onebody} \\ \text{*anotherbody} \end{Bmatrix}$.

(69)   We looked $\begin{Bmatrix} \text{somewhere} \\ \text{everywhere} \\ \text{*thatwhere} \\ \text{*onewhere} \end{Bmatrix}$.

Now let us consider phrases such as *somebody nice*. As we saw above, within our original analysis it was necessary to make special provision for examples of this sort. Specifically, we were in effect forced to make a special exception to a restriction on Relative Clause Reduction. But within the new analysis, we no longer need a special condition. In the first place, Relative Clause Reduction applies to single-word modifiers as well as to phrasal modifiers, converting a tree such as (70a) into (70b).

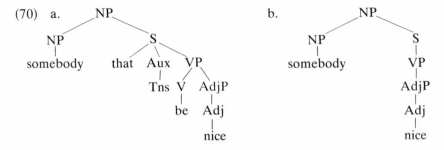

In the second place, Modifier Shift will correctly be prevented from applying to the tree in (70b), since there is no noun to the left of the reduced relative clause. We thus automatically end up with the correct result, without having to impose any special condition to either Relative Clause Reduction or Modifier Shift. On this score, then, the new analysis, incorporating a rule of Modifier Shift, appears to come out ahead of the original analysis, which did not include such a rule.

Before concluding this discussion of the new analysis, which we shall refer to as the *modifier shift analysis*, we might inquire into the possibility of replacing the phrase-structure rule (1) by rule (71):

(1)   NP → (Det) (Adj) N

(71)   NP → (Det) N

For NP's such as *the tall man* and *a red chair*, we can clearly get along perfectly well with the latter rule, since Relative Clause Reduction and Modifier Shift will automatically yield these NP's from the more complex structures *the man that is tall* and *a chair that is red*. However, there are other prenominal modifiers for which such a derivation is problematical. In each of the following pairs, we have a perfectly well-formed *Adj N* sequence, whose corresponding *N that is Adj* sequence is ungrammatical:

(72) a.   a total stranger
     b.   *a stranger that is total

(73) a.   an utter fool
     b.   *a fool that is utter

(74) a.   the main reason
     b.   *the reason that is main

(75) a.   an occasional visitor
     b.   *a visitor that is occasional

(76) a.   the inner door
     b.   *the door that is inner

These examples appear to indicate that it is necessary to introduce at least some modifiers into prenominal position in deep structure. Under the modifier shift analysis, then, prenominal modifiers such as *tall*, *red*, and *murdered* will be analyzed as arising by way of underlying relative clauses, whereas those such as *total, utter,* and *main* will be treated as deep structure prenominals.[2]

13.5 A PROBLEM FOR THE MODIFIER SHIFT ANALYSIS

The modifier shift analysis developed in the preceding section implies a particularly close correspondence between permissible prenominal modifiers and permissible predicate modifiers. The rules of Relative Clause Reduction and Modifier Shift together yield the prediction that any word that is permissible after *be* in a relative clause will also be a possible prenominal modifier. Thus, it must be counted a serious problem for this analysis that not all predicate modifiers may occur grammatically in prenominal position. The following pairs of NP's exhibit this contrast in grammaticality:

(77) a. the boy that is ill
     b. *the ill boy

(78) a. a man that is afraid
     b. *an afraid man

A similar problem is provided by adjectives that may occur as prenominal modifiers, but without one of the interpretations that they allow in predicate position. One such adjective is *right*. A noun phrase such as *the girl that was right* allows the interpretation 'the girl who made a correct statement.' In fact, this is its most natural interpretation. By contrast, the phrase *the right girl* does not permit this interpretation, but is interpreted instead as a paraphrase of something like 'the girl that was supposed to be chosen (for some specified reason).' If we assume the view outlined in Chapter 9 that deep structures are sufficient for the semantic interpretation of sentences, and if we adopt the rules of Relative Clause Reduction and Modifier Shift, then we would incorrectly expect that *the right girl* would receive the same interpretation as *the girl that was right*.

Faced with examples like these, we might attempt to save the modifier shift analysis by resorting to the types of rule features discussed in section 10.6. For instance, we might consider specifying the adjective *afraid* as a negative exception to the rule of Relative Clause Reduction; in this way, we avoid deriving *a man afraid* by Relative Clause Reduction from *a man that is afraid*. Consequently, no structure is provided from which *an afraid man* can be developed. Likewise, we might give two different entries in the lexicon for the adjective *right*, and specify one of these (the "say something correct" reading) as a negative exception to Relative Clause Reduction. Then we would avoid deriving *the right girl* from *the girl that is right*, and consequently we would no longer be left with the incorrect prediction that the former is interpreted as a paraphrase of the latter.

Such a strategy has problems of its own, however. When we examine the behavior of larger phrases headed by *afraid*, we find that Relative Clause Reduction gives entirely good results:

(79)   Any man or woman (that is) afraid of overeating can simply call toll-free the number listed below.

Similarly, we find that multi-word adjective phrases headed by *right* can undergo Relative Clause Reduction, in cases in which the adjective phrase contains other material besides the adjective itself:

(80)   I don't see how any girl (that was) right on so many other occasions could be wrong on this one.

We fare no better if we attempt to account for the behavior of these words by marking them as negative exceptions to Modifier Shift instead of to Relative Clause Reduction. To be sure, such a move would block the generation of *an afraid man* while allowing the generation of *any man or woman afraid of overeating*. Unfortunately, however, it would have the unfavorable consequence of allowing the generation of *a man afraid*.

Let us now return to our original analysis, in which no rule of Modifier Shift was assumed, and see what can be done within the outlines of this analysis to account for the data that have proved problematical for the modifier shift analysis. As the original analysis stands at present, it will give us the same ungrammatical NP's that proved to be problematical for the modifier shift analysis. Specifically, since such words as *ill* and *afraid* are marked with the category feature $\langle \text{Adj} \rangle$ for the purposes of inserting them into predicate position, they will also be insertable into the prenominal position provided by our original phrase structure rules. Clearly, then, even within the original analysis, something must be said to distinguish a word such as *tall*, which can occur in both prenominal and predicate position, from a word such as *ill*, which can occur only in the latter position.

One general possibility would be to specify separately for each adjective in the lexicon which of the two underlying positions it may assume, in somewhat the same fashion as we specified possible environments for verbs (section 2.4). More specifically, we could provide the lexical entry of *long* with the features $_{\text{AdjP}}\langle(\text{Deg})\text{———}\rangle_{\text{AdjP}}$ and $_{\text{Prenom}}\langle(\text{Deg})\text{———}\rangle_{\text{Prenom}}$. The first feature would indicate that *long* could be inserted into a full-fledged adjective phrase, of the sort that our phrase structure rules allow in predicate position. The second feature would permit the insertion of *long* into the prenominal constituent. The adjective *ill*, on the other hand, would carry only the single feature $_{\text{AdjP}}\langle(\text{Deg})\text{———}\rangle_{\text{AdjP}}$. It would thus be allowed only in predicate position. The adjective *inner*, by contrast, would carry only the feature $_{\text{Prenom}}\langle(\text{Deg})\text{———}\rangle_{\text{Prenom}}$; this adjective would thus be limited to prenominal position.

In this elaborated version of the old analysis, then, there is no generalization implied at all that would link possible prenominal modifiers to possible predicate modifiers. While this might seem at first glance to be an undesirable state of affairs, it is not really so unless it can be shown that some worthwhile generalization of this type really does exist. If, on the other hand, a certain generalization is not valid, then the fact that our grammar does not imply that generalization must count as a point in favor of the grammar, rather than against it.

Even if we adopt an analysis in which no direct connection is implied between prenominal and predicate modifiers, we might still be able to give at least some general rules for determining which adjectives may occur pre-nominally. For instance, one fairly sound generalization appears to be that any adjective denoting color may be used in prenominal position. Similar generalizations appear to be warranted for adjectives denoting size and those denoting shape. If generalizations of this type prove to be more reliable than those that are implied by the modifier shift analysis, then we have grounds for preferring our original analysis, in which prenominal adjectives appear as such in deep structure.

EXERCISE

1. We have seen several examples of prenominal adjectives that were themselves modified by degree modifiers such as *very*, *extremely*, and so forth:

(i)   He is $\left\{ \begin{array}{l} \text{a } \textit{very argumentative } \text{man} \\ \text{an } \textit{appallingly insensitive fellow} \end{array} \right\}$.

In order to allow the generation of these prenominal phrases within the old analysis, we introduced the following phrase structure rules:

(ii)   NP → Det (Prenom) N

(iii)   Prenom → (Deg) Adj

Unfortunately, not all degree modifiers are grammatical with prenominal adjectives. In particular, such modifiers as *that* or *so* give good results only when the adjective that they modify occurs in predicate position or in postnominal position:

(iv)   *The only that intelligent man is John.

(v)   The only man that intelligent is John.

(vi)   The only man that is that intelligent is John.

If we assume the general outlines of the original analysis, then the following alternative proposals might be put forward in order to account for the sentences in (iv) through (vi):

Proposal A: Sentence (v) above has a deep structure in which the phrase *that intelligent* occurs in prenominal position. There is then an obligatory rule that moves Prenom constituents containing *that* and *so* to the right of the modified noun.

Proposal B: Sentence (v) above has the same deep structure as (vi). The rule of Relative Clause Reduction, which ordinarily does not allow the reduction of AdjP's that contain no complements, must make an exception when an adjective is preceded by *that* or *so*. In addition, the lexical entries for *that* and *so* must indicate that they are not eligible for insertion into the Prenom constituent.

Which of these two proposals is favored by the following data?

(vii)   *No that ill man should run for governor.

(viii)   No man that ill should run for governor.

(ix)   No man that is that ill should run for governor.

Explain your answer carefully.

Suggestions for Further Reading

The analysis of prenominal adjectives as arising from predicate adjectives is developed in Chomsky 1957, Chapter 7, and in Smith 1964. Many papers include discussions of prenominal adjectives for which such an analysis does not seem appropriate: Winter 1965, Bolinger 1967, Levi 1973, Berman 1974a, Chapter 3. The last three of these works suggest some alternative generalizations about the possibilities for prenominal modification.

Notes

1. The idea of deriving prenominal modifiers from predicate modifiers is presented in Chomsky 1957, Chapter 7. The hypothesis of a connection between prenominal modifiers and reduced postnominal modifiers was first proposed in Smith 1964.

2. Given the second type of rule feature described in section 10.6, it is possible to derive even these prenominal modifiers from underlying predicate adjectives. Each of these exceptional adjectives could be marked with the rule feature $\langle +\text{Modifier Shift}\rangle$. This feature specification would have the effect of ruling out any derivation in which an adjective that was so marked had failed to undergo Modifier Shift. For example, if the adjective *inner* was specified as a positive exception to this rule, then (i) below would be allowed, whereas (ii) and (iii) would not be:

(i)   The inner door was locked.

(ii)   *The door was inner.

(iii)   *The door that was inner was locked.

As noted in Chapter 10, there are some serious theoretical problems with the use of rule features; these problems will be examined in Chapter 17.

14

The Internal Structure
of Noun Phrases

In this chapter we will be concerned with two alternative analyses of noun phrases such as:

(1)   the man that John saw

One of the analyses is that with which we are already familiar. In this analysis, the NP is divided into two basic parts, the first a smaller NP, *the man*, and the second a relative clause. As we noted earlier, the basic phrase structure rules for developing structures of this sort are the following:

(2) a.   NP → NP   S
    b.   NP → Det   N

The surface structure tree that (1) is assigned in this analysis is:

(3)

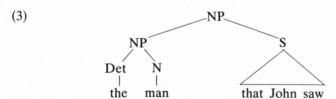

This old analysis will be referred to in this chapter as the *NP-S analysis.*[1]

The new analysis will be presented in section 1. In section 2 we will discuss an English construction that appears to provide support for the new analysis; in section 3 we will look at some other data from English that appear to be accounted for more readily within the older analysis.

14.1 AN ALTERNATIVE ANALYSIS OF NOUN PHRASES WITH RELATIVE CLAUSES

The new analysis that we will present here requires a quite different division of the NP in (1), one in which the two basic parts of the NP as a whole are: first the determiner *the*, and second, the sequence *man that John saw*. This latter sequence we will label *Nom*; we will divide it in turn into a smaller Nom, consisting only of the noun *man*, and an S:

(4)

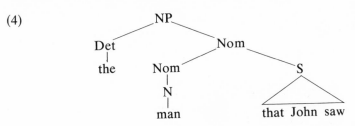

In order to develop trees of this type, we require the following as our basic phrase structure rules for NP's:

(5)   NP → Det Nom
        Nom → Nom S
        Nom → N

Our new analysis will be referred to as the *Det-Nom analysis*.[2]

Solely for the purposes of discussion, we will assume that prenominal modifiers arise by the transformational rules of Relative Clause Formation, Relative Clause Reduction, and Modifier Shift, rather than being generated directly in the deep structure. For the NP-S analysis, the statements of these rules given in the preceding chapter will suffice. For the Det-Nom analysis, however, modifications are required in Relative Clause Formation and Modifier Shift. In the alternate version of the former rule, we require, not identity of two NP's, but rather identity of an upper Nom constituent and one in the underlying relative clause structure:[3]

(6)   Relative Clause Formation   (Det-Nom version)

$$X - {}_{Nom}[Nom - {}_{S}[Y - {}_{NP}[Det - Nom]_{NP} - Z]_{S Nom} - W$$

        1   2   3   4   5   6   7

        Condition: 2 = 5

        ⇒ 1, 2, *that* + 3, 0, 0, 6, 7   (Obligatory)

The way that this structural description is satisfied in the generation of (1) is shown below:

(7)

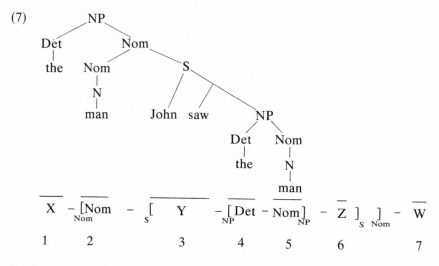

In the version of Modifier Shift that will be best suited for the Det-Nom analysis, we stipulate that the adjective or participle in question be moved across the preceding Nom:

(8)   Modifier Shift (Det-Nom version)

$$X - {}_{Nom}[\text{ Nom } - {}_{S}[{}_{VP}[\text{ Y } \begin{Bmatrix} Adj \\ V \end{Bmatrix}]_{VP}]_{S}]_{Nom} - Z$$
$$1 \qquad 2 \qquad\quad 3 \qquad\qquad\quad 4$$
$$\Rightarrow 1, 3 + 2, 0, 4$$

This rule applies to change intermediate structures such as (9) into structures such as (10):

(9)   (10)

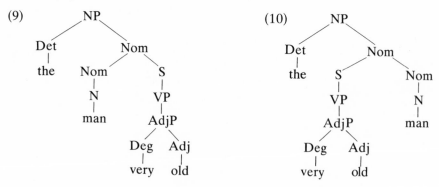

EXERCISES

1. For each of the following sentences, give the deep structure that would be assigned to it in the Det-Nom analysis sketched in this section, and also

the surface structure that would result from the application of the relevant transformational rules:

(i)   The car that Bill is driving belongs to the bank.

(ii)   A toothless crone walked into the room.

(iii)   The man from France deplaned in Washington.

2.   Given the Det-Nom analysis, the sentence given below has two distinct deep structures and two distinct surface structures:

   The old man from France departed.

What are they? (This consequence of the Det-Nom analysis will prove important in the next section.)

14.2 *ONE* SUBSTITUTION

The basic argument that we will give in support of the new analysis arises out of a consideration of the rule of *One* Substitution, which was developed in a tentative initial form in Chapter 10 to account for sentences such as the following:

(11)   Fred owns an old *car* and a new *one*.

The optional transformational rule that we developed there had the effect of replacing any count noun by *one* if there was an identical noun somewhere preceding it:

(12)   *One* Substitution   (first preliminary version)

$$X - N - Y - \underset{\langle +\text{count} \rangle}{N} - Z$$

$$1 \quad 2 \quad 3 \quad \quad 4 \quad \quad 5$$

Condition: $2 = 4$

$\Rightarrow 1, 2, 3,$ *one*, 5   (Optional)

Before getting down to the real business of this section, it will be useful to make two modifications in this rule.

In the first place, some provision must be made for choosing correctly between the singular form *one* and the plural form *ones*:

(13)   The *tickets* that are available now are more expensive than the

$$\begin{Bmatrix} tickets \\ *one \\ ones \end{Bmatrix} \text{that were available then.}$$

We will assume (for the moment arbitrarily) the feature treatment of the singular/plural distinction, that is, the treatment outlined in section 4 of Chapter 10. What we must then do is arrange for the number feature on the replaced noun to be carried over to the occurrence of *one* that is substituted for it. We can do this by making use of the notation developed in Chapter 10 for number and gender agreement rules:

(14)   *One* Substitution   (second preliminary version)

$$X - N - Y - \underset{\substack{\langle +\text{count}\rangle \\ \langle \alpha\ \text{plur}\rangle}}{N} - Z$$

$$\begin{array}{ccccc} 1 & 2 & 3 & 4 & 5 \end{array}$$

Condition: 2 = 4

$$\Rightarrow 1,\ 2,\ 3,\ \underset{\langle \alpha\ \text{plur}\rangle}{one},\ 5$$

What the reference to "$\langle \alpha$ plur$\rangle$" accomplishes here is to assign the feature $\langle -\text{plur}\rangle$ to *one* if the replaced noun is $\langle -\text{plur}\rangle$, and to assign $\langle +\text{plur}\rangle$ to *one* if the original noun was positively specified for this feature.

In the second place, not every environment permits the replacement of the noun by *one* or *ones*, as the following sentences show:

(15)   Jack's old *car* runs better than Harry's new $\left\{ \begin{array}{l} car \\ one \end{array} \right\}$.

(16)   The *cars* that were sold yesterday brought a higher price than the $\left\{ \begin{array}{l} cars \\ ones \end{array} \right\}$ that were sold last week.

(17)   Jack's *car* runs better than Harry's $\left\{ \begin{array}{l} car \\ *one \end{array} \right\}$.

(18)   The three *cars* that were sold yesterday brought a higher price than the two $\left\{ \begin{array}{l} cars \\ *ones \end{array} \right\}$ that were sold last week.

In order to generate the grammatical sentences above while avoiding the ungrammatical ones, we must say something about the left-hand environment of the noun to be replaced. Although matters are actually quite complicated, it will be sufficient for our present discussion to require that the replaced noun be preceded by either an adjective or the definite article *the*.[4] The revised rule, then, is as follows:

(19)   *One* Substitution   (third preliminary version)

$$X - N - Y - \left\{ \begin{array}{l} \text{Adj} \\ \text{the} \end{array} \right\} - \underset{\substack{\langle +\text{count}\rangle \\ \langle \alpha\ \text{plur}\rangle}}{N} - Z$$

$$\begin{array}{cccccc} 1 & 2 & 3 & 4 & 5 & 6 \end{array}$$

Condition: 2 = 5

$$\Rightarrow 1,\ 2,\ 3,\ 4,\ \underset{\langle \alpha\ \text{plur}\rangle}{one},\ 6$$

Quite clearly, the statement of *One* Substitution given in (19) will give exactly the same results whether we adopt the NP-S analysis or the Det-Nom analysis. Matters become more interesting, however, when we notice that there are many instances in which the form *one* may be interpreted as standing for more than just a noun by itself. The following example provides a first illustration:

(20)   The man from Cleveland that you talked with was more polite than the *one* that I talked with.

In this sentence, the word *one* can be understood as standing for *man*, as we would be led to expect by *One* Substitution in its present form. However, it can also be understood as standing for *man from Cleveland*. Additional examples can be constructed to show other possibilities. Although the sentences below are ambiguous in much the same way as (20) is, the italicization will in each case indicate only the interpretation in which the word *one* is understood as corresponding to the largest possible preceding sequence:

(21)   Fred talked with the *old fat man* from Cleveland and also with the *one* from New York.

(22)   The *tiny old brick house* that Frank bought was more expensive than the *one* that Shirley bought.

(23)   The old fat *man from Cleveland* was more helpful than the young thin *one*.

(24)   Gregory didn't want to talk either to the *short fat fellow from Cleveland that talked to you* that was wearing tennis shoes, or to the *one* that was wearing purple trousers.

Let us now inquire as to what revisions in the *One* Substitution rule are required by these additional sentences, first, if we assume the NP-S analysis, and second, if we assume the Det-Nom analysis.

Given the NP-S analysis, the tree structures assigned to the crucial noun phrases in (21) through (24) are given below, with the underscoring indicating the material replaced by *one*:

(25)

(26)

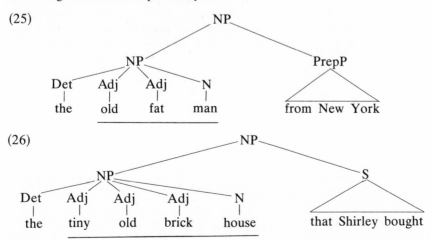

(27)

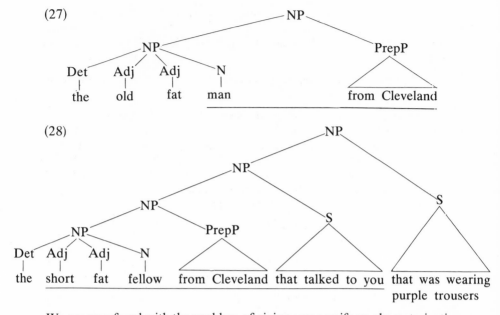

(28)

We are now faced with the problem of giving some uniform characterization to the sequences that have been replaced, so that we can put together a structural description. The task is made difficult by the fact that the replaced sequences in general do not make up single constituents. Furthermore, we cannot simply list in detail all of the types of replaceable sequences, since there is no clear limit on the number of adjectives that can be replaced, or on the number of relative clauses. We are forced, then, to put together a structural description in which variables play a critical role. We might notice that all of the replaced sequences in these examples go all the way to the right side of some NP, even though it is not necessarily the topmost one. In the four trees given in (25) through (28), the replaced material goes to the right-hand boundary of the top NP in one instance, and to the right-hand boundary of the second NP down in the other three instances. We make use of this circumstance in the following revised version of *One* Substitution:

(29)   *One* Substitution   (NP-S version)

$$X_1 - X_2 \ \ N \ \ X_3 - X_4 - {}_{NP}[\ X_5 - \begin{Bmatrix} Adj \\ the \end{Bmatrix} -$$

$$\quad 1 \qquad \quad 2 \qquad \quad 3 \qquad 4 \qquad 5$$

$$X_6 \quad \underset{\substack{\langle +\text{count} \rangle \\ \langle \alpha \ \text{plur} \rangle}}{N} \quad X_7 \ ]_{NP} - X_8$$

$$\qquad \quad 6 \qquad\qquad\qquad 7$$

Condition: $2 = 6$

$$\Rightarrow 1, \ 2, \ 3, \ 4, \ 5, \quad \underset{\langle \alpha \ \text{plur} \rangle}{one} \ , \ 7$$

This rule, as it is stated now, will give all of the sentences with *one* that we have considered thus far.

Unfortunately, however, we can find instances in which the variable terms in this rule allow us too much leeway, with the result that ungrammatical sentences are generated. A simple illustration is provided by the following structure:

(30)

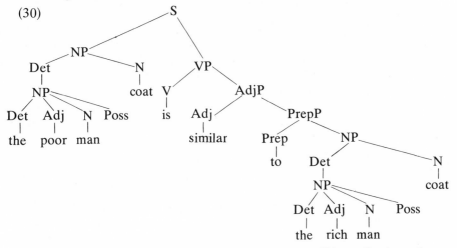

If *One* Substitution does not apply at all, we get (31); if it applies in such a way as to replace the second occurrence of *man*, we get (32):

(31)   The poor man's coat is similar to the rich man's coat.

(32)   The poor man's coat is similar to the rich one's coat.

But there is a second way to divide this tree in conformity with the rule given in (29):

(33)

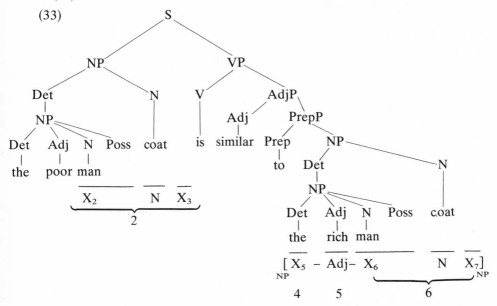

Replacement of the material assigned to term 6 in this division of the tree gives the ungrammatical version of (34):

(34)   The poor man's coat is similar to the rich $\left\{ \begin{array}{l} \text{man's coat} \\ \text{*one} \end{array} \right\}$.

Thus, even the fairly complex statement given in (29) does not do quite what it should do.

Let us turn now to the Det-Nom analysis and see how it fares with the data considered so far. We begin by examining the trees that would be assigned to the crucial noun phrases in (21) through (24) in this analysis, where, as before, the underscoring indicates the material replaced by *one*:

(35)

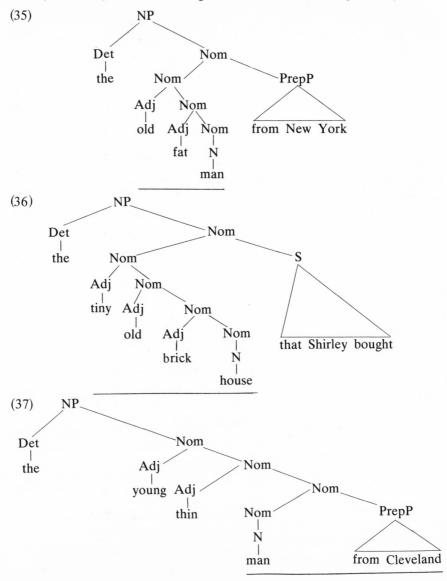

(36)

(37)

(38)

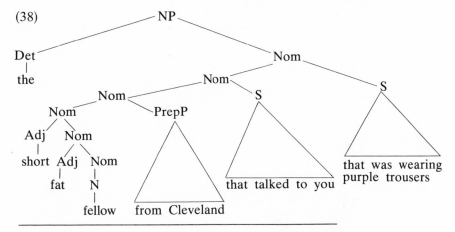

As an inspection of these trees will show, the replaced sequences are all single constituents originating in Nom nodes. Thus, it would appear that the rule of *One*-Substitution can be restated as follows:

(39)   *One* Substitution   (first Det-Nom version)

$$X - Nom - Y - \begin{Bmatrix} Adj \\ the \end{Bmatrix} - Nom - Z$$

1   2   3   4   5   6

Condition: $2 = 5$

$\Rightarrow$ 1, 2, 3, 4, *one*, 6

Not only is this version of the rule simpler than the one in (29), but in addition it does not give rise to the ungrammatical version of (34), which we repeat here:

(34)   The poor man's coat is similar to the rich $\begin{Bmatrix} \text{man's coat} \\ \text{*one} \end{Bmatrix}$.

The reason is quite simply that in the Det-Nom analysis the replaced material does not make up a Nom constituent:

(40)

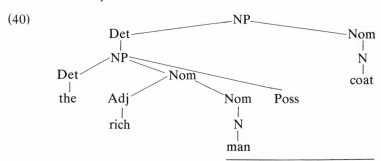

Now, however, we face a bothersome problem: in restating *One* Substitution as a rule that applies to Nom constituents rather than to nouns, we have not carried over the critically important restriction that the noun down inside the replaced Nom must be a count noun. In addition, we have apparently made it impossible to choose correctly between the singular *one* and the plural *ones*.

How can this shortcoming in the rule as stated in (39) be remedied? At first glance, it might appear that we could simply rewrite the fourth term of the structural description in such a way that the critical noun is specifically mentioned. For instance, we might restate the rule as follows:

(41)   *One* Substitution (second Det-Nom version)

$$X - \text{Nom} - Y - \begin{Bmatrix} \text{Adj} \\ \textit{the} \end{Bmatrix} - {}_{\text{Nom}}[\; Z \quad \underset{\substack{\langle +\text{count}\rangle \\ \langle \alpha \text{ plur}\rangle}}{N} \quad W \;]_{\text{Nom}} - U$$

$$1 \qquad 2 \qquad 3 \qquad 4 \qquad\qquad 5 \qquad\qquad 6$$

Condition: $2 = 5$

$$\Rightarrow 1, \; 2, \; 3, \; 4, \quad \underset{\langle \alpha \text{ plur}\rangle}{\textit{one}} \quad , \; 6 \quad \text{(Optional)}$$

Besides being more complicated than (39), this rule does not even do what it was designed to do. What the rule actually says is that any Nom constituent that is identical with some earlier Nom and also contains a count noun can optionally be replaced by *one*. But this statement allows too much.

The type of ungrammaticality that results is illustrated by the following sentence:

(42)   The milk from that store that we bought today is not as fresh as
$\begin{Bmatrix} \text{the milk from that store} \\ \text{*the one} \end{Bmatrix}$ that we bought yesterday.

The sequence *milk from that store* meets all of the requirements of term 5 of the structural description, as we can see:

(43)

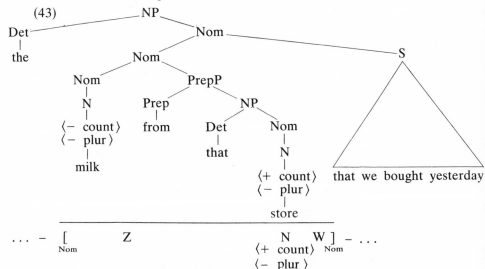

Unfortunately, then, it is not sufficient to require merely that some random noun be a count noun. Although the rule stated in (41) gives no hint of this, the critical noun in this structure is in fact the noun *milk*, which in traditional grammatical studies would be referred to as the *head noun*. The rule as stated in (41), however, fails to pick out the head noun to the exclusion of other nouns that may happen to be included in the Nom constituent.

The choice between singular *one* and plural *ones* can be made incorrectly for exactly the same reason. For instance, if we wish to replace *box containing blueberries* in (44) below, the result will be correct if we take the singular *box* as the critical noun and use the singular form *one*:

(44)   The first box containing blueberries is heavier than the second $\left\{\begin{array}{l}\text{box containing blueberries}\\\text{one}\end{array}\right\}$.

Unfortunately, the rule as stated in (41) also allows us to take the specification for the feature of plurality from the noun *blueberries*, giving the ungrammatical (45):

(45)   *The first box containing blueberries is heavier than the second ones.

Consequently, it might appear that not even the Det-Nom analysis enables us to formulate a rule of *One* Substitution that gives correct results.

An interesting solution to this problem is possible, however. Instead of trying to write a transformational rule in which the head noun is somehow singled out in the structural description, let us simply begin with (39), the rule that we started with, and add the features $\langle+\text{count}\rangle$ and $\langle\alpha\text{ plur}\rangle$ to the Nom itself:

(46)   *One* Substitution   (final Det-Nom version)

$$X - \text{Nom} - Y - \left\{\begin{array}{l}\text{Adj}\\\textit{the}\end{array}\right\} - \begin{array}{c}\text{Nom}\\\langle+\text{count}\rangle\\\langle\alpha\text{ plur}\rangle\end{array} - Z$$

$$\begin{array}{cccccc}1 & 2 & 3 & 4 & 5 & 6\end{array}$$

Condition: 2 = 5

$$\Rightarrow 1, 2, 3, 4, \begin{array}{c}\textit{one}\\\langle\alpha\text{ plur}\rangle\end{array}, 6$$

To be sure, nothing that has been said up to this point gives us any license to apply this rule to a tree in which the part corresponding to term 5 has a structure such as the following:

(47)

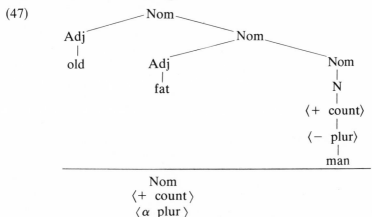

Given our current understanding of the way in which transformational rules operate, we would have to say that the sequence *old fat man* does not qualify to be replaced by *one*, since the Nom constituent involved does not itself carry specifications for either of the features mentioned in term 5.

But here we might propose a new convention regarding the interpretation of features in transformational rules:

(48)   Any feature of an N is automatically understood as being assigned to any node that dominates it, up to and including the first NP node above it.

This convention in effect gives an implicit definition of what we mean by "head noun": a certain noun is the *head noun* of a given constituent if there is no NP intervening on the path from the noun in question up to the node dominating the constituent. The convention then goes on to state that a requirement of a certain feature on a constituent such as Nom or NP is satisfied if the head noun of that constituent has the required feature specification.

The effect of this requirement can be illustrated by referring again to some of the sentences discussed earlier. To begin with, let us look at a legitimate instance of *One* Substitution which gives a grammatical result:

(21)   Fred talked with the *old fat man* from Cleveland and also with the *one* from New York.

The relevant underlying NP, on the Det-Nom analysis, is that given in (49), with the boxed Nom being the candidate for replacement by *one*:

(49)

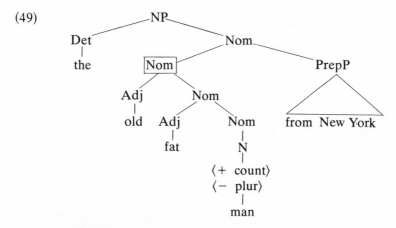

Since the only nodes between the N and the boxed Nom are two other Nom nodes, the noun *man* counts as the head noun of the boxed Nom, and the features ⟨+count⟩ and ⟨−plur⟩ found on the noun *man* can be made use of by the boxed Nom. Consequently, given the rule as stated in (46) and the convention stated in (48), we correctly predict that the sequence *old fat man* can be replaced by *one*.

Now let us turn to the ungrammatical version of (42), which we used to illustrate the shortcomings of the structural description of *One* Substitution as stated in (41):

(42)   *The milk from that store that we bought today is not as fresh as the one that we bought yesterday.

The relevant underlying NP here is that given in (50), and the boxed Nom is the candidate for replacement by *one*:

(50)

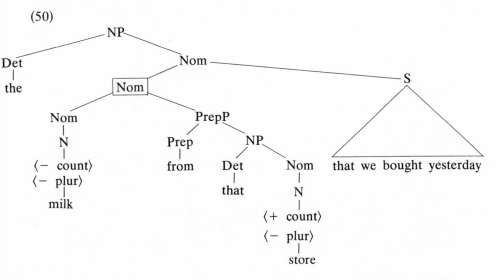

The boxed Nom dominates two nouns, *milk* and *store*, the first marked ⟨−count⟩ and the second marked ⟨+count⟩. The ⟨−count⟩ marking associated with *milk* is available to the boxed Nom node. By contrast, the ⟨+count⟩ marking associated with *store* is not available, because of the NP node that dominates the sequence *that store*. Thus, since the boxed Nom does not have a ⟨+count⟩ feature specification that it can legally borrow from an N below it, we correctly predict that *One* Substitution as stated in (46) cannot apply in such a way as to replace this particular Nom. Consequently, we succeed in avoiding the generation of the ungrammatical version of (42).

In similar fashion, the statement of the rule given in (46), together with condition (48), allows us to choose number correctly when we substitute for a phrase such as *basket containing blueberries*, for which we assume roughly the following structure:

(51)

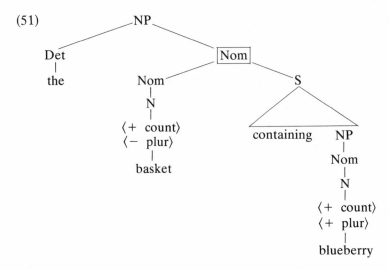

Since there are no NP nodes between the noun *basket* and the boxed Nom node, *basket* qualifies as the head noun of this Nom constituent and can make its feature specifications ⟨+count⟩ and ⟨−plur⟩ available to this Nom. On the other hand, the noun *blueberry* cannot qualify because of the fact that there is an NP node intervening between *blueberry* and the boxed Nom; consequently, the feature specification ⟨+plur⟩ that we find associated with *blueberry* will be excluded, and properly so, from having any influence in determining whether the singular or plural form of *one* is to be used when the boxed Nom is replaced. Thus, by setting forth (48) as a general convention governing the interpretation of feature specifications in transformational rules, we are able to maintain the very simple statement of *One* Substitution given in (46), a rule that is effective only within the Det-Nom analysis.

Although this might seem to be a satisfactory ending to the argument, we would do well not to let matters rest here. Thus far, the only justification that we have given for convention (48) is that it solves a bothersome problem in the statement of one rule in English. The case for this convention is thus not yet very strong. Its fragility becomes clearer when we reflect that virtually any annoying problem in the syntax of English or any other language can be "solved" by the concoction of a suitable "general convention." Thus, one important question that we should try to answer is whether or not the convention has any independent support.

The phenomenon of gender agreement in French appears to afford some grounds for an affirmative answer to this question. The rule that we suggested in Chapter 10 was the following:

(52)   X –   N   – V – Adj – Y
            ⟨α gender⟩
        1   2   3   4   5
    ⇒ 1, 2, 3,   4   , 5
                ⟨α gender⟩

This rule gave us the required difference in the forms of the predicate adjectives found in the following two sentences:

(53)   Ce crime (masc.) etait ingénieux (masc.).
       'That crime was ingenious.'

(54)   Cette rime (fem.) etait ingenieuse (fem.).
       'That rhyme was ingenious.'

Although the rule in (52) suffices for the very simple sentences (53) and (54), it is either inapplicable or else applies incorrectly in sentences that contain a complex NP as subject. An example of the first case is:

(55)   La fille (fem.) qui rit est $\begin{cases} \text{*intelligent (masc.)} \\ \text{intelligente (fem.)} \end{cases}$.

       'The girl who is-laughing is intelligent.'

The difficulty here is that the head noun of the subject NP (*fille*, 'girl') is followed by a relative clause that ends in a verb (*qui rit*, 'who is-laughing'). Since the verb of the main clause (*est*, 'is') is not directly preceded by a noun, the rule of gender agreement as stated will be inapplicable. An example of the second type is provided by (56):

(56)   Le soldat (masc.) qui protège votre fille (fem.)

       est $\begin{cases} \text{intelligent (masc.)} \\ \text{*intelligente (fem.)} \end{cases}$.

'The soldier who is-protecting your daughter is intelligent.'

The noun which in fact should be used to determine the gender of the predicate adjective is *soldat*, the head noun of the subject NP. Unfortunately, however, Gender Agreement as stated in (52) picks out *fille*, the noun directly before the main verb, and incorrectly makes the predicate adjective feminine instead of masculine.

The difficulty here is similar to that which we encountered in trying to state *One* Substitution in English: we must somehow or other arrange for the head noun to determine gender agreement, wherever it happens to be in the subject NP and whatever other nouns happen to be keeping it company. Without some convention such as (48), we are forced to identify the head noun by mentioning in the rule every kind of element that can occur before it in an NP. As it happens, we get a fair approximation in the following rule:

(57) $[_{NP}$ (Det) (Numeral) (Adj) $-$ N $-$ X $]_{NP}$ $-$ V $-$ Adj $-$ Y
                                     $\langle \alpha \text{ gender} \rangle$

           1   2   3   4   5   6

       $\Rightarrow$ 1, 2, 3, 4,   5   , 6
                          $\langle \alpha \text{ gender} \rangle$

However, this rule would have to be considered complicated and unrevealing, attempting as it does to catalog everything that can occur before the head noun of a French noun phrase. On the other hand, if we adopt convention

(48), we can restate Gender Agreement in a much simpler fashion:

$$(58) \qquad \begin{array}{ccccc} NP & - & V & - & Adj & - & X \\ \langle \alpha\ gender \rangle & & & & & \\ 1 & & 2 & & 3 & & 4 \end{array}$$

$$\Rightarrow 1,\ 2, \qquad 3 \qquad,\ 4$$
$$\langle \alpha\ gender \rangle$$

Convention (48) in effect does the work of identifying the head noun for us; it then makes available the gender feature that is inherent with this particular noun to each higher node, up to and including the NP node that dominates the entire subject. The gender feature of the head noun can be referred to very readily by Gender Agreement as stated in (58), since it is now a feature of the subject NP as a whole. Thus convention (48), originally proposed to solve a problem in the statement of *One* Substitution in English, finds independent support in the fact that it solves another syntactic problem, this second one in French.

Let us now summarize briefly the argument in favor of the Det-Nom analysis. The basic assertion is that within the Det-Nom analysis we can state a very simple and revealing rule of *One* Substitution, whereas such a simple and effective rule is not possible within the NP-S analysis. Although this simple rule does not work unless we adopt a new convention governing the behavior of lexical features, we have tried to show that this convention is independently supported, in that it makes possible a more revealing description of French gender agreement than can be developed without it.

EXERCISES

1. The rule of *One* Substitution as stated in (46) does not allow the generation of the second variant in the following pair:

Joe bought a bobsled and Jack bought $\begin{Bmatrix} \text{a bobsled} \\ \text{one} \end{Bmatrix}$, too.

Any treatment proposed not only must allow the generation of both of the above variants, but in addition must not allow the derivation of the following:

 *Joe bought a bobsled and Jack bought a one, too.

What changes in *One* Substitution and/or what additional rules would you suggest as a means of accounting for these new data?

2. As noted in the preceding discussion, the possibility of replacement of a Nom constituent by *one* depends in part on the material to the left of the Nom under consideration. As was shown in (15) through (18), adjectives and the definite article allow the substitution of *one* following them, but number words such as *several* and possessives such as *my* do not. In some situations in which *one* cannot appear, we find that simple deletions are possible.

Sally ate just two sandwiches, but Sam ate $\left\{\begin{matrix}\text{several sandwiches}\\\text{several}\end{matrix}\right\}$.

In other situations, we find a deletion accompanied by a difference in the form of the preceding word:

Jack's car runs better than $\left\{\begin{matrix}\text{my car}\\\text{*my}\\\text{mine}\end{matrix}\right\}$.

   A. List as many environments as you can in which it is possible to substitute *one(s)*.

   B. List as many environments as you can in which only deletion is possible.

   C. List any environments you can find in which either deletion or substitution of *one(s)* is possible.

3.   It might appear plausible to derive a sentence such as *Your dog is fiercer than Oscar's* by way of an intermediate stage containing the sequence *Oscar's one*. An obligatory rule of "*One* Deletion," applying to instances of *one* preceded by possessive NP's, would reduce *Oscar's one* to *Oscar's*. This derivation can be outlined as follows:

Oscar's dog   ⇒   Oscar's one   ⇒   Oscar's
           (*One* substitution)   (*One* Deletion)

An opposing view would be that the reduction of *Oscar's dog* to *Oscar's* should not involve an intermediate stage *Oscar's one*, but should instead be carried out in a single step, by means of the following optional rule:

X – Nom – Y – Poss – Nom – Z
1   2   3   4   5   6
Condition: 2 = 5
⇒ 1, 2, 3, 4, 0, 6

Which, if either, of these two proposals is favored by the sentences given below?

Your furniture is more valuable than $\left\{\begin{matrix}\text{my furniture}\\\text{*my one}\\\text{mine}\end{matrix}\right\}$.

Your old furniture is more valuable than my $\left\{\begin{matrix}\text{new furniture}\\\text{*new one}\\\text{*new}\end{matrix}\right\}$.

State the reasons for your answer as clearly as possible.

4.   A.   Give examples to show that in checking for identity of terms 2 and 5 in the structural description of *One* Substitution as stated in (46), a difference between the two Nom's in the specification of the feature ⟨plur⟩ should be ignored, so that a Nom with a singular head noun and one with a plural head noun may count as identical.

   B.   Show the same for the feature ⟨count⟩. Here it is useful to observe that there are many nouns in English (e.g., *watermelon, cake, pie*) that may be used either as mass nouns or as count nouns. The reader may have found additional examples in the course of answering Exercise 2, section 10.1.

C. Chomsky 1965, pp. 176–182, attempts to give a general characterization of the situations in which "identity" between two terms of a structural description does not require identity of feature specifications. Study Chomsky's proposal; then evaluate it in the light of the facts concerning *One* Substitution.

5. Assuming *One* Substitution as stated in (46), which of the following structures would you want to assume for the noun phrase *the side of the cabinet*?

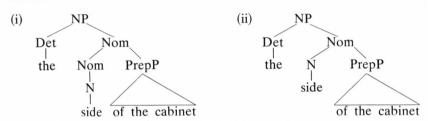

Justify your answer by reference to data concerning the possibilities of *One* Substitution here. Then answer the same question for the NP's *the student with long hair* and *the student of physics*.

6. In Chapter 10 the following rule of Number Agreement was suggested for English:

$$\begin{array}{cccccc} _{\text{NP}}[\text{Det} - & \text{N} & - \text{X}]_{\text{NP}} & - \text{Tns} - \text{Y} \\ & \langle \alpha \text{ plural} \rangle \\ 1 & 2 & 3 & 4 & 5 \end{array}$$

$$\Rightarrow 1, 2, 3, \quad 4 \quad , 5 \quad \text{(Obligatory)}$$
$$\langle \alpha \text{ plural} \rangle$$

A. Show that the rule as stated does not always pick out the correct noun in the subject NP as the noun that determines the form of the verb.

B. How can this rule be reformulated more simply and more accurately, given the convention stated in (48)?

14.3 SINGLE-WORD INDEFINITES

In this section we will examine an argument that might be put forward in favor of the NP-S analysis. This argument is based on constructions of the type illustrated below:

(59)   *Somebody that knows Bill* is coming to the party.

In the preceding chapter, when we were assuming the NP-S analysis without considering alternatives, we introduced expressions such as *something*, *somebody*, and *anyone* as indivisible NP's. As we noted then, the introduction of these expressions as indivisible NP's rather than as determiner-plus-noun sequences helped us to avoid the generation of ungrammatical expressions such as *thatbody* and *onewhere*.

Within the NP-S analysis, the derivation of the phrase *somebody that knows Bill* is perfectly straightforward. The derivation proceeds from the following deep structure:

(60)

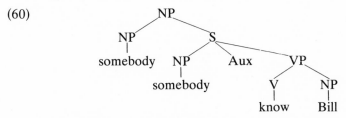

The rule of Relative Clause Formation stated in Chapter 4, which we originally devised for the purpose of generating relative clause modifiers for ordinary nouns, applies in obvious fashion to this structure, in line with the following division into factors:

(61)   ...   somebody   somebody   know Bill   ...

$$X - [_{NP} NP - [_S Y - NP - Z]_S]_{NP} - W$$
$$\quad 1 \qquad 2 \qquad 3 \qquad 4 \qquad 5 \qquad 6$$

The result is:

(62)

NP

NP — S
|
somebody   that   Aux   VP
V — NP
| |
know   Bill

An account of the same NP within the Det-Nom Analysis is not such a simple matter. If we are to make use of the version of Relative Clause Formation stated in (6), then we must assign sentence (59) the underlying tree structure given in (63).

(6) $X - [_{Nom} Nom - [_S Y - [_{NP} Det - Nom]_{NP} - Z]_S]_{Nom} - W$
        $\quad 1 \qquad 2 \qquad 3 \qquad 4 \qquad 5 \qquad 6 \qquad 7$
        Condition: $2 = 5$
        $\Rightarrow$ 1, 2, *that* + 3, 0, 0, 6, 7   (Obligatory)

(63)

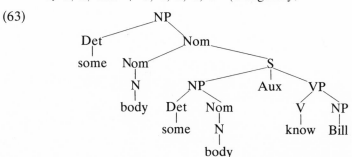

Unless we adopt a structure along these lines, we must either give up this version of Relative Clause Formation or else add a special new transformational rule whose function is to provide derivations for relative clauses that happen to modify single-word indefinites.

The problem posed by single-word indefinites becomes clear as soon as we consider what phrase structure rules and lexical rules are required if we are to get the deep structure in (63) and others like it:

(64) a.   NP → Det   Nom

   b.   Nom → Nom   S

   c.   Nom → N

   d.   *body* ⟨N⟩

   e.   *where* ⟨N⟩

Unfortunately, these rules allow the generation of the ungrammatical expressions that were mentioned in the preceding chapter:

(65)   Let's talk with $\begin{Bmatrix} *\text{thatbody} \\ *\text{onebody} \\ *\text{anotherbody} \end{Bmatrix}$.

(66)   We looked $\begin{Bmatrix} *\text{thatwhere} \\ *\text{onewhere} \end{Bmatrix}$.

If we are to maintain the tree structure in (63) without at the same time generating the ungrammatical sentences in (65) and (66), we must do something to ensure that *-body*, *-where*, and so on are not generally available as Nom's.

Although there are a number of conceivable approaches that might be pursued in attempting to solve this problem, we will mention just one here. This approach involves revising our framework so as to allow lexical entries for compound words to carry two separate category features instead of just one. With this revision in our framework, it would be possible to list the word *somebody* in the lexicon in the following manner:

(67)   some + body
        ⟨Det⟩ + ⟨N⟩

Each of the other single-word indefinites could be listed in the lexicon in the same way. The dual feature specification would allow these words to be inserted into any NP in which a determiner and a noun happened to be adjacent. The structure that would arise for (59) is:

(68)

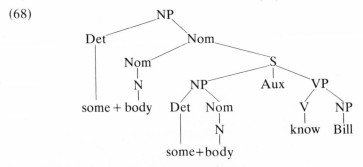

The word fragments *-body* and *-where*, on the other hand, would not have independent listings in the lexicon. Consequently, they could not be freely inserted into N positions, and the ungrammatical sequences in (65) and (66) would not be generated.

Although this new type of lexical rule helps to avoid a serious problem for the Det-Nom analysis, it is open to a possible objection of another sort, namely, that the addition of this rule-type to our descriptive framework has not been shown to have any justification outside of the very limited problem under discussion, and in fact is required there only on one of the two competing analyses. Without some independent justification, the widening of our descriptive framework in this way must be considered ad hoc, that is, devoid of any function other than that of saving the Det-Nom analysis from embarrassment. Thus, until some independent use is found for this new descriptive device, the NP-S analysis must be credited with a small but significant advantage over the Det-Nom analysis in the handling of single-word indefinites.

EXERCISE

1. Suppose for the purposes of discussion that we assume the Det-Nom analysis, with single-word indefinites being handled by means of dual-category specifications like (67). We might then compare two different analyses of prenominal adjectives:

(i)   The analysis given in section 1 of this chapter, in which prenominal adjectives originate in relative clauses, with the following transformational rules playing a role in their derivation:

a.   Relative Clause Formation   (Obligatory)

$$X- \quad [\text{Nom}- \quad [Y- \quad [\text{Det}-\text{Nom}] \quad -Z] \quad] \quad -W$$
$$\underset{\text{Nom}}{} \qquad \underset{S}{} \quad \underset{NP}{} \qquad \underset{NP}{} \quad \underset{S\,\text{Nom}}{}$$

1   2   3   4   5   6   7

Condition: 2 = 5

$\Rightarrow$ 1, 2, *that* + 3, 0, 0, 6, 7

b.   Relative Clause Reduction   (Optional)

$$X- \quad [\text{Nom}- \quad [that \text{ Tns } be-Y] \quad] \quad -Z$$
$$\underset{\text{Nom}}{} \qquad \underset{S}{} \qquad\qquad \underset{S\,\text{Nom}}{}$$

1   2   3   4   5

$\Rightarrow$ 1, 2, 0, 4, 5

c.   Modifier Shift

$$X- \quad [\text{Nom}- \quad [\quad [Y \quad \begin{Bmatrix} \text{Adj} \\ V \end{Bmatrix}] \;] \;] \quad -Z$$
$$\underset{\text{Nom}}{} \qquad \underset{S}{} \underset{VP}{} \qquad \underset{VP}{} \underset{S\,\text{Nom}}{}$$

1   2   3   4

$\Rightarrow$ 1, 3 + 2, 0, 4   (Obligatory)

(ii)   An analysis in which prenominal adjectives are introduced as such in deep structure, by the following phrase structure rules:

Nom → Prenom Nom
Prenom → (Adv) Adj

In Analysis (i), an NP such as *the old house* would be derived from the following deep structure:

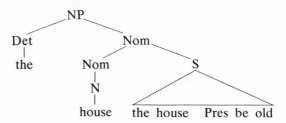

In Analysis (ii), by contrast, the same NP would have the following tree as both its deep and surface structure:

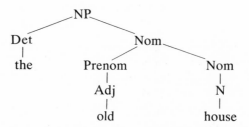

Which of these two analyses fits in most readily with the analysis of single-word indefinites based on dual-category lexical specifications? Justify your choice by giving one or more specific examples.

Suggestions for Further Reading

The two analyses evaluated in this chapter are also discussed in Chapter 7 of Stockwell, Schachter, and Partee 1973. A semantic argument in favor of the Det-Nom analysis is advanced in Partee 1972.

Notes

1. This analysis is proposed in Ross 1967a.
2. The Det-Nom analysis is one of three analyses of relative clauses presented and evaluated in Stockwell, Schachter, and Partee 1973, Chapter 7.

3. This version of the rule does not require that the deep structure determiners in the upper NP and the lower NP be the same. Kuroda 1968 in fact argues that in some cases a better account results if the determiners are assumed to be different.

4. In interpreting this statement, we will assume that numerals such as *two* and *three* are not classed as adjectives. Otherwise, the ungrammatical substitution of *ones* in (18) would be allowed.

Part IV

FURTHER ISSUES
IN
UNIVERSAL GRAMMAR

In this part, we shift our primary focus away from questions about the grammar of English and back to issues concerning the choice of an adequate general framework. Chapter 15 presents an argument in favor of assuming a more complex relation between the syntactic component of a grammar and the semantic component, while Chapter 16 argues a similar point with regard to the relation between syntax and phonology. The central objective of Chapter 17 is to show how revising our framework in the direction of greater restrictiveness can lead to increased success with the projection problem. In Chapter 18 the line of reasoning developed in Chapter 17 is used to evaluate the conflicting positions in a major syntactic controversy, that concerning the correct manner of describing nominal constructions such as *John's refusal to leave* and *the mayor's rejection of the proposal.*

15

Semantic Interpretation and Derived Structures

In Chapter 9 we presented a general descriptive framework in which semantic interpretive rules applied only to deep structures. It is clear that such a framework is viable only if all structural information necessary for the semantic interpretation of a sentence is present in its deep structure. In this chapter we examine an aspect of the semantic interpretation of English sentences that appears to require a rule that ties semantic representation directly to surface structure. Section 1 concerns the representation of sentences containing quantity words such as *many*, *all*, and *some*. In section 2 we turn to a consideration of what kind of semantic representation to assign when more than a single logical element is found within the same sentence. Actual rules of semantic interpretation are developed in section 3, and a special convention is proposed to govern their application. Finally, in section 4 we consider some evidence in support of the hypothesis that this convention must make reference to surface structure.

15.1 THE SEMANTIC REPRESENTATION OF QUANTITY WORDS

In Chapter 9 we introduced the kind of representation commonly used by logicians and philosophers for English affirmative sentences and their corresponding negatives. For instance, (1) below would have the representation in (2):

(1)   Bill is alive.

(2)   ALIVE (Bill).

This type of representation made it possible to state simple rules of inference to account for contradictory sentences such as:

(3)   John killed Bill, but Bill did not die.

A similar representation is frequently assumed for words such as *some*, *many*, *several*, and *all*, even though syntactically these words occur within NP's. These representations are inspired by paraphrases of the type given in (4b) for the ordinary English sentence (4a):

(4) a.   Many doctors are honest.
    b.   There are many x such that the following proposition is true: "x is a doctor and x is honest."

In more formal fashion, we can represent the semantic structure of (4a) as follows:

(4) c.   Many$_x$ ((Doctor (x)) AND (Honest (x))).[1]

The same sort of representation can be used for sentences in which there is more than just a single NP:

(5) a.   Jack saw many whales.
    b.   There are many x such that the following proposition is true: "x is a whale and Jack saw x."
    c.   Many$_x$ ((Whale (x)) AND (See (Jack, x))).

(6) a.   Jill showed the house to several customers.
    b.   There are several x such that the following proposition is true: "x is a customer and Jill showed the house to x."
    c.   Several$_x$ ((Customer (x)) AND (Show (Jill, the house, x))).

(7) a.   John gave many books to Alice.
    b.   There are many x such that the following proposition is true: "x is a book and John gave x to Alice."
    c.   Many$_x$ ((Book (x)) AND (Give (John, x, Alice))).

Similar representations can be given for sentences containing such quantity words as *several*, *three*, and so forth.

With words such as *all* and *every*, which we will translate into ALL, the general format will be the same. In these cases, however, we will want to have the two propositions joined by the predicate IMPLIES rather than by the predicate AND.

(8) a.   All cows eat grass.
    b.   For all x, the following proposition is true: "'x is a cow' implies the proposition 'x eats grass.'"
    c.   ALL$_x$ ((Cow (x)) IMPLIES (Eat $(x$, grass))).

(9) a.   Dr. Jones sends flowers to every patient.
    b.   For every x, the following proposition is true: "'x is a patient' implies the proposition 'Dr. Jones sends flowers to x.'"

c. ALL_x ((Patient (x)) IMPLIES (Send (Dr. Jones, flowers, x))).

The reason for not wanting to connect these propositions with AND in these latter two cases is quite simple: it would clearly be incorrect to infer from the truth of a sentence such as "Every miser is miserable" the truth of the proposition 'Every x is a miser.'

Let us now look at a rule of inference that makes reference to such representations. The rule in question is one that accounts for our judgment that the logical inference given in (10) is a valid one, that is, our judgment that the conclusion must be true if both premises are true:

(10)   Premise 1: All cows eat grass.
Premise 2: Elsie is a cow.
Conclusion: Elsie eats grass.

Such a judgment of validity is to be contrasted with the judgment that would be made in the following case:

(11)   Premise 1: Some cows eat grass.
Premise 2: Elsie is a cow.
Conclusion: Elsie eats grass.

In this instance, even though the conclusion might in fact be true of a certain cow named Elsie, the conclusion does not necessarily follow from the two premises, and the inference is thus *invalid*.

Given the kind of representation that we have developed for quantity words such as *all, many, some,* and so forth, we can account for the validity of (10) by establishing the following rule of inference:

(12)   Starting from two premises of the form

(a) ALL_x ($(R_2(x))$ IMPLIES $(R_1(..., x,...))$)

and

(b) $R_2(NP_1)$

it is valid to infer a proposition represented by the following:

$R_1(..., NP_1,...)$,

where any and all other arguments of R_1 are left unchanged.

Let us see now how this rule applies to the premises in (10). Translating these sentences into their semantic representations, we have:

(13)   Premise 1: ALL_x ((Cow (x)) IMPLIES (Eat $(x,$ grass))).
Premise 2: Cow (Elsie).

The rule of inference in (12) can apply when we let the predicate *Cow* take the place of R_2, let *Eat* take the place of R_1, and let *Elsie* take the place of NP_1. What we get when we do this is just the conclusion represented as follows:

(14)   Eat (Elsie, grass).

Rule (12) also applies when the first premise has a quantity word in some position other than the subject, as for example:

(15) a.   Premise 1: John avoids all cows.
     b.   Premise 2: Elsie is a cow.
     c.   Conclusion: John avoids Elsie.

Here the representations of the premises are as follows:

(16) a. ALL_x ((Cow (x)) IMPLIES (Avoid (John, x))).
     b.   Cow (Elsie).

In this instance, rule (12) is applicable if we let *Avoid* take the place of R_1, *Cow* take the place of R_2, and *Elsie* take the place of NP_1. The result is just (17), the semantic representation for the conclusion in (15):

(17)   Avoid (John, Elsie).

At this point, we might be justified in asking whether we could not just as well have achieved the same results without going to the trouble of treating the item ALL as a special kind of predicate. As an alternative, we might propose to replace the first representation in (13) above by the much simpler representation in (18):

(18)   Eat (All cows, grass).

With this alternative type of representation, we would replace the rule of inference given in (12) with the following:

(19)   Starting from two premises of the form

        $R_1(..., ALL\ N,...)$

        and

        $R_2(NP_1)$

        where R_2 is the predicate that translates N, it is valid to infer a proposition having the following representation:

        $R_1(..., NP_1,...)$

        where any and all other arguments of R_1 are left unchanged.

Given the representations in (20a–b) this rule of inference gives us (20c):

(20) a.   Eat (ALL cows, grass).
     b.   Cow (Elsie).
     c.   Eat (Elsie, grass).

This is the same result that we arrived at when we followed the other approach.

As a matter of fact, the examples given so far do not provide any grounds for preferring the more abstract type of representation for quantity words to the more concrete type of representation shown immediately above. As we will see in the following section, however, the concrete representations and their associated rules of inference are not adequate to account for the semantic properties of sentences that contain more than a single quantity word.

EXERCISE

1. The following sentences, taken together as a set, are contradictory:

(i)   Elsie is a cow.

(ii)   All cows eat grass.

(iii)   Elsie doesn't eat grass.

Give a semantic representation for each of these sentences, and indicate how the rules of inference presented in this section and in section 9.3 provide an account of the contradiction.

15.2 RELATIVE SCOPE OF LOGICAL ELEMENTS

Let us begin this section by examining the representations that will be assigned to sentences with more than one quantity word if we adopt the more abstract system of representation. A first example of such a sentence is:

(21) a.   Every committee received contributions from exactly three lobbyists.

As the first step in arriving at the abstract representation, we can paraphrase the sentence informally as follows:

(21) b.   For every x_1, if x_1 is a committee, then the following proposition holds: "there exist exactly three x_2 such that the following proposition holds: 'x_2 is a lobbyist and x_1 received contributions from x_2.'"

It was important in constructing this paraphrase to use two different letters x_1 and x_2 to distinguish the roles that are played in the basic proposition by the two NP's *every committee* and *exactly three lobbyists*. Had we used the same letter x for both NP's, we would have arrived at the following paraphrase:

(22)   For every x, the following proposition holds: "if x is a committee, then there exist exactly three x such that the following proposition holds: 'x is a lobbyist and x receives contributions from x.'"

This paraphrase is clearly deficient in that it fails to make clear whether it is the committees or the lobbyists that are receiving the contributions. Finally, we translate the informal paraphrase in (21b) into the more formal representation:

(21) c. ALL_{x_1} ((Committee (x_1)) IMPLIES (THREE_{x_2} ((Lobbyist (x_2)) AND (Receive $(x_1$, contributions, x_2)))))).

In describing representations such as (21c), we will frequently speak of one predicate as having *wider scope* than some other one. In (21c), in particular, the predicate ALL has wider scope than the predicate THREE. We may also speak of ALL as "including the predicate THREE within its scope."

A representation such as (21c) can now enter into logical inferences of the kind exhibited in the previous section. Suppose, for instance, that we are given the following premises and conclusion:

(23) a.   Premise 1: Every committee received contributions from exactly three lobbyists.

b.   Premise 2: The Council for Fair Play is a committee.

c.   Conclusion: The Council for Fair Play received contributions from exactly three lobbyists.

We already have a representation for (23a), namely, that given in (21c). The representation for the second premise is just (24):

(24)   Committee (The Council for Fair Play).

The rule of inference stated in (12) now operates on (21c) and (24), giving (25) as the representation of a valid conclusion:

(25) $THREE_{x_2}$ ((Lobbyist (x_2)) AND (Receive (The Council for Fair Play, contributions, x_2))).

This last formula is just the representation for (23c), the tentative conclusion. The prediction, then, is that sentence (23c) will be judged a logical consequence of the premises in (23a–b) by someone who understands English, a prediction that is borne out by the facts.

Now let us look at a second sentence containing more than a single quantity-word:

(26) a.   Exactly three lobbyists sent contributions to every committee.

This sentence is most appropriately paraphrased as follows:

(26) b.   There are exactly three x_2 such that the following proposition holds: "x_2 is a lobbyist and for every x_1 the following proposition holds: 'x_1 is a committee implies that x_2 sent contributions to x_1.'"

The formal translation is as follows:

(26) c. $THREE_{x_2}$ ((Lobbyist (x_2)) AND (ALL_{x_1} ((Committee (x_1)) IMPLIES (Send $(x_2$, contributions, x_1))))).

Let us see now what we can say about a corresponding set of premises and conclusion using sentence (26a) as the first premise:

(27) a.   Premise 1: Exactly three lobbyists sent contributions to every committee.

b.   Premise 2: The Council for Fair Play is a committee.

c.   Conclusion: Exactly three lobbyists sent contributions to the Council for Fair Play.

If we attempt again to apply the rule of inference given in (12), we find that in this instance we cannot do it, since the logical representation of the first premise does not have the predicate ALL as its outermost predicate. When we check our intuitions, we find that indeed the conclusion in (27c) does not follow automatically from the premises. In particular, it is quite easy to imagine situations in which the premises would be true but the conclusion false. For instance, both premises would be true if, given a group of six lobbyists (L_1 through L_6) and three committees (C_1, C_2, C_3), the contributions flowed in the manner indicated below:

(28) L_1 L_2 L_3 L_4 L_5 L_6

     $C_1 \; C_2$ $C_1 \; C_2 \; C_3$ $C_1 \; C_2 \; C_3$ $C_1 \; C_3$ $C_2 \; C_3$ $C_1 \; C_2 \; C_3$

(Let C_3 be the Committee for Fair Play.) Then we see that the two premises are satisfied, the first premise because there are exactly three lobbyists (L_2, L_3, and L_6) who sent contributions to every committee. However, the conclusion that exactly three lobbyists sent contributions to C_3 is certainly false: the number of lobbyists contributing to this committee is actually five.

With the kind of logical representation proposed here, then, together with the rule of inference given in (12), we are able to distinguish between the valid inference given in (23) and the invalid inference given in (27). Suppose, however, that we were to adopt the more concrete representation, in which quantity words stay within their NP's, so to speak. In the case of the inference given in (23), the results would be exactly the same as with the abstract treatment. However, in the case of the invalid inference given in (27), we would arrive at an erroneous prediction of validity. Specifically, the first premise of this inference would have a representation of the form given below:

(29) a.   Send (THREE lobbyists, contributions, every committee).
        R_1 (..., every   N)

The second premise would also be of the required form:

(29) b.   Committee (the Council for Fair Play).
        R_2 (NP_1)

Rule (19) then gives the following representation:

(29) c.   Send (THREE lobbyists, contributions, the Council for Fair Play).

But this is just the representation for (27c); thus this treatment would lead us to expect that the inference in (27) would be valid. Since we know in fact that this inference is not valid, we must count this treatment inferior to the more abstract one. We have thus provided some support for what at first glance might have seemed an unnecessarily abstruse form of semantic representation for quantity words.

When we turn our attention to sentences that contain a quantity word and a negative instead of two quantity words, we again find it useful to adopt representations in which relative scope is indicated clearly. As initial examples, let us examine the following:

(30) a. Not many doctors like George.

(31) a. Many doctors do not like George.

The logical structures of these sentences are brought out more clearly in the following informal paraphrases:

(30) b. It is not the case that there are many x_1 such that the following proposition is true: "x_1 is a doctor and x_1 likes George."

(31) b. There are many x_1 such that the following proposition is true: "x_1 is a doctor and it is not the case that x_1 likes George."

These paraphrases can be translated formally as follows:

(30) c. NOT (Many$_{x_1}$ ((Doctor (x_1)) AND (Like $(x_1$, George)))).

(31) c. Many$_{x_1}$ ((Doctor (x_1)) AND (NOT (Like $(x_1$, George)))).

With these representations in hand, we can make use of the rule of inference for negation proposed in Chapter 9 to account for the fact that the pair of sentences in (32) below is contradictory, whereas the superficially quite similar pair in (33) is not:

(32) a. Many doctors like George.
    b. Not many doctors like George.

(33) a. Many doctors like George.
    b. Many doctors do not like George.

The semantic representations for (32a–b) will be as follows:

(34) a. Many$_{x_1}$ ((Doctor (x_1)) AND (Like $(x_1$, George))).
    b. NOT (Many$_{x_1}$ ((Doctor (x_1)) AND (Like $(x_1$, George)))).

Now the rule of inference stated originally in Chapter 9 comes into play:

(35) Let R_1 and R_2 be propositions. Suppose that there is some proposition R_3 such that R_1 entails R_3 and R_2 entails NOT (R_3). Then R_1 and R_2 are contradictory.

Let us set $R_1 = $ (34a) and $R_2 = $ (34b). Here we need no other rules of inference. With R_3 set equal to (34a), we see immediately that R_3 is a consequence of R_1 and thus a consequence of the set as a whole. Similarly, NOT (R_3) is just R_2, so that it too is a consequence of the pair of representations. Hence, by rule (35), we correctly deduce that (32a) and (32b) will be judged contradictory.

Let us turn now to the pair of sentences in (33), which, as we noted, are not contradictory. The semantic representations for these sentences will be:

(36) a. Many$_{x_1}$ ((Doctor (x_1)) AND (Like $(x_1$, George))).

    b. Many$_{x_1}$ ((Doctor (x_1)) AND (NOT (Like $(x_1$, George)))).

Unlike the pair of representations in (34), there is no representation R_3 that can be derived along with its negation NOT (R_3) from these two representations. Consequently, we correctly refrain from deducing a contradiction in this case.

We should note here that the rules of inference that we might propose in a complete semantic theory would not provide us with an explicit method for taking an arbitrary set of sentences and determining whether or not the sentences are contradictory. One of the major results of modern logic is a theorem to the effect that such a method is in principle impossible to construct. Thus, when we evaluate a set of rules of inference that are intended to account for judgments of contradiction and noncontradiction, the most that we can ask is that the following two conditions be satisfied *to the best of our knowledge*:

(37) a.   For every set of sentences that is judged contradictory, there is a deduction of this contradiction based on the rules of inference;

    b.   It should not be possible to deduce a contradiction from any set of sentences that is not in fact felt to be contradictory.

Having provided some justification for a type of representation in which scope relations of quantity words and negatives are clearly indicated, we must attempt to say what kinds of semantic interpretive rules we need if we are to make a correct matching between sentences and their semantic representations. This is the business of the next section.

EXERCISE

1.   Describe as clearly as you can the semantic difference between (i) and (ii):

(i)   Each professor thinks that each professor will receive a pay raise.

(ii)   Each professor thinks that he will receive a pay raise.

What semantic representations might one propose for these sentences?

15.3 INTERPRETIVE RULES
FOR QUANTITY WORDS AND NEGATION

Let us begin by developing rules to match some simple sentences, including some of those already considered, with their semantic representations. Let us take (38a) as an initial example:

(38) a.   Jack saw many whales.

The representation that we want our rules to yield for this sentence is just:

(38) b. Many_{x_1} ((Whale (x_1)) AND (See (Jack, x_1))).

In informal terms, what we need is a rule that in effect picks out the *many* within the NP *many whales*, and takes it up out of the S that contains it, leaving the variable x_1 behind in its place. Our rule must also conjoin to this S a proposition asserting the class that x_1 is allowed to refer to, in this case, the class of whales. What will then remain in the original S is just *Jack see* x_1. To that structure, we can now apply a rule of the type illustrated in Chapter 9, that is, a rule that converts this remainder into a predicate-plus-argument structure.

The following is a rule that will have just the desired effect in the interpretation of the sentence under discussion:

(39)   Given a syntactic structure of the form

$$[X - [many - N] - Y],$$
$$\,_S \qquad \,_{NP} \qquad \,_{NP} \qquad \,_S$$

interpret this structure as follows:

$$\text{Many}_{x_i} \quad ((N\ (x_i))\ \text{AND}\ ([\ X - [\ x_i\ ] - Y\ ])),$$
$$\,_S \qquad \,_{NP}\ \,_{NP} \qquad \,_S$$

where x_i is a variable that is not already found within the S in question.[2]

This rule takes as its input the syntactic structure in (40) below to give the combined syntactic and semantic structure in (41):

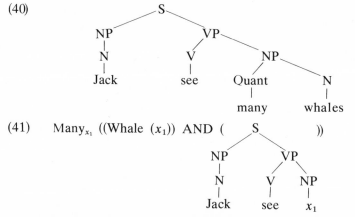

(40)

(41) Many_{x_1} $((\text{Whale}\ (x_1)))$ AND (

An interpretive rule for *see* now applies to the left-over S, and the result is just the representation given in (38).[3]

For the interpretation of sentences with *every* and *all*, we can set up rules that are similar in every respect except for yielding a representation containing the predicate IMPLIES rather than the predicate AND. The following rule would serve to interpret sentences with *every*:

(42)   Given a syntactic structure of the form

$$[X [every - N] - Y]$$
$$\,_S \quad \,_{NP} \qquad \,_{NP} \qquad \,_S$$

interpret this structure as

$$\text{ALL}_{x_i} ((\text{N} (x_i)) \text{ IMPLIES } ([\underset{S}{} \text{ X} - \underset{\text{NP}}{} [x_i] \underset{\text{NP}}{} - \text{Y}]_{S})),$$

where x_i is a variable that does not already occur in the representation.

A rule identical except for the particular word mentioned in the syntactic structure would suffice to interpret sentences containing *all*.

Let us now attempt to set up a rule for the interpretation of *not*. Once again, we begin by looking at a simple sentence and the representation that we want to obtain for it:

(43)   John does not see Marsha.

(44)   NOT (See (John, Marsha)).

As with *many*, what we need is essentially a rule that pulls the *not* out of the sentence in which it occurs, and makes it a predicate with the left-over part of the sentence as its argument. Such a rule is:

(45)   Given a structure of the form

$$\underset{S}{} [\text{X } not \text{ Y}] \underset{S}{},$$

where the S in question is the S most immediately dominating *not*; interpret this structure as follows:

$$\text{NOT } (\underset{S}{} [\text{XY}] \underset{S}{}).$$

Applied to (46a), this gives the mixed semantic and syntactic structure in (46b):[4]

(46)   a.   b.   NOT (S   )

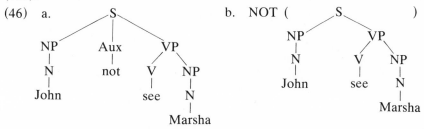

The only other thing to be done in associating a semantic representation with this sentence is to assign a representation to the left-over part of the original S, that is, to the structure that appears in the argument position of (46), so that the representation in (43) would result.

We can now examine the operation of these rules in sentences that contain both *many* and *not*. First, let us see how the semantic representation of (47) might be derived from the structure in (48):

(47)   Many doctors do not like George.

(48)

Application of rule (39), the rule for interpreting *many*, gives us:

(49) $\text{Many}_{x_1}((\text{Doctor}\ (x_1))\ \text{AND}\ ($))

```
              S
          ╱   │   ╲
        NP   Aux   VP
        │     │    ╱  ╲
        x₁   not  V    NP
                  │     │
                 like   N
                        │
                      George
```

Then we apply (45), the interpretive rule for *not*, to the left-over part of the S. This gives us:

(50) $\text{Many}_{x_1}\ ((\text{Doctor}\ (x_1))\ \text{AND}\ (\text{NOT}\ ($)))

```
              S
          ╱       ╲
        NP         VP
        │        ╱    ╲
        x₁      V      NP
                │       │
               like     N
                        │
                      George
```

Finally, an interpretive rule for *like* gives us:

(51) $\text{Many}_{x_1}\ ((\text{Doctor}\ (x_1))\ \text{AND}\ (\text{NOT}\ (\text{Like}\ (x_1,\ \text{George})))).$

This is just the semantic representation that we suggested earlier as the appropriate one for the sentence under consideration.

At first glance, we might appear to have dealt satisfactorily with the problem of assigning a semantic representation to (47). However, an unresolved difficulty remains. Instead of applying the *many* rule first and then the *not* rule, suppose that we had applied the *not* rule first. The *not* rule would give the structure in (52) below, and subsequent application of the *many* rule would give (53):

(52)   NOT (   )

```
                 S
            ╱         ╲
          NP           VP
        ╱    ╲        ╱   ╲
     Quant    N     V      NP
       │      │     │       │
      many doctors like     N
                            │
                          George
```

(53)   NOT (Many$_{x_1}$ ((Doctor (x_1))) AND (   )))

```
              S
          ╱       ╲
        NP         VP
        │        ╱    ╲
        x₁      V      NP
                │       │
               like     N
                        │
                      George
```

Operating in this order, then, these two semantic interpretive rules will give a representation in which NOT has wider scope than MANY, which is just the opposite of what we desire in a representation for (47), *Many doctors do not like George.*

We might at first suppose that the way to avoid this unwanted represent-ation for (47) is to specify an order on these rules of semantic interpretation, to the effect that the *many* rule, if applicable, must always precede the *not* rule. In the semantic interpretation of the sentence in question, this would be sufficient to give the correct result. But there are other sentences containing both *not* and *many* which require just the opposite order of these interpretive rules. Examples are (54) below, which we have already considered, and also (55):

(54)   Not many doctors like George.

(55)   George doesn't like many doctors.

Both of these sentences require representations in which the NOT has wider scope than the *Many*, yet we would arrive at just the opposite relative scope if we were first to apply (39), the *many* rule. Some other solution is clearly called for.

A more promising possibility comes to light when we look at the actual word order in the three sentences (47), (54), and (55). When we write the sentences down, and indicate the desired semantic representation to the right of each sentence, an interesting correlation becomes apparent:

(47)   *Many* doctors do *not* like George. $\text{Many}_{x_1} (\ldots \text{NOT} (\ldots$

(54)   *Not many* doctors like George. $\text{NOT} (\text{Many}_{x_1} (\ldots$

(55)   George does *not* like *many* doctors. $\text{NOT} (\text{Many}_{x_1} (\ldots$

The relative scope of Many_{x_1} and NOT corresponds exactly to the left-to-right order of the words *many* and *not*. We can thus achieve the desired matching between the sentences considered so far and their semantic representations by adopting the following convention:

(56)   Left-to-Right Convention
        In applying rules of interpretation to quantity words and negative words, go through the tree from left to right.[5]

This convention dictates that the *many* rule be applied first in the semantic derivation of (47), but that the *not* rule have precedence in the derivation of (54) and (55). We thus get the desired results when the rules are applied in this fashion.

15.4 A PROBLEM FOR DEEP STRUCTURE INTERPRETATION

Now that we have tentatively sketched some rules for determining relative scope of negatives and quantifiers, and suggested a convention governing their application, let us see whether this treatment is consistent with the deep structure framework outlined in section 9.5. The examples discussed so far in this section provide absolutely no difficulties: if we apply the interpretive rules to the deep structures of these examples, we get perfectly satisfactory results. However, when we turn to sentences that have undergone a more complex transformational derivation, we find that the representations we get are not always those that we desire. As a first example, consider the following tree:

(57)

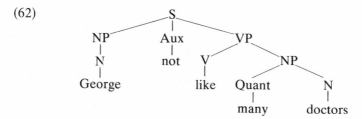

This tree is presumably the deep structure for all three of the following sentences:

(58)   Many doctors do not like George.

(59)   George is not liked by many doctors.

(60)   Many doctors, George is not liked by.

Applying the interpretive rules from left to right through (57), we arrive at (61) as a semantic representation for these three sentences:

(61) $Many_{x_1}$ ((Doctor (x_1)) AND (NOT (Like $(x_1,$ George)))).

For the first and third of these sentences, this representation is just what we want, but for the second sentence, this is the wrong representation. For that sentence, a representation is required in which NOT has the wider scope.

As a second example, let us look at the tree in (62), which serves as the deep structure for (63), (64), and (65):

(62)

(63)   George does not like many doctors.

(64)   Many doctors are not liked by George.

(65)   Many doctors, George does not like.

The left-to-right application of the interpretive rules through this tree gives the following semantic representation for these sentences:

(66)   NOT ($Many_{x_1}$ ((Doctor (x_1)) AND (Like (George, x_1)))).

This representation is correct for (63), but not for (64) or (65). For these latter two sentences, we need representations in which $Many_{x_1}$ rather than NOT has the wider scope.

At first, we might be tempted to give up the Left-to-Right Convention and to look for some other convention in its place. Alternatively, though, we might consider the possibility that the trouble lies not with the Left-to-Right Convention, but instead with our attempt to have the convention operate on the basis of deep structure word order. As a matter of fact, the three out of the six examples given above which were assigned the wrong representations are exactly those in which the relative order of *many* and *not* in surface structure differs from the order of the same two words in deep structure. By contrast, all three of the sentences that were interpreted correctly show the same order of *many* and *not* in surface structure as in deep structure. In two of these cases, (58) and (63), no major transformational rules figured in the derivations, whereas in (60), the relative order of the two critical words was changed by the Passive rule and then was changed back again by a second transformation, the rule of Topicalization (section 8.1). In light of these considerations, suppose that we maintain our Left-to-Right Convention in essentially its original form, except to specify that the determination of the left-to-right relationship is to take place at surface structure:

(67)   In interpreting a sentence containing quantity words and negative words, apply the interpretive rules to the relevant words in the order in which these words appear *in the surface structure of the sentence*.[6]

For the sake of having a more concrete picture, we can imagine that it is the deep structure of a sentence that is actually converted by the interpretive rules into a partial semantic representation, with the surface structure providing the information necessary to a determination of the order in which words in the deep structure are to be interpreted. For instance, in deriving a semantic representation for (65), *Many doctors, George does not like*, we start out with the pairing of a deep structure and a surface structure:

(68) a.   S (Surface Structure)   b.   S (Deep Structure)

many doctors Georges does *not* like   George *not* like *many doctors*
       1st   2nd   2nd   1st

Since *many* occurs to the left of *not* in surface structure, we let the *many* rule apply to the deep structure first, giving the following:

(69) $Many_{x_1}$ ((Doctor (x_1))) AND (

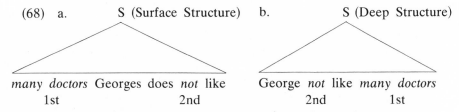

))

Only now can the *not* rule apply.

It is worth noting that this version of the Left-to-Right Convention continues to hold good when a sentence contains more than two words of the relevant types. One such sentence is:

(70)   Many books are not read by many doctors.

Here we want to get the following semantic representation:

(71) $Many_{x_1}$ ((Book (x_1))) AND (NOT ($Many_{x_2}$ ((Doctor (x_2))) AND (Read (x_2, x_1))))))).

The relevant pairing of deep and surface structure is:

(72)   a.

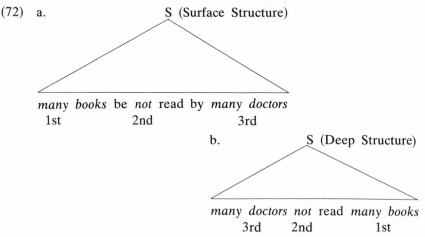

Application of the relevant rules to the deep structure in the order indicated by the numerals under the surface structure tree yields exactly the desired representation.

What we appear to have found, then, is a certain aspect of the semantic interpretation of English sentences that can be determined in a revealing way only if certain interpretive rules are allowed access to information about surface structure word order. Such a finding dictates that the deep structure framework must be exchanged for one that can be represented schematically as in (73) on the following page.

It is worth mentioning here that essentially the same conclusion about the connection between semantic representations and surface structures arises even in some treatments of English that are quite different from ours in the syntactic rules assumed. In one well-known alternative treatment, for example, there is no well-defined level of deep structure distinguishable from the level of semantic representations.[7] In such a treatment, words like *many* and *not* are assigned the same sort of underlying status as ordinary verbs. For example, sentences (47) and (54) would in one of these analyses be assigned the respective underlying structures in (74) and (75):[8]

(47)   Many doctors do not like George.
(54)   Not many doctors like George.

(73)

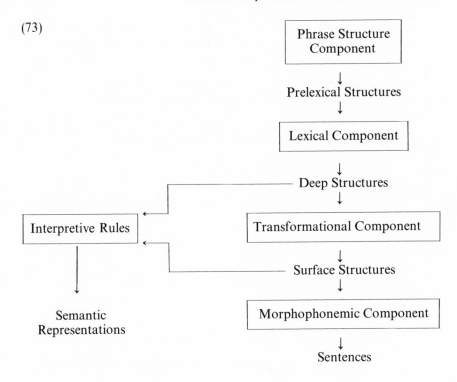

(74)

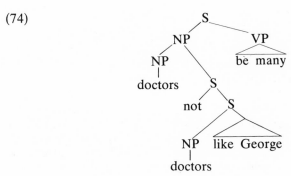

(75)

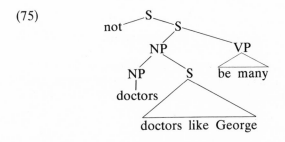

Given underlying structures of this sort, the rules involved in the derivation of surface structures must include rules which are roughly the reverse of the interpretive rules sketched earlier in this section. Specifically, they must take quantifiers like *many* down into the NP's in which they occur in surface structure and they must take *not* into the S in which it is eventually found on the surface. Although there has been a good deal of debate pro and con concerning the support for such underlying syntactic structures, we will concentrate here on only one point, namely, that this type of analysis, like our earlier one, requires some statement relating the scope of logical elements to their order in surface structure.

A consideration of (76) and (77) will be sufficient to show why some constraint is necessary:

(76)   George doesn't like many doctors.

(77)   Many doctors aren't liked by George.

Suppose that we start with the very abstract representation below:

(78)

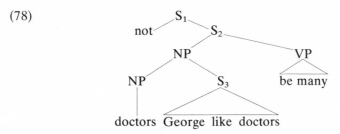

We can derive sentence (76) from this structure as follows. On the S_3 cycle, nothing happens. On the S_2 cycle, *many* is lowered into the NP *doctors* in S_3, and the remaining structure in S_2 that is outside S_3 is deleted. On the S_1 cycle, the *not* is incorporated into the Aux of S_3. With the application of *Do* Support, the derivation is completed. We have thus succeeded in matching up sentence (78) with an abstract deep structure in which the relative scope of the logical elements *not* and *many* is reflected directly in their relative height in the tree.

The only problem here is that the tree in (78) is also available as a source for sentence (77). The derivation of (77) would proceed in the same way as the derivation of (76) did, except that Passive would apply in the S_3 cycle. Incorporation of *many* on the S_2 cycle and *not* on the S_1 cycle would give (77). Unfortunately, the relative scope of the logical elements *not* and *many* is inversely related to their relative height in the tree in (78), instead of being directly related as in the preceding example. What we would prefer instead as a deep structure for (77), assuming an approach like this, is a tree in which *many* is higher than *not*. Such a tree is given below:

(79)

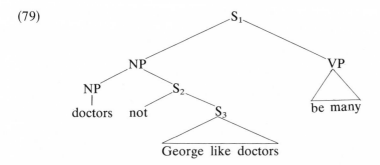

George like doctors

One suggestion as to how this problem might be solved is that a special "filtering" constraint be set up, which in effect rules out any pairs of deep structure and surface structure in which the top-to-bottom order of logical elements in the deep structure is not paralleled by the left-to-right order of the corresponding elements in surface structure. Thus, for example, the derivation of (76) from (78) would be allowed, as would the derivation of (77) from (79). By contrast, the derivation of (77) from (78) would be disallowed, since *not* is higher than *many* in the tree in (78), but occurs to the right of it in the surface structure of sentence (77).

Although literally speaking this alternative analysis does not require a rule of semantic interpretation that refers to surface structure, it still does require a statement that makes mention of both an (abstract) deep structure and surface structure. Thus, a more general conclusion remains unchanged: the correct matching of actual sentences with representations in which scope of logical elements is represented in some straightforward way apparently requires reference to surface-structure word order.

Before concluding, we should mention that there is much more to be said about the type of data discussed in this section, and many important questions remain. To begin with, there are many respects in which the Left-to-Right Convention is not quite accurate as it stands. For one thing, at least some sentences appear to allow a secondary interpretation, in which the understood scope is not that which would be predicted by (67). One such sentence is:

(80)   Many books were read by several people.

In addition to the primary reading, one in which Many has wider scope than Several, there is also a reading in which the relative scope is reversed. On this reading the sentence is synonymous with:

(81)   There were several people who read many books.

In similar fashion, there exists a possibility of a second reading for a sentence such as (63), which we considered earlier:

(63)   George does not like many doctors.

On this second reading, the sentence is interpreted as:

(82)   There are many doctors that George doesn't like.

In the latter sentence, Many has wider scope than NOT.[9]

By contrast, there are other instances in which such secondary readings do not seem to be available. For example, sentence (58), where *many* occurs to the left of *not*, does not appear to have any interpretation except that in which Many has wider scope than NOT:

(58)   Many doctors do not like George.

Thus, it seems necessary in a more detailed account of such sentences to distinguish cases in which a secondary interpretation is permitted from those in which it is not.

In addition to attempting to come up with increasingly accurate constraints for the interpretation of logical elements in English, we might also ask questions about the status of such constraints: are they all part of English grammar proper, or are they attributable at least in part to universal grammar? On the basis of the very limited evidence now available, it appears that the Left-to-Right Convention should tentatively be divided into two different statements, with these statements being assigned different statuses. One statement concerns the scope relations existing between negatives and other logical elements. Here there appears to be some variation from one language to another. Although English, as we have seen, generally requires a negative element to be to the left of any quantifier that falls within its logical scope, such a requirement is not found in Japanese, where negation always occurs sentence-finally. This location to the right of any and all quantifiers does not prevent the Japanese negative element from including these quantifiers in its logical scope.

The second statement concerns the relation between two quantifiers. In this area, English and Japanese do not differ so markedly. In Japanese as in English, the preferred interpretation seems to be given by a left-to-right convention. The convention as it applies only to quantifiers, then, appears to stand a better chance of being universal, and hence is a candidate for inclusion in our universal grammar rather than merely in our description of English.

EXERCISES

1. Sketch a semantic representation for each of the following sentences:

(i)   Many books, many doctors don't read.
(ii)   Many books, not many doctors read.

2.   At first glance, it might appear that the following should be a contradictory sentence:

All of the books were read by many of the doctors, but not many of the doctors read all of the books.

A. Describe a situation in which such a sentence would be true. (The construction of such a situation suffices to show that the sentence is not contradictory.)

B. Give the semantic representation for this sentence. Assume that *but* is essentially to be translated as AND.

3.   Sentence (i) below is an interesting example of a sentence that permits two distinct readings, both of which are entirely natural:

(i)   Many people visit Japan every year.

Sketch the two semantic representations that would be appropriate. Now look at (ii):

(ii)   Every year many people visit Japan.

What representation or representations would be appropriate for this sentence? (Based on **Kuno 1971**.)

4.   Corresponding to sentence (i) below, we have the synonymous elliptical sentence in (ii):

(i)   Jane isn't liked by many doctors, and Sally isn't liked by many doctors, either.

(ii)   Jane isn't liked by many doctors, and Sally isn't, either.

The appropriate semantic representation for both of these sentences is the following:

(iii)   (NOT (Many$_{x_1}$ ((Doctor (x_1))) AND (Like $(x_1,$ Jane))))) AND
           (NOT (Many$_{x_1}$ ((Doctor (x_1))) AND (Like $(x_1,$ Sally))))).

A. Sketch a very rough syntactic derivation for (ii), assuming an analysis along the lines developed earlier in this book.

B. Why does this sentence pose a problem for the hypothesis that the Left-to-Right Convention refers to surface structures? Explain your answer briefly but clearly. (Based on **Lakoff 1970b**.)

5.   In many early transformational treatments of English, sentence (i) below would be derived from the fuller sentence (ii) by the optional rule of Conjunction Reduction discussed in Chapter 11.

(i)   Three of the men ate barbecue and drank beer.

(ii)   Three of the men ate barbecue and three of the men drank beer.

A. Sketch semantic representations for (i) and (ii), indicating clearly the difference in the way that they are interpreted.

B. Explain why, given such an analysis, it is not possible to determine the semantic representation of a conjoined sentence by looking only at its deep structure.

C. Suggest a condition that determines whether or not a quantifier is to be understood as falling within the logical scope of AND. (Based on Partee 1970 and Lakoff 1970b.)

Suggestions for Further Reading

The treatment of English quantifiers and negatives outlined in this chapter is an "interpretive" account, much in the spirit of Jackendoff 1972, Chapter 8. (An earlier version of this chapter appeared in article form as Jackendoff 1969.) Chomsky 1971 and Jackendoff 1972 also suggest interpretive treatments for other areas of English syntax and semantics.

In an alternative description of quantifiers and negatives, they are treated as predicates of higher S's in deep structure, along lines suggested first in Lakoff 1970a, Appendix F. Similar attempts to develop underlying structures that could serve as semantic representations are made in McCawley 1968b, Keenan 1971 and 1972, and in Seuren 1972. Within this general approach, attention was first given to the relation between logical scope and surface structure order in Lakoff 1971. This approach to quantifiers and negatives was one of the identifying positions of a movement within generative-transformational grammar known as "generative semantics" or "semantic syntax."

"Interpretive semantic" critiques of the "generative semantic" position on quantifiers and negatives include Partee 1970 and Jackendoff 1971b. Lakoff 1970b is a reply to the Partee paper. Partee 1971a gives an overview of the controversy.

Another thesis that came to be identified with the generative semantic position was the thesis that some transformational applications preceded certain lexical insertions, so that the level of deep structure as defined in Chomsky 1965 could not exist. Arguments for this position can be found in Postal 1970b and in Lakoff 1971. The earlier view is defended against these criticisms in Chomsky 1972.

A decidedly different treatment of English quantifiers was developed by the logician Richard Montague. An introduction to his system of syntactic and semantic analysis is provided in Partee 1975.

Notes

1. In this chapter, we will use capital letters in semantic representations when the concept represented appears to be a good candidate for inclusion in a universal list of primitive predicates. Unfortunately, it will not be possible in this chapter to

give a similarly explicit representation to every word that we encounter. In particular, we face a problem in interpreting English words such as *doctor* or *whale*. On the one hand, these words almost certainly do not stand for the sort of simple basic concepts that words such as *all* and *not* stand for. Consequently, we would not be entitled to translate them as DOCTOR and WHALE. On the other hand, as was noted in Chapter 9, nothing approaching a coherent and complete system of primitive predicates has ever been proposed from which an appropriately complex representation for *doctor* or *whale* could be constructed. Whenever in the course of this chapter we use an expression such as "Doctor(x)" as part of a semantic representation, we will understand it as an abbreviation for a definition in terms of some set of primitive predicates, even though such a set is not presently available. This lack of explicitness will have little if any bearing on the matters of primary concern here.

2. This last condition is necessary so that we avoid assigning incorrect interpretations to sentences with more than one quantity word. Without such a condition, rule (39) and others like it would give the incoherent representation in (ii) below as a possible representation of the sentence in (i):

(i)   Every committee received contributions from exactly three lobbyists.

(ii)   ALL$_{x_1}$ ((Committee (x_1)) IMPLIES (THREE$_{x_1}$ ((Lobbyist (x_1))
        AND (Receive $(x_1$, contributions, $x_1)))))$.

This type of misrepresentation was discussed in the text in connection with (21a).

3. As is perhaps clear from the way in which we constructed the semantic representation in the tree in (40), we will adopt a convention to the effect that the interpretive rules apply "anti-cyclically," that is, from the top of the tree down rather than from the bottom up.

4. We omit all Tns nodes from the deep structure trees in this discussion, both because it simplifies the exposition to do so, and because the immense semantic complexity of the tense system in English has so far resisted any explicit and systematic treatment.

5. We will have more to say later about the status of such a constraint. Specifically, we will want to determine whether the constraint should be viewed as a part of English grammar or whether it should be attributed to universal grammar.

6. For an indication that the critical level may be some intermediate level slightly short of surface structure, see exercise 4 at the end of this section.

7. This alternative treatment results from the application to English of a descriptive framework commonly referred to as "generative semantics" or "semantic syntax." This framework is developed in many papers; several are listed at the end of this chapter.

8. The underlying structures in (74) and (75) are of the type proposed in Lakoff 1970a, Appendix F.

9. Even more problematical is the fact that sentences with *every* and *all* often have preferred interpretations that are inconsistent with the Left-to-Right Convention:

(i)   a. *Every* dog does*n't* distrust Fred.

(ii)   a. *All* cows are*n't* black.

For each of these sentences, the normal interpretation is one in which the *not* has wider scope than the quantity-word:

(i)   b. NOT (ALL$_x$ ((Dog (x)) IMPLIES (Distrust $(x$, Fred)))).

(ii)   b. NOT (ALL$_x$ ((Cow (x)) IMPLIES (Black (x)))).

Even with these sentences, though, the effects of the Left-to-Right Convention are felt. When offered a choice, most speakers of English will rate (ia) and (iia) somewhat less acceptable than the respective paraphrases:

(i)　　c. Not every dog distrusts Fred.

(ii)　　c. Not all cows are black.

In these more acceptable sentences, the Left-to-Right Convention is not violated.

16

Syntax
and Phonology

In this chapter, we explore some questions concerning the relation between the syntactic rules of a language and the *phonological rules*, i.e., the rules that specify how sentences are pronounced. In section 1 we give a brief introduction to the types of data with which phonological description concerns itself, and then sketch informally a descriptive framework within which data of this sort can be accounted for. In section 2 we begin our investigation of the relation between syntax and phonology by showing a phonological rule that requires reference to syntactic constituent structure. Furthermore, we consider arguments for the view that the structure to which this rule applies is not surface structure, but rather the structure that is found at the end of each syntactic cycle. Finally, in section 3, we look at a movement rule of English which putatively makes reference to a certain phonological property of the element to be moved.

16.1 AIMS OF A PHONOLOGICAL DESCRIPTION

Thus far in this book, we have proceeded as if we were interested in generating sentences of *written* English. The representations that we have provided for sentences have all been based on the Roman alphabet and the orthographic conventions peculiar to English. Such representations have been completely sufficient for our purposes, since, first, we have not set out to specify how the sentences in question are actually pronounced by speakers of English, and second, it has not been necessary so far to make reference to facts of pronunciation in rules of the type we have developed.

In order to describe the pronunciation of English sentences, the first thing that we need is a set of terms for characterizing phonetic properties of utterances. Many such sets of terms are now in common use. By way of illustration, we will g.ve a description of the pronunciation of the word *piece* that makes use of a traditional classification system based primarily on articulatory properties of sounds:

(1) a. The word in question is a sequence of three segments. (Here we must be careful not to be misled by the fact that the conventional English spelling makes use of five alphabetic characters.)

b. The first segment is a consonant. More particularly, it is a *stop* (there is a complete blockage of the air coming out through the vocal tract). In addition, it is *bilabial* (the blockage of air is effected by placing the two lips together), *voiceless* (it is pronounced without any accompanying vibration of the vocal cords), and *aspirated* (it is released with a distinct puff of air).

c. The second segment is a *vowel*. It is *high* (the highest part of the tongue is very near to the roof of the mouth), *front* (the highest part of the tongue approaches the front of the roof of the mouth), *tense* (the entire vocal apparatus is in a state of relatively high tension), and *unrounded* (there is no rounding of the lips).

d. The third segment is a *consonant*. It is a *fricative* (its production involves a continuous noisy flow of air through a partial obstruction of the vocal tract). In addition, it is *alveolar* (the obstruction is made by holding the apex of the tongue against the alveolum, the bony ridge directly behind the upper front teeth), and finally, it is *voiceless*.

At first glance, it might appear that all we need to do to give an adequate description of English pronunciation is simply to provide a description of the sort given in (1), for every English word. We could in fact list the phonetic characterization of the word as part of the lexical entry, along with the various syntactic features. The entire lexical entry for the word that we spell in English as *piece* would be:

(2)   Phonological information:

consonant	vowel	consonant
stop	high	fricative
bilabial	front	alveolar
voiceless	tense	voiceless
aspirated	unrounded	

Syntactic information:

$\langle N \rangle$, $\langle +\text{count} \rangle$, $\langle \text{——} \ (of\ \text{NP}) \rangle$

Semantic information: (Here we might require one or more semantic interpretive rules, of the type outlined in Chapter 9.)

We can imagine the entire entry being inserted into a tree in the course of the lexical insertion process, which applies after the application of phrase structure rules. The phonological information is carried along with all of the other lexical information through the syntactic derivation, and serves its function at the end of the derivation by providing necessary information about the pronunciation of that part of the sentence which corresponds to this single word.

Although it might be literally possible to account in part for the pronunciation of English sentences in this way, there are many respects in which such a description would be unnecessarily complicated and unrevealing. Although there is a great deal of very special information that has to be provided about the pronunciation of each word in English, some aspects of the pronunciation of English words can be accounted for by general rules.

Our phonetic description of *piece* provides a simple initial example of this difference between "nonpredictable" and "predictable" phonetic information. The voicelessness of the initial segment does not follow from any general rule of English. Indeed, there are many pairs of words that begin with sounds differing only in voicing: *pit/bit, few/view, came/game, chip/gyp*, and so on. Similarly, the specification that the vowel segment is tense cannot be given by a general rule. This is shown by the following pairs, which differ only in the fact that the vowel segment of the first is tense, whereas the vowel segment of the second is nontense: *beat/bit, chase/chess, wooed/would*. By contrast, however, the lack of rounding is not a special characteristic of the vowel in *piece*, but is completely predictable, given that the segment is a *front* vowel. That is, in English (though not in French, German, or Turkish), front vowels are always unrounded. In similar fashion, the aspiration of the initial consonant segment is not a special characteristic of this word. Instead, it is completely predictable: in English (though not in Hindi or Chinese), all voiceless stops are aspirated when they come at the beginning of a word. There is an equally general rule to the effect that voiceless stops occurring after word-initial [s] are *unaspirated*; a comparison of the [p] in *peach* and the [p] in *speech* will show this difference clearly.[1] Given this predictability of vowel rounding and stop aspiration, it would be unrevealing indeed to specify the presence or absence of rounding for each vowel segment in the lexicon and the presence or absence of aspiration for each stop. A better approach would be to make no mention of rounding or aspiration in the lexicon, and assign these features to the appropriate segments by one or more *phonological rules*, of the type suggested informally above.

Summarizing briefly, we will assume that the phonetic specifications in the lexical entry of a word, which will be referred to as its *phonological representation*, will in general be incomplete. In particular, it will not mention properties of the word that are predictable by general rule. To this representation apply the phonological rules of the language, for example, the English rules mentioned above that give specifications for vowel rounding and stop aspiration. The end result is a representation in which every sound segment is described completely. This last type of representation, exemplified by (2) above, will be called a *phonetic representation*.

Before passing on to some less elementary examples of English phonological rules, we should note one difference that exists between phonological and phonetic representations. In the actual stream of speech itself, there are no divisions or identifiable phonetic effects which always appear just in the places corresponding to spaces between words in written English. Consequently, there is no reason for the phonetic representation of an entire sentence to be broken down into groups of segments corresponding to words.

An interesting question arises at this point: can we do without such divisions in the *phonological* representations, or is some indication of boundaries between words essential there? The answer is in fact already implied in the informal rule that we have given above for determining aspiration in English voiceless stops: all *word-initial* voiceless stops are aspirated. This rule makes crucial reference to the idea of a *word*, and without some indication in the phonological representations as to where one word stops and the next one begins, it would be impossible to apply this rule correctly. For instance, in both *place pies* and *play spies*, we have, in our actual pronunciation, an [s] sound followed immediately by a voiceless stop [p]. In the pronunciation of the first of the two sequences, the [p] is aspirated, whereas in the second it is not. Without some indication of word boundaries in the phonological representation, however, the rules that we gave above would not have sufficient information to apply correctly. That is, if phonological representations contained no information except the specification of segments, then there would be no way of determining whether or not a given voiceless stop or a given [s] was "word-initial."

At this point, the relation between phonological and phonetic representations may seem fairly straightforward. In particular, it may appear that the only difference between the two is that the latter are just more fully filled out versions of the former. To dispel this impression, and to give a truer idea of the complexity of the relationship between the two sets of representations, we turn now to a discussion of a phonological rule of English which, instead of merely giving a more detailed specification for some segment, actually changes some of the feature specifications already there.

If asked to say whether the first vowel in the word *catastrophe* is the same vowel as the first vowel in *catastrophic*, most speakers of English would be tempted to say that the two vowels are identical. Yet a more careful examination of the two vowels will reveal that they do not have the same quality at all. The first vowel in *catastrophic*, which is ordinarily transcribed by the symbol [æ], can be characterized as a nontense low front vowel. By contrast, the first vowel in *catastrophe* is a mid-to-high vowel, made in roughly the center of the mouth rather than in the front part. This vowel is generally transcribed by the so-called *schwa* symbol [ə].

When we look at the second vowels of the two words, we find another surprise. This time it is *catastrophe* that has the nontense low front vowel [æ], whereas *catastrophic* shows the mid-to-high central vowel [ə]. A final surprise is in store when we look at the third vowels. In *catastrophic* we find a low central-to-back vowel, generally transcribed as [a],[2] whereas in *catastrophe*, we once more find [ə]. We can represent the situation more clearly by writing the relevant portions of the two words one above the other, and then indicating by phonetic symbol the phonetic quality of the relevant vowels:

(3) a.   c a t a s t r o p h e
               (ə) (æ)   (ə)
           c a t a s t r o p h i c
               (æ) (ə)   (a)

As can be seen from (3), in each of the three pairs of corresponding vowels that we have considered, the two vowels in the pair are different.

As a first reaction to examples like these, we might feel compelled to say that the first three vowels of *catastrophe* have to be specified in the lexicon as [ə], [æ], and [ə], respectively, and that the first three vowels in *catastrophic* must be specified separately as [æ], [ə], and [a]. English affords innumerable other examples in which we see the same type of alternation between pairs of corresponding vowels in related words. Some examples are listed below:

(3) b.   s y n o n y m
             (I) (ə) (I)
           s y n o n y m o u s
             (ə) (a) (ə)

(I represents a nontense mid-front vowel.)

    c.   r e p e t i t i v e
             (ə) (ɛ) (ə)
           r e p e t i t i o n
             (ɛ) (ə) (I)

(ɛ represents a nontense high-front vowel.)

    d.   d e m o c r a t i c
             (ɛ) (ə) (æ)
           d e m o c r a c y
             (ə) (a) (ə)

    e.   g e r u n d
             (ɛ) (ə)
           g e r u n d i v e
             (ə) (ʌ)

(ʌ represents a nontense low-central vowel.)

If we were to follow the approach just suggested for the description of the vowels in *catastrophe* and *catastrophic*, we would have to list all of the vowels separately within each of these additional pairs of words, too. In this situation, it might be well for us to see if some more revealing account of these English vowel alternations can be found. More specifically, we might look for some other critical difference in pronunciation to which all of the vowel differences could be tied.

When we listen carefully to the pronunciation of these pairs of words, we note that there is another marked difference from one member of each pair to the other, a difference in *stress*, or "accent" as it is often referred to in everyday speech. We will denote the highest (*primary*) stress by the symbol ´ over a vowel, slightly lower (*nonprimary*) stress by the symbol ˋ, and the absence of stress by the absence of any marking at all. The stress patterns in the words considered above are as follows:

(4) a. c a t á s t r o p h e
       (ǎ/ə) (á/æ) (o/ə)
       c à t a s t r ó p h i c
       (à/æ) (a/ə) (ó/a)

b. s ý n o n ý m
       (ý/ɪ) (o/ə) (ý/ɪ)
       s y n ó n y m o u s
       (y/ə) (ó/a) (y/ə)

c. r e p é t i t i v e
       (e/ə) (é/ɛ) (i/ə)
       r è p e t í t i o n
       (è/ɛ) (e/ə) (í/ɪ)

d. d e m ó c r a t i c
       (e/ɛ) (o/ə) (á/æ)
       d e m ó c r a c y
       (e/ə) (ó/a) (a/ə)

e. g é r u n d
       (é/ɛ) (u/ə)
       g e r ú n d ì v e
       (e/ə) (ú/ʌ)

A careful examination of (4) shows a clear pattern: all of the unstressed vowels are schwas, but none of the stressed vowels are.

If we are willing to allow phonological rules that make quite drastic changes in the specification of individual segments, then we can account for the vowel alternations in these words by a single very simple phonological rule, without the necessity of specifying in the lexicon different sets of vowels for each of two related words. We can do this by allowing, for example, *catastrophe* and *catastrophic* to share the part of their lexical entry that concerns their phonological representation (except for the different endings on the two words). This shared representation will contain specifications for the vowels that appear under stress. Thus, if we use individual phonetic symbols as a shorthand abbreviation for sets of features, the phonological representations of *catastrophe* and *catastrophic* are as follows:

(5)   k æ t æ s t r a f i
       k æ t æ s t r a f ɪ k

As the reader will note, these representations do not directly reflect the vowels actually pronounced in either of the words *catastrophe* or *catastrophic*. What we need if we are to get from the phonological representations in (5) to the correct phonetic representations is a phonological rule along the following lines:

(6)   Vowel Reduction
      Any vowel which is completely unstressed is replaced by [ə] (i.e., by a nontense mid-to-high central vowel).[3]

This rule applies as follows in the phonological derivation of *catastrophe* and *catastrophic*, where boxes mark stressless vowels:

(7) a.   k [æ] t ǽ s t r [a] f – i   ⇒ k [ə] t ǽ s t r [ə] f – i
         k æ t [æ] s t r á f – ɪ k ⇒ k ǽ t [ə] s t r á f – ɪ k

Similar derivations are possible for the other pairs of words discussed above:

(7) b.   s í n [a] n ɪ̀ m   ⇒ s í n [ə] n ɪ̀ m
         s [ɪ] n á n [ɪ] m [a] s ⇒ s [ə] n á n [ə] m [ə] s
    c.   r [ɛ] p ɛ́ t [ɪ] t ɪ v   ⇒ r [ə] p ɛ́ t [ə] t ɪ v
         r ɛ̀ p [ɛ] t í t i o n   ⇒ r ɛ̀ p [ə] t í t i o n
    d.   d ɛ̀ m [a] k r ǽ t ɪ k   ⇒ d ɛ̀ m [ə] k r ǽ t ɪ k
         d [ɛ] m á k r [æ] s i   ⇒ d [ə] m á k r [ə] s i
    e.   j ɛ́ r [ʌ] n d   ⇒ j ɛ́ r [ə] n d
         j [ɛ] r ʌ́ n d ì v   ⇒ j [ə] r ʌ́ n d ì v

It might appear at this point that we could set up a combined phonological representation for each of the pairs given above, since the vowel specifications are no longer different. For example, we might attempt to combine the lexical entry for *catastrophe* and that for *catastrophic* as follows:

$$(8) \quad \text{k æ t æ s t r a f} \begin{cases} -\text{ i } \langle\text{N}\rangle \\ -\text{ ɪ k } \langle\text{Adj}\rangle \end{cases}$$

But there is still one obstacle standing in the way of such a combination of phonological specifications: the stress patterns of the two words are completely different. Thus, even though we have managed to arrive at phonological representations in which the corresponding vowels are identical, we are still unable to combine the two representations into a single one. We appear to be left, then, with the following entirely separate phonological representations:

(9)   k æ t ǽ s t r a f – i ⟨N⟩
      k æ̀ t æ s t r á f – ɪ k ⟨Adj⟩

Rather than letting matters rest here, however, we might investigate the possibility of predicting the stress patterns themselves by general rules. If such rules could be found, then no indication of stress would need to be given in the lexical entries of individual words.

It should be clear immediately that no single simple rule will do the job, no rule, that is, as simple as the stress rules in Finnish (where stress is always assigned to the first syllable of a word) or in Polish (where it is always assigned to the next-to-last syllable). But traditional and modern investigators have uncovered many quite dependable general rules, which when taken together account for stress in a substantial majority of English words. One of the simplest of these rules is the one that accounts for the placement of primary stress in one-syllable words such as *cat*, *dog*, *walk*, *short*, and so on:

(10)   In monosyllabic words, assign primary stress to the vowel.[4]

Another simple rule (a bit more interesting than the first) is the one that accounts for the placement of primary stress in the words *catastrophic*, *philosophical*, and *democratic*:

(11)   In adjectives ending in the suffix -*ic(al)*, assign primary stress to the vowel of the syllable immediately preceding the suffix.

For the assignment of primary stress in many other words, and also for the assignment of nonprimary stress, the rules are more complicated, depending on a variety of factors. In the first place, stress location may depend on whether or not a certain critical vowel belongs to the class of what have in traditional dictionaries of English been called "long" vowels. Thus, in *horizon*, where the middle vowel is "long," the stress falls on this long vowel, whereas in *venison*, where the middle vowel is not long, the stress appears on the preceding syllable. In the second place, it may make a difference whether a certain vowel is followed by a single consonant or by more than one. For example, stress falls on the next-to-the-last vowel of *gerundive* because there are two consonants following this vowel. By comparison, it falls on the third-from-the-last syllable of *repetitive* because the next-to-the-last vowel is followed by only a single consonant.

More abstract properties of words may also be relevant. In the first place, some rules appear to require reference to specific lexical classes. For example, the difference in lexical class between *elicit* (verb) and *javelin* (noun) has been cited as the critical factor underlying the difference in the placement of stress. In the second place, the correct placement of stress sometimes requires information as to whether or not the word in question is derived from some other word. For example, the fact that the noun *permit* is derived from a corresponding verb, whereas the noun *hermit* is not, has been offered as an explanation for the fact that the final syllable of the former but not of the latter receives secondary stress. A similar explanation has been offered for the difference of primary stress placement between *advocacy* and *economy*, on the assumption that the former but not the latter is derived from a verb.[5]

For our present purposes, it is sufficient to note that to the degree that general rules can be given which predict the location of stress in English words, it is unnecessary to provide specification of stress in lexical entries. As regards the set of illustrative examples under discussion, success in setting up general stress-assignment rules means that in each pair of words, identical parts of the phonological representations can be combined:

(12) a.   k æ t æ s t r a f $\begin{array}{l} {}^- \text{i} \quad \langle \text{N} \rangle \\ {}^- \text{ı k} \; \langle \text{Adj} \rangle \end{array}$

    b.   s ı n a n ı m $\bigl\langle\begin{array}{l} {}^- \quad\quad \langle \text{N} \rangle \\ {}^- \text{a s} \; \langle \text{Adj} \rangle \end{array}$

c. $r \varepsilon p \varepsilon t I t <^{- \; I \; v \quad \langle Adj \rangle}_{- \; i \; o \; n \; \langle N \rangle}$

d. $d \varepsilon m a k r æ <^{t \; - \; I \; k \; \langle Adj \rangle}_{s \; - \; i \quad \langle N \rangle^{6}}$

e. $j \varepsilon r \wedge n d <^{- \qquad \langle N \rangle}_{- \; I \; v \; \langle Adj \rangle};\; \langle N \rangle$

The kind of phonological derivation that we assume can be summarized as follows, using the word *synonymous* as an illustration. To begin with, we have some surface structure tree which contains the form /s ɪ n a n ɪ m – a s/, under the domination of an Adj node as required by the category feature associated with it in the lexicon.[7] We then apply the phonological rules, beginning with those that assign stress. The relevant stress rule gives (13) as an intermediate stage in the derivation:

(13)   s ɪ n á n ɪ m a s

This intermediate stage now undergoes Vowel Reduction, which converts three of the four vowels to [ə]:

(14)   s ə n á n ə m ə s

Correspondingly, for *synonym* we have the following derivation:

(15)   s ɪ n a n ɪ m   (phonological representation)

s í n a n ì m   (by relevant rules of stress assignment)

s í n ə n ì m   (by Vowel Reduction)

This last line is the desired phonetic representation.

The phonological processes that we have discussed in this section represent only a small fraction of those that have an important role in English phonology. In particular, there are many very complex vowel alternations that we have not attempted to describe. But even with no more than this brief sketch of a very few processes, we are in a position to note two striking parallels between the syntactic description of a language and its phonological description. In the first place, we have seen that it is sometimes fruitful to describe the pronunciation of the words of a language in terms of abstract representations which do not themselves coincide with any actual allowable phonetic representation of the language. For example, the phonological representation that we set up for *repetition* was /r ɛ p ɛ t ɪ t – ion/, a representation which, if taken as an actual phonetic representation, would not correctly represent the pronunciation of *repetition* or of any other word of English. We found ourselves in many similar situations in syntax, for example when we argued that a revealing treatment of the distribution of certain inflectional forms of verbs in sentences like (16) below could be framed most easily if we posited (17) as a more abstract structure from which the sentence was derived, a structure which was not itself a well-formed sentence of English:

(16)   John has been working.

(17)   John Pres have en be ing work.

As regards their relative degree of abstractness, then, the relation between phonological representations and phonetic representations parallels very closely that between deep structures and surface structures.

The second important parallel is between transformational rules and phonological rules: both sets of rules are to be understood as applying *in sequence*, and in both cases something must be said about which sequences of rule applications are permissible. In syntax, a good example is afforded by the interaction of Passive and Number Agreement, which must apply in sequence (with Passive ordered first) to generate well-formed passive sentences. In phonology, a parallel example is afforded by the interaction of the stress rules with the rule of Vowel Reduction. In order to get the correct result (in fact, in order to avoid reducing far too many vowels to [ə]), we must apply the rules in sequence, with the stress rules ordered before Vowel Reduction. In recent detailed studies of English phonology, many additional phonological rules have been proposed, and the proper ordering of these rules appears to be every bit as critical as in syntax, if not more so. Similar extensive ordering statements have been argued for in the phonologies of other languages.

Before closing this section, it will be useful to provide in schematic form a general picture of the relations of the various components of a comprehensive syntactic and phonological description, as these relations have been assumed to be up to the present point in the discussion:

(18)

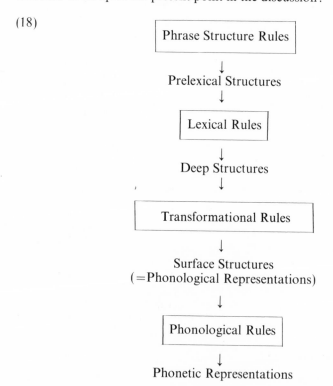

Phrase Structure Rules

↓

Prelexical Structures

↓

Lexical Rules

↓

Deep Structures

↓

Transformational Rules

↓

Surface Structures
(=Phonological Representations)

↓

Phonological Rules

↓

Phonetic Representations

Just as in recent chapters we have considered arguments in favor of giving up the simple picture of the syntax-semantics relation sketched at the end of Chapter 9, so now we will examine two arguments in favor of a less straightforward relation between syntax and phonology.

EXERCISES

1. The following pairs of words show an alternation between aspirated stops (p', t') and unaspirated stops ($p^=$, $t^=$):

(i)   telep$^=$athy
        telep'athic
(ii)   opp'ose
        opp$^=$osition
(iii)   phot'ographer
        phot$^=$ographic
(iv)   automat$^=$ic
        automat'icity

The rules given in the text for determining aspiration apply only to stops that are word-initial and to stops that are preceded by the sound *s* within the same word. These rules are clearly not applicable in the examples given immediately above. Devise a simple rule that accounts for the aspiration or lack of it in these words. Then determine whether your rule has to be ordered with respect to any of the phonological rules discussed in this section.

2. In many traditional dictionaries, a distinction is made between "long" vowels and "short" vowels, along the lines illustrated in the following examples:

LONG		SHORT	
light	[ay]	lit	[ɪ]
fate	[ey]	fat	[æ]
peek	[iy]	peck	[ɛ]
verbose	[ow]	verbosity	[a]

In general, the "long" vowels are tense, whereas the "short" vowels are lax. How is this classification useful in revising Vowel Reduction so as to prevent it from incorrectly reducing the unstressed vowels enclosed in boxes below?

(i)   g $\boxed{e}$ ó g r a p h $\boxed{y}$
(ii)   p s $\boxed{y}$ c h ó l o g $\boxed{y}$
(iii)   c á l i c $\boxed{o}$
(iv)   v $\boxed{a}$ c á t i o n
(v)   p h $\boxed{o}$ t ó m e t r y
(vi)   r h $\boxed{i}$ n ó c e r o s

16.2 ENGLISH SENTENCE STRESS

In the preceding section, we took note of distinctions of stress within individual English words, and indicated how these distinctions might be accounted for by phonological rules. We now turn our attention to distinctions of stress that are found in sequences consisting of more than a single word. An initial example is afforded by the phrase *secondary education*, as pronounced by speakers of American English. If the two words that make up this phrase were spoken in isolation, their respective stress patterns would be as follows:

(19)   sécondàry

(20)   èducátion

However, when they are spoken together as a single phrase, we can perceive that the third syllable in *education* is slightly more prominent than the first syllable in *secondary*, even though this syllable of *secondary* is still the most highly stressed syllable within the word. The degree of stress found on the initial syllable of *secondary* is often represented in transcriptions by the symbol ˆ, which stands for a stress level intermediate between the stress levels represented by ´ and ˎ. With this new symbol, we can now represent the stress pattern of the noun phrase *secondary education* as follows:

(21)   sêcondàry èducátion

Following a more recent usage, we will for convenience represent these three stress levels by positive whole numbers, with "1" standing for highest stress (replacing ´), "2" standing for the next-highest stress (replacing ˆ), and "3" standing for the lower level (replacing ˎ). With this change, the transcriptions given above are to be replaced by the following:

(22)   sec$\overset{1}{\text{ond}}$ar$\overset{3}{\text{y}}$

(23) $\overset{3}{\text{e}}$duc$\overset{1}{\text{a}}$tion

(24)   s$\overset{2}{\text{e}}$cond$\overset{3}{\text{a}}$ry $\overset{3}{\text{e}}$duc$\overset{1}{\text{a}}$tion

Some other examples of stress contours in noun phrases will be useful at this point.

(25)   a m$\overset{2}{\text{e}}$dical m$\overset{1}{\text{i}}$racle

(26)   the sp$\overset{2}{\text{e}}$ctor of r$\overset{2}{\text{a}}$bid n$\overset{1}{\text{a}}$tional$\overset{3}{\text{i}}$sm

(27)   the h$\overset{2}{\text{o}}$use in the w$\overset{1}{\text{o}}$ods

Each of these phrases contains two or more words which in isolation would be pronounced with a primary stress. In each of these phrases, however, only one primary stress occurs, with all of the other syllables receiving a stress no higher than secondary.

Our account of the stress patterns found in these phrases will rest on two fundamental assumptions. The first is that at some level prior to the level of phonetic representation, the stress pattern assigned to a word within a phrase is the same as that assigned to it in isolation.[8] Thus, the phrases given above will have the following as intermediate representations:

(28) $\overset{1}{\text{se}}\overset{3}{\text{con}}\text{dary }\overset{3}{\text{e}}\text{du}\overset{1}{\text{ca}}\text{tion}$

(29)   a $\overset{1}{\text{me}}$dical $\overset{1}{\text{mi}}$racle

(30)   the $\overset{1}{\text{spe}}$ctor of $\overset{1}{\text{ra}}$bid $\overset{1}{\text{na}}$tio$\overset{3}{\text{na}}$lism

(31)   the $\overset{1}{\text{hou}}$se in the $\overset{1}{\text{woo}}$ds

The second assumption is that these intermediate forms undergo a rule which has the effect of adjusting the stresses on all except the last word of the phrase:

(32)   Nuclear Stress Rule
Within a constituent, reduce to secondary stresses any and all primary stresses except for the one farthest to the right.[9]

Applying within NP's, this rule will have the effect of converting the intermediate stress patterns in (28) through (31) into the actual stress patterns found in (24) through (27).

When we examine sentences instead of noun phrases, we find stress patterns that are exactly parallel to those described above:

(33) $\overset{2}{\text{Ho}}$race $\overset{1}{\text{sta}}$yed.

(34) $\overset{2}{\text{Ho}}$race $\overset{2}{\text{sta}}$yed a$\overset{1}{\text{wa}}$y.

(35) $\overset{2}{\text{Ja}}$ck $\overset{2}{\text{stu}}$dies $\overset{2}{\text{se}}$con$\overset{3}{\text{da}}$ry $\overset{3}{\text{e}}$du$\overset{1}{\text{ca}}$tion.

(36) $\overset{2}{\text{Ge}}$orge is $\overset{2}{\text{ea}}$ger to $\overset{2}{\text{gi}}$ve a $\overset{1}{\text{le}}$cture.

(37) $\overset{2}{\text{Fi}}$do was $\overset{2}{\text{stu}}$ng by a $\overset{1}{\text{bee}}$.

Since an entire sentence is itself a constituent, these patterns are automatically accounted for by the Nuclear Stress Rule as formulated in (32), under the assumption that at an intermediate level the sentences above have the following representations:

(38) $\overset{1}{\text{Ho}}$race $\overset{1}{\text{sta}}$yed.

(39) $\overset{1}{\text{Ho}}$race $\overset{1}{\text{sta}}$yed a$\overset{1}{\text{wa}}$y.

(40) $\overset{1}{\text{Ja}}$ck $\overset{1}{\text{stu}}$dies $\overset{1}{\text{se}}$con$\overset{3}{\text{da}}$ry $\overset{3}{\text{e}}$du$\overset{1}{\text{ca}}$tion.

(41) $\overset{1}{\text{Ge}}$orge is $\overset{1}{\text{ea}}$ger to $\overset{1}{\text{gi}}$ve a $\overset{1}{\text{le}}$cture.

(42) $\overset{1}{\text{Fi}}$do was $\overset{1}{\text{stu}}$ng by a $\overset{1}{\text{bee}}$.

The rule simply changes all primary stresses to secondary stresses, except for the rightmost primary stress in each sentence.

None of the examples considered so far provides any difficulties for the Nuclear Stress Rule itself or for the view that it applies to surface structures, i.e., to structures that have already undergone a complete syntactic derivation. There are some English sentences, however, that exhibit a stress pattern different from what we would be led to expect. An initial example is:[10]

(43) $\overset{2}{\text{John}}$ $\overset{2}{\text{has}}$ some $\overset{1}{\text{books}}$ to $\overset{2}{\text{read}}$.

What we would expect here is the stress pattern given in (44a), a pattern that is appropriate only if reading is being contrasted with some other activity. as in (44b):

(44) a. $\overset{2}{\text{John}}$ $\overset{2}{\text{has}}$ some $\overset{2}{\text{books}}$ to $\overset{1}{\text{read}}$.

  b. John has some books to $\overset{1}{\text{read}}$, but he doesn't have any to $\overset{1}{\text{review}}$.

Since it is the most neutral, noncontrastive stress pattern that the Nuclear Stress Rule is intended to account for, and since the most neutral pattern for the sentence under consideration is that given in (43), the failure of the Nuclear Stress Rule to assign that pattern must be accounted a problem for the treatment of sentence stress suggested so far.

Another problematic example is provided by a sentence such as (45):

(45) Alex is washing the car that Marsha bought.

The most neutral stress pattern for this sentence is one in which primary stress falls on *car*:

(46) $\overset{2}{\text{Alex}}$ is $\overset{2}{\text{washing}}$ the $\overset{1}{\text{car}}$ that $\overset{2}{\text{Marsha}}$ $\overset{2}{\text{bought}}$.

Unfortunately, the treatment proposed thus far assigns primary stress to the verb *bought*, yielding a stress pattern which in fact would be most readily interpreted as implying some contrast between *buying* and some other method of acquisition:

(47) $\overset{2}{\text{Alex}}$ is $\overset{2}{\text{washing}}$ the $\overset{2}{\text{car}}$ that $\overset{2}{\text{Marsha}}$ $\overset{1}{\text{bought}}$.

At first glance, it might seem that the fault would have to lie with our formulation of the Nuclear Stress Rule, and that some complication of this rule would be the most effective way to solve the problem raised by the two sentences just discussed. However, there is another distinct possibility worth considering: the Nuclear Stress Rule may be satisfactory as stated, but we may not be applying it in the most effective manner. In particular, we have been assuming that all stress rules apply to surface structures. At this point let us consider an alternative convention:

(48) a. Rules assigning stress to words apply prior to the syntactic derivation.

  b. Rules assigning stress to S's apply at the end of each cycle of the syntactic derivation.

This manner of application is depicted in (49):

(49)

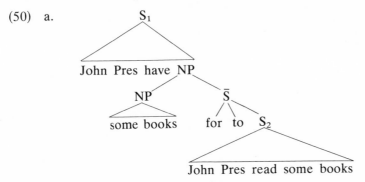

Step 0: Apply rules which determine stress within words.

Step 1a: Apply relevant transformational rules in S_3.

Step 1b: Apply Nuclear Stress Rule in S_3.

Step 2a: Apply relevant transformational rules in S_2.

Step 2b: Apply Nuclear Stress Rule in S_2.

Step 3a: Apply relevant transformational rules in S_1.

Step 3b: Apply Nuclear Stress Rule in S_1.

We will refer to this new proposal about the manner in which phonological rules apply as the "Ordering Hypothesis," and will use the term "Surface Structure Hypothesis" for the manner of application assumed earlier.

We begin our examination of the Ordering Hypothesis with a reconsideration of (43), which as we observed is most naturally stressed on the word *books*:

(43)   John has some books to read.
        (² ² ¹ ²)

A plausible deep structure for this sentence might be (50a), given that *John* is the "understood subject" of *read*, and *books* is the "understood object":

(50) a.
S_1

John Pres have NP

NP $\bar{S}$

some books   for to S_2

John Pres read some books

Application of the word-stress rules gives:

(50) b.   [John Pres have some books [for to [John Pres read some books]$_{S_2}$]$_{\bar{S}}$]$_{S_1}$
           (with ¹ stress marks on John, have, books, John, read, books)

In the lower sentence, S_2, no syntactic rules apply. Application of the Nuclear Stress Rule in S_2 reduces the stress on *John* and *read*, giving the following intermediate result:

(50) c. $_{S_1}$[John Aux hàve some boóks $_{\bar{S}}$[for to $_{S_2}$[Jòhn rèad some

boóks]]].
$\quad_{S_2\ \bar{S}S_1}$

We now proceed to the domain of S_1. Here it is necessary to apply a number of transformational rules, including Affix Insertion, Identical-NP Deletion, and Complementizer Deletion. The most critical rule for our purposes, however, is a rule similar in effect to Relative Clause Formation, which deletes the embedded object under identity with the corresponding NP next to the subordinate structure. In the present instance, this rule deletes a phrase (*some books*) that happens to be carrying a primary stress at this point in the derivation. When all of these syntactic rules have applied, the resulting structure is as follows:

(50) d.   Jòhn Aux hàve some boóks $_{\bar{S}}$[$_S$[to rèad]] .
$\qquad\qquad\qquad\qquad\qquad\qquad_{S\ \bar{S}}$

Having finished with the transformational rules in the S_1 domain, we again apply the Nuclear Stress Rule, reducing all primary stresses except the rightmost primary to secondary stresses. Because of the prior application of the Nuclear Stress Rule on the earlier cycle, the embedded verb *read* does not carry a primary stress, and hence the rightmost primary stress in the sentence as a whole is on the word *books*. Application of the Nuclear Stress Rule to (50d) reduces the stresses on *John* and *have*, but leaves the primary stress on *books* intact. The result is just that given earlier as the most normal stress pattern for this sentence:

(43)   Jòhn hàs some boóks to rèad.

A similar derivation is available for (46):

(46)   Àlex is wàshing the càr that Màrsha boùght.

The deep structure for this sentence would be:

(51) a.

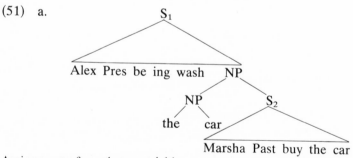

Assignment of word-stress yields:

(51) b. $_{S_1}$[Álex Pres be ing wàsh the càr $_{S_2}$[Mársha Past buy the

càr]] .
$\quad_{S_2\ S_1}$

On the S_2 cycle, no transformational rules apply. Application of the Nuclear Stress Rule gives:

(51) c. [1] [Alex Pres be ing wash the [1] car [Marsha Past [1] buy the
S_1 S_2

[1] car]] .
$S_2 S_1$

On the S_1-cycle, the critical syntactic rule is Relative Clause Formation, which yields:

(51) d. [Alex [1] Pres be ing wash the [1] car [that [2] Marsha Past [2] buy]] .
S_1 S_2 $S_2 S_1$

In this structure, the rightmost primary stress is on *car*. Consequently, when the Nuclear Stress Rule applies at the end of the S_1-cycle, the primary stress on *car* remains, whereas the two primary stresses to the left of *car* are reduced to secondary stresses:

(51) e. [2] Alex is [2] washing the [1] car that [2] Marsha [2] bought.

This is just the desired stress pattern.[11]

A particularly striking contrast for which this analysis has been suggested as an explanation is that exhibited by the following two sentences:

(52) I [2] found some [1] pictures that [2] John would [2] like.

(53) I [2] found [2] something that [2] John would [1] like.

Stress is assigned to (52) in exactly the same way that it was assigned to (46). The mysterious sentence in this pair, if we accept the Ordering Hypothesis, would appear to be (53), in which the final verb of the relative clause receives primary stress. In fact, the stress on this sentence might appear to favor the Surface Structure Hypothesis. But if we consider the embedded sentence from which the relative clause in (53) is formed, we can see why the primary stress in the complex sentence falls on the verb of the relative clause. The corresponding simple sentence is:

(54) [2] John would [1] like [2] something.

The critical property of this sentence, for our present purposes, is that primary stress does not fall on the object NP, but instead falls on the verb. Indefinite words such as *something, somebody, someone*, and *somewhere* characteristically do not attract the primary stress of a simple sentence, even when, as in (54), they are in a position in a sentence in which a full NP such as *some pictures* would always receive primary stress. In order to account for the stress pattern in a simple sentence such as (54), we might amend the Nuclear Stress Rule in such a way as to prevent it from leaving a primary stress on one of these indefinite words. Alternatively, we might suppose that when these words are inserted into trees, they have an underlying secondary stress instead of an underlying primary. Under this alternative, the initial stress pattern for (54) would be (55):

(55) $\overset{1}{\text{John}}$ Past will $\overset{1}{\text{like}}$ $\overset{2}{\text{some}}$thing.

Application of the Nuclear Stress Rule will reduce the stress on *John* to secondary, leaving the primary stress on *like* intact.

As soon as we take care of stress assignment in the simple sentence (54), we find that stress assignment in the corresponding relative clause sentence (53) is consistent with the Ordering Hypothesis. The derivation of (53) begins with (56a):

(56) a. $[\underset{S_1}{\text{I Past find }} \overset{1}{\text{find}} \overset{2}{\text{something}} [\underset{S_2}{\text{John Past will }} \overset{1}{\text{like}} \overset{1}{\text{some}}\overset{2}{\text{thing}}]]_{S_2 S_1}$.

Application of the Nuclear Stress Rule in S_2 gives exactly the same results as in the corresponding simple structure:

(56) b. $[\underset{S_1}{\text{I past }} \overset{1}{\text{find}} \overset{2}{\text{something}} [\underset{S_2}{\text{John Past will }} \overset{1}{\text{like}} \overset{2}{\text{some}}\text{thing}]]_{S_2 S_1}$.

On the higher cycle, Relative Clause Formation gives:

(56) c. $[\underset{S_1}{\text{I Past }} \overset{1}{\text{find}} \overset{2}{\text{something}} [\underset{S_2}{\text{that }} \overset{2}{\text{John}} \text{ Past will } \overset{1}{\text{like}}]]_{S_2 S_1}$.

The Nuclear Stress Rule now applies in the sentence as a whole. The primary stress on *like* remains intact, since it is the rightmost primary stress. The only remaining one, that on *find*, is reduced to secondary. The resulting stress pattern is just:

(56) d.   I $\overset{2}{\text{found}}$ $\overset{2}{\text{some}}$thing that $\overset{2}{\text{John}}$ would $\overset{1}{\text{like}}$.

In this instance, then, an apparent oddity in the stress pattern of a complex sentence is seen to follow, given the Ordering Hypothesis, from a special adjustment that must be made in the description of stress assignment in simple sentences.

Thus far in this section, we have presented a series of arguments in favor of the Ordering Hypothesis as against the Surface Structure Hypothesis. In each case, we attempted to show that if the Ordering Hypothesis was adopted, some superficially peculiar stress properties of complex sentences would follow from the stress properties of the simple sentences that made them up. At this point, it will be instructive to consider one particular rejoinder that has been made on behalf of the Surface Structure Hypothesis which takes the form of a counterattack.

In Exercise 2 at the end of Chapter 7, we sketched a widely accepted transformational analysis of the construction illustrated in the following sentence:

(57)   John is easy for Alice to please.

Under the analysis given there, the derivation of this sentence would commence with the structure sketched in (58a), which contains an underlying direct object for the verb *please*:

(58) a.

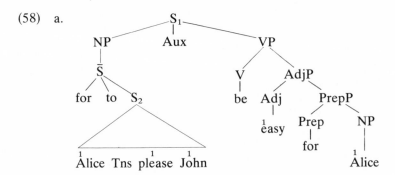

Application of the Nuclear Stress Rule in S_2 at the end of the first cycle gives the following intermediate stress pattern for S_2:

(58) b.

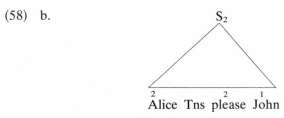

On the S_1 cycle, application of Extraposition, Affix Insertion, Identical-NP Deletion, and Complementizer Deletion gives the following structure:

(58) c.

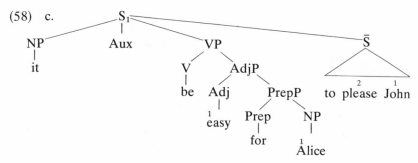

To this structure, Object Raising can apply, giving:

(58) d.   John Aux be easy for Alice to please.

Application of the Nuclear Stress Rule on the top cycle reduces all of the primary stresses except that on *Alice*, giving the following stress pattern as a result:

(58) e.   John is easy for Alice to please.

Unfortunately, this is not the most natural stress pattern for this sentence, except when *Alice* is understood as being contrasted with someone else. The most natural stress pattern is:

(58) f.   John is easy for Alice to please.

Moreover, this correct stress pattern is just the one that would have been obtained had the Nuclear Stress Rule been applied in conformity with the Surface Structure Hypothesis, since under this original hypothesis, we would never have had occasion to reduce the primary stress on the verb *please* as we did in the Ordering Hypothesis derivation given above. Thus, the Surface Structure Hypothesis appears to enjoy an advantage here.

Here a surprising defense might be offered for the Ordering Hypothesis. Suppose that we assume a different analysis for sentences such as (57). Under this alternative analysis, the infinitival phrase starts out in deep structure as a predicate VP instead of as a subject S, and the rule of Object Raising is reformulated to move an NP from this complement VP into the main clause subject position, replacing an empty NP.[12] Under this reanalysis, the deep structure for (57) would be:

(59)   a.

```
                        S₁
         ┌──────────────┼──────────────┐
        NP             Aux             VP
         │                           ╱    ╲
         Δ                          V     AdjP
                                    │    ╱    ╲───────────┐
                                   be  Adj   PrepP        VP
                                        │    ╱  ╲        ╱  ╲
                                      easy  for Alice  to please John
```

Suppose that in addition we assume that the Nuclear Stress Rule, when it applies in the generation of full sentences, is like ordinary cyclic transformational rules, in that S's are the only domains in which it applies.[13] This latter assumption will mean that we have only a single application of the Nuclear Stress Rule in the structure given in (59a). Furthermore, the Ordering Hypothesis dictates that this application of the Nuclear Stress Rule must follow the application of all syntactic rules. Thus, Object Raising (in a slightly revised form) will already have applied, yielding:

(59)   b.   John is easy for Alice to please.

With this alternative deep structure, the Nuclear Stress Rule does not have a chance to apply until after the underlying object of *please* is removed by Object Raising. Consequently, there is never any occasion to reduce incorrectly the primary stress on *please* to secondary. With this reanalysis of Object Raising complements, then, the Ordering Hypothesis can be kept alive, and sentence (57) no longer constitutes an advantage for the Surface Structure Hypothesis.

At this point, the proponent of the Surface Structure Hypothesis is entitled to issue another challenge. Although he may grant that the adoption of this VP analysis of Object Raising complements provides a way of saving the Ordering Hypothesis, he is within his rights to ask whether there is any independent justification for adopting this analysis as against the original one. If none can be found, then this new analysis must be considered ad hoc, its only virtue being that it saves the Ordering Hypothesis from a serious embarrassment. On the other hand, if independent justifications can be found, then the defense must be counted more successful.

Such independent justification has in fact been offered for assigning underlying VP status to Object Raising complements. The argument rests on the existence of ill-formed sentences such as the following:[14]

(60)   *That judge would be easy for Sally to be sent to prison by.

Within the analysis in which Object Raising complements are underlying $\bar{S}$'s, this ungrammatical sentence is generated. By way of illustration, we give a transformational derivation for (60) on the original analysis, beginning with the deep structure:

(61)   a.

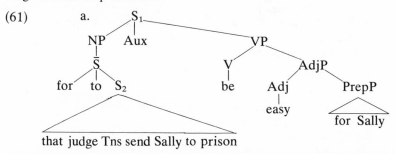

Application of Passive in S_2 yields a structure in which *Sally* is the derived subject:

(61) b.   ...$_{S_2}$[Sally Tns be en send to prison by the judge]$_{S_2}$ ...

The derivation continues on the S_1 cycle as follows:

(61) c.   it Aux be easy for Sally $_{\bar{S}}$[for to Sally Tns be en send to prison by

that judge]$_{\bar{S}}$. (by Extraposition)

    d.   it Aux be easy for Sally $_{\bar{S}}$[to be en send to prison by that judge]$_{\bar{S}}$.

(by Affix Insertion, Identical-NP Deletion, and Complementizer Deletion)

    e.   that judge Aux be easy for Sally to be en send to prison by.
(by Object Raising)

After the appropriate morphophonemic rules apply, we find that we have generated the ungrammatical sentence (60).

By contrast, suppose that we were to assume that Object Raising complements are underlying VP's, contained in a structure of the sort sketched below:

(62)

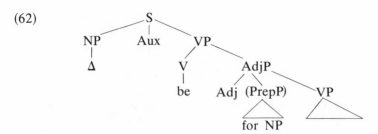

From a structure of this type, there would be no way of deriving a sentence, such as (60), with a passive infinitive. The reason is quite simple: an underlying VP will provide no opportunity for the application of Passive, since there must be a subject NP present if the structural description of Passive is to be satisfied. Hence, given a VP analysis of Object Raising complements, we succeed in avoiding the generation of sentence (60).

Sentence (60), then, can be viewed as providing an argument in favor of the VP analysis of Object Raising complements. As it happens, though, there are at least some passive infinitival phrases that appear to give much more acceptable results, among them the following:[15]

(63)   Such flattery is easy to be fooled by.

Such an example, if it is well-formed, provides evidence against the VP analysis. Furthermore, it suggests that a different explanation should be given for the ill-formedness of (60).

At this point, it would be well to review the progress of this argument, in order to reemphasize the way in which the controversy between the Ordering Hypothesis and the Surface Structure Hypothesis is related to the controversy between the S analysis of Object Raising complements and the VP analysis of the same construction. We began by noting that under the S analysis, the Nuclear Stress Rule, if applied in conformity with the Ordering Hypothesis, does not assign stress correctly to a sentence such as (57), *John is easy for Alice to please.* We also noted that the Surface Structure Hypothesis does not suffer from this embarrassment: it gives the correct stress even with the S analysis. Thus, if the S analysis is assumed, the Ordering Hypothesis must be given up, whereas the Surface Structure Hypothesis can continue to be maintained.

On the other hand, with the VP analysis of these complements, we get a correct stress assignment for this sentence even if we apply the Nuclear Stress Rule in conformity with the Ordering Hypothesis. Thus, if we adopt the VP analysis, we are not forced to give up the Ordering Hypothesis. As a consequence of all this, the possibility of keeping the Ordering Hypothesis afloat in the face of examples such as (57) depends critically on how effective a case can be made for the VP analysis of Object Raising complements as against the S analysis. The ill-formed passive complement in (60) appeared to provide the basis for an independent argument in favor of the VP analysis, but the well-formedness of (63) appeared to tip the scales in the opposite direction.

Let us conclude this section with a brief summary. In the Ordering Hypothesis, we have a new claim concerning the manner in which syntactic and phonological rules interact, specifically, that the phonological rules of a language apply at the end of each syntactic cycle instead of waiting until the end of the entire syntactic derivation. This hypothesis drew its support from its usefulness in removing several apparent counterexamples to the Nuclear Stress Rule in English. These examples were presented in (43) and (46). On the debit side, the Ordering Hypothesis appeared to yield incorrect consequences for Object Raising sentences. An alternative syntactic analysis was suggested for these sentences under which the Ordering Hypothesis would not give bad consequences. However, this alternative analysis was seen to be somewhat vulnerable. We are thus in much the same sort of situation with the Ordering Hypothesis as we were with the Cyclic Convention itself at the end of Chapter 7. In both cases, the hypothesis in question had some very interesting favorable consequences, but yielded some questionable results as well. Finally, in neither case is it evident whether the most fruitful approach will be to modify the general hypothesis, or to change our views concerning the particular rules of English.

EXERCISES

1.   Which (if either) of the two hypotheses, the Ordering Hypothesis or the Surface Structure Hypothesis, comes out ahead in accounting for the following sentence:

(i)   We met a man to whose children Martha gave a bȯok.

Answer the same question for the following sentence:

(ii)   We found a book that Martha gave to Joe's chi̇ldren.

2.   Study the following sentence:

Let me tell you about something strȧnge that happened.

     A. Show that the Ordering Hypothesis and the Nuclear Stress Rule as stated in (32) do not assign the correct stress to this sentence.
     B. Provide some evidence that the fault lies with the Nuclear Stress Rule rather than with the Ordering Hypothesis.

3.   In several recent generative studies, it has been suggested that the underlying NP that is deleted in the course of deriving the relative clause construction is not a full NP but rather a definite pronoun. For instance, the approximate deep structure of (i) below would on this new analysis be (iii) rather than (ii):

(i)   The man that John introduced you to is a thief.
(ii)   *The man* $_s$[John introduced you to *the man*]$_s$ is a thief.
(iii)   *The man* $_s$[John introduced you to *him*]$_s$ is a thief.

Show that if this new analysis is adopted, sentence (46), repeated below, no longer provides an argument in favor of the Ordering Hypothesis:

(46)   Álex is wáshing the cár that Mársha bóught.

(In order to show this, you will first have to observe something about the stress behavior of definite object pronouns in simple sentences.) This problem is based on an observation given in Berman and Szamosi 1972, p. 306, fn. 2.

4. In Bresnan 1971, an analysis of questions is assumed that differs in one significant respect from the one developed in this book. In this alternative analysis, there is a complementizer *WH* (roughly equivalent to our *Q*) that serves to attract questioned constituents. The difference in the two proposals can be seen in the differing deep structure trees assigned to the question in (i):

(i)   Which book did John give to Peggy?

(ii)

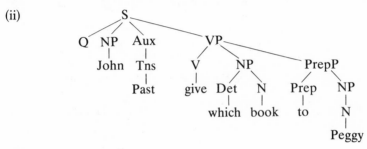

(iii)

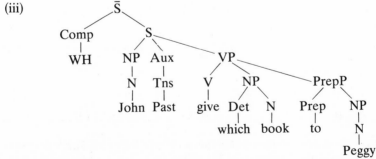

In addition to assuming the deep structure in (iii), Bresnan assumes that there is a separate S̄ cycle, on which the rule of Question Formation applies, and on which the Nuclear Stress Rule can reapply.

   A. Show how, with this last assumption and the tree in (iii), the following stress contour would be accounted for:

   What bóoks has Jóhn réad?

   B. Show that the Nuclear Stress Rule, if applied as dictated by the Ordering Hypothesis, would assign a different stress pattern to this sentence if one assumed the type of deep structure for this sentence shown in (ii) above, rather than that shown in (iii).

16.3 AUXILIARY SHIFT IN ENGLISH

In the preceding section we saw a case in which it could be argued that a phonological rule (the Nuclear Stress Rule) had to have access to syntactic information not present in surface structure if it was to function with maximum effectiveness. In this section we will examine a purported instance of an entirely different sort, an instance of a syntactic rule that appears to require access to a certain kind of phonological information.

The rule in question is one that we must set up in order to account for the relative position of the adverb and initial helping verb in the following sentences:

(64)   Fred will *probably* be working when you arrive.

(65)   Fred has *always* been fond of Sheila.

(66)   Fritz was *never* informed of the decision.

(67)   They were *probably* being kept under surveillance.

(68)   Max is *usually* communicative.

In each of the above sentences, an adverb intervenes between the first helping verb and the material that follows it. As a matter of fact, in the sentences in question, the adverb is found in exactly the position in which we find the word *not* in the otherwise identical sentences:

(69)   Fred will *not* be working when you arrive.

(70)   Fred has *not* been fond of Sheila.

(71)   Fritz was *not* informed of the decision.

(72)   They were *not* being kept under surveillance.

(73)   Max is *not* communicative.

In Chapter 3 we proposed to introduce *not* into deep structures as an optional first element in the Aux constituent. We accounted for its position in surface structure by means of a transformational rule that shifted Tns plus the first helping verb over the left of *not*, or shifted Tns alone when no helping verb was present. It might now appear that the same treatment is appropriate for adverbs such as *probably, always, never*, and *usually*. That is, we might generate them in deep structure as optional elements of the Aux constituent, and reorder the first helping verb by a transformational rule. In fact, we might even be tempted to reformulate *Not*-HV Inversion in such a way that it would apply not only in the presence of *not*, but also in the presence of these other adverbs.

A consideration of additional examples, however, shows that there are significant differences between the behavior of *not* and the behavior of these other adverbs. For one thing, we find that the presence of these additional adverbs does not bring about *Do* Support in the way that *not* does:

(74)   Joe does not enjoy a good meal.

(75)   *Joe does $\left\{ \begin{matrix} \text{never} \\ \text{always} \end{matrix} \right\}$ enjoy a good meal.

On the other hand, these adverbs, unlike *not*, may occur grammatically without *do*:

(76)   *Joe not enjoys a good meal.

(77)   Joe $\left\{ \begin{matrix} \text{never} \\ \text{always} \end{matrix} \right\}$ enjoys a good meal.

At the very least, then, the rule that accounts for the position of these adverbs must somehow be kept from applying in such a way as to move a Tns element when it is not followed by a helping verb. Otherwise, our grammar would generate ungrammatical sentences such as those in (75). We will assume the following statement as a first approximation of the rule accounting for the relative position of adverbs and helping verbs:

(78)   Auxiliary Shift

$$\text{NP} - \text{Adv} - \text{Tns} \left\{ \begin{matrix} \text{M} \\ \text{have} \\ \text{be} \end{matrix} \right\} - \text{Y}$$

$$\begin{matrix} 1 & 2 & 3 & 4 \end{matrix}$$

$$\Rightarrow 1, 3 + 2, 0, 4$$

A second major difference between the behavior of *not* and the behavior of these other adverbs is that there are no circumstances in which *not* remains to the left of a tense-inflected helping verb, whereas there are two situations in which the helping verb does not shift across these other adverbs. One situation is that in which the helping verb is emphasized:

(79)   Fritz probably WILL be working when you arrive.

(80)   Fred always HAS been fond of Sheila.

(81)   Fritz never WAS informed of the decision.

(82)   They probably WERE being kept under surveillance.

(83)   Max usually IS communicative.

These sentences should be compared with the decidedly more awkward sentences given below, in which the emphasized helping verb precedes the adverb instead of following it:

(84)   ?*Fritz WILL probably be working when you arrive.

(85)   ?*Fred HAS always been fond of Sheila.

(86)   ?*Fritz WAS never informed of the decision.

(87)   ?*They WERE probably being kept under surveillance.

(88)   ?*Max IS usually communicative.

We might tentatively account for the contrast in grammaticality between the sentences in (79) through (83) and those in (84) through (88) by stating as a special condition on the Auxiliary Shift Rule that the helping verb in question must not be emphasized.

The second situation in which adverbs must retain their underlying order before the first helping verb is illustrated in the following sentences:

(89)   John has admired Sue only since last year, but Bill ALWAYS has.

(90)   John has taken more money from you in the past few days than Bill EVER has from me.

(91)   I'm not certain how gentle they EVER are with lame-duck presidents.

These should be compared with the following sentences, in which the relative order of adverb and helping verb has been switched:

(92)   *John has admired Sue only since last year, but Bill has ALWAYS.

(93)   *John has taken more money from you in the past few days than Bill has EVER from me.

(94)   *I'm not certain how gentle they are EVER with lame-duck presidents.

The one common property to be found in sentences (89) through (91) that distinguishes them from all of the sentences discussed previously is that in each of the three sentences something has been moved or deleted immediately after the helping verb in the course of the transformational derivation. In (89) it is the phrase *admired Sue*, in (90) it is the verb *taken*, and in (91) it is the questioned adjective phrase *how gentle*. In fact, in parallel sentences in which the critical material is not moved or deleted, it is perfectly permissible to shift the helping verb to the left of the adverb:

(95)   John has admired Sue only since last year, but Bill *has ALWAYS* admired Sue.

(96)   John has taken more money from you in the past few days than Bill *has EVER* taken from me.

(97)   I'm not certain that they *are EVER* very gentle with lame-duck presidents.

We might account for these new distinctions, then, by adding a second restriction to the rule of Auxiliary Shift: this rule may not apply if some constituent following the critical helping verb has been moved or deleted in the course of the transformational derivation.

At this juncture, we appear to be left with two entirely unrelated restrictions on the rule of Auxiliary Shift. However, a closer examination of the second environment in which the rule is blocked will show that the two restrictions actually follow from a single more general restriction on the rule.

To set the stage, let us take note of a peculiar fact about the pronunciation of English helping verbs. As a general rule, the various full vowels that we hear when we pronounce these words in isolation or when we emphasize them are replaced by the reduced vowel [ə] when the words are pronounced unemphatically in sentences. For instance, in isolation the word *shall* is pronounced with the same full vowel [æ] that we find in *pal*. By contrast, when it occurs in a sentence such as the following, it is ordinarily pronounced with the reduced vowel [ə]:

(98)   We shall [šəl] all profit by this experience.

There is a similar contrast between the pronunciation of the word *could* in isolation (in this situation it rhymes with *hood*) and its pronunciation in a sentence such as the following:

(99)   We could [kəd] tell that something was amiss.

There are many other monosyllabic words in English which show the same variation between a full and a reduced pronunciation. These include prepositions such as *at* and *from*, conjunctions such as *and* and *but*, and a variety of other words.[16]

As a preliminary account of this variation, let us assume that all occurrences of these words are initially assigned primary stress by rule (10) in section 1, that is, by the general rule that assigns primary stress to monosyllables. The unstressed pronunciation of these words will be attributed to the operation of the following rule:

(100)   Stress Weakening
        In circumstances in which they are not emphasized, English helping verbs, and also prepositions, conjunctions, articles, and certain other words, have their stress removed.

For example, the helping verb *shall* in (98) above will first be assigned primary stress: [šǽl]. Subsequently, application of Stress Weakening will give [šæl]. This form is now eligible for Vowel Reduction, which we developed in section 1 to account for vowel alternations in words of more than one syllable. The result of applying Vowel Reduction will be the desired phonetic representation: [šəl].

Now that we have developed an account of the appearance of reduced vowels in these helping verbs, let us look at a rather surprising situation in which the full vowels are maintained, contrary to what we should expect from the Stress Weakening rule. In each of the following sentences, the first helping verb has a reduced vowel, but the second does not:

(101)   John has [həz] admired Sue for a long time, and Bill has [hæz], too.

(102)   John has [həz] taken more money from you than Bill has [hæz] from me.

(103)   I think that they are [ər] gentle with senile senators, but I don't know how gentle they are [ar] with lame-duck presidents.

In order to account for these unreduced vowels, let us add a special restriction to Stress Weakening:

(104)   Stress Weakening is inapplicable when something has been moved or deleted after the word in question.

With this new condition, Stress Weakening will not apply to the second helping verb in any of the above sentences. The helping verbs will retain their underlying stress, and consequently the conditions necessary for Vowel Reduction will not be satisfied. We have thus accounted for the persistence of the full vowel in these occurrences of helping verbs.

Let us now return to the problem that we encountered in trying to specify the environments in which Auxiliary Shift did not take place. The problem was that we were faced with what seemed to be two entirely unrelated restrictions on the application of this rule. The first was that the rule did not apply when the helping verb in question was emphasized. The second was that it did not apply when some material had been moved or deleted immediately following the helping verb. But we are now in a position to see what these two situations have in common: *it is in precisely these two situations that the helping verb retains some degree of stress*. On the other hand, the helping verbs that do undergo the rule of Auxiliary Shift are just those whose stress has been lost by the rule of Stress Weakening. Consequently, we can do the work of both of the original restrictions on Auxiliary Shift simply by including in the structural description the specification that the helping verb in question be *unstressed*:[17]

(105) Auxiliary Shift (revised version)

$$\text{NP} - \text{Adv} - \begin{Bmatrix} \text{M} \\ have \\ be \end{Bmatrix} \text{Tns} - \text{X}$$
$$\langle -\text{stress} \rangle$$

$$1 \quad\quad 2 \quad\quad\quad 3 \quad\quad\quad 4$$
$$\Rightarrow 1, 3 + 2, 0, 4$$

Let us turn now to the implications of this analysis for our universal grammar. To begin with, it is clear that the analysis is incompatible with a descriptive framework of the type represented schematically in (18), which requires that all syntactic rules apply before any phonological rules. In particular, Auxiliary Shift (a movement rule) cannot apply until after the application of Stress Weakening (a phonological rule).

A second implication concerns the type of rules that the framework allows. Nothing that we have said prior to this chapter would have allowed us to make reference to a phonological property such as stress in the statement of a movement rule. The inclusion of such a rule in our grammar of English thus would commit us to a more "permissive" framework, one that allows a wider range of rules for the grammars of individual languages.

Although we can use a single rule like Auxiliary Shift to argue for a more permissive framework, this one rule will not give us much indication of exactly how much more permissive the new framework should be. One extreme would be to allow syntactic rules to make reference to any phonological properties of words. The little evidence available at the present time suggests that such an increase in permissiveness would be unnecessarily broad. It would allow syntactic rules that referred to the voicing of the first sound of a word, or to the presence or absence of a consonant cluster at the end of a word. As a matter of fact, no such syntactic rules have ever been discovered in any language. A more appropriate increase in permissiveness might result if we were to modify our framework in such a way as to allow syntactic rules to refer to only a few specific phonological properties. The Auxiliary Shift rule as stated in (105) would clearly require that the relative degree of stress be one of the permitted properties. Another phonological property that has figured in some syntactic rules is the number of syllables in a word. To give one example, the rule that determines the word order of pronouns in Tagalog must apparently distinguish between pronouns of one syllable and those that contain two syllables.[18] Further investigations in a wide range of languages may uncover other phonological properties that are relevant for syntactic descriptions, and may give a clearer idea of exactly how permissive our framework should be in this regard.

EXERCISES

1. Give a brief informal account of the variation in pronunciation found in the following sentences:

(i)   He's looking at [ət] one of the pictures, but we're not sure which one he's looking at [æt].

(ii) Ted knows some [səm] songs that everyone likes, and Alfred knows some [sʌm] that no one can stand.

2. It is well-known that in English many of the helping verbs have optional contracted forms. These contracted forms are regularly represented as such in the standard English orthography:

(i) $\begin{Bmatrix} \text{I am} \\ \text{I'm} \end{Bmatrix}$ leaving.

(ii) $\begin{Bmatrix} \text{Sheila is} \\ \text{Sheila's} \end{Bmatrix}$ fed up with her old typewriter.

(iii $\begin{Bmatrix} \text{That cat has} \\ \text{That cat's} \end{Bmatrix}$ done it again.

(iv) $\begin{Bmatrix} \text{They will} \\ \text{They'll} \end{Bmatrix}$ just have to come back later.

Two facts about this type of contraction were noted in early generative grammars of English (Lees 1960, Fillmore 1965). First, an emphatic sentence such as (v) is not interpretable as (vi), but only as (vii):

(v)   THEY'LL say something.

(vi) They WILL say something.

(vii) THEY will say something.

Second, it is impossible to contract a helping verb that occurs at the end of a sentence:

(viii)   Harry isn't broke, but $\left\{ \begin{array}{l} \text{I am} \\ \text{*I'm} \end{array} \right\}$.

(ix)   Alfred isn't as tall as $\left\{ \begin{array}{l} \text{Sam is} \\ \text{*Sam's} \end{array} \right\}$.

What simple specification in the contraction rule will prevent its application in the undesired cases illustrated above?

3.   In this section, we have noted the existence of both weakened and un-weakened forms of a number of helping verbs, including *shall, could, have*, and *is*. We can as a matter of fact find the same type of contrast in the pro-nunciation of the helping verb *do*. We find the weakened variant in situations such as the following:

(i)   Harold's monograph does [dəz] not address the issues.
(ii)   Does [dəz] George really believe that story?

On the other hand, we find unweakened variants when the *do* is emphatically stressed, and also when it appears immediately before a deletion:

(iii)   Harold's monograph DOES [dʌz] address the issues.
(iv)   Martin flies to Dallas more often than he does [dʌz] to California.

Using these facts, show that Affix Hopping precedes Auxiliary Shift. (Hint: we argued in an earlier chapter that Affix Hopping must be ordered before *Do* Support; in this chapter, we suggested that Auxiliary Shift must follow Stress Weakening.) The ordering of Auxiliary Shift later than Affix Hopping justifies the relative order of the helping verb and the Tns element in the statement of Auxiliary Shift given in (105).

4.   A. Explain briefly why Subject-HV Inversion must be ordered well before Auxiliary Shift.

    B. What modification is necessary in rule (i) (the version of Subject-HV Inversion presented in Chapter 4) if we are to account for questions such as (ii) and (iii)?

(i)   Q – NP – Tns $\left(\left\{ \begin{array}{l} \text{M} \\ \textit{have} \\ \textit{be} \end{array} \right\} \right)$ – X

           1   2   3   4
           ⇒ 1, 3 + 2, 0, 4   (Obligatory)

(ii)   Does Charles always eat peas with his knife?
(iii)   Could Chris conceivably have called last night?

    C. Given the modifications that you suggest, see if you can find an argument based on the following sentences for requiring that Auxiliary

Shift apply only to verbs to which Tns has been attached:

(iv)   The guests will both have left.
(v)   *The guests will have both left.
(vi)   Will the guests both have left?
(vii)   *Will the guests have both left?

Suggestions for Further Reading

There are a number of introductory texts in phonology for the reader who desires a more extensive background in the subject: Harms 1968, Schane 1973, Hyman 1975, and Anderson 1975. Chomsky and Halle 1968 includes a detailed discussion of English stress. Alternatives are suggested in Lee 1969 and Ross 1972, and a revision in the basic stress rule is set forth in Halle 1973.

The source of the Ordering Hypothesis is Bresnan 1971. The hypothesis is criticized in Berman and Szamosi 1972, Lakoff 1972, and Bolinger 1972. Schmerling 1974 provides an interesting discussion of the difficulties that stand in the way of giving an intelligible definition of "normal stress."

The behavior of English helping verbs provides the focus for several papers, including Zwicky 1970, King 1970, and Baker 1971.

For general discussions of the relation between syntax and phonology, see Zwicky 1969 and Hetzron 1972.

Notes

1. There are other aspects of the environment of a voiceless stop that have an effect in determining whether or not it is aspirated. Some of these are dealt with in Exercise 1 at the end of this section.

2. There is actually a good deal of dialectal variation in the pronunciation of the third vowel in *catastrophic*, and also in the pronunciation of vowels spelled with *o* which appear in other words discussed in this section. The transcription given here represents the author's pronunciation. The reader can get some idea of the dialectal variation in the pronunciation of these vowels in American English by referring to Kenyon and Knott 1953.

3. The rule as stated here requires an additional restriction, which is developed in Exercise 2 at the end of this section.

4. There are a number of significant exceptions to this rule, which we will have occasion to mention in section 2 and will deal with more completely in section 3.

5. For detailed studies of English stress, see Chomsky and Halle 1968, Chapters 2 and 3, and Ross 1972.

6. In at least one study, an even more abstract representation is suggested for

democracy, in which the consonantal segment before the ending is given as a *t* rather than as an *s* (Chomsky and Halle 1968, p. 229).

7. The reason for giving the vowel of the suffix *-ous* as /ə/ in the phonological representation is that in some cases we find related words in which an [a] is pronounced in the corresponding position:

luminous	luminosity	curious	curiosity
[ə]	[a]	[ə]	[a]

8. Examples (29) through (31) suggest that some kind of exception must be made for articles and prepositions. Later examples will suggest the same thing with regard to helping verbs. More will be said about some of these special words in section 3.

9. Although this rule yields the same assignment of primary stresses in phrases as does the rule of the same name in Chomsky and Halle 1968, their rule and the manner in which it is assumed to apply have the effect of allowing reduction of secondary stress to an indefinite number of lower degrees. This point is discussed by Bierwisch 1968 and Bresnan 1971, pp. 272–273.

10. The existence of problematic stress patterns of this type was noted originally by Newman 1946. The solution proposed below is due to Bresnan 1971.

11. As will be seen in Exercise 3 at the end of this section, the success of the Ordering Hypothesis in yielding the stress pattern in (51e) depends on the deep structure that is assumed for the relative clause.

12. The particular location of the complement VP in deep structure does not have any bearing on the topic of primary concern here. As an incidental matter, though, it is worthwhile to point out the justification for making this VP part of the AdjP. The crucial piece of evidence is the possibility of grammatical questions such as:

(i)   *How easy to please* do you think John will be _____?

Interestingly enough, the corresponding structure whose subject is the *it* of Extraposition does not permit the fronting of the infinitival phrase along with the adjective:

(ii)   **How easy to please John* do you think it will be_____?

Thus, the sequence *how easy to please* in (i) acts like a single phrase, whereas the sequence *how easy to please John* in (ii) does not.

13. In the presentation of the Ordering Hypothesis given in Bresnan 1971, it is assumed that NP's as well as S's serve as domains for the application of both syntactic rules and the Nuclear Stress Rule. Since the point of view in the present discussion is that secondary stresses are not reduced further by reapplications of the Nuclear Stress Rule, it makes no difference for the examples under consideration here whether the Nuclear Stress Rule applies in both NP and S or only in S.

14. This argument in favor of a deep structure VP analysis for Object Raising complements is due to Lasnik and Fiengo 1974.

15. This example is given in Chomsky 1964, p. 35.

16. For a thorough discussion of the English words that vary between full and reduced forms, see Jones 1960, Chapter 16.

17. The justification for specifying term 3 of this rule with Tns to the right of the helping verb rests on a result developed in Exercise 3, at the end of this section, which concerns the relative ordering of several critical rules.

18. Tagalog pronoun position is discussed in detail in Schachter 1974.

17

A More Restricted
Syntactic Framework

At many points earlier in this book, we have tested a certain framework in new areas of English grammar only to find that the framework in question was too restrictive in the range of grammars that it allowed. For instance, in Chapter 3 we tested the phrase structure framework developed in the previous chapter by trying to apply it to the description of yes-no questions in English. In the course of this test, we found that it was impossible to give a revealing description of this construction within the confines of the phrase structure framework. As a remedy, we proposed to modify our framework by making transformational rules available for inclusion in the grammars of individual languages. Within the resulting more permissive framework, we were able to formulate a much more revealing account of English questions. In subsequent chapters there were other instances in which particular revisions in our framework were designed to permit revealing accounts of areas of English syntax, accounts that would not have been permitted within the terms of the unrevised framework. The most recent suggestion of this type was the proposal to allow movement rules to make reference to certain kinds of phonological information, a suggestion that arose from the consideration of the rule of Auxiliary Shift in Chapter 16.

Our object in this chapter will be to suggest some respects in which the framework developed up to now is deficient in just the opposite direction. That is, instead of looking at cases in which the framework is too restrictive in the range of grammars that it allows, we will look at cases in which it is not restrictive enough. These considerations will lead us to examine some proposals for making our framework less permissive, so that the range of permitted grammars is narrowed significantly. Before looking at particular cases, we will devote a preliminary section to a discussion in the abstract of the grounds on which we can charge a given framework with being overly permissive.

17.1 CONSEQUENCES
OF AN OVERLY PERMISSIVE FRAMEWORK

Let us imagine a hypothetical linguist who has developed a tentative universal grammar consisting of a syntactic framework and an evaluation measure. The linguist sets out to test this universal grammar, to see whether or not it might provide a solution to the projection problem. He obtains a record of some one person's basic data; his hope is that his universal grammar will permit him to derive correct predictions about the person's adult judgments from a consideration of his basic data. The linguist begins by drawing up as many grammars as he can which, first, conform to the terms of his framework, and second, are compatible with the set of basic data. To the resulting collection of grammars, he applies the evaluation measure. But the evaluation measure, instead of picking out just one grammar from this set as the strongest candidate for descriptive adequacy, fails to distinguish between two top contenders, G_x and G_y. This situation is summed up graphically below:

(1)

$$
\text{Basic Data} \rightarrow \boxed{\text{Framework}} \rightarrow \left\{ \begin{array}{l} G_1 \\ G_2 \\ G_3 \\ \vdots \\ G_x \\ \vdots \\ G_y \\ \vdots \end{array} \right\} \rightarrow \boxed{\begin{array}{l} \text{Evaluation} \\ \text{Measure} \end{array}} \begin{array}{l} \rightarrow G_x \\ \rightarrow G_y \end{array} \text{???}
$$

Upon further investigation, the linguist discovers, much to his chagrin, that G_x and G_y, despite their equivalence with regard to the limited set of basic data, yield markedly different sets of predictions concerning the adult judgments of the person in question. In every case in which the predictions of the two *individual grammars* differ, the logical result is that no clear prediction is made by the *universal grammar* as to the expected adult judgment. When he checks the conflicting predictions of G_x and G_y against the actual judgments of the adult speaker, he finds that G_x fares much better than G_y. The linguist may take some satisfaction in the fact that G_x, one of the two grammars selected by his universal grammar, is very successful outside of the basic data. However, he must still count it against his universal grammar that it did not allow him to select G_x as his best candidate for descriptive adequacy *in advance* of any testing on new data. Thus, his tentative universal grammar proves to be inadequate as a solution to the projection problem.

His initial attempts to find a solution to his difficulties center around the evaluation measure. Specifically, he tries to find an alternative measure that would select G_x as the single most promising grammar out of the set of grammars compatible with the basic data. But every plausible measure that he can think of is just as ineffectual as the original in making G_x come out ahead of G_y as the predicted "best grammar." At this point, he has reason to believe that the difficulty resides in his choice of framework. In particular, he suspects that his framework is at fault in permitting too many grammars that look equally attractive when only basic data are taken into account. He now tries to define a more restricted framework, one that still permits his good grammar G_x, but that excludes from consideration in advance the seductive but ultimately inadequate competitor G_y. He now repeats the test which he carried out before, using the new, more restrictive framework. He again draws up as many grammars as he can that, first, conform to the terms of the framework (this time the new one), and second, are compatible with the basic data. The resulting set of grammars is much smaller than the set that he arrived at with his original framework. Significantly, he finds that the set no longer contains G_y, since G_y does not satisfy the conditions of the new framework. When he applies his original evaluation measure this time, G_x is selected unambiguously. This state of affairs is summarized schematically below:

(2)

$$\text{Basic Data} \rightarrow \boxed{\begin{array}{c}\text{Framework}\\\text{(Revised)}\end{array}} \rightarrow \left\{\begin{array}{c}-\\G_2\\G_3\\\vdots\\G_x\\\vdots\\-\\\vdots\end{array}\right\} \rightarrow \boxed{\begin{array}{c}\text{Evaluation}\\\text{Measure}\end{array}} \rightarrow G_x$$

The linguist now has a universal grammar which shows some initial promise of being satisfactory. This revised universal grammar has made it possible to predict a descriptively adequate grammar (G_x) for a certain person on the basis of that person's basic data.

Further tests for this revised framework will of course be desirable, in particular, tests that involve the selection of grammars for other languages. These further tests may provide additional support for the revised framework. On the other hand, they may also point up remaining inadequacies. They may show that the framework is in need of still more stringent restrictions. Or they may show that some of the restrictions already imposed are too severe, with the result that the revised framework does not allow any revealing grammars at all for some language. The linguist's goal is to arrive ultimately at a framework that is restrictive and narrow in just the places where it needs to be in order to exclude seductive but misleading grammars in advance, but that is still permissive enough to allow a revealing grammar for every language.

At first glance, there may seem to be little reason to suppose that our current framework might suffer embarrassments of the sort just outlined. It might seem much more reasonable to suppose that the basic data to which an English-speaking child is exposed is so extensive and varied that only one transformational grammar of English would be both compatible with that data and tempting from the point of view of a reasonable evaluation measure. This view of matters might appear to receive some plausibility from the enormous amount of data that we have cited in the preceding chapters in arguing for one transformational grammar of English as against another.

In this respect, however, our discussions in previous chapters may have been deceptive. The reason is simple: a fluent adult has introspective access to many kinds of information about his language that a child is rarely or never provided with. One such general body of information consists of the adult's judgments that certain sentences are not grammatical. We have seen hundreds of such judgments in previous chapters of this book; they have been of striking usefulness to us in constructing tentative grammars of English, and in comparing two or more competing grammars. A child learning English, by contrast to an adult, has available at best a very limited supply of this sort of information. Such information as he gets about sentences that are not grammatical would have to come chiefly in the form of corrections of ungrammatical sentences that he happens to utter. For instance, suppose that he uttered (3a), and obtained (3b) as a response:

(3) a.   John knows what will we do.   (child)
    b.   John knows what we will do.   (adult)

The child might conceivably interpret (3b) as a correction of his original utterance, in the form of an indication as to the correct way to express what he had in mind. If he did see that the adult's utterance was intended in this way, he would then have succeeded in obtaining the information that his original sentence was ungrammatical. Such negative information could then conceivably serve as one item in his set of basic data.

Recent studies of child language use tend to suggest that such negative information in the form of corrections is not available to children in very large quantities or on a very systematic basis.[1] They suggest a wide variation in the ability of individual parents to notice grammatical mistakes in their children's speech and a correspondingly large variation in their propensity for making corrections. They also suggest that children quite frequently either resist a correction when it is made, or else do not understand it. There is thus some room for doubt as to whether such corrections as are made actually play a critical role in leading a child toward the system of rules that he eventually acquires.

A further consideration is relevant here. Although some of the types of ungrammatical sentences that we have cited in earlier chapters actually occur in the speech of children, there are other types, including some of major significance for the study of English grammar, that children never utter in the first place. In cases of this sort, there is no possibility that the child could gain access to the information that sentences of these types are ungrammatical, since no occasion is provided for parental corrections. In Chapter 8 we saw some initial examples of this sort, which we used to support constraints on movement rules:

(4)   *This is the girl whom John hit the boy that threw a snowball at.

(5)   *What did you buy peaches and?

There are other kinds of information which are available to adults through introspection, but which appear not to be similarly available to children. One significant type is semantic information concerning whether or not given sentences are ambiguous. An adult speaker of English can provide us with the information that the following sentence is ambiguous:

(6)   Flying planes can be dangerous.

However, it would appear that such information is rarely if ever made available to children.

The critical point of this discussion of the disparity between adult data and basic data can now be stated. In many discussions of alternative transformational descriptions of English (including several in this book), negative data of the sort available only to adults play a critical role in deciding between competing analyses. If such information were not used, that is, if no appeal were made to any data outside of the type to which a child has access, then it would be impossible to make a choice between the competing analyses. These situations are represented schematically below:

(7)

$$\text{Adult's Data} \rightarrow \boxed{\text{Transformational Framework}} \rightarrow \left\{\begin{array}{l} G_1 \\ G_2 \\ \vdots \\ G_x \\ \vdots \end{array}\right\} \rightarrow \boxed{\text{Evaluation Measure}} \rightarrow G_x$$

(8)

$$\text{Child's Data} \rightarrow \boxed{\text{Transformational Framework}} \rightarrow \left\{\begin{array}{l} G_1 \\ G_2 \\ G_3 \\ \vdots \\ G_x \\ \vdots \\ G_y \\ \vdots \end{array}\right\} \rightarrow \boxed{\text{Evaluation Measure}} \begin{array}{l} \rightarrow G_x \\ \rightarrow G_y \end{array} ???$$

In (7), because of the wealth of negative information present in the adult data, the set of transformational grammars compatible with that set of data is relatively small. As a consequence, application of the evaluation measure to this set of grammars results in a clear choice of G_x, a descriptively adequate grammar. By contrast, when, as in (8), we attempt to select a descriptively adequate grammar on the basis of the child's data alone, the absence from this set of data of the types of negative information found in the adult data results in a much wider and more perplexing range of compatible grammars. Precisely because of the absence of this crucial negative data, some tempting alternative grammar G_y is permitted in the competition. If we had access to all of the negative information that an adult has access to, we could rule out G_y immediately. But with only the child's data to go on, we find ourselves unable to dismiss it in advance as we should like our theory to force us to do.

We turn now to a consideration of some situations in English in which our current transformational framework suffers exactly the type of embarrassment shown in (8), and an examination of some proposals for modifying this framework in the direction of greater restrictiveness.

17.2 THEORETICAL IMPLICATIONS OF *ONE* SUBSTITUTION

In section 14.2 we compared two competing analyses of English NP's as regards the basis that they formed for the treatment of the English word *one*, as used in sentences such as:

(9)   I would like to tell you another funny story, but I've already told you the only *one* I know.

(10)   The old man from France was more erudite than the young *one*.

In one analysis, which we referred to as the Det-Nom analysis, the NP was divided into two constituents, a determiner and a Nom constituent, the latter consisting of the noun and its modifiers. The following trees illustrate the structures that arise in this analysis.

(11)   a.

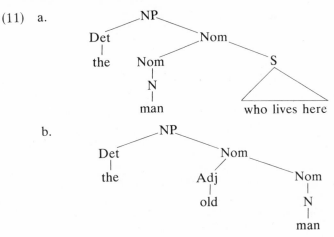

b.

c.

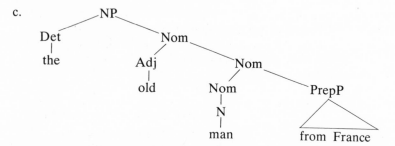

In the second analysis, which we referred to as the NP-S analysis, the N and its modifiers did not make up a single constituent. The structures arising from this analysis are illustrated in (12).

(12) a.

b.

c.

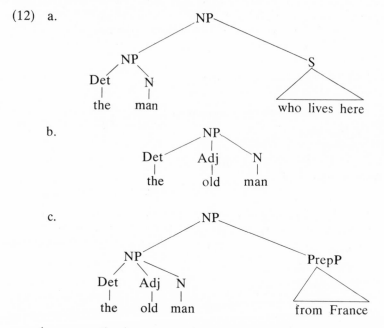

As we saw, the data concerning *one* clearly favored the Det-Nom analysis. One argument was that in sentences such as (9), two interpretations are permitted, one in which the word *one* has the sense of *funny story* and another in which it has the sense of *story*. Similarly, the word *one* in (10) can be understood either as *man from France* or merely as *man*. If the Det-Nom analysis was assumed, then these facts about the possible interpretations of *one* could be accounted for by a simple transformational rule that optionally replaced a Nom by *one* when there was an identical Nom earlier in the sentence. By contrast, the structures that arose in the NP-S analysis required a much more complicated formulation of the rule of *One* Substitution to account for the same judgments.

We also noted that another fact could be accounted for by stating *One*

Substitution as replacing a Nom constituent.[2] Suppose that NP's such as *the student of chemistry* were assigned the structure below.

(13)

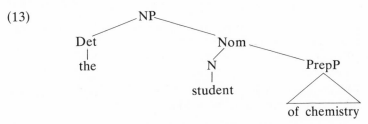

Then it would immediately follow that the replacement of the noun alone in sentences such as the following would give bad results:

(14)   The student of chemistry was more thoroughly prepared than the

$\begin{Bmatrix} \text{a. student} \\ \text{b.*one} \end{Bmatrix}$ of physics.

Thus, on the basis of these data, we were able to argue for a particular analysis of English NP's and a particular formulation of *One* Substitution.

Let us imagine now that we had not had access to the information that sentences like (9) and (10) are ambiguous, or that *One* Substitution in sentences like (14) gives an ungrammatical result. Suppose instead that we had been provided only with data of the following sort:

(15) a.   Some sentences containing *one*, for example:
            You keep the big cup, and I'll take the small one.
            John has a large glass, and Alice has one, too.

b.   Some accompanying data to indicate that *one*, unlike such forms as *hat* or *ball*, must have its sense interpreted by reference to some earlier expression.

c.   Sentences illustrating the variety of constituents that could occur with nouns inside of NP's, including relative clauses, prepositional phrases, and prenominal adjectives.

One very simple account for data of just this sort is the Det-Nom analysis, with a *One* Substitution rule that replaces Nom. As well as being consistent with the hypothetical basic data in (15), this account would allow us to predict that *one* could replace a sequence such as *man from France* as well as the word *man* by itself. In addition, if the proper structure were assigned to *the student of chemistry*, it would allow us to predict that *one* could not replace the word *student* in this expression.[3]

Unfortunately, there is also another account that is equally simple and equally consistent with the limited data given in (15). This is just the NP-S analysis, with a rule of *One* Substitution that replaces N's instead of Nom's. This alternative analysis, although equivalent to the Det-Nom analysis when only the limited data in (15) is concerned, gives quite different predictions outside this set. In the first place, it assigns sentence (16a) below only one underlying structure, one in which the material to be replaced by *one* consists only of the noun *story*. As a consequence, it leads us to the incorrect prediction that sentence (16a) can be understood as a paraphrase of (16b), but not as a paraphrase of (16c):

(16) a.   I would like to tell you another funny story, but I've already told you the only *one* I know. (=9)

     b.   I would like to tell you another funny story, but I've already told you the only *story* I know.

     c.   I would like to tell you another funny story, but I've already told you the only *funny story* I know.

It also leads us to expect that a sentence such as (17) should be grammatical:

(17)   *The student of chemistry was more thoroughly prepared than the one of physics. (=14b)

When we consider these facts that lie outside the limited data in (15), then, the NP-S analysis with an N-replacement rule for *one* is seen to be clearly inferior to the Det-Nom analysis with a Nom-replacement rule for *one*. But this eventual superiority of the latter analysis was in no way apparent when we had available only the limited data in (15). Thus, although our current framework does have the merit of making available at least one account of the limited data in (15) that turns out to do well with new data, it has the disadvantage of leaving this good account in competition with an equally simple alternative whose inferiority is not at all apparent until these new data are considered.

At this point, it might seem that we engaged in a rather artificial and pointless exercise when we asked what grammars we could have formulated on the basis of the very limited data in (15), when we in fact had access to much additional information. However, this exercise finds a very strong justification in the considerations raised in the preceding section. Specifically, the kinds of data that we chose to exclude from the list in (15) were of precisely the types to which children learning English do not appear to have reliable access.

Let us begin with the data concerning the possible interpretations of *one*. Under what sorts of conditions could a child conceivably obtain the information that *one* can stand for sequences consisting of more than just a noun alone? At first glance, it might appear that hearing a sentence such as (18) in a situation in which both John and Alice have large glasses would be sufficient to indicate the possibility of an Adj-N interpretation for *one*:

(18)   John has a large glass, and Alice has one, too.

This utterance in this situation, however, would not provide clear evidence at all, since the interpretation in which *one* stands for *glass* alone is not in the least ruled out by the external situation. Whenever it is true that Alice has a large glass, it is also true that she has a glass. A somewhat more unusual set of circumstances would be required, for example, the utterance of a sentence such as (19) when Alice has a glass that is red instead of blue:

(19)   John has a blue glass, but Alice doesn't have one.

In this situation, the interpretation in which *one* stands for *glass* alone is ruled out. Hence, the child would be led to interpret *one* as standing for *blue glass*, since only this interpretation would be consistent with the external facts.

Although we can construct hypothetical situations of this last sort, they must certainly be extremely uncommon in a child's early experience, if in fact they occur at all. If English speakers had to depend on this kind of evidence in childhood to acquire a system of rules, we might expect there to be a split in adult judgments about sentence (18), where the judgment made by each person would depend on whether he had been fortunate enough to be presented with sentences like (19) under a specific set of favorable circumstances. However, in view of the uniformity with which adult speakers of English interpret (18), we have grounds for doubting that the possibility of the Adj-N interpretation is something for which speakers require specific evidence during childhood. Thus, when we try to determine the kinds of data that should be classified as *basic data*, we would probably do well to exclude data concerning the various possibilities for interpreting *one*.

Let us turn now to the information that sentences such as (17) are ungrammatical: *The student of chemistry was more thoroughly prepared than the one of physics. As noted previously, recent studies in the use of language by children have tended to raise serious doubts concerning the availability of negative data in general. Moreover, the particular type of grammatical violation illustrated in (17) is not to be found at all in the existing records of ungrammatical utterances made by children. Thus, we have strong reason to doubt that English-speaking children are provided with any direct evidence that replacements like the one shown in (17) give ungrammatical results.

To summarize the problem, then, we have seen two types of adult judgments for which there probably does not exist any direct evidence in an English-speaking child's basic data. When we tried to formulate grammars within our current framework on the basis of the kinds of data that appear to be most readily available to the child, we found that there were at least two grammars that were consistent with this limited data. Since both grammars are permitted by the transformational framework, and since it would be difficult to devise a plausible evaluation measure that would clearly favor the Det-Nom analysis, we have no way of predicting in advance that the Det-Nom analysis will be much superior to the NP-S analysis in accounting for "nonbasic" judgments of the two kinds that we have been considering. As noted repeatedly throughout this book, the fundamental question to be asked in judging a certain syntactic framework is whether or not the framework (together with some evaluation measure) allows us to select a descriptively adequate grammar on the basis of the kind of data available to a child, i.e., the question of whether or not the framework provides part of a solution to the projection problem. The present situation, in which such a selection is not possible, thus constitutes an embarrassment for our current framework.

The fundamental source of this shortcoming is quite clearly the enormous variety of phrase structure rules and transformational rules that are made available by our current framework for possible inclusion in the grammars of individual languages. A logical approach to remedying this shortcoming would be to seek to revise our framework in such a way as to reduce drastically the range of available rules. In particular, we might aim for a revised framework in which we could exclude from consideration in advance such initially attractive but ultimately misleading grammars as the NP-S analysis with *one* substituting for N. If we were then to reexamine the limited set of basic data in (15) with this more restricted framework in hand, the Det-Nom analysis would be selected by default. As a consequence, we would be able to make clear predictions about the judgments concerning the possibilities for interpreting *one* and the impossibility of replacing certain nouns by themselves.

As an initial step in developing this more restricted framework, let us consider a proposal that has received a good deal of attention in modern syntactic work, namely, that there is some small fixed set of phrase structure rules from which all languages draw. In particular, suppose that we specify the following rule-types as the only allowable types for giving the phrase structure of NP's:

(20) a.   A rule specifying NP as a sequence of Det and Nom, the order to be specified in the grammar of each language.[4]

   b.   A rule specifying Nom as a sequence of Nom and S, Nom and Adj, Nom and PrepP, and so forth, with the order again to be specified in the grammar of each individual language.

   c.   A rule specifying Nom as a sequence of N and various NP's, PrepP's, etc., with the order again to be specified in the grammar of each language.

The initial impact of such a proposal is readily apparent: we have succeeded in limiting our linguistic framework in such a way that the NP-S analysis of English constituent structure is no longer allowed.

However, even after making these severe restrictions on possible phrase structure rules, we are still left with the possibility of an alternative grammar that gives the same bad results for *One* Substitution as did the NP-S grammar. Specifically, nothing that we have said so far excludes a description in which the Det-Nom constituent structure goes hand in hand with the *One* Substitution rule that replaces N's instead of Nom's. Such an analysis is fully consistent with the limited body of data in (15). In order to exclude such a transformational rule from consideration, we might make restrictions on transformational rules as well as on phrase structure rules. In the present instance, we could specify as part of our general framework the types of constituents that are eligible to be replaced under identity with other elements in the sentence. One possibility would be some principle such as the following:

(21)   In any rule that replaces one of two identical elements by some special form, only phrase structure categories higher than the lexical categories N, V, Adj, etc. are eligible to figure in the rule as the specification of the replaced category.

With our framework restricted in this way, a rule that substitutes *one* for N is no longer available as a candidate for inclusion in a grammar of English. Thus, this restriction results in selection by default for a rule that mentions Nom. The total effect, then, of the phrase structure restrictions spelled out in (20) and the transformational restriction spelled out in (21) is to make the Det-Nom analysis with *one* replacing Nom virtually the only analysis available as an account of the very limited basic data in (15). The tempting but misleading competitors have been ruled out ahead of time by the more restricted framework that results when the principles in (20) and (21) are adopted as part of our framework.

The selection of the Det-Nom analysis and the version of *One* Substitution that replaces Nom virtually ensures the possibility of interpreting *one* to stand for such expressions as *funny story* and *man from France*. However, we are still not quite in a position to predict the cases in which *one* may not replace nouns such as *student* in larger expressions. The difficulty is that nothing that we have said so far guarantees that we will assign constituent structures to particular phrases in a way that will allow *One* Substitution to apply in just the correct instances. For instance, the word *student* in the phrase *student with long hair* must be granted the status of Nom in its own right:

(22)

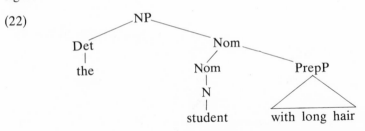

This structure is necessary to ensure the possibility of generating sentences such as:

(23)   The student with short hair is taller than the one with long hair.

By contrast, we must somehow ensure that the same word in the phrase *student of physics* is categorized only as an N, not as a Nom:

(24)

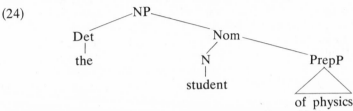

If the word *student* in this latter phrase were assigned Nom status in its own right, we would incorrectly expect (25) to be grammatical:

(25)   *The student of chemistry was more thoroughly prepared than the one of physics.   (=17)

An equally troublesome problem of the same sort is posed by a surprising variation in the possibilities for *One* Substitution in phrases like *English king*. Sentence (26a) below is ambiguous, being paraphraseable as either (26b) or (26c):

(26) a.   The French king is more powerful than the English king.

b.   The king who is French is more powerful than the king who is English.

c.   The king of France is more powerful than the king of England.

By contrast, sentence (26d), in which the second occurrence of *king* in (26a) has been changed to *one*, allows only the 'king who is English' reading:

(26) d.   The French king is more powerful than the English one.

Whereas George I of England (who was German by birth) could legitimately be referred to by the phrase *the English king* in (26a), he could not legitimately be referred to by the corresponding phrase *the English one* in (26d).

The facts would follow from a rule of *One* Substitution that replaced Nom, provided that phrases such as *the English king* are assigned the distinct structures given below, corresponding to the two different interpretations:

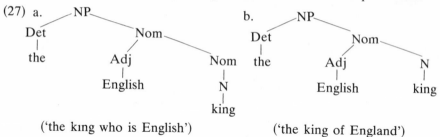

(27) a.

('the king who is English')   ('the king of England')

Without such a difference in structure, we would have no way of predicting the difference in susceptibility to *One* Substitution that we actually find associated with these two interpretations.

What sort of basic data might English speakers have received that would lead them to select just the constituent structures that are required for correct application of *One* Substitution? As before, we would do best to assume that the basic data contain no direct indication of when *One* Substitution is not permitted. We might begin by looking at a child's basic data to see if there are any utterances that they typically hear or corrections that they typically receive that could serve as an indication as to the correct assignment of constituent structure to specific phrases. Unfortunately, in the cases in question, there appears to be very little relevant information of this type available to the child.

Here we might consider a more surprising possibility, namely, that part of the basic data necessary to a child when he learns his language is some indication, from the situation in which an utterance occurs, of the intended semantic interpretation, and that it is this type of data that provides the basis for choosing correct constituent structures for various specific noun phrases. As an initial step in seeing what form such an account might take, let us compare the semantic properties of *the student with long hair* and *the student of physics*. A fundamental part of our interpretation of the first of these phrases is that when we use it to refer to someone, we are implicitly committing ourselves to the truth of two quite independent propositions about him, first, that he is a student, and second, that he has long hair. If we were to replace *student* by other nouns that happened to describe him correctly, the resulting phrases would still make good sense:

(28) a.   the man with long hair.
   b.   the Norwegian with long hair.
   c.   the football player with long hair.

By contrast, when we use the phrase *the student of physics* to refer to someone, we are really committing ourselves to a single proposition, roughly, the proposition that the person in question studies physics. In this phrase, the attempt to replace *student* by other nouns that happen to describe the person in question results in nonsense:

(29) a.   *the man of physics
   b.   *the Norwegian of physics
   c.   *the football player of physics

These differences in semantic properties can be represented quite directly in the type of semantic representation developed in Chapters 9 and 15. The representation appropriate for *the student with long hair* would be a representation containing two propositions joined by AND:

(30)   the x ((Student (x)) AND (HAVE $(x$, long hair))) 'the x such that x is a student and x has long hair'

The representation for *the student of physics*, by contrast, would contain only a single proposition:

(31)   the x (Study $(x$, physics)) 'the x such that x studies physics'

A similar contrast in semantic representation is appropriate for the two interpretations of the phrase *the English king*. For the interpretation paraphraseable by 'the king who is English,' we desire a representation that contains two independent propositions:

(32)   the x ((King (x)) AND (English (x))) 'the x such that x is a king and x is English'

The 'king of England' reading, on the other hand, is best represented by a formula containing only a single proposition:

(33)   the x (King $(x$, England)) 'the x such that x is king of England'

With this background, we are in a position to propose a pair of complementary principles of universal grammar that dictate syntactic constituent structure in part on the basis of semantic structure. The first is a rule that assigns Nom status to what we might call "minimal" Nom's:

(34)   Given a syntactic expression consisting of a noun and any and all of
the constituents that represent arguments of the predicate represented by the noun, assign the entire expression the status of Nom.

This principle would assign Nom status to "intransitive" nouns such as *man*
and *tree*. It would also assign Nom status to the noun *student* in the expression
student with long hair, since here the expression *with long hair* does not represent an argument of the predicate expressed by *student*. On the other hand,
given the expression *student of physics*, it would assign Nom status to the
entire expression, since here the following PrepP represents an argument of
the predicate represented by *student*. It would correspondingly assign Nom
status to a sequence such as *English king*, on the reading in which *English*
was interpreted as representing an argument of the predicate represented
by *king*.

We now require a second principle, to provide Nom status for certain
larger expressions:

(35)   Given a syntactic expression consisting of a Nom and some other
constituent, where the semantic representation of the expression is
in the form of a conjunction of the proposition expressed by the
Nom and the proposition expressed by the other constituent, assign
Nom status to the entire expression.

The way in which this principle works can be illustrated by looking at the
constituent structure that would be assigned to the expression *student with
long hair*. Since the sequence *with long hair* does not represent an argument
of *student*, the first of the above principles operates to assign Nom status to
student by itself:

(36)

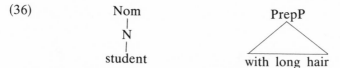

At this point, we can check for applicability of the second principle. We have
an expression consisting of a Nom and another constituent; furthermore, as
we can see by looking at the semantic representation in (30), repeated below,
the semantic condition set forth in (35) is satisfied.

(30)   the *x* ((Student (*x*)) AND (HAVE (*x*, long hair))) 'the *x* such that *x*
is a student and *x* has long hair'

Principle (35) thus dictates that we assign a higher Nom here, which gives:

(37)

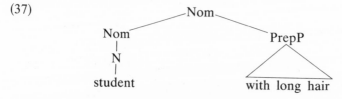

Principle (35) could reapply if we had this Nom within an even larger expression. For instance, it would assign a third Nom in the structure of the expression *student with long hair who came late*:

(38)

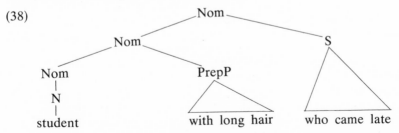

In the cases under discussion, then, the tentative universal conventions proposed in (34) and (35) give the desired result, provided that the critical information is available concerning the semantic representation of the phrases in question. In order for these conventions to have an effect in an explanation of the adult speaker's judgments, we must assume that the child is able to infer something about the semantic representation of a phrase from the circumstances in which he hears the phrase uttered. Thus, in proposing principles such as those in (34) and (35) as part of an account of language acquisition, we are in effect committing ourselves to the position that certain types of semantic information are critical in the successful acquisition of English syntax.

Let us pause here to review our explanation for the adult judgments concerning the possibilities of *One* Substitution. Two basic sets of assumptions entered into this explanation. The first set consists of tentative principles of universal grammar, specifically, principles that help to define a narrower syntactic framework:

(39) a.   A specification of a small set of phrase structure rules from which the grammars of individual languages can draw.

   b.   A specification of the constituent types that may figure in rules that replace material under identity.

   c.   A highly constrained set of possible semantic representations.

   d.   A principle that dictates possible constituent structures for certain expressions on the basis of their semantic representations.

The second set of assumptions, hardly less tentative than the first, concerns the type of material that a child's basic data must include:

(40) a.   Some examples of sentences containing *one*.

   b.   Some accompanying indication that *one*, unlike forms such as *hat* or *ball*, must have its sense interpreted by reference to other expressions.

   c.   Sentences illustrating the range of constituents that can occur with N's within NP's.

   d.   Some accompanying indication of the circumstances in which various expressions were used.

The data in (40c, d), together with the universal principles mentioned in (39a, c, d), would determine the basic phrase structure rules of English, and the particular structures to be associated with a variety of individual phrases. The data in (40a, b), together with the universal principle (39b), would then dictate the inclusion in English grammar of a rule of *One* Substitution, which replaces a Nom constituent by the word *one* under the influence of an identical Nom constituent earlier in the discourse.

Before concluding, we would do well to consider two possible objections that might be raised against the direction that the discussion in this section has taken. In the first place, it might appear that the number of universal principles proposed has been somewhat excessive, in view of the small amount of "nonbasic" adult data that they played a role in explaining. It is entirely possible, though, that the same principles will prove useful in explaining the relationship between basic data and adult judgments in languages other than English. In addition, there may be other "nonbasic" judgments within English that these principles could help to explain. To cite just one illustration, adult speakers of English uniformly judge the change in the order of prepositional phrases shown in (41) below much more satisfactory than the change shown in (42):

(41) a.   the student from France with long hair
     b.   the student with long hair from France

(42) a.   the student of physics with long hair
     b.   *the student with long hair of physics

The ungrammaticality of (42b), like the ungrammaticality of *the one of physics*, is not a judgment for which children appear to have any direct evidence in the form of a correction. An explanation for the judgment is provided by principles (39a, c, d), on the basis of data of the types specified in (40c, d). These principles, applied to these basic data, yield phrase structure rules that allow either (a) or (b) in (41), but only (a) in (42). Thus, even without going outside of English, we begin to find additional nonbasic data of a kind that provides independent support for some of the proposed universal principles.

The second objection that might be raised can be put in the form of a question: how can we justifiably propose the principles in (39) for tentative inclusion in universal grammar when we have considered only data from English? The justification arises from our initial definition of the goal of universal grammar as that of making it possible to predict a human being's adult linguistic judgments on the basis of his early linguistic experience. The existence of nonbasic English data of the sorts considered in this section in effect compels us to set forth, even if tentatively, some fairly specific principles of universal grammar. Without such principles, the nonbasic judgments simply resist explanation.

This is not in the least to say, of course, that material in other languages is irrelevant to the evaluation of these principles. On the one hand, we might find material that provided further support for these principles. On the other, we might come upon material that would force us to abandon or modify one or more of them. Having said this, we should note that the project of testing these principles in even one other language is not necessarily a simple undertaking. Because the principles are quite abstract and manifest themselves indirectly, we have no way of knowing ahead of time just what data in some new language will be relevant to testing them. This point can perhaps be made clear by looking at the relevant English data again: even though English has been the subject of intensive study for many years, many of the nonbasic judgments that we have cited as supporting the principles in (39) are not of the sort that one could find by reading standard grammatical works about English. As a matter of fact, such data from a language rarely come to light until some attempt is made to construct a detailed and explicit generative grammar of the language, a project whose magnitude and complexity should at this point in the book be readily apparent. Even then, critical data may go unnoticed, or if noticed, their relevance for testing the proposed principles of universal grammar may pass unobserved. The tentative formulation of universal principles in itself frequently serves to help bring relevant data to light.

EXERCISE

1.   In Chapter 2 (sections 2.3 and 2.4), an argument in favor of an evaluation measure was presented. The argument took the following form. The phrase structure framework as defined in section 2.2 was not by itself sufficient to get from the hypothetical set of basic data in (20) of section 2.3 to a clear set of predicted judgments of grammaticality concerning the new sentences in (23). However, when we added an evaluation measure that selected the grammar with the lowest number of symbol occurrences as the "predicted best grammar," we obtained the desired predictions concerning these sentences.

In the present section, we have outlined a framework that contains the beginning of a much more restricted definition of "permissible phrase structure rule." The definition mentions particular phrase structure types (e.g., NP, Adj, Nom) and states a restricted set of possibilities concerning the way in which these categories may be related. Suppose that we assume a more restricted definition along these lines, one that includes the statements in (20) of this section, and also perhaps some statements of a similar sort outlining a limited set of possibilities for expanding S and VP. Do the basic data in (20) of section 2.3 and the corresponding nonbasic data in (23) still provide support for an evaluation measure, or is an evaluation measure unnecessary with this more restricted framework? Explain your answer as carefully as possible.

17.3 PROBLEMS OF OVERGENERALIZATION

In this section we will consider some evidence of a different sort in favor of putting severe restrictions on the transformational rules that are available for the description of individual languages. We will look at a number of transformational rules for English that appear very attractive at first, but that prove to have troublesome exceptions. In each case, we will see that there are alternative descriptions which are not open to the same criticism. We will then suggest how our current framework might be replaced by a much more restricted framework, one that would not allow the undesirable grammars in the first place.

As an initial step, let us consider various kinds of linguistic exceptions, in order to be able to distinguish those exceptions which do not constitute an embarrassment for a certain framework from those which do. It would clearly be unreasonable to insist that no linguistic description of English that contained exceptional statements could possibly be correct. From our understanding of our goal in constructing a linguistic framework, the difference between embarrassing exceptions and benign exceptions follows immediately: any exceptional statements in a grammar are harmless if there is some basic data available to a child learning the language that indicates the necessity of making those exceptional statements. On the other hand, exceptional statements for which a child's basic data provide no evidence are troublesome, and any grammar that contains such exceptional statements is immediately suspect.

A simple example of a benign exceptional statement is provided by the statement that must be made to account correctly for the behavior of the colloquial interrogative phrase *how come*. This phrase is unlike other question phrases, including the synonymous expression *why*, in that it does not trigger the rule of Subject-HV Inversion:

(43) a.   How come he's still here?
     b.   *How come is he still here?

(44) a.   *Why he's still here?
     b.   Why is he still here?

In order to account for this exceptional behavior, we might include the following statement with the general rule of Subject-HV Inversion:

(45)   The phrase *how come* does not trigger Subject-HV Inversion.

In this instance, there is information in the basic data that might serve to motivate such an exceptional statement. In the first place, the child must at some point know that Subject-HV Inversion is an obligatory rule. We can be sure of this because of the adult judgment that sentences such as (44a) above are ungrammatical. In the second place, the child's elders provide him with many positive examples of questions containing *how come*, which serve to indicate clearly that *how come* does not undergo Subject-HV Inversion. Thus, the child could conceivably learn about the exceptional status of *how come* without ever being corrected for uttering a sentence like (43b). In general, any exception to an obligatory rule can be readily detected solely on the basis of fully grammatical sentences.

A similar situation holds with regard to idiosyncratic inflectional forms, given the kinds of frameworks commonly assumed in studies of morphology in various languages. For instance, one very simple framework would allow a range of morphological rules running from very general to very special, with the convention that the more special rules take precedence. On the basis of only positive data from English, we would be led to formulate the following rules, the first one very special and the second very general:

(46)   *choose* Past → *chose*

(47)   V *Past* → V *ed*

These two rules, together with the convention just mentioned, yield two correct predictions, the first that *chose* is an allowable past tense form of *choose*, and the second that **choosed* is not. Hence we do not need to be supplied with prior negative data in order to determine that *choose* does not undergo the regular rule for deriving past tense forms.

An initial example of a rule whose exceptions have a more discomforting status is the rule of Dative Movement set forth in section 10.6:

(48)   Dative Movement

$$X - V - NP - to - NP - Y$$
$$1 \quad 2 \quad 3 \quad 4 \quad 5 \quad 6$$
$$\Rightarrow 1, 2 + 5, 3, 0, 0, 6 \quad \text{(Optional)}$$

This rule has the effect of deriving the (b) sentences below from the structures underlying the (a) sentences:

(49) a.   We sent the book to George.

b.   We sent George the book.

(50) a.   John gave the wine from France to his grandmother.

b.   John gave his grandmother the wine from France.

As was noted in Chapter 10, several verbs constitute exceptions to this rule: when structures containing these verbs undergo Dative Movement, the resulting sentences are ungrammatical:

(51) a.   George contributes one-tenth of his pay check to the church.

b.   *George contributes the church one-tenth of his pay check.

(52) a.   We reported the accident that you saw to the police.

b.   *We reported the police the accident that you saw.

We suggested that the ungrammaticality of sentences such as (51b) and (52b) might be accounted for by adding the rule feature ⟨−Dative Movement⟩ to the lexical entries of *contribute* and *report*, and to the entries of other verbs that may not undergo this rule.

In this instance, positive data alone would not suffice to motivate the exceptional markings in the grammar. To see this, let us suppose that we are provided with just the following positive data from English:

(53) a.   We sent the book to George.

b.   We sent George the book.

(54) a.   John gave the wine from France to his grandmother.

b.   John gave his grandmother the wine from France.

(55) a.   George contributes one-tenth of his pay check to the church.

(56) a.   We reported the accident that you saw to the police.

One immediately tempting description that is compatible with these data is just the transformational description that we have been discussing, in which the rule of Dative Movement plays a central role in the derivation of (53b) and (54b). Since nothing in this positive data suggests the necessity of negatively marked rule features, none are listed in the lexical entries of any of the four verbs *send, give, contribute,* or *report.* Consequently, the resulting set of rules incorrectly predicts fully grammatical status for each of the following sentences:

(55) b.   *George contributes the church one-tenth of his pay check.

(56) b.   *We reported the police the accident that you saw.

The only kind of basic data that could help us here would be some indication that sentences with *report* and *contribute* which had undergone the rule were ungrammatical. This information could be a part of an English-speaking child's basic data only if he uttered sentences like (55b) and (56b) and then was corrected. Unfortunately, there is no evidence that errors of this sort are made spontaneously by children. Without such errors, though, there would be no occasion for adult corrections of the required type, and hence no source for the information that such sentences are ungrammatical. The problem for a description of English that contains a rule of Dative Movement can be summarized as follows: if we assume such a rule, then we are left with a number of exceptions to it, whose existence is left unexplained by the basic data to which a child learning English has access.

Transformational studies of English contain many other examples of optional rules that are beset with exceptions for which a child's basic data would contain no evidence. One such rule is a rule sometimes referred to as "*To-Be* Deletion," whose effect is to derive sentences such as (57b) and (58b) as optional reduced versions of the corresponding (a) sentences:[5]

(57) a.   John seems to be sleepy.

     b.   John seems sleepy.

(58) a.   John appears to be reluctant to leave.

     b.   John appears reluctant to leave.

The rule in question can be stated as follows:[6]

(59)   *To-Be* Deletion

$$X - V - to\ be - Y$$
$$1 \quad 2 \quad\ \ 3 \quad\ \ 4$$
$$\Rightarrow 1,\ 2,\ 0,\ 4 \quad \text{(Optional)}$$

Suppose that we have a set of basic data that includes the sentences in (57) and (58), and also the following additional sentences:

(60) a.   John happens to be sleepy.

(61) a.   Archie tends to be reckless at the wheel.

On the basis of this set of data, a grammar that included a rule such as (59) would seem a reasonable choice. Furthermore, nothing in the data serves to indicate that this rule should be limited in any way in its application. Unfortunately, though, *happen* and *tend* (and also a great many other verbs) do not allow *to be* to be absent:

(60) b.   *John happens sleepy.

(61) b.   *Archie tends reckless at the wheel.

Again, just as with the exceptions to the hypothesized rule of Dative Movement, the exceptional markings necessary to keep this rule from applying too widely can be motivated only by the information that certain sentences are ungrammatical. Once more, however, there is no evidence that children learning English utter sentences such as (60b) or (61b) in the first place. Consequently, we have reason to doubt that they are provided with the corrections that would be necessary to motivate marking verbs such as *happen* and *tend* with the rule feature ⟨ − *To-Be* Deletion⟩. If we assume such a rule as part of English grammar, the basic data available to an English-speaking child provide us with no reason to expect the exceptions that in fact exist.

A final example of a putative optional process with troublesome exceptions is that expressed in the interacting rules of Relative Clause Reduction and Modifier Shift, which were introduced in Chapter 13. These rules had the effect of deriving an NP such as *the tall man* from the complex NP *the man who is tall*. As was noted in Chapter 13, there are a number of adjectives in English which would have to be marked as not undergoing reduction and preposing across a noun:

(62) a.   the man who is awake
     b.   *the awake man

(63) a.   the boy who is ill
     b.   *the ill boy

Once again, it seems doubtful on the basis of currently available evidence about children's language use that they are provided with direct evidence, in the form of corrections, for the ungrammaticality of phrases such as (62b) and (63b). Hence, if we adopt this analysis of prenominal adjectives in English, we are unable to explain the exceptional status of adjectives such as *awake* and *ill*.

For each of the sets of data discussed above, there is a grammar that does not show the defects of the treatment that incorporates an optional transformational rule. Let us begin by looking once again at the following hypothetical basic data:

(53) a.   We sent the book to George.
     b.   We sent George the book.

(54) a.   John gave the wine from France to his grandmother.
     b.   John gave his grandmother the wine from France.

(55) a.   George contributes one-tenth of his pay check to the church.

(56) a.   We reported the accident that you saw to the police.

Instead of setting up a transformational rule for deriving one type of dative construction from the other, we might simply provide two phrase structure rules, one for each type:

(64) a.   VP → V   NP   PrepP
     b.   VP → V   NP   NP

We could then provide subcategorization features to indicate which environments a given verb appears in. For the hypothetical basic data given above, the following features would be necessary:

(65) a.   send ⟨____NP   to   NP⟩, ⟨____NP   NP⟩
     b.   give ⟨____NP   to   NP⟩, ⟨____NP   NP⟩
     c.   contribute ⟨____ NP   to   NP⟩
     d.   report ⟨____ NP   to   NP⟩

In effect, this analysis represents a highly conservative account of the data: verbs are not assumed to occur in the ⟨____ NP   NP⟩ environment unless the basic data specifically include examples of such occurrences. As a consequence, this analysis does not suffer from the same embarrassment as the account that includes a Dative Movement rule. In particular, it does not yield the incorrect predictions that sentences such as (55b) and (56b) are grammatical:

(55) b.   *George contributes the church one-tenth of his pay check.

(56) b.   *We reported the police the accident that you saw.

A similar alternative could have been devised for the grammatical sentences containing *seem, appear, happen,* and *tend*:

(57) a.   John seems to be sleepy.
     b.   John seems sleepy.

(58) a.   John appears to be reluctant to leave.
     b.   John appears reluctant to leave.

(60) a.   John happens to be sleepy.

(61) a.   Archie tends to be reckless at the wheel.

Instead of deriving the (a) and (b) sentences in (57) and (58) from a common deep structure, we could have posited two distinct deep structure configurations for each of these two verbs, perhaps of the sort sketched in (66):

(66) a.

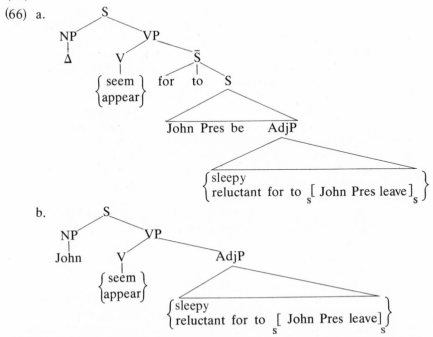

The verbs *seem* and *appear*, which occur in both environments, would have two separate subcategorization features in their lexical entries, whereas the verbs *happen* and *tend* would have only one. As with the second treatment of indirect-object verbs, this alternative treatment of *seem* and *appear* represents a very conservative account of the relevant positive data, one that is not overly general in the way that the transformational account is. In particular, this second account would not yield incorrect predictions about sentences such as (60b) and (61b):

(60) b.   *John happens sleepy.

(61) b.   *Archie tends reckless at the wheel.

In the case of predicate and prenominal adjectives, we have already seen an account that relied on multiple subcategorization rather than on a transformational derivation of the latter from deep structures containing the former. This was the analysis given in section 13.5, in which prenominal and predicate adjectives were generated independently by rules of the phrase structure component and the lexicon.

Let us pause here to summarize the problem that we face with our current framework. Although in each case this framework allows us an ultimately successful account of some limited set of positive data, it also allows us an account that is less successful by virtue of overgeneralizing, that is, by virtue of generating many new sentences that are not grammatical. Moreover, it is difficult to discern any clear difference in formal complexity that might enable an evaluation measure to favor the sets of rules relying on phrase structure over those making use of transformations.

Again, as in our discussion of *one* earlier in this chapter, we might seriously consider the possibility of narrowing the range of permissible transformational rules in such a way as to exclude in advance such tempting but ultimately misleading rules as Dative Movement, *To-Be* Deletion, and Adjective Preposing. One general proposal along these lines would be to replace the very broad formal definition of transformational rule by a fixed list of very narrowly defined rule-types.[7] That is, instead of giving a definition of "transformational rule" that is broad enough to encompass such widely varying rules as Passive, Subject-HV Inversion, Relative Clause Formation, and *One* Substitution, we would attempt to make a list of specific rule types (e.g., subject creation rules, verb inversion rules, relative clause rules, anaphoric substitution rules, and so forth). For each type of rule, we would attempt to give a general characterization. For instance, we might define a class of anaphoric substitution rules in such a way as to include rules like *One* Substitution and *Do-So* Substitution. Furthermore, we might include, as one of the defining features of rules of this type, just the constraint proposed in the preceding section, to the effect that such replacement rules only be allowed to replace nonlexical constituents. Other properties of such rules might be specified: for instance, that their domains of application are discourses rather than individual sentences.

Our major aim in carrying out a project of this sort would be to separate out the vast set of attractive but misleading rules that our current framework allows. The difference in inclusiveness between our current framework and one developed along the lines suggested above can be represented graphically as follows:

(67) a. Current Framework (Transformational Component)

Rule Type Examples from English

Transformational Rules	Passive Subject Raising *There* Insertion ??Dative Movement Subject-HV Inversion *Not*-HV Inversion Relative Clause Formation ??Relative Clause Reduction ??Modifier Preposing *One* Substitution *Do-So* Substitution VP Deletion (Post-HV Deletion) ??*To-Be* Deletion

b.   Revised Framework   (Restricted and subdivided Transformational Component)

Rule Type   Examples from English

Subject Creation Rules	Passive Subject Raising *There* Insertion

??Dative Movement

Verb Inversion Rules	Subject-HV Inversion *Not*-HV Inversion

Relative Clause Rules	Relative Clause Formation

??Relative Clause Reduction
??Modifier Preposing

Anaphoric Substitution Rules	*One* Substitution *Do-So* Substitution

Anaphoric Deletion Rules	VP Deletion (Post-HV Deletion)

??*To-Be* Deletion

Diagram (67a) represents the situation that we find ourselves in if we maintain our current framework. In developing a single very general definition of "transformational rule," we in effect cast our net so widely that we allow not only the genuinely general rules of English, but also some rules (those indicated by question marks) which represent attractive but spurious generalizations. Diagram (67b), on the other hand, shows what might be achieved if we could construct a framework in which we cast a series of smaller nets, a strategy that would still allow us access to those rules that express fruitful generalizations about English, but that would exclude in advance the kinds of ultimately undesirable rules that we have discussed in this section.

The preceding discussion, then, gives an idea of one general approach that we might take in attempting to solve certain problems of overgeneralization. It should be evident that diagram (67b) is not itself an explicit framework for grammatical description, but only a preliminary sketch of the lines on which one might be developed. Devising a detailed framework will require additional work in several areas.

One major project will be to reexamine the transformational rules that have been suggested for English. If we are to maintain a degree of logical consistency with the arguments against Dative Movement, *To-Be* Deletion, and Modifier Shift, then we must give serious attention to any instance in which a putative transformational rule is overly general. In some cases, it may be desirable to follow the strategy adopted in this section, eliminating the transformational rule from our grammar and arranging for a corresponding tightening in our general framework. In other cases, though, we may find that a rule which appears at first to be overly general can nevertheless be left in its simplest form, with an explanation for the overgenerality being provided by some independent linguistic principle. In Chapter 8, for example, we examined some interesting cases of ungrammaticality that resulted from the application of general rules like Question Movement and Relative Clause Formation. Rather than concluding that a grammar of English should not contain these rules, we left the rules in their most general form and added conventions to our universal grammar that put appropriate limitations on the application of the rules.

Other problems of overgenerality in our rules for English may be solvable by an appeal to semantic properties of particular English constructions. One problem of this type arises in connection with the Passive rule. The new framework sketched in (67b) has been designed to allow this rule, even though there are verbs in English that give bad results when they appear in the passive construction:

(68)   *John is resembled by Fred's brother.

(69)   *Two dollars is cost by this coat.

The justification for retaining the Passive rule, while trying to exclude other rules that are plagued with exceptions, is that there appears to be a much better possibility of giving a simple semantic explanation for the apparent exceptions to the Passive rule.[8] In an account of this kind, the ill-formedness of a passive sentence such as (68) would be attributed to an incompatibility between the interpretation assigned to the verb *resemble* and a general interpretation assigned to the passive construction. If a semantic explanation for these deviant passive sentences can indeed be found, then we will be able to maintain a simple Passive rule, without having to include rule features in the lexical entries of individual verbs. The Passive rule would thus not be open to the objection that was leveled against Dative Movement, *To-Be* Deletion, and Modifier Shift.

A second major project that will be necessary as part of the attempt to fill in the sketch in (67b) will be to carry out intensive studies of syntactic rules in languages other than English. To take one example, we listed a rule-type "Verb Inversion Rule" in (67b), and included in this class two English rules (Subject-HV Inversion and *Not*-HV Inversion). We can have some confidence in framing an explicit definition of this rule type only to the extent that we have examples of similar rules from other languages. These additional examples would give us a clearer idea than we could get from the two English rules alone of exactly what possibilities our general definition should allow. Similar comments hold for the various other classes of rules suggested tentatively above.

EXERCISE

1.   Consider the following statements about the English rule of Subject-HV Inversion in questions:

  a. It is obligatory in direct questions (e.g., *Who has he seen?* vs. **Who he has seen?*).
  b. It does not apply in subordinate questions (e.g., *I know who he has seen* vs. **I know who has he seen*).

There is a simple but incorrect idea about the facts that we might arrive at if we were provided only with examples of well-formed questions and sentences.

  A.   What is this incorrect alternative?

  B.   What restrictions might we build into our descriptive framework in order to exclude the alternative idea in advance?

Suggestions for Further Reading

Very little specific work has been done in searching for restrictions on permissible grammars with the aim of helping to solve the projection problem, even though this approach has been advocated in general terms in a number of works by Chomsky, including Chomsky 1965, 1970, and 1973. Several useful studies have appeared, though, in which some array of similar constructions are examined in a variety of unrelated languages. These include Greenberg 1963 (a general survey of word-order tendencies), Bach 1965 and Schachter 1974 on relative clauses, and Bach 1971 on questions. Such studies give some indication of the actual range of variation among languages, which will have to be allowed for in a more restrictive syntactic framework of the type suggested in section 3 of this chapter.

Notes

1. See in particular Braine 1971 and Brown and Hanlon 1970.
2. See Exercise 5, section 14.2.
3. We will have something to say later in this section about how the appropriate structure might be assigned.

4. Actually (20a) represents a considerable oversimplification, in that it provides no structure for various more complicated determiner and quantifier constructions. However, this simplification is irrelevant to the main point of this discussion.

5. See, for example, Borkin 1973.

6. Actually, there is an even simpler rule:

X – *to be* – Y
1   2   3
⇒ 1, 0, 3

It is left to the reader to see how badly this rule errs on the side of overgenerality. A good starting point would be to calculate the results of applying it to the first sentence of Hamlet's soliloquy.

7. First proposed by Bach 1965 and 1971.

8. For one suggestion concerning a semantic explanation, see Jackendoff 1972, Chapter 2.

18

Nominal Constructions

In the preceding chapter we examined several arguments in favor of making restrictions in the previously developed descriptive framework, that is, in the specification of "allowable grammars." In each case, the burden of the argument was that the more restricted framework would make it possible to choose an adequate grammar for English on the basis of a much smaller amount of primary data than would be required if the less restrictive framework were assumed. Of special interest were the situations in which the theory incorporating the less restrictive framework required certain types of negative data in order to arrive at a correct choice of grammar, data of a sort not generally available in the course of ordinary language acquisition.

One final example of a restrictive proposal merits a chapter of its own, in part because of the immense complexity of the area of grammar with which it deals, and also because of the large amount of attention that it has received in the literature. At issue is the manner in which the full sentences in (1) and the so-called "derived nominals" in (2) should be related in a grammar of English:

(1) a. The stranger disappeared.
    b. The secretary destroyed the files.
    c. Michael refused to resign.

(2) a. The stranger's disappearance
    b. The secretary's destruction of the files
    c. Michael's refusal to resign

The view that prevailed in early work in generative grammar was that the NP's in (2) were to be assigned deep structures containing the corresponding full sentences in (1).[1] Essential to this analysis was a transformational rule whose effect was to convert the various parts of the full sentence into the corresponding parts of the nominal construction. A recent alternative view is that the nominal constructions in (2) do not have the full sentences in (1) as part of their derivations, but instead have deep structures that do not differ significantly from their surface structures.[2] Following current terminology, we will refer to these opposing views as the "Transformationalist" position and the "Lexicalist" position, respectively.

18.1 THE TRANSFORMATIONALIST POSITION AND ITS EARLY JUSTIFICATION

During the early years of the generative study of English syntax, restrictions on the environments in which verbs could appear were stated not in terms of subcategory features of the sort introduced in Chapter 2, but rather in terms of so-called "context-sensitive" phrase structure rules. By the use of such rules, one could make a certain expansion of some node dependent on the other nodes to be found in its neighborhood. The use of such a device is illustrated in (3), a set of rules that generates the sentences of (1):

(3) a. $S \rightarrow NP \quad Aux \quad VP$

b. $VP \rightarrow V \ (NP)$

c. $VP \rightarrow V \quad S$

d. $V \rightarrow V_1$ in the environment ____ $]_{VP}$

e. $V \rightarrow V_2$ in the environment ____ $NP \ ]_{VP}$

f. $V \rightarrow V_3$ in the environment ____ $\bar{S} \ ]_{VP}$

g. $V_1 \rightarrow$ *disappear*

h. $V_2 \rightarrow$ *destroy*

i. $V_3 \rightarrow$ *refuse*

These rules allowed trees such as those below, in which the different types of verbs occurred in the appropriate environments:

(4) a.   b.

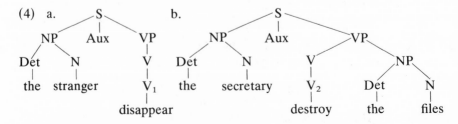

c.

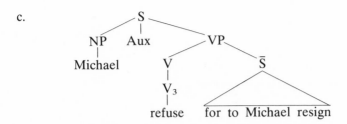

On the other hand, they did not allow the following sentences, in which the verbs are not correctly matched with their environments:

(5) a.   *The secretary destroyed.

   b.   *The stranger disappeared the files.

Given this general approach to the correct restriction of environments in which verbs appeared, there seemed to be essentially only two options available for the description of the corresponding nominals in (2). The first option was to generate the nominals by the same sort of context-sensitive phrase structure rules that had been used to develop the VP's. Taking this approach, the following rules might have been proposed for expanding the NP's in (2):

(6) a. $NP \rightarrow Poss \quad Nom$

   b. $Nom \rightarrow N \ (of \ NP)$

   c. $Nom \rightarrow N \ \bar{S}$

   d. $N \rightarrow N_1$ in the environment $[\underline{\quad}]_{Nom}$

   e. $N \rightarrow N_2$ in the environment $[\underline{\quad} of \ NP]_{Nom}$

   f. $N \rightarrow N_3$ in the environment $[\underline{\quad} \bar{S}]_{Nom}$

   g. $N_1 \rightarrow disappearance$

   h. $N_2 \rightarrow destruction$

   i. $N_3 \rightarrow refusal$

This treatment had what appeared to be a highly undesirable aspect: the work which was done to specify the environments for various verbs had to be done all over again for the corresponding nouns, producing an apparently unrevealing duplication of effort.

The other option that was considered was to generate full sentences by the phrase structure rules in (3), and then to treat the nominals in (2) as transformed versions of the sentential structures that arose by the operation of the phrase structure rules. For instance, the deep structure for the nominal *the stranger's disappearance* was presumed to be a tree of approximately the form given below:

(7)   a.

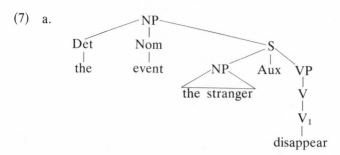

With this deep structure, the contextual restrictions on the occurrence of the noun *disappearance* are already taken care of by the phrase structure rules that insert *disappear* into the VP. What is required now is a rule to convert (7a) into the desired surface structure, a tree presumably something like (7b):

(7)   b.

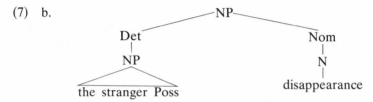

In similar fashion, the presumed deep structure and surface structure for *the secretary's destruction of the files* would be:

(8)   a.

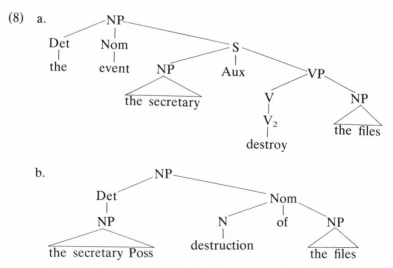

b.

If we ignore momentarily the presence of the word *of* in (8b), the essential properties of the conversion from (7a) to (7b) and from (8a) to (8b) can be formulated as follows:

(9)   Nominalization
       Given a structure of the form

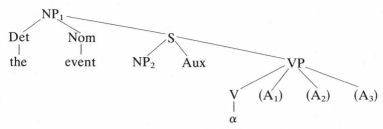

       where α is some actual verb (e.g., *disappear*, *destroy*), convert this
       structure into the following:

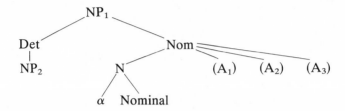

We also require additional rules. One rule inserts the word *of* into sequences
of the following form:

(10)   [N NP]
        Nom   Nom

Another rule adds a possessive marker to an NP under the domination of a
determiner. Finally, we need special rules to spell out the actual noun forms
of what started out as verbs:

(11) a.   *disappear* + *Nominal* → *disappearance*
     b.   *destroy*   + *Nominal* → *destruction*
     c.   *refuse*   + *Nominal* → *refusal*

    It is important to note at this juncture that the Nominalization rule has
one property that distinguishes it sharply from the transformational rules
that we have seen up to this point. In two instances it has the effect of replacing one node label by another. The V which dominates the verb in the S is
replaced by N, and the VP that encompasses the V and its sister constituents is replaced by Nom. Thus, although this rule is "transformational"
in the loose sense of converting one tree into another, it is not "transformational" in the more narrow sense of being formulable in terms of a structural
description and a structural change of the type that we have studied
previously.
    As noted in the previous chapter, it is generally preferable to maintain
the definition of "possible rule" in as narrow a form as we can. However,

a wider specification of allowable rule-types is justified when we find a sound generalization about a language which cannot be readily expressed without a framework that is more permissive in just this way. If rules that have the effect of changing node labels permit simple expressions of certain sound generalizations about English, and if these generalizations cannot be expressed directly and simply within a framework that does not permit such rules, then we have reason to favor the wider, more permissive framework. In the present instance, we have already seen that the rule of Nominalization stated in (9) expresses in straightforward fashion a far-reaching generalization about English that cannot be expressed directly within a phrase structure framework. What still remains to be done is to investigate the soundness of the generalization expressed in this rule.

18.2 NOMINAL PRODUCTIVITY

The Nominalization rule in (9) provides derivations for an enormous number of nominal phrases in English from corresponding verb phrases, of which the following is a small sample:

(12) a.   The committee adopted the plan.

     b.   The committee's adoption of the plan

(13) a.   The brigade retreated across the mountains.

     b.   The brigade's retreat across the mountains

(14) a.   Smith isolated the virus.

     b.   Smith's isolation of the virus

(15) a.   Sally attempted to avoid Fred.

     b.   Sally's attempt to avoid Fred

With a slight reformulation of the rule, we can also account for nominals that are related to adjectives rather than to verbs:

(16) a.   The man was eager to leave.

     b.   The man's eagerness to leave

(17) a.   The manager was obstinate.

     b.   The manager's obstinacy

(18) a.   The explanation was clear.

     b.   The clarity of the explanation[3]

Unfortunately, an analysis of nominals of the sort sketched above leaves us with no explanation for a large number of nominal phrases which could be generated by the rule, but which are in fact ungrammatical. The clearest cases are those in which the nominalized form of the verb is grammatical in some nominal contexts but not in others. For example, it is possible to form a nominal with *belief* which corresponds to the sentence in (19a):

(19) a.   Virginia believes in Santa Claus.

     b.   Virginia's belief in Santa Claus

By contrast, the following sentence has no corresponding nominal form:

(20) a.   Virginia believes that story.

b.   *Virginia's belief of that story

In similar fashion, the nominal *neglect* is more limited in its occurrence than is the corresponding verb:

(21) a.   Pepperdine neglected his offspring.

b.   Pepperdine's neglect of his offspring

(22) a.   Pepperdine neglected to lock the outer door.

b.   *Pepperdine's neglect to lock the outer door

Quite remarkably, the semantically very similar nominal *failure* does allow infinitival phrases:

(23) a.   Pepperdine failed to lock the outer door.

b.   Pepperdine's failure to lock the outer door

We might consider accounting for the negative judgments concerning (20b) and (22b) by using negative rule features. In each instance where a verb was possible in an environment in which the corresponding nominal was not possible, we could attach to the relevant subcategorization feature the additional specification ⟨−Nominalization⟩. For example, the lexical entries for *believe* and *neglect* might include the following feature specifications:

(24)   *believe* ⟨V⟩, ⟨ ___ in NP⟩, ⟨___ NP⟩
⟨−Nominalization⟩

(25)   *neglect* ⟨V⟩, ⟨ ___ NP⟩, ⟨ ___ S̄⟩
⟨−Nominalization⟩

Although employment of negative rule features makes possible an accurate account of the judgments of English speakers concerning the nominals in (19) through (22), we can raise the same questions about the use of such features here as we raised against their use in the previous chapter. Specifically, we must first ask what kind of evidence would serve to motivate such negative markings with individual verbs. Again as before, the answer appears to be that the necessity for such negative specifications would be motivated during the acquisition process only by some indication that such nominals as *Virginia's belief of that story* and *Pepperdine's neglect to lock the outer door* were ungrammatical. In the absence of some such indication, we should necessarily expect these nominals to be well-formed. We are then entitled to ask whether such negative information is actually available to novice speakers of English on some more or less uniform basis. Once more, the answer appears to be that it is not, judging from the existing literature on the acquisition of English as a first language. Thus, if we adopt a framework that allows a Nominalization rule like that given in (9) and relies on negative rule features to block the application of this rule in exceptional cases, then the absence of the requisite basic data in the early experience of an English-speaking child leaves us without an explanation of the English-speaking adult's rejection of the ungrammatical nominals.

18.3 A LEXICALIST FRAMEWORK

We now find ourselves in a peculiar situation. During the first part of our discussion, we made the factual assumption that the environments in which a verb is allowed will be closely paralleled by the environments that allow the corresponding nominal. Based on this assumption, we proposed the addition to syntactic theory of a rule-type that would allow this generalization to be expressed simply within a grammar of English. But then on closer examination, we found many troublesome exceptions to this generalization, which are difficult to explain on the basis of the types of data that children learning English are actually exposed to.

At this juncture, then, it is natural to ask whether the rejection of the pure phrase structure approach might not have been too hasty. What initially appeared to be a defect of that approach, namely, its failure to permit any simple generalization from data about possible verb phrases to predictions about possible nominals, turns out on more detailed examination to be something of a virtue. We will now consider the development of a more restricted framework, in which rules such as (9) are not made available for inclusion in the grammars of individual languages. We will henceforth use the word "Lexicalist" to refer to such a framework.[4]

Once we adopt a more restricted framework of this sort, we are virtually compelled to select a grammar for English in which nominal phrases are described independently of verb phrases.[5] Just as *disappear* would be listed in the lexicon with a feature that identified it as a $\langle V \rangle$ and also one that indicated that it was insertable into intransitive VP's, so also the word *disappearance* would be listed as an $\langle N \rangle$, with the further specification that it could be inserted into an "intransitive" Nom. There would be similar correspondences in the lexical entries for *destroy* and *destruction*, and also for *refuse* and *refusal*. By contrast, the lexical entry for *believe* would contain the two subcategory features $\langle \_\_\_ \text{ NP} \rangle$ and $\langle \_\_\_ \text{ in NP} \rangle$, whereas the entry for the noun *belief* would contain only the one feature $\langle \_\_\_ \text{ in NP} \rangle$. As with some of the examples in the preceding chapter, the empirical claim about acquisition inherent in the Lexicalist position as defined here is that an adult speaker would judge a nominal in a given environment as grammatical only if he had been provided with actual instances of that nominal in that environment during the period of his acquistion.

As part of the Lexicalist analysis of English, we must of course include special phrase structure rules for expanding the various types of Nominal constituents. The following is a brief sample of the types of Nom environments to be provided for:

(26)   The stranger's *death*

(27)   The secretary's *destruction of the files*

(28)   Virginia's *belief in Santa Claus*

(29)   My *attempt to interview the colonel*

(30)   The brigade's *retreat across the mountains*

(31)   Our *nearness to San Diego*

(32)   Your *discussion of the fee with the attorney*

(33)   The professor's *claim that the earth is flat*

From these examples, it is clear that we need at least the following phrase structure rules:

(34) a.   Nom → N (PrepP) (PrepP)

b.   Nom → N S̄

We might at first glance suspect that no such rules would be needed in a Transformationalist analysis of English, since the various phrase-types would be accounted for entirely by the phrase structure rules expanding the VP. However, there are many nouns which have no plausible derivation from any verb, but which nevertheless occur in the environments given by the rules in (34):

(35)   The stranger's *demise*

(36)   Virginia's *faith in Santa Claus*

(37)   My *effort to interview the colonel*

(38)   The brigade's *trip across the mountains*

(39)   Our *proximity to San Diego*

Thus the rules in (34) are required in a Transformationalist analysis no less than in a Lexicalist analysis.[6]

EXERCISE

1.   The purpose of this problem is to explore the consequences of adopting a special abbreviatory convention for the lexicon. In the preceding section we assumed that lexical entries for verbs and their related nouns are to be kept entirely separate. For example, the verb *refuse* and the noun *refusal* would have two separate entries, despite the close similarity of the environments for which they are subcategorized:

(i)   *refuse* ⟨V⟩, ⟨___ NP⟩, ⟨___ *for to* S⟩
       refusal ⟨N⟩, ⟨___ NP⟩, ⟨___ *for to* S⟩

(We assume for the purposes of this problem that the *of* which shows up after *refusal* is provided by a transformational rule of the sort sketched earlier.) Let us now consider an alternative convention, one that allows subcategorization restrictions on verbs and related nouns to be combined.

This type of representation is shown as follows:

(ii) $\begin{cases} refuse \ \langle V \rangle \\ refusal \ \langle N \rangle \end{cases}$, $\langle \underline{\quad\quad} NP \rangle, \langle \underline{\quad\quad} for \ to \ S \rangle$

Now study the following basic data from English:

(iii)   a. John neglected his children.
       b. John's neglect of his children surprised us.
       c. Fred neglected to lock the door.

What is the predicted grammatical status of the nominal in (iv), if we assume a framework in which combined lexical entries are *not* permitted?

(iv)   *Fred's neglect to lock the door.

What is the predicted status in a framework in which combined lexical entries *are* permitted. (Note: With each framework, assume an evaluation measure that dictates that the predicted best grammar is the grammar *within that framework* that contains the smallest number of feature specifications.)

18.4 NOMINALS AND TRANSFORMS

In the preceding discussion, we have passed over one question that might be raised about the derivation of an NP such as:

(40)   Michael's refusal to resign

Within the Transformationalist approach, this nominal can be generated very simply. The underlying structure is:

(41)
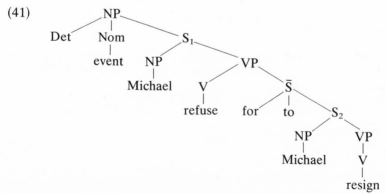

Identical-NP Deletion as originally stated applies in the S_1 cycle. Consequently, when a higher cycle is reached and the Nominalization rule applies, the deletion of the lower occurrence of *Michael* has already been accomplished.

Within the Lexicalist approach, such a derivation is of course not possible, since there would never be any point in the derivation of (40) at which the rule of Identical-NP Deletion would have a suitable S within which to apply. However, before concluding that (40) serves as compelling evidence against the Lexicalist position, we might consider a surprising alternative view of the operation of rules like Identical-NP Deletion. Instead of assuming, as we have up to now, that transformational rules apply only in S's, we might propose to reformulate the rules in such a way that they could apply in NP's as well. Suppose, in particular, that we assume roughly the following deep structures for the sentence with *refuse* and the corresponding nominal with *refusal*:

(42)   a.

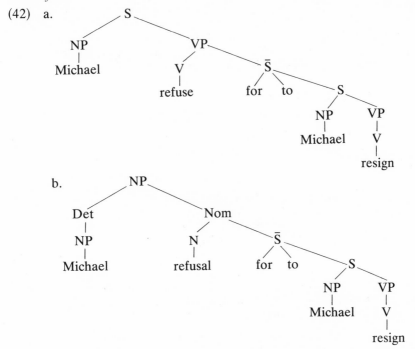

b.

In view of the striking overall similarities between these two structures, we might now reformulate the rule of Identical-NP Deletion as follows:

(43) $[X-NP-(\left\{\begin{matrix}V\\N\end{matrix}\right\})-\underset{\bar{S}}{[}(for)-\underset{S}{[}NP-Y]_S]_{\bar{S}}\underset{\{{}^S_{NP}\}}{]}$
        $\underset{\{{}^S_{NP}\}}{}$
          1   2   3   4   5 6
        Condition: 2 = 5
        ⇒ 1, 2, 3, 4, 0, 6   (Obligatory)

This generalized transformational rule suffices to derive *Michael's refusal to resign* from the Lexicalist deep structure given in (42b). With rule (43), then, it is no longer necessary to assume that the noun phrase *Michael's refusal to resign* goes back to a deep structure containing essentially the sentence *Michael refused to resign*.

The revision of our descriptive framework to permit transformational rules that apply in both S's and NP's makes it very tempting to account for new types of NP structures (whenever possible) as arising from the application of transformational rules already developed for S's. In the case of Identical-NP Deletion, an NP such as (40) would serve to motivate the replacement of the original Identical-NP Deletion rule by the generalized version of the rule given in (43). In this case, all currently available evidence appears to indicate that the extension of the rule to NP's is perfectly sound.

We can test this proposal further by looking for other cases in which such generalizations to NP's might appear tempting on the basis of some set of positive basic data. If the generalization, once made, turns out to have been a sound one, then the proposal to allow such generalizations receives additional support. On the other hand, if the generalizations that such a proposal makes attractive turn out to be unsound and misleading, then we have grounds for making such generalizations available only in quite restricted circumstances.

A test case of just this sort is provided by the following pair of nominals:

(44) a.   The chairman's expulsion of the egg-thrower
     b.   The egg-thrower's expulsion by the chairman

The relation between these nominals is very close to that between these full sentences:

(45) a.   The chairman expelled the egg-thrower.
     b.   The egg-thrower was expelled by the chairman.

The only apparent difference in the relation between the two nominals and that between the two sentences is that the noun *expulsion* shows no change in form corresponding to the insertion into the sentence of the special helping verb *be* and the inflectional marker *-en*. On the basis of examples such as these, a descriptive framework allowing generalization of transformational rules to NP's would make it very tempting to adopt the following composite version of the Passive rule:

$$(46) \quad \underset{\{ \substack{\langle S \rangle \\ NP} \}}{[\ NP\ -} \begin{Bmatrix} V \\ N \end{Bmatrix} - NP\ -\ X\ ]_{\{ \substack{\langle S \rangle \\ NP} \}}$$

$$\qquad\qquad 1 \qquad\quad 2 \qquad 3 \quad 4$$

$$\Rightarrow 3,\ \langle be\ +\ en\ +\ \rangle\ 2,\ 0,\ 4\ +\ by\ +\ 1 \quad \text{(Optional)}$$

Here we use angled brackets to indicate that the *be en* is included in the structural change only when the rule applies to an S.

Suppose that this rule is adopted. We must now ask whether this step which the theory made attractive is really a safe one. As it happens, there are at least two respects in which NP passivization is more restricted than passivization in S's. In the first place, there are many verb-noun pairs which allow passivization only with the verb. For example, the verbs *hate* and *resent* are perfectly grammatical in either an active or passive construction:

(47) a.   The sheriff $\begin{Bmatrix} \text{hates} \\ \text{resents} \end{Bmatrix}$ Joe.

     b.   Joe is $\begin{Bmatrix} \text{hated} \\ \text{resented} \end{Bmatrix}$ by the sheriff.

By contrast, the nouns *hatred* and *resentment* can appear only in an active nominal:

(48) a.   The sheriff's $\begin{Bmatrix} \text{hatred} \\ \text{resentment} \end{Bmatrix}$ of Joe.

     b.   *Joe's $\begin{Bmatrix} \text{hatred} \\ \text{resentment} \end{Bmatrix}$ by the sheriff.

As a general rule, nouns that denote attitudes are not hospitable to a *by*-phrase to the same degree as the corresponding verbs are. But this result is unexpected, given the generalized Passive rule in (46). We thus have a problem for a descriptive framework that makes available such a "generalized" passive rule.

Another problem for the idea that nominals with *by*-phrases arise from a generalized version of the Passive rule becomes apparent as soon as we broaden the rule for sentences in such a way as to generate passives from structures in which a preposition directly follows the verb:[7]

(49) a.   The duke submitted to the king.

     b.   The king was submitted to by the duke.

Such a passive would justify the inclusion of an optional preposition in the structural description of a Passive rule for S's:

(50)   NP $-$ V (Prep) $-$ NP $-$ X
      1   2   3   4

     $\Rightarrow$ 3, *be* $+$ *en* $+$ 2, 0, 4 $+$ *by* $+$ 1   (Optional)

This more comprehensive version of the Passive rule for S's would generalize to NP's as indicated below, in the absence of specific negative evidence against such a generalization:

(51) $[\text{NP} - \begin{Bmatrix} \text{V} \\ \text{N} \end{Bmatrix}$ (Prep) $-$ NP $-$ X]
     $\begin{Bmatrix} \langle S \rangle \\ NP \end{Bmatrix}$ $\begin{Bmatrix} \langle S \rangle \\ NP \end{Bmatrix}$
       1   2   3   4

     $\Rightarrow$ 3, $\langle be + en + \rangle$ 2, 0, 4 $+$ *by* $+$ 1   (Optional)

Unfortunately, though, the application of this rule in NP's gives bad results in those instances in which a preposition intervenes between the N and the underlying NP which is to be fronted:

(52) a.   The duke's submission to the king

     b.   *The king's submission to by the duke

Here, then, we have another respect in which the initially attractive proposal to let the Passive rule generalize to NP's turns out to have undesirable consequences.

Another case in which a generalization of a transformational rule to NP's looks promising at first glance is provided by nominal constructions based on the noun *tendency*:[8]

(53)   John's tendency to forget appointments annoys his colleagues.

In the case of sentences containing the verb *tend*, there is evidence in favor of a derivation involving the rule of Subject-Raising, a derivation of the same sort as that proposed earlier for *appear* and *seem*. Like *appear* and *seem*, *tend* can take the existential *there* as its surface structure subject:

(54)   There tend to be many traffic accidents on national holidays.

In addition, we find the same kind of active–passive synonymy with *tend* that we found with these other two verbs, but not with such verbs as *hope*:

(55) a.   Hasty readers tend to overlook small errors.
     b.   Small errors tend to be overlooked by hasty readers.
           (a=b)

(56) a.   The police appear to admire Jones.
     b.   Jones appears to be admired by the police.
           (a=b)

(57) a.   George hopes to meet Bill at the airport.
     b.   Bill hopes to be met at the airport by George.
           (a≠b)

In view of the Subject Raising derivation for *tend*, we might naturally consider the possibility that nominals with *tendency* arise by a generalized version of Subject Raising. We could posit the tree below as the deep structure for the subject NP in (53).

(58)

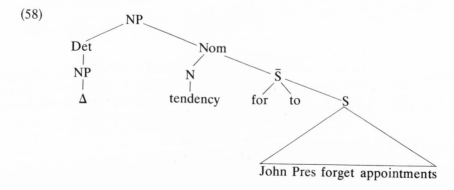

Application of a generalized Subject Raising rule (together with Affix Insertion and Complementizer Deletion) would give:

(59)

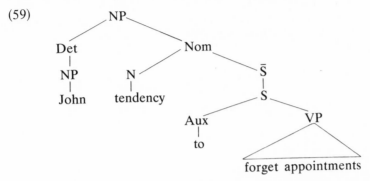

This structure would eventually come out as the nominal with which we are concerned:

(60)   John's tendency to forget appointments

A Subject Raising analysis of *tendency*, as attractive as it might seem at first glance, turns out on closer examination to have much less to recommend it than does the parallel analysis of the verb *tend*. In the first place, the existential *there*, which was allowed with *tend*, does not occur with *tendency*:

(61) a.   There tend to be many traffic accidents on national holidays.

b.   *There's tendency to be many traffic accidents on national holidays

It should be noted that the ungrammaticality of (61b) is not necessarily an embarrassment for the Subject-Raising analysis of *tendency*, in view of the general impossibility of using a genitive form of *there*:

(62) a.   John was annoyed at Fred's being present at the meeting.

b.   *John was annoyed at there's being only three people present at the meeting.

On the other hand, though, the ungrammaticality of (61b) robs the Subject Raising analysis of *tendency* of an argument parallel to the argument that the existential *there* provided for Subject Raising in S's.

In the second place, the synonymy noted between active and passive versions of *tend*-sentences is not found in NP's with *tendency*. In fact, the passive version is in many instances odd:

(63) a.   Alice tends to mistake John for his brother.

b.   John tends to be mistaken for his brother by Alice.

(64) a.   Alice's tendency to mistake John for his brother

b.   ?John's tendency to be mistaken for his brother by Alice

If (64b) can be interpreted at all, it is not synonymous with (64a). The NP in (64a) clearly refers to some characteristic of Alice, whereas (64b) must be understood as referring to some characteristic of John. If we were to derive a *tendency* nominal such as (64a) by means of a generalized version of Subject Raising, we would have every reason to expect that (64b) should be synonymous with (64a) and equally well-formed. The fact that it is not thus counts as an embarrassment for this analysis of NP's with *tendency*.

What other analysis might we propose for *tendency*? One possibility is to assign it a deep structure similar to that assigned earlier to *refusal*:

(65)

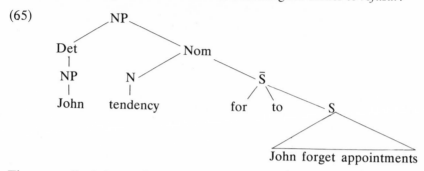

The generalized form of Identical-NP Deletion could now apply to this structure, resulting in the desired surface form *John's tendency to forget appointments*. For this latter analysis, the nonsynonymy of the active and passive nominals in (64) does not constitute an embarrassment. The two NP's would be assigned distinct deep structures, those given in (66a, b):

(66) a.

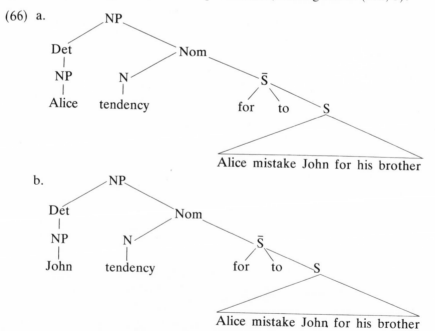

b.

Consequently, we would not necessarily expect the resulting NP's to be synonymous.

We have thus seen a second example of a nominal construction for which an initially appealing analysis that incorporates a generalized transformation turns out on closer examination to have undesirable consequences. In view of these two cases, then, we would do well to consider putting very heavy restrictions on the possibilities for stating transformational rules in generalized form. The most conservative proposal would be not to allow any such generalizations at all. This proposal would in effect require that any transformational rule proposed for NP's be justified solely on the basis of data concerning NP's. For example, the rule for so-called "passive" nominals such as (44b), *The egg-thrower's expulsion by the chairman*, would have to be based solely on data about nominals. It would not be possible, given this proposal, to "borrow" any aspects of the rule for passive *sentences* and apply them to the description of nominals. A somewhat less conservative approach would be to allow some types of transformational rules to generalize, while excluding generalizations of other types. For example, on the basis of the very limited sample of rules discussed here, we might tentatively advance the following hypothesis:

(67)   Rules involving identity of two NP's generalize readily, whereas those involving movement do not generalize at all.

Further investigation might suggest some other proposals concerning which types of rules should be allowed to generalize to NP's. Here, as with other questions about the treatment of nominals, there is still much work to be done in determining what logically possible generalizations are actually sound. Such an effort is necessary if we are to make an intelligent choice among the variety of ways that nominals might be accounted for.

EXERCISE

1.   As is shown in (i) and (ii) below, an NP within another NP may sometimes serve as the antecedent for a reflexive pronoun:

(i)   *John's* faith in *himself* was responsible for his success in the auto parts business.

(ii)   Alice's conversation with *Fred* about *himself* produced no tangible improvement in his behavior.

In other instances, however, the attempt to reflexivize under identity with an NP inside a larger NP gives bad results:

(iii)   **John's* efforts to leave the country caused *himself* some embarrassment.

(iv)   **Fred's* claim that Martha will marry *himself* is preposterous.

(v)   **John's* sister's view of *himself* has not been made public.

(vi)   *Martha's faith in *Harry* moved *himself* to tears.

A. Assuming the Lexicalist Hypothesis, which (if any) of the ungrammatical sentences (iii)–(vi) is blocked by the clause mate condition on Reflexivization (section 6.3)?

B. Try to suggest a replacement for the clause mate condition. This replacement should handle all of the examples that the original condition accounted for, and in addition should fare well with all of the examples in (iii) through (vi) above.

Suggestions for Further Reading

The major works on the subject of nominals in English are Lees 1960, Lakoff 1970a, and Chomsky 1970. The latter article is reviewed in McCawley 1975, section 1. Postal 1974, Chapter 10, offers several putative cases of nominals in whose derivation Subject Raising applies. Jackendoff 1975 discusses several proposals for a lexicalist theory of the lexicon.

Notes

1. This position is outlined most explicitly in Lees 1960, pp. 64–69.

2. First advocated in Chomsky 1970.

3. The nominal in (18b) serves to illustrate a general regularity of English: when a genitive NP is inanimate, the postnominal form with *of* is generally preferred to the prenominal form:

(i)   The clarity of the explanation

(ii)   ?The explanation's clarity

(iii)   The explosion of the bomb

(iv)   *The bomb's explosion

4. The proposal that grammatical rules not be allowed to change node labels is put forth most explicitly in Jackendoff 1972, p. 13.

5. This statement holds true only so long as the part of our framework that specifies the form of lexical entries is left the same. For an indication of what happens when this part of our framework is modified in a certain way, see Exercise 1 at the end of this section.

6. For an account of these nominals within a transformationalist framework which avoids the introduction of rules such as those in (34), see Lakoff 1970a, Chapter 5. The general idea is that nouns that require following phrases are to be derived from "abstract" verbs. For instance, the nouns *faith* and *effort* would be derived from abstract verbs *to faith* and *to effort*, respectively. These verbs would be marked as positive exceptions to the rule of Nominalization, thus assuring that any derivation in which they failed to be nominalized would be discarded as ill-formed.

7. This argument against a generalized passive rule is due to McCawley 1975.

8. An extensive discussion of nominals with *tendency* is to be found in Postal 1974, Chapter 10. Postal uses data about *tendency* to argue for the Transformationalist view of nominals. The problems that *tendency* nominals pose for this approach are essentially the same ones that arise in the approach being discussed in this section. These problems are described below.

Bibliography

AKMAJIAN, ADRIAN (1975), "More Evidence for an NP Cycle," *Linguistic Inquiry* VI: 115–129.

AKMAJIAN, ADRIAN, and TOM WASOW (1975), "The Constituent Structure of VP and AUX and the Position of the Verb BE," *Linguistic Analysis* 1: 205–245.

ANDERSON, STEPHEN R. (1975), *The Organization of Phonology.* New York: Academic Press.

ANDREWS, AVERY D. (1971), "Case Agreement of Predicate Modifiers in Ancient Greek," *Linguistic Inquiry* II: 127–151.

BACH, EMMON (1965), "On Some Recurrent Types of Transformations," in C. W. Kreidler, ed., *Report of the Sixteenth Annual Round Table Meeting on Linguistics and Language Studies* (*Georgetown University Monograph Series on Languages and Linguistics 18*) Georgetown University, Washington, D.C.

_____ (1971), "Questions," *Linguistic Inquiry* II: 153–166.

BAKER, C. L. (1970), "Notes on the Description of English Questions: The Role of an Abstract Question Morpheme," *Foundations of Language* 6: 197–219. Reprinted in Pieter A. M. Seuren, ed. (1974), *Semantic Syntax.* London: Oxford University Press.

_____ (1971), "Stress Level and Auxiliary Behavior in English," *Linguistic Inquiry* II: 167–181.

BERMAN, ARLENE (1974a), *Adjectives and Adjective Complement Constructions in English,* Report No. NSF-29 to the National Science Foundation, Department of Linguistics, Harvard University, Cambridge, Mass.

_____ (1974b), "On the VSO Hypothesis," *Linguistic Inquiry* V: 1–37.

BERMAN, ARLENE, and MICHAEL SZAMOSI (1972), "Observations on Sentential Stress," *Language* 48: 304–325.

BIERWISCH, MANFRED (1968), "Two Critical Problems in Accent Rules," *Journal of Linguistics* 4: 173–178.

BLOOMFIELD, LEONARD (1933), *Language*. New York: Holt, Rinehart and Winston.

BOLINGER, DWIGHT (1965), "The Atomization of Meaning," *Language* 41: 555–573.

———— (1967), "Adjectives in English: Attribution and Predication," *Lingua* 18: 1–34.

———— (1972), "Accent Is Predictable (If You're a Mind-reader)," *Language* 48: 633–644.

BORKIN, ANN (1973), "*To Be* and Not *To Be*," in Claudia Corum, T. Cedric Smith-Stark, and Ann Weiser, eds., *Papers from the Ninth Regional Meeting of the Chicago Linguistic Society*, The Chicago Linguistic Society, Chicago.

BRAINE, MARTIN D. S. (1971), "On Two Types of Models of the Internalization of Grammars," in Dan I. Slobin, ed., *The Ontogenesis of Grammar: A Theoretical Symposium*. New York: Academic Press.

BRESNAN, JOAN W. (1970), "On Complementizers: Toward a Syntactic Theory of Complement Types," *Foundations of Language* 6: 297–321.

———— (1971), "Sentence Stress and Syntactic Transformations," *Language* 47: 257–281. Reprinted in Michael K. Brame, ed. (1972), *Contributions to Generative Phonology*. Austin: University of Texas Press.

———— (1972), "Stress and Syntax: A Reply," *Language* 48: 326–342.

———— (1975), "Comparative Deletion and Constraints on Transformations," *Linguistic Analysis* 1: 25–74.

———— (1976), "On the Form and Functioning of Transformational Rules," *Linguistic Inquiry* 7: 3–40.

BROWN, ROGER, and CAMILLE HANLON (1970), "Derivational Complexity and Order of Acquisition in Child Speech," in John R. Hayes, ed., *Cognition and the Development of Language*. New York: John Wiley and Sons. Reprinted in *Psycholinguistics: Selected Papers by Roger Brown*. New York: The Free Press, 1970.

BURT, MARINA K. (1971), *From Deep to Surface Structure: An Introduction to Transformational Syntax*. New York: Harper and Row.

CHOMSKY, NOAM (1957), *Syntactic Structures*. The Hague: Mouton.

———— (1962), "A Transformational Approach to Syntax," in A. A. Hill, ed., *Proceedings of the Third Texas Conference on Problems of Linguistic Analysis in English, 1958*, The University of Texas, Austin. Reprinted in Jerry A. Fodor and Jerrold J. Katz, eds. (1964), *The Structure of Language: Readings in the Philosophy of Language*. Englewood Cliffs, N.J.: Prentice-Hall, Inc.

———— (1964), *Current Issues in Linguistic Theory*. The Hague: Mouton.

———— (1965), *Aspects of the Theory of Syntax*. Cambridge, Mass.: MIT Press.

———— (1968), *Language and Mind*. New York: Harcourt, Brace & World.

———— (1970), "Remarks on Nominalization," in Roderick A. Jacobs and Peter S. Rosenbaum, eds., *Readings in English Transformational Grammar*. Waltham, Mass.: Ginn and Company.

———— (1971), "Deep Structure, Surface Structure, and Semantic Interpretation," in Danny Steinberg and Leon Jakobovits, eds., *Semantics: An Interdisciplinary Reader in Philosophy, Linguistics, and Psychology*, New York: Cambridge University Press.

———— (1972), "Some Empirical Issues in the Theory of Transformational Grammar," in Stanley Peters, ed., *Goals of Linguistic Theory*. Englewood Cliffs, N.J.: Prentice-Hall Inc.

CHOMSKY, NOAM (1973), "Conditions on Transformations," in Stephen R. Anderson and Paul Kiparsky, eds., *A Festschrift for Morris Halle*. New York: Holt, Rinehart and Winston.

CHOMSKY, NOAM, and MORRIS HALLE (1968), *The Sound Pattern of English*. New York: Harper & Row.

ELGIN, SUZETTE HADEN (1973), *What is Linguistics?* Englewood Cliffs, N.J.: Prentice-Hall, Inc.

EMONDS, JOSEPH E. (1969), "A Structure-Preserving Constraint on NP Movement Transformations," in Robert I. Binnick, Alice Davison, Georgia Green, and Jerry Morgan, eds., *Papers from the Fifth Regional Meeting of the Chicago Linguistic Society*, Department of Linguistics, University of Chicago.

FILLMORE, CHARLES J. (1963), "The Position of Embedding Transformations in a Grammar," *Word* 19: 208–231.

_____ (1965), *Indirect Object Constructions in English and the Ordering of Transformations*. The Hague: Mouton.

_____ (1966), "Deictic Categories in the Semantics of 'Come,'" *Foundations of Language* 2: 219–227.

_____ (1968), "The Case for Case," in Emmon Bach and Robert T. Harms, eds., *Universals in Linguistic Theory*. New York: Holt, Rinehart and Winston.

_____ (1970), "The Grammar of *Hitting* and *Breaking*," in Roderick A. Jacobs and Peter S. Rosenbaum, eds., *Readings in English Transformational Grammar*. Waltham, Mass.: Ginn and Company.

_____ (1971), "Verbs of Judging: An Exercise in Semantic Description," in Charles J. Fillmore and D. T. Langendoen, eds., *Studies in Linguistic Semantics*. New York: Holt, Rinehart and Winston.

FROMKIN, VICTORIA, and ROBERT RODMAN (1974), *An Introduction to Language*. New York: Holt, Rinehart and Winston.

GLEASON, H. A., Jr. (1961), *An Introduction to Descriptive Linguistics*, rev. ed. New York: Holt, Rinehart and Winston.

GLEITMAN, LILA R. (1965), "Coordinating Conjunctions in English," *Language* 41: 260–293. Reprinted in David A. Reibel and Sanford A. Schane, eds. (1969), *Modern Studies in English: Readings in Transformational Grammar*. Englewood Cliffs, N.J.: Prentice-Hall, Inc.

GREENBERG, JOSEPH H. (1963), "Some Universals of Grammar with Particular Reference to the Order of Meaningful Elements," in Joseph H. Greenberg, ed., *Universals of Language*. Cambridge, Mass.: MIT Press.

GREENOUGH, J. B., G. L. KITTREDGE, A. A. HOWARD, and BENJAMIN D'OOGE (1903), *Allen and Greenough's New Latin Grammar*. Boston: Ginn and Company.

GROSU, ALEXANDER (1973), "On the Nonunitary Nature of the Coordinate Structure Constraint," *Linguistic Inquiry* IV: 88–92.

_____ (1974), "On the Nature of the Left-Branch Condition," *Linguistic Inquiry* V: 308–319.

HALLE, MORRIS (1973), "Stress Rules in English: A New Version," *Linguistic Inquiry* IV: 451–464.

HARMS, ROBERT T. (1968), *Introduction to Phonological Theory*. Englewood Cliffs, N.J.: Prentice-Hall, Inc.

HASEGAWA, KINSUKE (1968), "The Passive Construction in English," *Language* 44: 230–243.

HETZRON, R. (1972), "Phonology in Syntax," *Journal of Linguistics* VIII: 251–265.

HOCKETT, CHARLES F. (1958), *A Course in Modern Linguistics*. New York: The Macmillan Company.

HYMAN, LARRY M. (1975), *Phonology: Theory and Analysis*. New York: Holt, Rinehart and Winston.

JACKENDOFF, RAY S. (1969), "An Interpretive Theory of Negation," *Foundations of Language* 5: 218–241.

———— (1971a), "Gapping and Related Rules," *Linguistic Inquiry* II: 21–35.

———— (1971b), "On Some Questionable Arguments about Quantifiers and Negation," *Language* 47: 282–297.

———— (1972), *Semantic Interpretation in Generative Grammar*. Cambridge, Mass.: MIT Press.

———— (1975), "Morphological and Semantic Regularities in the Lexicon," *Language* 51: 639–671.

———— (1976), "Toward an Explanatory Semantic Representation," *Linguistic Inquiry* 7: 89–150.

JACOBS, RODERICK A., and PETER S. ROSENBAUM (1968), *English Transformational Grammar*. Waltham, Mass.: Blaisdell.

JESPERSEN, OTTO (1965), *The Philosophy of Grammar*. New York: W. W. Norton.

JONES, DANIEL (1960), *An Outline of English Phonetics*, 9th ed. Cambridge, England: W. Heffer & Sons.

KARTTUNEN, LAURI (1971), "Implicative Verbs," *Language* 47: 340–358.

KATZ, JERROLD J., and JERRY A. FODOR (1963), "The Structure of a Semantic Theory," *Language* 39: 170–210. Reprinted in Jerry A. Fodor and Jerrold J. Katz, eds. (1964), *The Structure of Language: Readings in the Philosophy of Language*, Englewood Cliffs, N.J.: Prentice-Hall, Inc.

KATZ, JERROLD J., and PAUL M. POSTAL (1964), *An Integrated Theory of Linguistic Descriptions*, Cambridge, Mass.: MIT Press.

KAUFMAN, ELLEN S. (1974), "Navajo Spatial Enclitics: A Case for Unbounded Rightward Movement," *Linguistic Inquiry* V: 507–533.

KEENAN, EDWARD L. (1971), "Quantifier Structures in English," *Foundations of Language* 7: 255–284.

———— (1972), "On Semantically Based Grammar," *Linguistic Inquiry* III: 413–461.

KENYON, JOHN S., and THOMAS A. KNOTT (1953), *A Pronouncing Dictionary of American English*. Springfield, Mass.: G. & C. Merriam Company.

KIMBALL, JOHN P. (1973), *The Formal Theory of Grammar*. Englewood Cliffs, N.J.: Prentice-Hall, Inc.

KING, HAROLD V. (1970), "On Blocking the Rules for Contraction in English," *Linguistic Inquiry* I: 134–136.

KIPARSKY, PAUL, and CAROL KIPARSKY (1970), "Fact," in Manfred Bierwisch and Karl Erich Heidolph, eds., *Progress in Linguistics*. The Hague: Mouton.

KLIMA, EDWARD S. (1964), "Negation in English," in Jerry A. Fodor and Jerrold J. Katz, eds., *The Structure of Language: Readings in the Philosophy of Language*. Englewood Cliffs, N.J.: Prentice-Hall, Inc.

KOHRT, MANFRED (1975), "A Note on Bounding," *Linguistic Inquiry* VI: 167–171.

KOUTSOUDAS, ANDREAS (1971), "Gapping, Conjunction Reduction, and Coordinate Deletion," *Foundations of Language* 7: 337–386.

———— (1972), "The Strict Order Fallacy," *Language* 48: 88–96.

KUNO, SUSUMU (1971), "The Position of Locatives in Existential Sentences," *Linguistic Inquiry* II: 333–378.

_____ (1973), "Constraints on Internal Clauses and Sentential Subjects," *Linguistic Inquiry* IV: 363–385.

_____ (1975), "Conditions for Verb Phrase Deletion," *Foundations of Language* 13: 161–175.

KURODA, S.-Y. (1968), "English Relativization and Certain Related Problems," *Language* 44: 244–266. Reprinted in David A. Reibel and Sanford A. Schane, eds. (1969), *Modern Studies in English: Readings in Transformational Grammar*. Englewood Cliffs, N.J.: Prentice-Hall, Inc.

LAKOFF, GEORGE (1970a), *Irregularity in Syntax*. New York: Holt, Rinehart and Winston.

_____ (1970b), "Repartee, or a Reply to 'Negation, Conjunction and Quantifiers,'" *Foundations of Language* 6: 389–422.

_____ (1971), "On Generative Semantics," in Danny Steinberg and Leon Jakobovits, eds., *Semantics: An Interdisciplinary Reader in Philosophy, Linguistics, and Psychology*. London: Cambridge University Press.

_____ (1972), "The Global Nature of the Nuclear Stress Rule," *Language* 48: 285–303.

LAKOFF, GEORGE, and STANLEY PETERS (1966), "Phrasal Conjunction and Symmetric Predicates," in *Mathematical Linguistics and Automatic Translation*, Report No. NSF-17, Harvard University Computation Laboratory, Cambridge, Mass. Reprinted in David A. Reibel and Sanford A. Schane, eds. (1969), *Modern Studies in English: Readings in Transformational Grammar*. Englewood Cliffs, N.J.: Prentice-Hall, Inc.

LAKOFF, GEORGE, and JOHN R. ROSS (1966), "Criterion for Verb Phrase Constituency," in *Mathematical Linguistics and Automatic Translation*, Report No. NSF-17, Harvard University Computation Laboratory, Cambridge, Mass.

LANGACKER, RONALD W. (1973), *Language and Its Structure: Some Fundamental Linguistic Concepts*, 2nd ed. New York: Harcourt Brace Jovanovich.

_____ (1974), "The Question of Q," *Foundations of Language* 11: 1–38.

LANGENDOEN, D. TERENCE (1970), "The 'Can't Seem To' Construction," *Linguistic Inquiry* I: 25–35.

LASNIK, HOWARD, and ROBERT FIENGO (1974), "Complement Object Deletion," *Linguistic Inquiry* V: 535–571.

LEE, GREGORY (1969), "English Word-Stress," in Robert I. Binnick, Alice Davison, Georgia Green, and Jerry Morgan, eds., *Papers from the Fifth Regional Meeting of the Chicago Linguistic Society*, Department of Linguistics, University of Chicago.

LEES, ROBERT B. (1960), *The Grammar of English Nominalizations*. The Hague: Mouton.

LEES, ROBERT B., and EDWARD S. KLIMA (1963), "Rules for English Pronominalization," *Language* 39: 17–28. Reprinted in David A. Reibel and Sanford A. Schane, eds. (1969), *Modern Studies in English: Readings in Transformational Grammar*. Englewood Cliffs, N.J.: Prentice-Hall, Inc.

LEHMANN, TWILA (1972), "Some Arguments Against Ordered Rules," *Language* 48: 541–550.

LEHMANN, WINFRED P. (1972), *Descriptive Linguistics: An Introduction*. New York: Random House.

LEVI, JUDY (1973), "Where Do All Those Other Adjectives Come from?" in Claudia Corum, T. Cedric Smith-Stark, and Ann Weiser, eds., *Papers from the Ninth*

Regional Meeting of the Chicago Linguistic Society, Chicago Linguistic Society, Chicago.

LIGHTFOOT, DAVID (1975), "The Theoretical Implications of Subject Raising," *Foundations of Language* 13: 115–143.

LYONS, JOHN (1968), *Introduction to Theoretical Linguistics*. London: Cambridge University Press.

MCCAWLEY, JAMES D. (1968a), "Lexical Insertion in a Transformational Grammar Without Deep Structure," in *Papers from the Fourth Regional Meeting of the Chicago Linguistic Society*, Department of Linguistics, University of Chicago.

———(1968b), "The Role of Semantics in a Grammar," in Emmon Bach and Robert T. Harms, eds., *Universals in Linguistic Theory*. New York: Holt, Rinehart and Winston.

———(1970a), "English as a VSO Language," *Language* 46: 286–299. Reprinted in Pieter A. M. Seuren, ed. (1974), *Semantic Syntax*. London: Oxford University Press.

———(1970b), "Where Do Noun Phrases Come from?" in Roderick A. Jacobs and Peter S. Rosenbaum, eds., *Readings in English Transformational Grammar*. Waltham, Mass.: Ginn and Company.

———(1971), "Tense and Time Reference in English," in Charles J. Fillmore and D. T. Langendoen, eds., *Studies in Linguistic Semantics*. New York: Holt, Rinehart, and Winston.

———(1975), Review of: Noam Chomsky, *Studies on Semantics in Generative Grammar*. The Hague: Mouton, 1972. In *Studies in English Linguistics* 3: 209–311.

NEWMAN, STANLEY (1946), "On the Stress System of English," *Word* 2: 171–187.

PARTEE, BARBARA HALL (1970), "Negation, Conjunction, and Quantifiers: Syntax Vs. Semantics," *Foundations of Language* 6: 153–165.

———(1971), "On the Requirement that Transformations Preserve Meaning," in Charles J. Fillmore and D. T. Langendoen, eds., *Studies in Linguistic Semantics*. New York: Holt, Rinehart, and Winston.

———(1972), "Some Transformational Extensions of Montague Grammar," in Robert Rodman, ed., *Papers in Montague Grammar (Occasional Papers in Linguistics, No. 2)*, Department of Linguistics, University of California, Los Angeles.

———(1975), "Montague Grammar and Transformational Grammar," *Linguistic Inquiry* VI: 203–300.

PERLMUTTER, DAVID M. (1971), *Deep and Surface Structure Constraints in Syntax*. New York: Holt, Rinehart and Winston.

———(1972), "Evidence for Shadow Pronouns in French Relativization," in Paul M. Peranteau, Judith N. Levi, and Gloria C. Phares, eds., *The Chicago Which Hunt: Papers from the Relative Clause Festival, April 13, 1972*, Chicago Linguistic Society, Chicago.

PETERS, STANLEY (1972), "The Projection Problem: How Is a Grammar to Be Selected?" in Stanley Peters, ed., *Goals of Linguistic Theory*, Englewood Cliffs, N.J.: Prentice-Hall, Inc.

POSTAL, PAUL M. (1970a), "On Coreferential Complement Subject Deletion," *Linguistic Inquiry* I: 439–500.

———(1970b), "On the Surface Verb 'Remind,'" *Linguistic Inquiry* I: 37–120.

———(1971), *Crossover Phenomena*. New York: Holt, Rinehart and Winston.

_____(1974), *On Raising: One Rule of English Grammar and Its Theoretical Implications*. Cambridge, Mass.: MIT Press.

QUICOLI, A. CARLOS (1972), *Aspects of Portuguese Complementation*, unpublished Ph.D. dissertation, State University of New York at Buffalo. Available from University Microfilms, Ann Arbor, Michigan.

REICHENBACH, HANS (1947), *Elements of Symbolic Logic*. New York: The Free Press.

RINGEN, CATHERINE (1972), "On Arguments for Rule Ordering," *Foundations of Language* 8: 266–273.

ROSENBAUM, PETER S. (1967), *The Grammar of English Predicate Complement Constructions*. Cambridge, Mass.: MIT Press.

ROSS, JOHN ROBERT (1967a), *Constraints on Variables in Syntax*, unpublished Ph.D. dissertation, M.I.T., Cambridge, Mass. Available from the Indiana University Linguistics Club, Bloomington.

_____(1967b), "On the Cyclic Nature of English Pronominalization," in *To Honor Roman Jakobson*, III. The Hague: Mouton. Reprinted in David A. Reibel and Sanford A. Schane, eds. (1969), *Modern Studies in English: Readings in Transformational Grammar*. Englewood Cliffs, N.J.: Prentice-Hall, Inc.

_____(1969), "Auxiliaries as Main Verbs," in William Todd, ed., *Studies in Philosophical Linguistics*, Series One. Evanston, Ill.: Great Expectations Press.

_____(1970), "Gapping and the Order of Constituents," in Manfred Bierwisch and Karl Erich Heidolph, eds., *Progress in Linguistics*. The Hague: Mouton.

_____(1972), "A Reanalysis of English Word Stress (Part I)," in Michael K. Brame, ed., *Contributions to Generative Phonology*. Austin: University of Texas Press.

SAPIR, EDWARD (1921), *Language*. New York: Harcourt Brace & World.

SCHACHTER, PAUL (1973), "Focus and Relativization," *Language* 49: 19–46.

_____(1974), "Constraints on Clitic Order in Tagalog," in George Bedell, ed., *UCLA Papers in Syntax 5*, Department of Linguistics, University of California, Los Angeles.

SCHANE, SANFORD A. (1973), *Generative Phonology*. Englewood Cliffs, N.J.: Prentice-Hall, Inc.

SCHMERLING, SUSAN F. (1974), "A Re-examination of 'Normal Stress,'" *Language* 50: 66–73.

SEUREN, PIETER A. M. (1972), "Autonomous versus Semantic Syntax," *Foundations of Language* 8: 237–265. Reprinted in Pieter A. M. Seuren, ed. (1974), *Semantic Syntax*. London: Oxford University Press.

SLEDD, JAMES (1959), *A Short Introduction to English Grammar*. Chicago: Scott Foresman.

SMITH, CARLOTA S. (1964), "Determiners and Relative Clauses in a Generative Grammar of English," *Language* 40: 37–52. Reprinted in David A. Reibel and Sanford A. Schane, eds. (1969), *Modern Studies in English: Readings in Transformational Grammar*. Englewood Cliffs, N.J.: Prentice-Hall, Inc.

STOCKWELL, ROBERT, PAUL SCHACHTER, and BARBARA HALL PARTEE (1973), *The Major Syntactic Structures of English*. New York: Holt, Rinehart and Winston.

WASOW, THOMAS (1975), "Anaphoric Pronouns and Bound Variables," *Language* 51: 368–383.

WEINREICH, URIEL (1966), "Explorations in Semantic Theory," in Thomas A. Sebeok, ed., *Current Trends in Linguistics*, Volume 3. The Hague: Mouton.

Wɪɴᴛᴇʀ, Wᴇʀɴᴇʀ (1965), "Transforms without Kernels?" *Language* 41: 484–489.

Zᴡɪᴄᴋʏ, Aʀɴᴏʟᴅ M. (1969), "Phonological Constraints in Syntactic Descriptions," *Papers in Linguistics* 1: 411–463.

_____(1970), "Auxiliary Reduction in English," *Linguistic Inquiry* I: 323–336.

———(1973), "Linguistics as Chemistry: The Substance Theory of Semantic Primes," in Stephen R. Anderson and Paul Kiparsky, eds., *A Festschrift for Morris Halle*. New York: Holt, Rinehart and Winston.

Index